WAL

\

From Soviet Republics to EU Member States

Studies in EU External Relations

Edited by

Marc Maresceau
Ghent University

Editorial Board

VOLUME 2

From Soviet Republics to EU Member States

A Legal and Political Assessment of the Baltic States' Accession to the EU

By

Peter Van Elsuwege

MARTINUS
NIJHOFF
PUBLISHERS

LEIDEN • BOSTON
2008

This book is printed on acid-free paper.

Library of Congress Cataloging-in-Publication Data

Elsuwege, Peter Van.
  From Soviet republics to EU member states : a legal and political assessment of the
Baltic states' accession to the EU / by Peter Van Elsuwege.
      p. cm. — (Studies in EU external relations ; v. 2)
  Includes bibliographical references and index.
  ISBN 978-90-04-16945-6 (hardback : alk. paper) 1. European Union—Baltic States.
2. European Union countries—Relations—Baltic States. 3. Baltic States—Relations—
European Union countries. I. Title.

    HC240.25.B29E47 2008
    341.242'2—dc22

                                                                              2008023114

ISSN   1875-0451
ISBN   978 90 04 16945 6

PRINTED IN THE NETHERLANDS

CONTENTS

PART ONE

THE BALTIC STATES IN EUROPE: HISTORICAL,
LEGAL AND GEOPOLITICAL CONTEXT

PART TWO

THE LEGAL FRAMEWORK OF RELATIONS
BETWEEN THE EC/EU AND THE BALTIC
STATES BEFORE ACCESSION TO THE EU

PART THREE

THE BALTIC STATES AND THE EU'S PRE-ACCESSION STRATEGIES

PART FOUR

THE ACCESSION NEGOTIATIONS:
A POST-FACTUM ANALYSIS

PART FOUR

THE ACCESSION NEGOTIATIONS:
A POST-FACTUM ANALYSIS

CHAPTER ONE

THE LEGAL FRAMEWORK OF EU
ACCESSION NEGOTIATIONS

§ 1. *The Scope of Accession Negotiations*

Preparation for membership is incomplete unless agreement has been reached upon the terms of admission and the necessary adjustments to the Treaties as provided under Article 49 EU. This agreement is the result of accession negotiations between the EU Member States and each applicant country. The negotiations are characterised by an asymmetrical relationship between the parties involved. This is the result of (i) the unanimity requirement for the accession of new Member States, which implies that it is very difficult for an applicant to change the compromises reached at EU level[1] and (ii) the fact that the conditions for accession are unilaterally defined by the EU Member States (cf. *supra*). Accordingly, the scope for negotiation is rather limited.[2]

New Member States are expected to apply, implement and enforce the entire *acquis* upon accession.[3] When a candidate country faces difficulties in complying with a specific chapter of the *acquis*, flexible solutions are sought within the process of accession negotiations. The main instrument of flexibility is the temporary postponement of the application of parts of the *acquis*. Such transition periods can be requested by both parties and should be limited in scope and duration. Each request is analysed on a case-by-case basis, "taking into account the country's interests and the likely impact of each request on the functioning of the

---

[1] L. Friis, A. Friis, "Countdown to Copenhagen: Big Bang or Fizzle in the EU's Enlargement Process", Copenhagen, Danish Institute of International Affairs, 2002, p. 13.

[2] For this reason, Phedon Nicolaides argues that the term 'accession negotiations' is misleading. Alternatively, he suggests the term 'entry examination' because the largest part of this exercise is devoted to checking whether a prospective member fulfils the conditions for membership whereas the actual negotiating part is rather small. See: P. Nicolaides, "Negotiating Effectively for Accession to the European Union: Realistic Expectations, Feasible Targets, Credible Arguments", *Eipascope* 1 (1998), p. 8.

[3] Agenda 2000. For a Stronger and Wider Union. COM (97) 2000 final, p. 61.

Union and the interest of the other applicant states".[4] In principle, the acceptance of a transitional measure in one case does not constitute a precedent for others nor do transitional measures granted in previous accessions create a precedent for ongoing negotiations.[5] In practice, however, it seems that parallel negotiations with different countries create a group dynamic which puts the EU in a position to offer all applicants a similar transitional arrangement on specific chapters of the *acquis* (cf. *infra*).[6]

Apart from the classical transitional periods, applicant countries may also ask for (financial) assistance to be able to comply with the *acquis*. A good example can be found in Lithuania's negotiating position on the energy chapter. Given the high cost involving the decommissioning of the Ignalina Nuclear Power Plant, Lithuania argued that it could only satisfy the EU demands on the condition of additional financial support. Lithuanian negotiators asked for € 376 m for 2004–2006 and an equivalent amount for beyond 2006.[7] The EU finally agreed to attribute € 285 m between 2004–2006 with a commitment to provide "adequate additional Community assistance to the decommissioning effort beyond 2006".[8] As part of the Ignalina compromise, Lithuania may also apply for authorisation to take specific measures if energy supply would be disrupted. This possibility applies until 31 December 2012.[9] The latter provision is not a traditional transitional measure but

---

[4] European Commission, "Enlargement Strategy Paper. Report on Progress Towards Accession by each of the Candidate Countries", COM (2000) 700, Brussels, 8 November 2000, p. 26.

[5] *Ibid.*

[6] See: L. Friis, "Breaking the Waves: The European Union's Enlargement Negotiations with EFTA and Central and Eastern Europe", in: O. Elgstrom, C. Jonsson, (eds.), *European Union Negotiations: Processes, Networks and Institutions*, London, Routledge, 2005, pp. 204–209.

[7] M. Kovalick, "High Costs of Closing Down Ignalina Plant", *Baltic Times*, 25 April 2002; X, "Lithuania says Ignalina can be closed by end of 2009, provided that EU pays for it", *Uniting Europe* 188 (2002), p. 5.

[8] Protocol No. 4 to the 2003 Treaty of Accession on the Ignalina Nuclear Power Plant in Lithuania, *OJ* (2003) L 236/945. On this basis, the Commission already proposed a sum of € 815 million from the Community budget to fund the decommissioning of the Ignalina NPP over the period from 2007 to 2013. Proposal for a Council Regulation on the implementation of Protocol No. 4 on the Ignalina nuclear power plant in Lithuania, as annexed to the Act concerning the conditions of accession to the European Union of the Czech Republic, Estonia, Cyprus, Latvia, Lithuania, Hungary, Malta, Poland, Slovenia and Slovakia, COM (2004) 624 final.

[9] Article 4 of Protocol No. 4 on the Ignalina Nuclear Power Plant in Lithuania, *Ibid.* On the interpretation of this clause, see *infra* at § 4.2.

a so-called safeguard clause. This instrument allows for exemptions from the *acquis* only if the need arises. Consequently, it was not imperative to work out specific derogations during the negotiations.[10]

Accession negotiations do not exclusively deal with flexibility instruments but also include technical issues such as, for example, the share of Community fishing opportunities to be allocated to the new Member States.[11] In this respect, the EU Member States and the candidate country involved discuss technical adjustments to the Community legislation. Latvia, for instance, requested the inclusion of Baltic sprat into the list of fish species to which the intervention mechanism for fresh and chilled fish can be applied and argued for a specific management regime in the entire Gulf of Riga.[12] In the light of the scientific information provided by Latvia concerning the particular situation of this area, the EU Member States agreed to adapt Council Regulation 104/2000 on the common organization of the markets in fishery and aquaculture products and Regulation 88/98 laying down certain technical measures for the conservation of fishery resources in the waters of the Baltic Sea.[13] Another example of technical adjustments to the *acquis* in the light of specific circumstances is provided by Estonia's insistence on amendments to the so-called habitats directive[14] in order to allow the hunting of brown bears, wolves, lynx and beavers.[15]

The examples of Estonia, Latvia and Lithuania illustrate that, in spite of their asymmetrical nature and limited scope, accession negotiations are extremely important to ensure the smooth integration of new Member States in the EU and to avoid negative social-economic

---

[10] Nicolaides, *op. cit.*, footnote 2, p. 10.

[11] Upon accession, new Member States take part in the EC Common Fisheries Policy, which *inter alia* implies that the Community takes over the execution of these countries' fisheries agreements.

[12] Latvia's position paper on the fisheries chapter is available at: http://www.am.gov .lv/data/file/e/chapter08.pdf.

[13] See: http://www.europa.eu.int/comm/enlargement/negotiations/chapters/ chap8/index.htm.

[14] Directive 92/43/EEC on the conservation of national habitats and of wild fauna and flora, *OJ* (1992) L 206/7.

[15] The EU Member States and Estonia agreed to exclude the Estonian populations of wolf, lynx and beaver from annex IV of Directive 92/43/EEC (species in need of strict protection) to include them in Annex V (species whose taking in wild and exploitation may be subject to management measures). Concerning the geographical exception for lynx, the Commission will present a report by 1 May 2009 and the Council may on this basis decide to terminate its further application acting by QMV. Hunting of brown bears is allowed in Estonia under specific circumstances and subject to specific procedures set out in Article 16 (2) and (3) of Directive 98/43/EEC.

consequences of enlargement in both the old and new Member States. In addition, the negotiating process plays a key role in the Europeaniza-tion[16] of the national institutions and administrations of the acceding countries. It forms the final stage of a gradual process of preparing their public administrations to become full players in the multi-level system of EU policy- and decision-making.[17]

§ 2. *Structures, Institutions and Procedures of the Accession Negotiations*

Accession negotiations are conducted within bilateral Intergovernmental Conferences (IGCs) between the EU Member States and each indi-vidual applicant country. After the multilateral and bilateral screening exercise, negotiations start when a candidate presents its negotiating position on a certain chapter of the *acquis* to the Presidency of the Council. This so-called 'position paper' includes an overview of the implementation of the *acquis* for this chapter and a description of the candidate's administrative capacity.[18] The candidate country also indicates potential problems and/or requests for transitional periods. On the basis of this information, the Commission draws up the EU's draft negotiating position. After discussion of this proposal in the Council Enlargement Working Group and the COREPER, the General Affairs Council adopts the official 'EU Common Position' by unanimity. At this point, the chapter can be 'opened' and negotiations can begin.[19]

---

[16] This concept essentially refers to the increasing impact of European integration upon the functioning of national institutions. On the academic debate surrounding the definition of 'Europeanization', see: C. Radaelli, "The Europeanization of Public Policy", in: K. Featherstone, C. Radaelli, (eds.), *The Politics of Europeanization*, Oxford, Oxford University Press, 2003, pp. 28–34; J.P. Olsen, "The Many Faces of Europe-anization", 40 *Journal of Common Market Studies* 5 (2002), pp. 921–952.

[17] See: B. Lippert, G. Umbach, *The Pressure of Europeanisation. From Post-Communist State Administrations to Normal Players in the EU System*, Baden-Baden, Nomos, 2005, 203 p.; B. Lippert, G. Umbach, W. Wessels, "Europeanization of CEE Executives: EU Mem-bership Negotiations as a Shaping Power", 8 *Journal of European Public Policy* 6 (2001), pp. 980–1012.

[18] L. Maurer, "Negotiations in Progress", in: A. Ott, K. Inglis, (eds.), *Handbook on European Enlargement. A Commentary on the Enlargement Process*, The Hague, Asser, 2002, p. 120.

[19] In the accession negotiations with Turkey and Croatia, a new instrument has been introduced. In order to improve the quality and transparency of the negotiations, the European Commission prepares "benchmarks", i.e. measurable criteria before the opening and closing of negotiating chapters. See: Communication from the European Commission to the European Parliament and the Council, "Enlargement Strategy and Main Challenges 2006–2007", COM (2006) 649, Brussels, 8 November 2006, p. 6.

Formal negotiations take place in the IGC with Ministers from the Member States and the candidate country. More substantial negotiations are conducted at the 'deputies level', between the Permanent Representatives of the EU Member States and the chief negotiator of the candidate country. Whereas the Member States' representatives are assisted by working groups of officials in the Council, the Chief Negotiator of the candidate state can count on a negotiating team of experts. The negotiating delegations of the Baltic States all had a more or less comparable structure with, on the one hand, a core group of high level officials and, on the other hand, the heads of specific working groups.[20] The main delegation consisted of the Minister of Foreign Affairs, operating as the official head of the delegation, the chief negotiator,[21] senior officials of the ministries together with the head of the national mission to the EU and, in the case of Estonia, the head of the Office of European Integration of the State Chancellery. The members of this core group carried responsibility for the formulation and timely completion of their country's negotiating positions. For this task, they could count on the preparatory work of specific Working Groups, dealing with the different chapters of the *acquis*. The Working Groups were led by ministerial officials which were also official members of the negotiating delegation. A Task Force under the Ministry of Foreign Affairs in the case of Estonia and a Secretariat of the Delegation for EU accession negotiations in Latvia and Lithuania co-ordinated the work of the Working Groups and the core group of the delegation. These institutions also informed the Government and the Parliamentary European Affairs Committees on the progress of the negotiations. In Estonia, a Consultative Committee, composed of representatives of Estonian non-governmental organizations, academic and business circles, was also established in order to create a link with the civil society as an additional source of information for the drafting

---

[20] For a an overview of the structure and composition of the negotiating delegations of the Baltic States, see: http://www.vm.ee/eng/euro/aken_prindi/2759.html for Estonia; http://www.latvija-eiropa.gov.lv/en/organizations/government/delegation for Latvia and http://www.euro.lt/upl_images/20020828090106.doc for Lithuania.

[21] For Estonia, the Chief Negotiator was Alar Streimann, the deputy under-secretary for European Integration of the Ministry of Foreign Affairs; for Latvia it was Andris Kesteris, under-secretary of state of the Ministry of Foreign Affairs and for Lithuania this function was occupied by Petras Austrevicius, the Director General of the European Committee under the Government, assisted by Rytis Martikonis, Secretary of the Ministry of Foreign Affairs.

of Estonia's negotiating positions.[22] Hence, accession negotiations are prepared on different institutional levels with the Commission as a sort of mediator between the candidate and the Member States.[23]

When all parties agree on a common position, the chapter in question will be 'provisionally closed'. The Union always reserves the right to reopen negotiations until agreement has been reached on all negotiating chapters. If it turns out difficult to find a compromise on certain issues, negotiators can also decide to 'set aside' those chapters to be revisited at the end as part of a global package deal. At this final stage, negotiations will no longer respect the neat division into chapters but rather focus on the horizontal balance of the Accession Treaty. If no breakthrough can be achieved within the formal negotiating structures, the European Council will be involved to decide on the most sensitive issues.[24] This was also the case in the framework of the fifth enlargement wave. For instance, the EU Member States decided to transfer discussions on the financial consequences of the decommissioning of the Ignalina NPP together with other financial issues such as the creation of a cash-flow and Schengen facility to the end of the negotiations. At the 12–13 December 2002 Copenhagen European Council, the Heads of State or Government managed to strike a deal on the cost of enlargement, which paved the way for the formal conclusion of accession negotiations and the drafting of the Accession Treaty.[25] Before analysing the legal status of the Accession Treaty, a comparative analysis of the accession negotiations with the Baltic States intends to give a more profound insight in the preparation of the transitional arrangements and technical adjustments as included in this Treaty.

---

[22] In spite of this formal provision, the EU's Economic and Social Committee (ESC) has criticized Estonia for its limited co-operation with the country's socio-economic organizations in the process of EU accession preparations. See: Opinion of the Economic and Social Committee on Estonia's progress towards accession, REX/028, Brussels, 12 July 2000.

[23] A. Mayhew, "Enlargement of the European Union: An Analysis of the Negotiations with the Central and Eastern European Candidate Countries", *SEI Working Paper* 39 (2000), pp. 67–69, available at: http://www.sussex.ac.uk/sei/documents/wp39.pdf. On the role of the Commission see also: Maurer, *op. cit.*, footnote 18, p. 118. The role of the Commission has further extended in the ongoing negotiating process with Turkey and Croatia due to the introduction of opening and closing benchmarks. See supra at note 19.

[24] *Ibid.*, p. 69.

[25] Presidency Conclusions Copenhagen European Council (12–13 December 2002), *Bull. EU* 12 (2002), I.3.3.

CHAPTER TWO

ACCESSION NEGOTIATIONS IN PRACTICE:
THE CASE OF THE BALTIC STATES

§ 1. *Starting with the 'Easy Chapters'*

Formal accession negotiations started with Estonia on 31 March 1998 and with Latvia and Lithuania on 10 February 2000. For practical reasons, the *acquis* had been divided into 31 negotiating chapters. As a rule, negotiators first deal with the so-called 'easy chapters' and gradually contend with the more complicated issues under discussion. An analysis of the negotiating process with the Baltic States confirms this picture. As can be derived from the tables in Annex, the first chapters to be closed included statistics, industrial policy, small and medium size enterprises, science and research, education and training and Common Foreign and Security Policy. In all these areas the competences of the EU are rather limited. Hence, the *acquis* of these chapters is not extensive and does not require major investments on the part of the candidate countries. The main efforts for the Baltic States included the adoption of administrative changes and the introduction of new procedures (for example as regards the collection of data).[26] No single request for transitional periods or derogations to the principle of immediate or full application of the *acquis* was put forward.

§ 2. *The Chapter on External Relations:*
Illustrating the Paradoxes of the Negotiating Process

The first real political and legal discussions came to the fore in connection with the external relations chapter. Preparations for membership in this field require candidate countries to denounce their own trade and economic agreements with third countries, adhere to the agreements concluded by the Community and its Member States and take over the

---

[26] R. Vilpisauskas, "Baltic States Negotiating the EU Entry: Process, Patterns and Results", *Lithuanian Political Science Yearbook* (2002), p. 131.

commitments taken by the EC in international trade fora such as the WTO.[27] For the Baltic States, those requirements *inter alia* implied the termination of bilateral free trade agreements with important trading partners such as Ukraine and, most importantly, the trilateral Baltic Free Trade Agreement (BFTA) in case the three countries would join the EU at different stages. In this respect, Latvia and Lithuania insisted on a transitional arrangement to maintain the BFTA until all three Baltic States would become full members of the EU. Lithuania also requested the continuation of its preferential trade regime with Ukraine for a period of five years after EU accession.[28] Estonia's chief negotiator, on the other hand, stressed that his country was prepared to accept the external relations *acquis* without any transitional period or derogation.[29]

The different positions of Estonia, on the one hand, and Latvia and Lithuania on the other aroused political tensions among the Baltic States. The Latvian and Lithuanian chief negotiators criticized Estonia's lack of political solidarity and called for a better co-ordination of the Baltic States' negotiating positions "in order to secure a better deal for all three applicants in the EU accession talks".[30] Estonian representatives, however, minimised the importance of the BFTA for Estonia and even accused Latvia and Lithuania of taking measures that were not in line with their regional commitments.[31] As such, the controversy in the Baltic States surrounding the EU accession negotiations on the external relations chapter illustrates the drawbacks of the EU's differentiation policy. The EU's position that a continuation of the BFTA and the Lithuanian-Ukrainian FTA was incompatible with the obligations of

---

[27] European Commission, "Enlargement of the European Union. Guide to the Negotiations. Chapter by Chapter", available at: http://europa.eu.int/comm/enlargement/negotiations/chapters/chap26/index.htm.

[28] See: Position Paper of the Republic of Latvia and the Republic of Lithuania on Chapter 26 "External Relations", available at: http://www.am.gov.lv and http://www.euro.lt respectively.

[29] X, "Lack of consensus among Baltic states about free trade agreement", *Uniting Europe* 95 (2000), p. 6; see also Estonia's Position Paper on Chapter 26, available at: http://www.vm.ee/eng/euro/kat_309/2770.html.

[30] X, "Latvia urges for better Baltic co-operation in accession talks", *Uniting Europe* 99 (2000), pp. 6–7.

[31] X, "Candidates comments after negotiating meeting of 6 April", *Uniting Europe* 95 (2000), pp. 5–6.

EU membership[32] further revealed the paradoxical interplay between the political and legal aspects of the EU enlargement process.

Being a politically inspired project, enlargement intends to create stability on the entire European continent. Accordingly, the EU's pre-accession strategies stimulated the development of regional co-operation initiatives such as the BFTA (cf. *supra*). From a legal perspective, however, enlargement implies an individualised procedure in the sense that each candidate is to be judged on its own merits, irrespective the situation in the other applicant countries. This individual treatment may be in conflict with the rather political ambitions of a regional co-operation programme. The Baltic States' negotiations on the external relations chapter clearly illustrated this paradox. The preferential ties between Estonia, Latvia and Lithuania, which were deemed important to improve regional stability, had to be cut down when the three States would not have joined the EU together in order to secure the proper functioning of the internal market and the EC's common commercial policy. A similar situation existed in Central Europe with the Czech-Slovak customs union. Against this background, Enlargement Commissioner Günter Verheugen declared his support for a group entry of the four Visegrád candidates [Czech Republic, Hungary, Poland and Slovakia]. Such a grouping was considered to be "politically logical" and would allow to "solve several practical problems".[33] Obviously, the tied economic links between those countries and the existence of the Czech-Slovak customs union inspired this political statement.

Latvia's chief negotiator, Andris Kesteris, used Verheugen's speech to deliver his own view on the EU's enlargement strategy.[34] On the one hand, he criticized the premature prioritisation of the Visegrád group. On the other hand, Kesteris fully endorsed the idea of grouping countries with similar economic and geographic particularities. In this respect, a joint accession of Estonia, Latvia and Lithuania was

[32] Obviously, a continuation of the above-mentioned agreements would be contrary to the EC's common commercial policy. In addition, it could affect the proper functioning of the common agricultural policy, the uniform implementation of the common customs tariff, disrupt the free movement of goods within the internal market and lead to distortions of competition. See: X, "EU Pressure on Lithuania over Baltic Free Trade After Membership", *Uniting Europe* 102 (2000), p. 8.

[33] X, "Group Entry of Poland, Hungary, Czech Republic and Slovakia is 'political priority', Commissioner says", *Uniting Europe* 96 (2000), pp. 1–2.

[34] X, "Latvia upset by 'premature' debate on possible joint entry of Visegrád countries", *Uniting Europe* 99 (2000), pp. 4–5.

recommended as "wise and logical". As part of his diplomatic offensive, Latvia's chief negotiator urged the Commission and the EU Member States to create the necessary prerequisites for Latvia to catch up with the countries of the Luxembourg group, and Estonia in particular. The answer to this request came with the presentation of the Commission's strategy to take the accession negotiations in a more substantial phase. This strategy included (i) a classification of requests for transitional measures; (ii) a detailed 'road map' for negotiations, providing a realistic timetable for the conclusion of the remaining chapters under the subsequent Council Presidencies in 2001–2002[35] and (iii) a more rapid method of opening remaining accession negotiation chapters with the Helsinki group.[36] Accordingly, the EU created the circumstances for the countries of the Helsinki group to catch up with the previous frontrunners. Latvia and Lithuania warmly welcomed this new strategy but Estonia remained sceptical, mainly because it feared delays on the road to accession. Estonia's chief negotiator, therefore, demanded that progress in the negotiations would not be restricted to a rigid timetable.[37] A response to the Estonian sensitivities was already provided in the Commission strategy paper, which explicitly referred to differentiation and individual progress on the basis of the Accession Partnerships as the key principles for progressing in the negotiations.[38] In other words, the basic logic of the enlargement process largely remained the same. The accession negotiations on the external relations chapter, however, clearly illustrated the advantages of a more geopolitical approach.

Pressure from the EU and progress in the negotiations forced Latvia and Lithuania to withdraw their requests for transitional arrangements in the field of external relations. Both countries accepted the EU's position that further tariff concessions for agricultural products under the Europe Agreements would automatically solve the problem of the BFTA in case of a differentiated accession of the Baltic States. In response to

---

[35] Accordingly, the Commission and the Nice European Council confirmed the Helsinki ambition to conclude negotiations with the best-prepared candidates by the end of 2002 (cf. *supra*).

[36] European Commission, "Enlargement Strategy Paper. Report on Progress Towards Accession by each of the Candidate Countries", COM (2000) 700, Brussels, 8 November 2000, pp. 25–31.

[37] X, "Frontrunners push for earlier end to talks than foreseen in Commission road map", *Uniting Europe* 122 (2000), pp. 1–7.

[38] European Commission, "Enlargement Strategy Paper. Report on Progress Towards Accession by each of the Candidate Countries", COM (2000) 700, Brussels, 8 November 2000, pp. 31–32.

the decision to abandon its free trade agreement with Ukraine, Lithuania announced to work keenly in favour of the further development of EU-Ukrainian relations, including support for the establishment of a free trade area, after its EU entry.[39] In spite of this political engagement, the legal prerequisites of the EC's common commercial policy clearly demonstrate the impact of accession upon a country's external (trade) policy as well as the effects of EU enlargement for countries left outside the EU.

In this respect, the Act of Accession explicitly proclaims that "from the date of accession, the new Member States shall withdraw from any free trade agreements with third countries".[40] Moreover, EU accession triggers the application of Article 307, which includes in its second paragraph an obligation for the Member States to eliminate the incompatibilities between agreements concluded before the date of their accession and the EC Treaty.[41] The Act of Accession, which only indirectly refers to this provision, further specifies that "if a new Member State encounters difficulties in adjusting an agreement concluded with one or more third countries before accession, it shall, according to the terms of the agreement, withdraw from that agreement".[42] On the other hand, EU enlargement also involves the accession of new Member States to international agreements concluded by the Community or the Union.[43] For mixed agreements, i.e. agreements concluded by both the Community and the Member States, the accession of new Member States requires the conclusion of a protocol between the Council, acting unanimously on behalf of the Member States, and the third party. The Commission conducts the negotiations on the Community side on the basis of unanimously approved negotiation directives from the Council

---

[39] X, "Lithuania progresses in talks after concessions on free trade with other Baltics and Ukraine", *Uniting Europe* 119 (2000), pp. 2–3.

[40] Article 6 (10) of the Act concerning the conditions of accession of the Czech Republic, the Republic of Estonia, the Republic of Cyprus, the Republic of Latvia, the Republic of Lithuania, the Republic of Hungary, the Republic of Malta, the Republic of Poland, the Republic of Slovenia and the Slovak Republic and the adjustments to the Treaties on which the European Union is founded, *OJ* (2003) L 236/35. A similar provision can be found in Article 6 (9) with regard to the new Member States' fisheries agreements, reflecting the Community's exclusive competence in this sphere.

[41] For an analysis of the case-law on Article 307 EC, see: M. Cremona, "The Impact of Enlargement: External Policy and External Relations", in: M. Cremona, (ed.), *The Enlargement of the European Union*, Oxford, Oxford University Press, 2003, pp. 162–172.

[42] Article 6 (10) Act of Accession.

[43] Article 6 (1) Act of Accession.

and in consultation with a Committee of Member States' representatives.[44] This procedure is important because in previous enlargement rounds the acceding countries themselves had to conclude separate agreements or protocols with third States.[45] It is obvious that the new *modus operandi*, where the Council so to say concludes accession protocols on behalf of the new Member States,[46] was advantageous for the Baltic States, particularly in the light of their politically and legally difficult relationship with Russia.

The discussions surrounding the conclusion of a protocol of extension to the Partnership and Co-operation Agreement with Russia clearly illustrated the complexity of this exercise. For the EU, the conclusion of such a protocol was seen as a technical and quasi-automatic operation. Russia, however, claimed compensation for the alleged negative consequences of enlargement and proceeded from the assumption that extending the PCA to the new Member States was a good opportunity to negotiate this question. In this respect, Moscow presented to the EU in January 2004 a list of fourteen concerns, mainly of an economic nature but also including the politically sensitive issue of protection of the sizeable Russian-speaking minorities in Estonia and Latvia.[47] Remarkably, a similar list was submitted to the Commission already in 1999.[48] In addition, Russia's 1999 Medium-Term Strategy on relations with the EU included a specific chapter on "securing the Russian interests in an expanded European Union", which *inter alia* referred to a possible refusal to extend the PCA.[49] In spite of these clear requests from the Russian side to proactively discuss the consequences of enlargement in the framework of the 'Strategic Partnership', the EU preferred a 'wait and see' approach, which lead to a crisis in the bilateral relations. Only few days before the accession of the new Member States both parties managed to find a mutually acceptable solution in the form of a Joint

---

[44] Article 6 (2) Act of Accession.

[45] M. Maresceau, "Bilateral Agreements Concluded by the European Community", 309 *Recueil des Cours The Hague Academy of International Law* (2004), p. 308.

[46] K. Inglis, "The Union's fifth Accession Treaty: New Means to Make Enlargement Possible", 41 *Common Market Law Review* (2004), p. 943.

[47] X, "Russia critical of minorities treatment in new EU Member States", *EUObserver.com*, 19 January 2004.

[48] X, "Russia seeks new Commission's understanding on enlargement request", *Uniting Europe* (1999) 66, pp. 3–4.

[49] Medium-term Strategy for Development of Relations between the Russian Federation and the European Union (2000–2010) [unofficial translation], available at: http://www.europa.eu.int/comm/external_relations/russia/russian_medium_strategy/.

Statement on "EU enlargement and EU-Russia relations" (cf. *infra*), which paved the way for the signature of the long-awaited Protocol on extension of the PCA.[50]

This example clearly illustrates that, even though the acceding countries agree with the obligations under the external relations chapter without any transitional arrangement, the full application of the *acquis communautaire* in this field requires the approval of third countries. The forced termination of the Baltic States' free trade arrangement with Ukraine further reveals that, notwithstanding the continuous rhetoric on the avoidance of new dividing lines, EU enlargement raises new legal barriers. As such, the extension of the external relations *acquis* to new Member States demonstrates the inherent tension between the legal and political consequences of enlargement.

§ 3. *The Internal Market Acquis: Illustrating the Limits of Differentiation*

The conclusion of the external relations chapter in April 2000 with Estonia and in November of the same year with Latvia and Lithuania, signified a first important breakthrough in the negotiating process. The December 2000 Nice European Council endorsement of the Commission's strategy to take the negotiations into a more substantial phase as well as the completion of the IGC on institutional reforms provided further impetus to tackle more sensitive chapters. In line with the proposed road map, the Swedish Presidency—taking place in the first half of 2001—primarily dealt with the four freedoms, company law, culture and audio-visual policy, social policy and environment.

The chapter on free movement of persons attracted specific attention, partly because the Baltic States secured the recognition of diplomas issued at the time of the Soviet Union but mainly because of the negotiations on the mobility of workers. Given their geographical location and limited populations, the Baltic States requested the immediate opening of the EU labour market. Taking into account the sensitivities and uncertainties surrounding this part of the *acquis*, the EU Member States decided to adopt a common position applicable to all Central

---

[50] Joint Statement on EU Enlargement and EU-Russia Relations and the Protocol to the Partnership and Co-operation Agreement are available at: http://www.europa. eu.int/comm/external_relations/russia/russia_docs/index.htm. On the political and legal consequences of PCA extension, see *infra* Part V, Chapter 1, § 1.2.

and East European candidate countries. The offer included a flexible 2+3+2 arrangement.[51] During the first two-year period from the date of accession, the old Member States (EU15) could apply their national regimes to regulate access of CEEC nationals on their labour market. Before the end of this period, the Council reviewed the functioning of the transitional arrangements on the basis of a report prepared by the Commission.[52] Each new Member State may request one additional review.[53] Under the EU's draft common position, the Council was given the power to decide, by unanimity, whether to shorten or lift the transition period on the basis of the Commission's assessment.[54] This option, however, was not preserved in the EU's final negotiating position and, eventually, in the Act of Accession. From a legal point of view, the review now only requires the EU15 to notify the Commission whether they will continue applying national measures.[55] This transitional arrangement should in principle come to an end five years after accession, but a Member State that notifies the Commission of serious disturbances of its labour market, or a threat thereof, may continue to apply national measures for an additional two years. Member States that have decided not to apply the transitional period may invoke a safeguard clause, i.e. suspend the application of Articles 1 to 6 of Regulation (EEC) 1612/69, after notification to the Commission and in case of serious disturbances of the labour market or a threat thereof until the end of the seventh year following the new Member States' accession.[56] As long as the EU15 apply national measures, new

---

[51] For a detailed analysis of this arrangement, see: A. Adinolfi, "Free Movement and Access to Work of Citizens of the New Member States: The Transitional Measures", 42 *CMLRev.* (2005), pp. 485–496.

[52] The Commission's report has been published on 8 February 2006. The report concluded that the mobility of Central and Eastern European workers had a positive impact on the economies of the EU Member States which had not applied national restrictions (Ireland, Sweden and the UK) and invited the other Member States "to consider whether the continuation of transitional arrangements is needed". Communication from the Commission to the Council, the European Parliament, the European Economic and Social Committee and the Committee of the Regions, Report on the Functioning of the Transitional Arrangements set out in the 2003 Accession Treaty (period 1 May 2004–30 April 2006), COM (2006) 48 final, Brussels, 8 February 2006.

[53] See e.g. for Estonia: Act of Accession, *OJ* (2003) L 236/812.

[54] "Enlargement: Commission proposes flexible transitional arrangements for the free movement of workers", Press Release 11 April 2001, IP/01/561.

[55] In the absence of such notification the *acquis* will apply.

[56] "The Commission shall decide on the suspension and on the duration and the scope thereof not later than two weeks after receiving such a request and shall notify the Council of such a decision. Any Member State may, within two weeks from the

Member States may apply equivalent measures with regard to nationals of the old Member State(s) concerned (reciprocity principle).

In spite of other provisions limiting the discretion of the EU15, such as a standstill clause,[57] preferential treatment of CEEC workers over other job-seekers from third countries[58] and declarations promising the rapid elimination of restrictive measures,[59] the Baltic States pointed out that such a transitional arrangement failed to observe the principle of differentiation because the EU's common position was clearly drafted for the bigger Central European countries.[60] The so-called 'flanking measures' for Austria and Germany, including restrictions to the temporary movement of workers in specific sensitive service sectors, illustrate this point.[61] The discussions on the free movement of workers, therefore, revealed another paradox of the negotiating process. Whereas the accession negotiations are conducted in bilateral IGCs and, in principle, proceed on an individual basis with each candidate country, the EU clearly applied a group approach by presenting a 'one size fits all' deal to all CEECs.[62] This strategy, in combination with the competitive nature of the accession process, stressed the asymmetric power relation between the EU and the candidates. After one country,

---

date of the Commission's decision, request the Council to annul or amend the decision. The Council shall act on such a request within two weeks, by qualified majority". Act of Accession, *OJ* (2003) L 236/812.

[57] This provision prevents the EU15 to apply conditions for access to work on citizens of the new Member States "which are more restrictive than those prevailing on the date of the signature of the Treaty of Accession", Act of Accession, *OJ* (2003) L 236/814.

[58] As long as the EU15 apply the transitional period, they should "give preference to workers who are nationals of the Member States over workers who are nationals of third countries as regards access to their labour market [...] Furthermore, in application of the principle of Community preference, migrant workers from third countries resident and working in [Estonia] shall not be treated more favourably than nationals of [Estonia]". Act of Accession, *OJ* (2003) L 236/814.

[59] For each new Member State from Central and Eastern Europe, the Act of Accession contains a declaration in which the EU15 promise to "make best use of the proposed arrangement to move as quickly as possible to the full application of the *acquis* in the area of free movement of workers". Act of Accession, *OJ* (2003) L 236/975.

[60] X, "Estonia feared being trapped in row over free movement of labour", *Uniting Europe* 102 (2000), p. 6; X, "Free Movement of Persons: Differentiation is Needed", *Uniting Europe* 139 (2001), p. 4.

[61] Arguably, this provision was included as a response to German and Austrians fears of massive labour immigration from its direct neighbours and Poland in particular. See e.g. comments of EU negotiators in: Friss, "The EU's Enlargement Negotiations", *op. cit.*, footnote 6, pp. 206–208.

[62] *Ibid.*

in this case Hungary, accepted the deal, it was presented as a *fait accompli* to the others. Aware of the limited chances to obtain more at a later stage, other countries followed suit. This was particularly the case with countries that tried to secure a place in the first enlargement group by closing chapters as quickly as possible. For this reason, it can be explained why Latvia closed the chapter on free movement of persons only few weeks after the ice-breaking deal with Hungary.

When the Czech Republic later managed to negotiate minor modifications, such as the possibility to limit the inflow of labour from other new Member States during the period when old Member States apply transitional measures, the EU immediately decided to offer this new solution to all countries that had already concluded this chapter. This practice illustrates the limits of the EU rhetoric on the principle of differentiation and individual treatment of each candidate. This observation aroused growing irritation among the Estonian negotiators. In the context of delays that occurred in the practical disbursement of the EU's pre-accession aid, Estonia's chief negotiator complained about the fact that:

> [A]lthough differentiation is always mentioned by the EU as a basic principle of the enlargement process, it has far from always being applied in practical terms. [...] The EU attitude often seems to be that the candidate countries have to receive the same treatment, and they have to be granted the same rights and benefits.[63]

The accession negotiations on the free movement of capital seemed to support this thesis. Confronted with requests for long transition periods by several Central European countries as regards the application of the *acquis* concerning the acquisition of agricultural, forestry and industrial land as well as secondary residences by EU citizens who do not reside on their territory, the EU proposed a 'one size fits all' solution. The EU common position included a seven-year transitional period for the acquisition of agricultural land and a five-year period for secondary residences. After the Czech Republic accepted this offer with minor amendments, a group dynamic could be observed because other applicants quickly accepted the same arrangement in spite of their different initial negotiating positions.[64] This development significantly

---

[63] X, "Estonia criticises delay on SAPARD Pre-Accession help", *Uniting Europe* 139 (2001), p. 5.

[64] Friis, "Countdown to Copenhagen", *op. cit.*, footnote 1, pp. 36–39.

affected the Baltic States' negotiations on this chapter. Initially, none of the three Baltic countries had applied for transitional periods. Accordingly, Estonia, Latvia and Lithuania provisionally closed the chapter without any transitional arrangement. Later on, taking into account the general scepticism of the farming population and the examples set by the Central European countries, the chapter was re-opened. This was particularly important for Lithuania because the full application of the *acquis* in this field required amendments to Article 47 of the Lithuanian Constitution (cf. *infra*). In this constitutional amendment process, the Lithuanian Parliament adopted a resolution recommending the government "to seek during the negotiations on the terms and conditions for accession to the European Union a transitional period of 7 to 10 years for acquisition of agricultural and forest land by foreign nationals, with the exception of farmers of the European Union Member States who have resided in Lithuania for at least 3 years on a permanent basis, have established a farm and have engaged in agriculture".[65]

During the final negotiating sessions, the EU accepted an identical arrangement for the three Baltic States, including a seven-year transitional period for the acquisition of agricultural and forestry land with a possibility to extend this period by three years in case of serious disturbances on the agricultural market or a threat thereof. This temporary derogation from the *acquis* does not apply to EU citizens who have been legally resident and active in farming in the respective states for at least three consecutive years.[66] The arrangement also includes a standstill and non-discrimination provision, which implies that EU citizens may not be treated less favourably in respect of the acquisition of agricultural land and forests than at the date of signature of the Accession Treaty[67] or be treated in a more restrictive way than a national of a third country. Reflecting the deal on the free movement of workers, a general review of the transitional measures is planned in the third year

---

[65] Seimas of the Republic of Lithuania, "Resolution on the expediency and time limits of the transitional period for acquisition of agricultural and forest land in Lithuania by foreign nationals", 1 July 2002, No. IX-1003.

[66] See e.g. for Estonia: Act of Accession, *OJ* (2003) L 236/814.

[67] Significantly, the Latvian Parliament adopted amendments to the law on the privatisation of rural land only one week before the signature of the Accession Treaty. The new amendments, introducing restrictions to the acquisition of agricultural land for EU citizens and other foreigners in line with the transitional arrangement, entered into force on 15 April 2003 with the Accession Treaty signed the following day. D. Akule, "Latvia makes last-minute changes in land purchase law", http://www.euobserver.com, 7 April 2003.

following the date of accession. In contrast to the provisions on free movement of workers, however, the Council can unanimously decide to shorten or terminate the transitional period on a proposal from the Commission.[68] In comparison to most other candidate countries the Baltic States did not negotiate a transitional period for the acquisition of summerhouses.

In spite of the parallel results of the accession negotiations in chapters such as the free movement of persons or free movement of capital, differentiation remained possible. Latvia, for instance, is the only Baltic State with transitional arrangements in the field of social policy and employment (all related to the adoption of health and safety requirements) whereas on the chapter of free movement of goods only Lithuania negotiated a transitional period until 1 January 2007 in the sub-sector of medical products for the renewal of marketing authorisations of medical products.[69] In general, however, the competitive nature of the EU accession process forced the candidate countries to adopt the EU's common positions without many deliberations in order to conclude as many negotiating chapters as fast as possible.[70] As a result, chapters involving significant adjustment efforts, such as the *acquis* on environmental protection, caused relatively little controversy. Arguably, the conclusion of the environment chapter with Slovenia at the end of March 2001 put some pressure on the other candidates.[71] Lithuania, for instance, quickly decided to withdraw five requests for transitional arrangements whereas the duration of the transitional periods was reduced in the remaining three cases. A similar pattern could be observed as regards Estonia and Latvia, which reduced their number of requests for transitional periods on this chapter from seven to four and twenty-three to nine respectively. This more flexible position of the candidate countries allowed the smooth proceeding of the accession talks. Lithuania and Latvia, in particular, made a remarkable progress under the Swedish Presidency. During the first half of 2001, both countries opened the remaining 13 chapters and closed eleven and seven chapters respectively. Estonia, in contrast, only closed three chapters within this period. Hence, the application of the new strategy

---

[68] See e.g. for Estonia: Act of Accession, *OJ* (2003) L 236/814.

[69] See Annex III.

[70] This practice has sometimes been called "chapter fetishism". See e.g. Friis, "Countdown to Copenhagen", *op. cit.*, footnote 1, p. 29.

[71] *Ibid.*, pp. 34–36.

for negotiations allowed Lithuania and Latvia to catch up with Estonia and the other Luxembourg group countries. This rapid catching up could partly be explained by the administrative and political efforts of the Lithuanian and Latvian negotiators and partly by the ambitious Swedish Presidency.[72]

§ 4. *Taxation and Energy: Tackling the Strategic Chapters*

4.1. *Estonia as a Special Case*

Belgium, taking over the EU Presidency for the second half of 2001, faced the challenge to continue the momentum created during the Swedish Presidency. On the agenda were, *inter alia*, negotiations on taxation and energy, arguably two of the most sensitive chapters for the Baltic States in general and Estonia in particular. Given the specific characteristics of Estonia's tax system, including a zero rate corporate income tax, low VAT rates for different goods and low excise duties compared to EU Member States, preparations for EU accession required significant legislative efforts. The *Riigikogu* had to adopt a new VAT Act, eliminating VAT exemptions on certain supplies of goods and services, and amendments to the Estonian Income Tax Act.[73] During the accession negotiations, several EU Member States criticized Estonia's practice of charging no income tax on reinvested corporate profits. Fearing unfair tax competition, the EU urged Estonia to tighten its tax regime.[74] Estonian representatives, however, rejected this demand because corporate

---

[72] R. Vilpisauskas, "Baltic States Negotiating EU Entry", *op. cit.*, footnote 26, p. 133; On the role of the Swedish Presidency, see also: R. Bengtsson, "EU Enlargement and the Swedish EU Presidency", Paper Presented at the Conference "Baltic States and EU Accession Negotiations: An Assessment", Riga, 14 December 2001, available at: http://www.svet.lu.se/Projekt/Presidency/Rigapaper.pdf.

[73] Estonia's new Income Tax Law entered into force in January 2000. Initially, this law exempted legal persons registered in Estonia and non-residents that had registered a branch or other permanent establishment in Estonia from paying income tax on re-invested profit. Amendments were adopted in October 2001, providing that profit distributions will be taxed regardless of whether the dividends are paid to resident or non-resident legal persons. See: European Commission 2000 and 2002 Regular Reports on Estonia's progress towards accession, available at: http://www.europa.eu.int/comm/enlargement.

[74] A. Lobjakas, "Commission Questions Estonia's Liberal Corporate Tax Regime", 8 March 2002, available at: http://www.eubusiness.com.

income tax does not fall within the scope of the *acquis communautaire*.[75] Estonia further wanted to maintain its zero VAT rate for hydroelectricity and wind energy up to the end of 2007, apply a reduced VAT regime on household heating resources until 30 June 2005, exempt small and medium size enterprises (SMEs) from compulsory VAT registration if they have a turnover below € 16,000 instead of € 5,000 as provided by the *acquis*, harmonise the tobacco excise tax rate gradually up to the end of 2010 and continue tax and duty free sales on board of ships for 6.5 years after accession.[76] A study of these five requests revealed that the Estonian government attributed most importance to the tobacco excise tax issue and the reduced VAT for household heating whereas the inclusion of the request for tax and duty free sales on ships was rather seen as an instrument to broaden the scope for negotiations.[77] The importance of each request can be linked to its economic, social and political consequences. A sharp increase in prices for household heating and cigarettes would directly affect the Estonian population and in particular the lowest incomes. In the case of tobacco products, fears of increased smuggling and declining budget revenues further supported the request for a transitional arrangement. Taking into account these arguments, the EU allowed Estonia to gradually raise the excise duties on tobacco products up to the minimum EU level by the end of 2009. As long as this transitional period applies, EU Member States may apply quantitative limits for cigarettes and other tobacco products brought into their territories from Estonia. A similar arrangement was agreed with Latvia and Lithuania, which had voiced similar concerns. For the supply of heating sold to private individuals, Estonia may maintain a reduced rate of no less than 5 per cent until 30 June 2007.[78] The EU also accepted Estonia's proposal to fix the

---

[75] In response to the zero rate corporate income tax in Estonia and the low corporate tax levels in many CEECs, France and Germany support the introduction of a minimum EU corporate tax, an idea which countries such as the UK and Estonia fiercely oppose. See: X, "France and Germany push for EU harmised corporate tax", *EurActiv*, 14 May 2004, available at: http://www.euractiv.com.

[76] L. Teras, "Estonia on the Road to the European Union: Hopes and Concerns in Accession Negotiations", in: J. Kapustans, (ed.), *Baltic States and EU Accession Negotiations: An Assessment*, Riga, Latvian Institute of International Affairs, 2002, p. 48.

[77] M. Kompus, K. Kallas, L. Saarniit, *Negotiating European Issues. National Strategies and Priorities. EU Accession Negotiations Chapter 10—Taxation*, OEUE Occasional Papers 2.2, available at: http://www.oeue.net/papers/estonia-euaccessionnegotiation.pdf.

[78] Latvia obtained a short-term exemption for VAT on household heating until 31 December 2004; Lithuania did not request a similar transitional arrangement.

VAT exemption threshold for SMEs at € 16,000.[79] The requests for a zero VAT rate on renewable energy resources and tax free sales on ships could, however, not be accepted.

Importantly, Estonia managed to obtain a temporary derogation from Article 5 (1) of the so-called parent-subsidiary directive, which prohibits withholding tax on profits distributed by a subsidiary to its parent company.[80] Given the broad interpretation of the ECJ to the scope of Article 5 (1),[81] Estonia's practice of charging income tax to profits distributed by Estonian subsidiaries to their parent companies established in other Member States clearly infringed EC law. The Act of Accession, however, allows Estonia to apply its corporate tax system up to the end of 2008.[82] Efforts of Estonian representatives to extend this derogation or amend Directive 90/435/EEC illustrate the importance of the taxation chapter, which was only provisionally closed in the summer of 2002 after a lengthy process of negotiations.[83] A similar process of long and difficult negotiations could be observed as regards the energy chapter.

For Estonia, the restructuring of the inefficient and highly polluting oil shale sector, responsible for up to 90 per cent of Estonia's energy

---

[79] For Latvia the threshold amounts € 17,200 and for Lithuania € 29,000. See: Act of Accession, *OJ* (2003) L 236/556.

[80] Council Directive 90/435/EEC of 23 July 1990 on the common system of taxation applicable in the case of parent companies and subsidiaries of different Member States, *OJ* (1990) L 225/6; Council Directive 2003/123/EC of 22 December 2003 amending Directive 90/435/EEC on the common system of taxation applicable in the case of parent companies and subsidiaries of different Member States, *OJ* (2004) L 7/41.

[81] In Case C-294/99 *Athinaiki Zihopiaa* [2001] ECR I-6797, the ECJ concluded that "[t]here is a withholding tax, within the meaning of Article 5 (1) of Council Directive 90/435/EEC of 23 July 1990 on the common system of taxation applicable in the case of parent companies and subsidiaries of different Member States, where national legislation provides that, in the event of distribution of profits by a subsidiary (a public limited company or equivalent company) to its parent company, in order to determine the taxable profits of the subsidiary its total net profits, including income which has been subject to special taxation entailing extinction of tax liability and non-taxable income, must be reincorporated into the basic taxable amount, when income falling within those two categories would not be taxable on the basis of the national legislation if they remained with the subsidiary and were not distributed to the parent company." See also: Case C-58/01 *Océ Van Der Grinten* [2003] ECR I-9809.

[82] Act of Accession, *OJ* (2003) L 236/816.

[83] In January 2005, Estonia's Finance Minister Taavi Veskimagi sent a letter to Tax and Customs Commissioner Laszlo Kovacs with a proposal to amend the parent-subsidiary directive in order to preserve Estonia's tax system. X, "Estonia asks for Commissioner's Opinion", *The Baltic Times*, 19 January 2005.

production, forms an extraordinary challenge.[84] In March 2001, the Estonian Ministry of Economic Affairs presented its "Restructuring Plan of the Estonian oil-shale sector 2001–2006".[85] This document stressed the strategic importance of oil shale for Estonia's economy. Taking into account the high cost of alternative solutions and the increasing dependency upon imported electricity from Russia or Lithuania in case energy production from oil shale would be abandoned, the Estonian government and parliament decided to continue oil shale based energy production until 2015.[86] Accordingly, Estonian negotiators requested a 'special status' for oil shale after accession to the EU and a treatment in EU policies equal to coal.[87] Apart from the economic and strategic relevance of continued oil shale production, Estonian representatives also pointed at the social consequences of closing oil shale mines. The production and consumption of oil shale is concentrated in the Ida-Viru county located at the Russian border in the North East of Estonia and populated mainly with Russian-speaking inhabitants. Given the already backward situation of this area, with the highest unemployment rates of the country and a relatively unfavourable investment climate, any reductions of workforce in the oil shale sector—the main employer of the region—create additional socio-economic problems.

Taking into account the unique character of Estonia's oil shale sector and its social and economic significance, Estonia was granted a temporary derogation as regards the application of Article 19 (2) of Directive 96/92, which required the Members States to have opened their national electricity markets for large-scale consumers of electricity by 1 July 2004. Pursuant to Section 8, point 2 of Annex VI to the Act of Accession, Estonia's transitional period ends on 31 December 2008.

---

[84] In its 1997 Opinion on Estonia's application for membership of the EU, the Commission observed: "Oil shale mining and burning are inefficient and present considerable environmental problems. They represent two thirds of Estonia's SO2 emissions. Reducing the dependency on oil shale will involve a major restructuring programme and Estonia will have to address its socio-regional consequences". Commission Opinion on Estonia's Application for Membership of the European Union, COM (97) 2006 final, Brussels, 15 July 1997, p. 80.

[85] Ministry of Economic Affairs of the Republic of Estonia, *Restructuring plan of the Estonian oil-shale sector 2001–2006*, available at: http://www.eib.ee/files/annex_06.pdf.

[86] *Ibid.*, p. 4.

[87] This request was already formulated by Estonian Prime Minister Toomas Hendrik Ilves in his opening statement on the start of accession negotiations (available at: http://www.vm.ee). Later on, Estonia's Chief Negotiator Alan Streimann regularly stressed the unique character of Estonia's oil shale sector (interview with Liina Teras, Attaché at the European Integration Department, Tallinn, 24 April 2002).

In view of the need for early implementation of an operational internal electricity market, as laid down in the conclusions of the March 2002 Barcelona European Council, the EU Member States also adopted a "Joint Declaration on oil shale, the internal electricity market and Directive 96/92/EC concerning common rules for the internal market in electricity", annexed to the Final Act of the Accession Treaty.[88] In this—from a legal point of view unbinding—document the Union recognizes that the specific situation related to the restructuring of the oil shale sector will require particular efforts until the end of 2012. Accordingly, the Estonian electricity market for non-household customers can only be gradually opened until that date.[89] The EU also acknowledged that Estonia reserves its position regarding future legislative developments regarding the internal electricity market.

A new legal situation emerged with the adoption of Directive 2003/54 concerning common rules for the internal market in electricity on 26 June 2003, i.e. some two months after the signature of the Treaty of Accession.[90] The new electricity Directive, which is based on Articles 47 (2) EC, 55 EC and 95 EC, wholly replaces and repeals Directive 96/92 and provides in its Article 21 for the complete opening of the electricity markets for all categories of customers by 1 July 2007 and for non-household customers by 1 July 2004. In response to these new circumstances, the Estonian government requested the Commission to adapt the derogation granted in Annex VI to the Act of Accession in respect of Article 19 (2) of Directive 96/92 so that it applied to Article 21 of Directive 2003/54. In addition, and with reference to the above-mentioned Joint Statement, Estonia requested an extended transitional period with regard to the full opening of its national electricity market. The Commission thereupon drafted a proposal for a Directive of the European Parliament and the Council, based upon Articles 47 (2) EC, 55 EC and 95 EC, amending Directive 2003/54 to the effect that Estonia was granted a temporary derogation from the application of Article 21 (1) (b) and (c) until 31 December 2012. Significantly, the Council adopted the amendment Directive (2004/85) including the new transitional arrangement for Estonia on

---

[88] Act of Accession, *OJ* (2003) L 236/975.
[89] *Ibid.*
[90] Directive 2003/54/EC of the European Parliament and of the Council of 26 June 2003 concerning common rules for the internal market in electricity and repealing Directive 96/92/EC, *OJ* (2003) L 176/37.

the legal basis of Article 57 of the Act of Accession, rather than on the grounds proposed by the Commission. Significantly, Article 57 AA does not require the participation of the European Parliament and allows the Council to adopt, by qualified majority on a proposal from the Commission, necessary adaptations to Community acts by reason of accession when those adaptations have not been included in the Act of Accession or its annexes. The application of Article 57 AA was deemed necessary because of the close link between the Commission's proposal and the Treaty of Accession and in view of the need to adapt Directive 2003/54 before its date of application, i.e. 1 July 2004. The European Parliament, however, did not accept such an extensive interpretation of Article 57 and brought the case before the ECJ in an action for annulment of Directive 2004/85 under Article 230 EC.[91]

This inter-institutional procedure raises interesting legal questions as regards the possibility to introduce new transitional measures with regard to legislation adopted in the period between the signature of the Accession Treaty and the date of accession. Whereas Article 55 AA permits new Member States to request derogations from acts adopted between the end of the accession negotiations and the date of signature of the Accession Treaty, no specific provisions have been included for legal developments after this period. Article 57 AA pursues a different objective than Article 55 AA in the sense that it is intended as a legal base for making necessary adaptations to Community acts which are indispensable for facilitating accession. Amendments going beyond this objective cannot be based on Article 57 AA.[92] According to Advocate-General Geelhoed, the introduction of new transitional arrangements is primarily a political decision and not a technical necessity under the terms of Article 57 AA.[93] Hence, the necessary implication is that the contested Directive should have been based on Articles 47 (2) EC, 55 EC, 95 EC in combination with Article 15 EC, which permits temporary derogations to Community acts in order to take account of differences in development between the economies of the Member States.

---

[91] ECJ, Case C-413/04, *European Parliament* v. *Council of the European Union*, ECR [2006] I-11221.

[92] ECJ, Case C-259/95, *European Parliament* v. *Council*, ECR [1997] I-5303 at para. 14. This case concerned an identically worded provision in the Act of Accession of 1994.

[93] Opinion of Advocate General Geelhoed in Case C-413/04, *European Parliament* v. *Council of the European Union*, at para. 57–59.

The ECJ largely followed the reasoning of the Advocate General but only partially annulled Directive 2004/85. On the one hand, the mere transposition of the original derogation (i.e. until the end of 2008) contained in Annex VI to the Act of Accession as regards Directive 96/92 to the new Directive 2003/54 could be validly adopted on the basis of Article 57 AA. With regard to the introduction of a new transitional arrangement until the end of 2012, on the other hand, the Court concluded that this clearly goes beyond the scope of Article 57 AA. Only the EC Treaty provisions form a legitimate basis for introducing new temporary derogations after the signature of the Accession Treaty. For acts that must be adopted before the date of accession, the acceding countries have the opportunity to assert their interests through the information and consultation procedure contained in an annex to the Treaty of Accession.[94] It is noteworthy that the possibility to permit temporary derogations in respect of Community acts adopted in the period between the end of the negotiations and the date of accession has been expressly included in Article 55 of the 2005 Act Accession with Bulgaria and Romania in order to remedy the apparent shortcomings of the pre-accession consultation procedure.[95] The Court, however, concluded that "the possible imperfections which the 2003 Act of Accession harbours in that regard cannot authorise recourse to an incorrect legal basis".[96] Hence, the partial annulment of Directive 2004/85 requires the adoption of a new directive in order to extend the transitional period for the opening of the energy markets until the end of 2012. Neither the Act of Accession nor the Joint Statement on the Estonian electricity sector provides a sufficient legal basis in this respect.

Pursuant to the Joint Declaration, the Commission closely monitors the development of electricity production and the possible changes in the electricity market in Estonia and in the neighbouring countries. From 2009 onwards any Member State, including Estonia, may request the Commission to assess the development of the electricity markets of the Baltic Sea region and, taking into account the unique character of oil shale and the socio-economic considerations related to the extraction,

---

[94] ECJ, Case C-413/04, *op. cit.*, footnote 91, para. 66.
[95] Article 55 of the Act concerning the conditions of accession of the Republic of Bulgaria and Romania and the adjustments to the treaties on which the European Union is founded, *OJ* (2005) L 157/219.
[96] ECJ, Case C-413/04, *op. cit.*, footnote 91, para. 76.

production and consumption of oil shale in Estonia on the one hand, and, the objectives of the Community regarding the electricity market on the other, the Commission shall report to the Council with appropriate recommendations.[97] This flexible solution was presented as one of the most important achievements of Estonia's negotiations. As part of the compromise on the energy chapter, the EU also agreed to include oil shale research in the list of activities eligible for funding from the ECSC Research Fund for Coal and Steel.[98] Finally, Estonia gained a transitional period until 31 December 2009 in order to build up minimum stocks of crude oil and/or petroleum products up to the level of 90 days emergency levels required by the EU *acquis*.[99] Latvia and Lithuania obtained a similar period to establish its oil reserves.

4.2. *The Question of Nuclear Safety: Consequences for Lithuania's Ignalina Nuclear Power Plant*

The presence of the Ignalina Nuclear Power Plant (NPP), responsible for more than 70 per cent of Lithuania's energy production, created specific challenges comparable to the situation of the oil shale sector in Estonia. The question of nuclear safety gave an additional dimension to the negotiations. In comparison to other areas, the EU does not have clear-cut common rules or legal standards for nuclear safety which the candidates have to comply with by the time of accession.[100] In spite of

---

[97] Act of Accession, *OJ* (2003) L 236/975.

[98] Since 24 July 2002 the ECSC Research Fund for Coal and Steel has come under the European Commission's administration. The Act of Accession added "oil shale" to Appendix A, point 1 of Decision 2002/234/ECSC of the Representatives of the Governments of the Member States, meeting within the Council, of 27 February 2002 on the financial consequences of the expiry of the ECSC Treaty and on the research fund for coal and steel (*OJ* (2002) L 79/42).

[99] See: Council Directive 68/414/EC of 20 September 1968 imposing an obligation on Member States of the EEC to maintain minimum stocks of crude oil and/or petroleum products, *OJ* (1968) L 308/14, as last amended by Council Directive 98/93/EC of 14 December 1998, *OJ* (1998) L 358/100.

At the end of the negotiations on the energy chapter, Estonia withdrew its request to include oil shale in its obligatory oil stocks. See: X, "Estonia closed negotiations on the complex energy chapter", *Uniting Europe* 198 (2002), p. 6.

[100] The main reason is the absence of a specific legal basis for the establishment of EU safety standards for nuclear installations. The ECJ's decision on the Community's accession to the Nuclear Safety Convention, however, opened the door to a Commission proposal for a Council Directive on the Safety of Nuclear Installations (COM (2003) 32 final of 30 January 2003). An amended proposal has been issued on

this situation, the European Council defined a high level of nuclear safety comparable to that in the EU as a strict condition for accession to the Union.[101] The European Commission, on its turn, presented the question of nuclear installation safety as part of the EU's "*non-binding acquis*".[102] Moreover, references to nuclear safety in the Europe Agreement with Lithuania provided a basis for discussing this issue in the framework of the association institutions.[103]

Given the lack of well-determined EU rules, the Council Enlargement Working Group set up an Atomic Questions Group (AQG) to prepare a methodology and documents on how to evaluate the candidate's capability and readiness to secure a "high level of nuclear safety".[104] The AQG presented its first report in November 2000 and instructed the creation of a Working Party on Nuclear Safety (WPNS) to conduct the monitoring of compliance with the requirements under a "peer review" mechanism.[105] For Lithuania, the AQG/WPNS suggested that Lithuania should provide clear and binding commitments regarding the final closure of Ignalina Unit 1 before 2005 and Unit 2 by the end of 2009.[106] In the context of the accession negotiations, the EU invited Lithuania "to examine these recommendations and to indicate, by the end of October 2001 at the latest in writing to the Accession

---

8 September 2004, COM (2004) 526. On the competence question, see: ECJ, Case C-29/99, *Commission* v. *Council* [2002] ECR I-11221, at para. 89. For comments, see: C. True, "Legislative Competence of Euratom and the European Community in the Energy Sector: the 'Nuclear Package' of the European Commission", 28 *European Law Review* 5 (2003), pp. 664–685.

[101] Presidency Conclusions Cologne European Council (3–4 June 1998), *Bull. EU* 6 (1999), I.23.60; Presidency Conclusions Helsinki European Council (10–11 December 1999), *Bull. EU* 12 (1999), I.3.7.

[102] Contribution of the Commission services to question no. 1 of the questionnaire submitted on 13 September by the Presidency to the Atomic Questions Group in the framework of the mandate given to it by the Coreper on 26 July 2006, Non-Paper, 29/09/2000, at: http://ec.europa.eu/energy/nuclear/safety/doc/non_binding_acquis.pdf.

[103] Arts. 70, 81 and 82 of the Europe Agreement, *OJ* (1998) L 51/3.

[104] Council Working Party on Enlargement, "Adoption of the mandate from the PRC to the Working Party on Atomic Questions concerning nuclear safety in the context of enlargement", Brussels, 25 July 2000, 10658/00.

[105] Council Working Party on Atomic Questions, "Nuclear Safety in the Context of Enlargement", Brussels, 24 November 2000, 13789/00, p. 12.

[106] Council General Secretariat, "Report on Nuclear Safety in the Context of Enlargement", Brussels, 27 May 2001, 9181/01, p. 16.

Conference that they are acceptable".[107] Confronted with this clear example of unilateral pressure from the EU, illustrating the asymmetric relationship in the accession negotiations, Lithuanian diplomats argued they could not commit themselves on the closure of the Ignalina NPP without firm guarantees of EU financial support.[108]

Lithuania's reluctance to accept the EU's common position can be understood in view of the considerable financial and social consequences the decommissioning of the nuclear reactors represents.[109] Ignalina has two of the most powerful commercial reactors in the world capable to provide electricity for the entire Baltic region. Closure of the NPP, therefore, implies a loss of hard currency for the country. Since Lithuania has no domestic natural energy resources such as coal, gas or oil, energy supply after Unit 2 has been shut down could be problematic. As is the case in Estonia, politicians fear a growing dependency on Russian oil, coal and gas. A closure of the NPP will also increase the domestic price of electricity, thereby worsening the competitive situation of the domestic heavy industry. Employment in the nuclear energy sector is another economic factor to be reckoned with.[110] Taking into account these arguments, the Commission acknowledged that "the decommissioning of the Ignalina Nuclear Power Plant is an extraordinary burden for Lithuania in view of the plant's economic importance relative to the country's size [...] this situation renders necessary additional support, which should continue for the next decades".[111] The EU's financial commitments paved the way for a compromise on the Ignalina issue, formalised in a legally binding protocol to the Act of Accession. The protocol provided that the EU would contribute € 285 million for the period 2004–2006 and contained a specific legal basis for the adoption

---

[107] Council General Secretariat, "Nuclear Safety in the Context of Enlargement", Brussels, 10 July 2001, 10729/01, p. 6.

[108] M. Mann, "Lithuania warns EU on nuclear plant closure", *Financial Times*, 1 April 2002; K. Maniokas, R. Stanionis, "Negotiations on Decommissioning Ignalina Nuclear Power Plant", in: K. Maniokas, R. Vilpisauskas, D. Zeruolis, (eds.), *Lithuania's Road to the European Union: Unification of Europe and Lithuania's EU Accession Negotiations*, Vilnius, Eugrimas, 2005, pp. 326–327.

[109] The Lithuanian Ministry of Economy estimated that the closure of the Ignalina NPP would cost € 2.4 billion by 2020. See: M. Kovalick, "High costs of closing down Ignalina Plant", *The Baltic Times*, 25 April 2002.

[110] X, "EBRD: Address Social Issues at Ignalina Nuclear Power Plant", available at: http://www.bankwatch.org/publications/issue_papers/2000/ignalina.pdf.

[111] Lithuanian European Integration Department, "Co-operation between Lithuania and the European Union", available at: http://www.urm.lt.

of a Council Regulation laying down the EU's financial contribution to the Ignalina Programme for the period from 1 January 2007 to 31 December 2013 (€ 837 million).[112] Lithuania, from its side, committed itself to close Unit 1 of the Ignalina NPP before 2005 and Unit 2 by 31 December 2009 at the latest and to the subsequent decommissioning of these units. Safeguard measures remain possible until the end of December 2012 if energy supply would be disrupted in Lithuania.[113]

§ 5. The Chapter of Justice and Home Affairs and the Kaliningrad Compromise: Illustrating the Importance of the Russian Dimension

5.1. The Limits of the EU's Enlargement Strategy

A fear of growing dependence on imported Russian energy clearly formed one of the considerations underlying the Estonian, Lithuanian and—to a lesser extent—Latvian negotiating positions on the energy chapter. The Russia dimension also played a role in the negotiations on the chapter of Justice and Home Affairs (JHA). Preparations for membership in this area *inter alia* included the strengthening of state border controls and the introduction of the EU's visa policy.[114] Accordingly, the Baltic States had to change or abolish temporary agreements with their eastern neighbours, most notably Russia, on simplified border crossing for citizens of those countries.[115]

---

[112] Council Regulation (EC) No. 1990/2006 of 21 December 2006 on the implementation of Protocol No. 4 on the Ignalina nuclear power plant in Lithuania to the Act of accession of the Czech Republic, Cyprus, Estonia, Latvia, Lithuania, Hungary, Malta, Poland, Slovenia and Slovakia, *OJ* (2006) L 411/10.

[113] Significantly, certain Lithuanian politicians hinted about the possibility to keep the Ignalina NPP open until 2015 in order to avoid an increased dependency on Russian gas imports. This hypothesis raises interesting legal questions concerning the interpretation of Protocol No. 4 to the Treaty of Accession. See *infra*, Part V, Chapter 3, § 2.

[114] The acquis in force requires that third country nationals listed in Annex 1 of Regulation 539/2001, as amended by Regulation 2414/2001, are in possession of visas attached to a valid travel document when crossing the external border of the Member States. This requirement also applies for transit as well as for short visits up to three months.

[115] Although Estonia, Latvia and Lithuania had already introduced a visa requirement for Russian citizens in 1993, a special regime was applied for borderland residents. Lithuania also preserved exemptions for the visa-free transit between Russia and Kaliningrad. See: O. Potemkina, "Ramifications of Enlargement for EU-Russia Relations and the Schengen Regime", in: J. Apap, (ed.), *Justice and Home Affairs in the EU. Liberty and Security Issues after Enlargement*, Cheltenham, Elgar, 2004, pp. 303–304.

A specific element in securing the Baltic States' eastern borders was the absence of formal border agreements with Russia. Remarkably, the EU remained relatively silent on this issue. Notwithstanding the remark in Agenda 2000 that "before accession, applicants should make every effort to resolve any outstanding border dispute among themselves or involving third countries",[116] the Commission Opinions on Estonia, Latvia and Lithuania as well as the annual progress reports for these countries ignored this issue. The EU welcomed the Baltic States' efforts on border demarcation but did not consider the implementation of formal border agreements a precondition for the conclusion of accession negotiations in the field of JHA. Obviously, the EU did not want to give Russia a veto right on the accession of the Baltic States.[117] Accordingly, the process of EU enlargement and bilateral EU-Russia relations were kept separately.

The limits of this approach became obvious when the Lithuanian government adopted in October 2001 a "draft plan for the implementation of the Schengen *acquis*". According to the plan, residents of Russia's Kaliningrad oblast were to lose their right of visa-free entry to Lithuania from 1 January 2003 onwards. Whereas the European Commission welcomed this step and insisted that the decision on the general introduction of visa requirements for the residents of Kaliningrad should be implemented,[118] the Russian Federation claimed that visa requirements for travel between different parts of the territory of Russia would be an unacceptable violation of the Russian citizens' right to move freely throughout the country. The Russian State Duma even accused the EU of violating "the commonly accepted norms and principles of international law".[119]

---

[116] Agenda 2000. For a Stronger and Wider Union. COM (97) 2000 final p. 59.

[117] The European Parliament Delegation to the EU-Estonia Joint Parliamentary Committee, for instance, clearly stated that "Estonia's progress towards membership of the EU should not be held up by any unwillingness on the part of Russia to finalize the border agreement". Report on the Communication from the Commission 'Agenda 2000'—for a stronger and wider Union, A4–0368/97, 19 November 1997, p. 169.

[118] European Commission, 2002 Regular Report on Lithuania's Progress towards Accession, SEC (2002) 1406, p. 117.

[119] This statement formed the basis for a discussion within the Council of Europe. The Council's Parliamentary Assembly concluded that Article 2, paragraph 1 of Protocol No. 4 to the European Convention on Human Rights "does not grant freedom of movement across international borders or transit through other states' territories. [...] The territorial sovereignty of the Russian Federation could not be affected by visa requirements following from the territorial sovereignty of Lithuania and Poland, and the Constitution of the Russian Federation could not grant the right to freedom of

Confronted with Russia's reaction, the European Commission issued an important staff working paper announcing that discussions with Russia on the Kaliningrad transit question would proceed within the context of the PCA institutional framework, in parallel to the accession negotiations on the JHA chapter.[120] Significantly, Lithuania managed to conclude the accession negotiations on this chapter in April 2002, i.e. before a compromise on Kaliningrad was found with Russia. This course of events clearly put further pressure on Russia and reflected the EU's position that only a flexible solution within the limits of the *acquis* would be acceptable. On several occasions, the Commission explicitly made clear that "granting visa free travel to residents of Kaliningrad even if they live in the immediate border area (so-called small border traffic) is not foreseen in the *acquis*".[121]

5.2. *The Commission Proposals and Reactions of the Parties Involved*

Proceeding from the basic line that an effective and flexible solution of the transit of persons and goods to and from Kaliningrad should be in compliance with the *acquis* and in agreement with the candidate countries concerned—as instructed by the June 2002 Seville European Council[122]—the Commission issued a groundbreaking document on Kaliningrad transit on 18 September 2002.[123] The Commission proposed the introduction of a special Facilitated Transit Document (FTD), equivalent to a multi-entry visa, for Russian citizens travelling frequently and directly between Kaliningrad and the Russian mainland.

---

movement outside the territory of the Russian Federation". See: Council of Europe Parliamentary Assembly—Political Affairs Committee (rapporteur L.M. Ragnarsdottir), "The Enlargement of the European Union and the Kaliningrad Region", Doc. 9560, 22 September 2002.

[120] Commission Staff Working Paper, "EU and Kaliningrad: Movement of Persons over Land Borders After Enlargement", SEC (2002) 49, Brussels, 15 January 2002, p. 2. In a reaction to the EU's proposals, the Russian Federation pushed for a specific and single forum to discuss the Kaliningrad question instead of splitting the various aspects of the issue among the different PCA sub-committees. The EU, however, refused this proposal. See: X, "Russia's Official Reaction to EU Proposals on Kaliningrad", *Uniting Europe* 138 (2001), p. 7.

[121] See e.g. Commission Staff Working Paper, *op. cit.*, footnote 120, p. 4; Copy of Letter of Commission President Romano Prodi to Vladimir Putin annexed to Council document 9299/02, Brussels, 28 May 2002.

[122] Presidency Conclusions Seville European Council (21–22 June 2002), *Bull. EU* 6 (2002) I.23.55.

[123] Communication from the Commission to the Council, "Kaliningrad: Transit", COM (2002) 510 final, Brussels, 18 September 2002.

This securised document would be issued at low cost by Lithuanian consulates after examination of lists of eligible persons provided by the Russian Federation. Russian internal documents could be accepted to deliver the FTD in a transitional period before the lifting of internal border controls. The Commission suggested that from 2005 onwards only international passports would be accepted. The Commission also envisaged a feasibility study of Russia's proposal to introduce a visa exemption for direct transit of passengers on non-stop high-speed trains. Significantly, any decision concerning this option was postponed until the EU accession of Lithuania. As a further gesture to reassure the Lithuanians, the Commission suggested legally binding guarantees that the arrangements on facilitated transit between Kaliningrad and mainland Russia would not prejudice the lifting of internal border controls and that Lithuania would receive appropriate financial assistance to implement the new regime. Importantly, discussions on the final modalities of the transit arrangement were explicitly kept outside the accession negotiations on the JHA chapter "as the basic principle of the *acquis*, in this case the visa requirement, would remain in place".[124] The Commission, in order words, intended to play a leadership role and wanted to avoid a delay in the negotiation process.

On 30 September 2002, the General Affairs Council approved the Commission's Communication as a basis for further discussions with Russia.[125] In a first reaction, the Russian Ministry of Foreign Affairs called the proposed FTD a "visa surrogate" that would only be issued to a limited, very vague category of Russians travelling frequently to and from Kaliningrad.[126] This proposal clearly failed to meet Russia's expectations of visa-free train and bus transit for all Russian citizens. In addition, Russia was not satisfied with the terms of the feasibility study for the non-stop train.[127] The Lithuanian Parliament, on the other hand, expressed its appreciation for the efforts of the Commission to seek technically flexible ways of solution.[128] At the same time,

---

[124] *Ibid.*, p. 10.
[125] 2450th Council Meeting, External Relations, 12134/02, Brussels, 30 September 2002.
[126] Ministry of Foreign Affairs of the Russian Federation, "Concerning Adoption of a Conclusion on Kaliningrad by the European Union External Relations Council at Foreign Ministers' Level", 2 October 2002, available at: http://www.ln.mid.ru.
[127] *Ibid.*
[128] Seimas of The Republic of Lithuania, "Resolution on the Position of the Seimas of the Republic of Lithuania on the Kaliningrad Issue", 10 October 2002, available at: http://www.lrs.lt.

the *Seimas* insisted that whatever special regime was eventually adopted should not be detrimental to Lithuania's sovereign rights and should not in any way prejudice the lifting of internal border controls inside the EU. In this regard, Lithuania's Minister of Foreign Affairs, Antanas Valionis, suggested that the Council should guarantee Lithuania's full membership of Schengen by 2006 provided that it fulfils all the necessary conditions according to the Schengen *acquis*.[129]

Based on the Commission proposals and the reactions of the parties involved, the Danish Council Presidency and the Commission held further consultations with representatives of Lithuania and the Russian Federation.[130] After meetings between the EU Troika and Russian Foreign Affairs Minister Ivanov and the President's special representative for Kaliningrad, Dmitri Rogozin, in October 2002, Russia's position gradually changed. Russia now accepted that the FTD scheme would be applied for transit by road (car and bus) but continued to insist on the continuation of the possibility of visa-free travel by train. Importantly, Russia stated that a final solution on Kaliningrad at the EU-Russia summit of 11 November 2002 would unlock its agreement to facilitate the opening of a new Lithuanian consulate in Sovetsk, to make efforts towards finishing within a short time the parliamentary procedures relating to the ratification of the Russian-Lithuanian border agreement and to conclude readmission agreements with Lithuania and Poland. In return, Russia expected EU commitments of financial, technical and other assistance for improving border infrastructure as well as for developing and reducing the prices of air and ferry transport. The Council Presidency welcomed these new developments and expressed its conviction that a compromise acceptable to all parties was within reach at the EU-Russia Summit on 11 November 2002.[131] In the run up to this important meeting, the Council finally approved the proposal made by the Commission in May 2002[132] that Russia should be recognized as a market economy and therefore becomes eligible for admission to the

---

[129] X, "Lithuania fears delayed entry into Schengen", available at: http://www.euobserver.com (16 October 2002).

[130] A report on contacts with Lithuania and Russia is included in Council Presidency Document 13345/02, Brussels, 21 October 2002.

[131] *Ibid.*

[132] Commission President Romano Prodi announced that the EU would be granting Russia the formal status and treatment of a 'market economy' on the occasion of the 29 May 2002 EU-Russia Summit. See: http://www.europa.eu.int/comm/external_relations/russia/summit_05_02/ip02_775.htm.

WTO.[133] This move to facilitate an agreement at the November summit was, however, overshadowed by a diplomatic row between Russia and the Danish Presidency over Chechnya. Denmark's refusal to extradite Chechen rebel leader Achmed Zakayev as well as the organization of a Chechen Congress in Copenhagen and critical statements concerning Russia's actions in Chechnya seriously deteriorated Russian-Danish relations. Given the potential negative effect of this bilateral dispute, the Danish Presidency decided to organize the crucial EU-Russia summit in Brussels instead of Copenhagen.[134]

5.3. *The 11 November 2002 Kaliningrad Compromise: A Legal Analysis*

In spite of the political tensions surrounding the 11 November meeting, the EU and Russia issued a "Joint Statement on Transit between the Kaliningrad Region and the rest of the Russian Federation".[135] This document, which primarily has a political rather than a legal value,[136] represents a final compromise accommodating Russian, Lithuanian and EU sensitivities. The different elements of this solution are "mutually complementary and are considered as a single package". The compromise nature of the Joint Statement becomes obvious in the following statement:

> The Russian Federation and the European Union note that from 1 January 2003 the Republic of Lithuania will, according to its agreement with the EU, implement national regulations for border control. The parties understand that these rules shall be applied in a flexible manner in order not to disrupt the traditional flow of transit passengers by rail. The parties recognize that the transit regime will not infringe upon the sovereign right of the Republic of Lithuania to exercise the necessary controls and to refuse entry into its territory.[137]

---

[133] Council Regulation (EC) No. 1972/2002 of 5 November 2002 amending Regulation (EC) No. 984/96 on the protection against dumped imports from countries not members of the European Community, *OJ* (2002) L 305/1.

[134] P. Ludlow, *The Making of the New Europe. The European Councils in Brussels and Copenhagen 2002*, Brussels, EuroComment, 2004, pp. 269–270.

[135] The text of this Joint Statement is available at: http://www.europa.eu.int/comm/external_relations/russia/summit_11_02/js_kalin.htm.

[136] M. Maresceau, "EU Enlargement and EU Common Strategies on Russia and Ukraine: An Ambiguous Yet Unavoidable Connection", in: C. Hillion, (ed.), *EU Enlargement: A Legal Approach*, Hart, Oxford, 2004, p. 197.

[137] See: http://www.europa.eu.int/comm/external_relations/russia/summit_11_02/js_kalin.htm [hereafter: EU-Russia Joint Statement 11 November 2002].

The first sentence reflects the EU's point of departure that a solution to the Kaliningrad transit issue should not prejudice the implementation of Lithuania's obligations under the *acquis* as agreed in the accession negotiations on the JHA chapter. The promise that this implementation will be done "in a flexible manner not to disrupt the traditional flow of transit passengers by rail" has clearly been inserted as a gesture to Russia.[138] Finally, the explicit recognition of Lithuania's sovereign right to exercise border controls and to refuse entry into its territory is designed to reassure Lithuania.

The central provision of the Kaliningrad package deal is certainly Russia's acceptance that transit of Russian citizens by land will only be possible on condition of a Facilitated Transit Document (FTD) scheme. In comparison to previous proposals, the Joint Statement distinguishes between two types of FTDs to be issued to Russian citizens. For transit by cars or buses, a multi-entry FTD can be obtained on the basis of an application to a Lithuanian consulate, subject to necessary checks and controls. Obviously, this document resembles the features of a visa. A more innovative solution has been introduced for Russian citizens intending to make single return trips by train through the territory of Lithuania. In this circumstance, a Facilitated Rail Transit Document (FRTD) can be obtained at the moment of purchasing a railway ticket. Two Council Regulations lay down the concrete application procedure and specify further technical details of the facilitated transit arrangement.[139] They have been adopted on the basis of Article 62 (2) EC and on the political and legal 'myth' that they were not directed specifically at Kaliningrad but apply in general to any 'enclave' situation. The cost for a FTD has been fixed at € 5. This document is valid for a maximum period of up to three years and can be used for multiple

---

[138] The Russian authorities estimated that, in 2001, the total number of border crossings between Kaliningrad and the rest of Russia were 960,000 by train and 620,000 by car. See: "Kaliningrad and the EU in facts and figures" at: http://europa .eu.int/comm/external_relations/north_dim/news/mem02_192.htm#border.

[139] Council Regulation (EC) No. 693/2003 of 14 April 2003 establishing a specific Facilitated Transit Document (FTD), a Facilitated Rail Travel Document (FRTD) and amending the Common Consular Instructions and the Common Manual, *OJ* (2003) L 99/8; Council Regulation (EC) No. 694/2003 of 14 April 2003 on uniform formats for Facilitated Transit Documents (FTD) and Facilitated Rail Transit Documents (FRTD) provided for in Regulation (EC) No. 693/2003, *OJ* (2003) L 99/15. The two Regulations constitute a development of the Schengen *acquis* in which Ireland, the United Kingdom and Denmark do not take part. On the other hand, its provisions are applicable to the Schengen associates Norway and Iceland.

entries within a transit time of maximum 24 hours. The FRTD is free of charge, can be used for a maximum period of up to three months and allows for a single entry and return by rail with a transit time of maximum 6 hours.[140] The FTD/FRTD have a legal status equivalent to transit visas and are territorially valid for the issue Member State and, if required, other transited Member States.[141]

The EU's acceptance of the FRTD as well as an intention to review the operation of the FTD scheme by the end of 2005—taking into account the objective not to disrupt the traditional flow of transit passengers by rail—was crucial for the Russian negotiators.[142] It implies that the agreed regime is temporary and might be abolished after Lithuania joined the Schengen area.[143] Arguably, Russia seemed to hope that by that time a high speed non-stop train between Kaliningrad and mainland Russia would have been operational, which could open the gates to visa free transit.[144] In order to support this case, a parallel could be drawn with the situation of airport transit passengers. In a ruling on airport transit arrangements, the ECJ indicated that for external border crossing not related to the entry into and movement within the internal market a visa may not be required.[145] Following this judgment, the Council has inserted in Article 2, second indent of Visa Regulation 539/2001 the provision that airport transit forms an exception to the general requirement of a visa for transit through the territory of one or several Member States.[146] Whereas the specific situation of airport

---

[140] Articles 2, 3 and 7 of Council Regulation (EC) No. 693/2003.

[141] Article 3 of Council Regulation (EC) No. 693/2003.

[142] This deadline to review the operation of the F(R)TD scheme was reformulated in Article 13 of Council Regulation 693/2003. Rather than "the end of 2005", as included in the political compromise, the Commission was under an obligation to report on the functioning of the facilitated transit regime "at the latest three years" after its entry into force. Accordingly, the Commission published its report only in December 2006. See: European Commission Report on the functioning of the facilitated transit for persons between the Kaliningrad region and the rest of the Russian Federation, COM (2006) 840 final, Brussels 22 December 2006. For comments on this assessment, see *infra* Part V, Chapter 2, § 3.

[143] Lithuania joined the Schengen area on 21 December 2007 together with Estonia, Latvia, Poland, Hungary, Malta, the Czech Republic, Slovakia and Slovenia. On the consequences of Lithuania's full application of the Schengen regime for the Kaliningrad transit regime, see *infra* Part V, Chapter 2, § 3.

[144] Potemkina, *op. cit.*, footnote 115, p. 314.

[145] ECJ, Case C-170/96, *Commission* v. *Council* [1998] ECR I-2763 at para. 22.

[146] Council Regulation (EC) No. 539/2001 of 15 March 2001 listing the third countries whose nationals must be in possession of visas when crossing the external border and those whose nationals are exempt from that requirement, *OJ* (2001) L 81/1.

transit is the only exception included in this Regulation, it could be argued that passengers on a high speed non-stop train should also fall within this category on the basis of the Court's reasoning in case C-170/96. In its Communication on Kaliningrad transit, the Commission already indicated that an adjustment of the *acquis* in this direction could not be excluded.[147] The introduction of the FRTD and a commitment on the part of the EU to launch a feasibility study on the high-speed non-stop train were, therefore, of major importance for Russia.[148] Other important EU concessions to Russia include the acceptance of Russian internal passports as a basis for issuing both types of FTD until the end of 2004 and a commitment of continued financial and technical assistance to promote the economic development of Kaliningrad and to strengthen cross-border co-operation between Russia and the enlarged EU.

Russia, for its part, has been willing to depart from its original demand for visa-free transit corridors and confirmed its intention to conclude a readmission agreement with Lithuania "covering persons of all nationalities" before 30 June 2003. Russia fulfilled this obligation in May 2003. Also in connection with the transit arrangement, the Russian State Duma finally ratified the border treaty with Lithuania, which was signed already in 1997. This important breakthrough illustrated the improved bilateral Russian-Lithuanian relationship. The Russian Federation explicitly acknowledged the sovereignty of Lithuanian territory and agreed on the expansion of the Lithuanian Consulate General in Kaliningrad and the opening of a new consulate in Sovetsk. Finally, Russia accepted the postponement of the feasibility study on visa-free transit by high-speed non-stop trains until after the EU accession of Lithuania and noted that decisions on this proposal could only be taken with the agreement of this country.[149]

---

[147] Communication from the Commission to the Council, Kaliningrad: Transit, COM (2002) 510 final, Brussels, 18 September 2002, p. 13.

[148] The feasibility study started in December 2003 and was finalised in August 2004. According to the final report of this study, the estimated cost for upgrading the existing infrastructure or the construction of new lines would be between € 350 and 500 million. This high amount of money seems to be hardly justifiable from an economic point of view and could explain the decreasing interest in this solution at the political level. See: Feasibility Study on High-Speed Non-Stop Trains Final Report, European Commission, DG Enlargement, 153 p.

[149] EU-Russia Joint Statement 11 November 2002, *op. cit.*, footnote 137.

Additional guarantees for Lithuania have been included in a protocol and a declaration to the Treaty of Accession. Already in the preamble to Protocol No. 5, it has been mentioned that "the transit of persons by land between the region of Kaliningrad and other parts of the Russian Federation through EU territory is a matter of concern concerning the Union as a whole and should be treated as such and must not entail any unfavourable consequence for Lithuania".[150] Accordingly, Article 1 of this Protocol clearly states that the Community arrangement on facilitated transit shall not delay or prevent the full participation of Lithuania in the Schengen *acquis*. The Community further promises assistance in implementing the transit rules—including a commitment to bear any additional cost linked to this implementation[151]—"with a view to Lithuania's full participation in the Schengen area as soon as possible". Declaration No. 12 to the Accession Treaty reiterates this commitment and anticipates that Lithuania "will be included in the first group of new Member States to participate fully in the Schengen *acquis*".[152] Finally, Article 3 of the Kaliningrad Protocol stipulates that any further decisions concerning the transit of persons between Kaliningrad and other parts of Russia can only be taken after Lithuania's EU accession on the basis of a unanimous Council decision on a proposal from the Commission. In other words, the Treaty of Accession provides Lithuania with a veto right on any further steps regarding Kaliningrad transit. This provision is highly relevant because the present Regulations on the establishment of the FTD scheme are based on Article 62 (2) EC and have been adopted according to the procedural rules of Article

---

[150] Protocol No. 5 to the 2003 Treaty of Accession on the transit of persons by land between the region of Kaliningrad and other parts of the Russian Federation, *OJ* (2003) L 236/946.

[151] In this respect, the EC and Lithuania signed a financial memorandum on 28 February 2003, providing Lithuania € 12 million financial support for the implementation of the facilitated transit procedures between Kaliningrad and mainland Russia. As an exception to the usual PHARE rules, the EC agreed to finance 100 % of the project. See: "Signature of EUR12m financing memorandum for Kaliningrad Transit", IP/03/3001, 28 February 2003. In addition, € 40 million have been provided under a special Kaliningrad Transit Programme for the period 2004–2006. See: Decision C (2003) 5213 of 13 December 2003 on financial assistance for Lithuania in implementing the Facilitated Transit Document (FTD) and Facilitated Rail Transit Document (FRTD) scheme established by Council Regulation (EC) No. 693/2003 and Council Regulation (EC) 694/2003.

[152] Declaration No. 12 to the 2003 Treaty of Accession on the transit of persons by land between the region of Kaliningrad and other parts of the Russian Federation, *OJ* (2003) L 236/976.

67 EC. The latter provision entails a possibility to adopt measures on the basis of qualified majority voting. The unanimity requirement is also highly relevant as regards potential amendments to Regulation 539/2001 necessary for the widening of the exceptions to the visa transit provisions. This Regulation falls within the scope of Article 62 (2) b) i) EC, which implies the application of qualified majority voting as provided by Article 67 (3) EC. Hence, the Kaliningrad Protocol raises interesting legal questions, in particular on the relationship between the Accession Treaty and EC Treaty provisions.

In principle, the accession conditions on the basis of Article 49 EU can only include technical adjustments and cannot amend the procedural rules of the EC Treaty.[153] The unanimity requirement for the specific situation of Kaliningrad in Article 3 of Protocol No. 5, therefore, seems to extend the traditional restrictive interpretation of this notion. It introduces a *lex specialis* on the matter of transit of persons between Kaliningrad and the Russian Federation. In this respect, it is significant that for equivalent provisions of Community law—in this case an article of an Accession Protocol and an EC Treaty provision which both have the status of 'primary law'—a later provision (*lex posterior*) prevails over an earlier one and a specific provision (*lex specialis*) over a general one.[154]

The Kaliningrad Protocol is of particular legal significance, mainly because it transformed the political guarantees included in the Joint Statement into a legally binding document. The limited scope of the Protocol, exclusively dealing with the interests of Lithuania but not including any reference to other aspects of the political compromise, implies that it does not affect the nature of the Joint Statement as a purely political act that cannot directly be invoked in legal proceedings. Of course, the situation is different with regard to the Regulations implementing the F(R)TD, which qualify for direct effect given

---

[153] ECJ, Case 185/73, *Hauptzollamt Bielefeld* v. *OHG Koenig* [1974] ECR 607 at para. 3. On the legal nature of the Accession Treaty, see *infra* Chapter 3, § 1.

[154] K. Lenaerts, P. Van Nuffel, *Constitutional Law of the European Union*, London, Sweet & Maxwell, 2005, p. 704. The ECJ has explicitly recognised the precedence of special legislation on environmental protection laid down in directives (ECJ, Case C-481/99 *Heininger* [2001] ECR I-9945, at para. 36–39; Case C-444/00 *Mayer Parry Recycling* [2003] ECR I-6163, at para. 57) whereas the Court of First Instance explicitly recognised that "the ECSC Treaty constitutes a *lex specialis* in derogation from the *lex generalis* represented by the EC Treaty". See: CFI, Case T-66/99 *ESF Elbe-Stahlwerke Feralpi* v. *Commissioni* [2001] ECR II-1523, at para. 102.

the clear and precise provisions on the application procedure for those documents.[155]

§ 6. *The Enlargement 'End Game':*
Discussions on Agriculture and the Final Financial Package

The political compromise reached at the November 2002 EU-Russia summit removed an important obstacle for EU enlargement. The Danish Presidency and the European Commission could now fully concentrate on the remaining issues, which were essentially of a financial nature. Given the budgetary implications of the remaining negotiating chapters on agriculture and regional policy, the Commission envisaged a 'global approach' linking those chapters to the negotiations on financial and budgetary provisions.[156] In this regard, it issued two information notes on the integration of the new Member States in the Common Agricultural Policy (CAP)[157] and concerning the "common financial framework 2004–2006 for the accession negotiations".[158] As a point of departure, the Commission clearly stated that any solution on the financial package should respect the expenditure ceilings agreed at the 1999 Berlin European Council even though the basic assumptions underlying the 1999 financial framework were no longer valid.

The 1999 Berlin agreement proceeded from the scenario that six new Member States would accede in 2002 whereas the evolutions in the accession process now required a financial framework for ten countries acceding in 2004.[159] This new context did not lead to a revi-

---

[155] Regulation 694/2003 on uniform formats for FTD/FRTD, for instance, contains clear and precise rules as regards data protection. Article 5 gives persons to whom the FTD and FRTD is issued "the right to verify the personal particulars contained in the FTD/FRTD and, where appropriate, to have them corrected or deleted".

[156] The Commission proposed this approach for the first time in its 2001 Enlargement Strategy Paper. See: European Commission, "Making a Success of Enlargement. Strategy Paper and Report of the European Commission on the progress towards accession by each of the candidate countries", http://www.europa.eu.int/comm/enlargement/report2001/strategy_en.pdf, pp. 20–21.

[157] European Commission, "Enlargement and Agriculture: Successfully integrating the new Member States into the CAP", Brussels, 30 January 2001, SEC (2002) 95 final.

[158] European Commission, "Common Financial Framework 2004–2006 for the Accession Negotiations", Brussels, 30 January 2002, SEC (2002) 102 final.

[159] J. Rollo, "Agriculture, the Structural Funds and the Budget after Enlargement", in: N. Neuwahl, (ed.), *European Union Enlargement. Law and Socio-Economic Changes*, Montréal, Editions Thémis, 2004, p. 126.

sion of the financial commitments. Arguably, the legal and political conditions for such a revision ruled out this option. From a legal point of view, the Berlin financial framework is a unanimously agreed legal limit on spending inserted in an Interinstitutional Agreement between the European Parliament, the Council and the Commission.[160] Fundamental changes to this legally binding document require the approval of all parties.[161] Clearly, this cumbersome procedure and the financial situation in several EU Member States facing serious budget deficits and controversial cuts in social spending excluded the chances of reopening the Berlin agreement.[162] Instead, the Commission proposed so-called "minor adjustments" in conformity with Article 25 of the Interinstitutional Agreement. This provision allowed adjustments to the financial perspective—within the limits included in the Berlin agreement—to take account of the expenditure requirements resulting from enlargement in accordance with the voting rules under the fifth subparagraph of Article 272 (9) EC, i.e. on proposal of the Commission and after agreement between the Council, acting by qualified majority, and the European Parliament, acting by a majority of its Members and three fifths of the votes cast. On this legal basis, the Commission suggested a number of significant changes to the EU's original position.[163] Most importantly, the Commission opened the door to direct income subsidies for farmers in the new Member States. This option was not foreseen

---

[160] Interinstitutional agreement of 6 May 1999 between the European Parliament, the Council and the Commission on budgetary discipline and improvement of the budgetary procedure, *OJ* (1999) C 172/1.

[161] Article 20 of the interinstitutional agreement distinguishes between two scenarios. Limited revisions to the financial perspective, i.e. below 0.03 % of the Community GNP within the margins for unforeseen expenditure, may be fixed by agreement between the Council, acting by a qualified majority, and the European Parliament, acting by a majority of its Members and three fifths of the votes cast. Any revision of the financial perspective above 0.03 % of the Community GNP within the margins for unforeseen expenditure requires unanimity in the Council. As a general rule, any proposal for revision must be presented by the Commission and adopted before the start of the budgetary procedure for the year or the first of the years concerned.

[162] A. Mayhew, "The Financial and Budgetary Impact of Enlargement and Accession", *SEI Working Paper* (2003) 65, p. 10. (available at: http://www.sussex.ac.uk/sei/documents/wp65.pdf).

[163] The Commission's information note paved the way for a formal proposal for a decision of the European Parliament and the Council on the adjustment of the financial perspective for enlargement, Brussels, 11 February 2003, COM (2003) 70 final, which on its turn resulted in decision 2003/429 EC of the European Parliament and the Council of 19 May 2003 on the adjustment of the financial perspective for enlargement, *OJ* (2003) L 147/25.

in Agenda 2000 or the Berlin financial framework. Confronted with strong pressure from the candidate countries to be fully integrated in all aspects of the CAP from the date of accession, the Commission acknowledged that the exclusion of new Member States from direct payments would be contrary to EC law:

> As direct payments are part of the CAP acquis as it currently stands the permanent exclusion of the new Member States from direct payments would not reflect the EC Treaty's concept of a single market for agricultural products that is inextricably linked with the existence of a common agricultural policy.[164]

This statement, however, did not imply the granting of direct payments to the new Member States at the same level as that applicable for the old Member States at the time of accession. In order to avoid negative effects on the restructuring of the candidate's agricultural sector, the Commission proposed a gradual introduction of direct payments for farmers of the new Member States after enlargement starting with 25 % of the level in the old Member States in 2004 and annually increasing up to 100 % in 2013. Although this proposal constituted a step forward in comparison to Agenda 2000, the candidate countries heavily criticized the differential treatment between farmers from the old and new Member States. In a joint reaction to the Commission proposals, the Baltic States rejected the idea of delaying full direct payments to new Member States' farmers. The Baltic representatives mainly tackled the suggestion of transitional arrangements going beyond the 1999–2006 financial framework.[165] Also in academic literature, the phasing in of direct payments until 2013, i.e. the end of the next financial perspective, has been heavily criticized. Alan Mayhew, for instance, concluded that "the agricultural proposals with respect to direct income subsidies are manifestly unfair".[166]

---

[164] European Commission, "Enlargement and Agriculture: Successfully integrating the new Member States into the CAP", Brussels, 30 January 2001, SEC (2002) 95 final, p. 5.

[165] X, "Baltic candidates agree on common line over farm talks", *Uniting Europe* (2002) 178, p. 3.

[166] A. Mayhew, "The Negotiating Position of the European Union on Agriculture, the Structural Funds and the EU Budget", *SEI Working Paper* (2002) 52, available at: http://www.sussex.ac.uk/sei/documents/wp52.pdf. On the discussions surrounding direct payments, see also: F. De Filippis, L. Salvatici, "The Eastward Enlargement of the European Union and the Common Agricultural Policy: the Direct Payments Issue", in: S. Manzocchi, (ed.), *The Economics of Enlargement*, Houndmills, Palgrave, 2003, pp. 311–347.

In order to accommodate the candidate countries, the Commission offered improved proposals on finance for rural development. This included a higher rate of Community co-financing, measures facilitating the implementation of rural development policy, a higher level of Cohesion Fund spending in total structural fund allocations and measures to help with the restructuring of semi-subsistence farms. In addition, the Commission proposed specific financial transfers to co-finance the closure of nuclear power plants in Lithuania (Ignalina) and Slovakia (Bohunice) as well as the creation of a special transition facility for institution building to cover actions that are not eligible under the existing Community programmes or structural funds.

A further significant concession was the explicit promise that "no new Member State should find itself in a net budgetary position which is worse than the year before enlargement".[167] This statement was important because several candidate countries faced potential cash flow problems as a result of the Union's insistence on the payment of full contributions to the EU budget from the first day of accession in combination with the expected slow absorption of structural funds and the practice that reimbursements from the EU budget for Member States' expenditure on direct payments is only made the year after their payment to farmers. To avoid scenarios where the new Member States would become net contributors during the first year after accession, the Commission proposed transitional arrangements for budgetary compensation.[168] As a basic principle, flexibility on the revenues side of the budget was excluded. Accordingly, transitional arrangements involved lump-sum budgetary transfers and temporary payments on the expenditure side of the budget. The decision to shift the date of accession from 1 January to 1 May 2004 also had important budgetary implications. The Commission calculated that this move considerably reduced the cash flow problems of the new Member States and allowed the EU to save € 117 million in direct payments, which could be used

---

[167] European Commission, "Common Financial Framework 2004–2006 for the Accession Negotiations", Brussels, 30 January 2002, SEC (2002) 102 final, p. 8.

[168] In order to forecast the net budgetary position of each new Member State after accession, the Commission proposed a methodology for the calculation of net budgetary balances, which was approved by the Council in September 2002. See: Council Secretariat General, "Methodological aspects related to the calculation of net budgetary balances", Brussels, 25 September 2002, 12372/02.

as 'spare' money to meet the demands of the candidate countries during the final stages of the negotiations.[169]

The October 2002 Brussels European Council laid down the limits for enlargement-related spending[170] and paved the way for the adoption of the EU Common Position on financial and budgetary provisions.[171] During the final stages of the negotiations, the Danish Presidency presented its own financial package.[172] In comparison to the EU Common Position, this final financial package included important new elements such as the possibility of 'topping up' direct income subsidies using funds reserved for rural development, the introduction of a 'Schengen facility' to finance the strengthening of the new external border of the Union and several country-specific and non-financial issues such as the hunting of lynx in Latvia and Estonia.[173] Discussions with the Baltic States primarily focused on the question of production quotas for agricultural products and especially the reference years used for the calculation of these quotas. The Commission originally proposed to quantify the various production quotas on the basis of "the most recent historical reference periods for which data are available, i.e. the time span from 1995 to 1999 (where available including 2000)".[174]

Estonia, Latvia and Lithuania argued that the proposed reference years were not representative for the actual or potential production levels because this was a special period of deep agricultural crisis as

---

[169] Ludlow, "The making of the new Europe", *op. cit.*, footnote 134, p. 233.

[170] In general, the Brussels European Council maintained that the Berlin financial framework must be respected, confirmed that the own resources *acquis* would apply to the new Member States from the date of accession and agreed to the Commission's proposals on direct income subsidies and transitional arrangements for budgetary compensation. Significantly, the European Council cut the proposed commitment appropriations for structural funds reserved for enlargement over the period 2004–2006 from € 25.5 billion proposed by the Commission to € 23 billion. Presidency Conclusions Brussels European Council (24–25 October 2002), *Bull. EU* (2002) 10, I.6.10.

[171] Council of the European Union, Enlargement group, "Preparation of the next enlargement conference with Cyprus, Malta, Hungary, Poland, Slovakia, Latvia, Estonia, Lithuania, the Czech Republic and Slovenia—Chapter 29: financial and budgetary provisions", Brussels, 7 November 2002, 13499/1/02.

[172] Report from the Presidency to the Council, "Enlargement", Brussels 7 December 2002, 15174/02.

[173] For a comparison between the EU Common Position of 8 November 2002 and the financial package proposed by the Danish EU Presidency on 25 November 2002, see: Mayhew, "The Financial and Budgetary Impact of Enlargement and Accession", *op. cit.*, footnote 162, p. 16.

[174] European Commission, "Enlargement and Agriculture: Successfully integrating the new Member States into the CAP", Brussels, 30 January 2001, SEC (2002) 95 final, p. 9.

a result of substantial restructuring and the 1998 Russian financial crisis. Consequently, the application of the envisaged reference period implied a risk of lower investments in the food industry and increasing unemployment. Hence, the Baltic agricultural ministers urged the EU Member States to reconsider the reference periods, taking into account the special situation of the Baltic agricultural sector in the 1990s.[175] In response to the concerns of the Baltic representatives, enlargement Commissioner Günter Verheugen promised that the EU would take into account the Baltic States' special historical background when negotiating the production quotas and other production management instruments.[176] An analysis of the Council enlargement group documents reveals, however, that the EU used the data from 1995 to 1999 (or 2000) as a basis for negotiation and only allowed other reference periods when the Baltic States could demonstrate the existence of exceptional conditions on the basis of clear and convincing evidence. The outcome of the negotiations shows that changes to the EU's original proposals turned out to be difficult. Estonia, for instance, requested a production quota of 10,000 tonnes of potato starch based on production level data from the period 1975–2000. The EU, however, only took into account the average production of 1997, 1998 and 1999 in order to set Estonia's national quota at 250 tonnes.[177] Notwithstanding the principle that further information on irreversible investments made before 1 February 2002 would be taken into account before finally attributing national quota, the Act of Accession effectively introduced the number of 250 tonnes.[178] The other Baltic States faced similar problems and decided, basically for the first time in the accession negotiations, to join efforts.

Last minute negotiations, taking place against the background of the December 2002 Copenhagen European Council, allowed the three Baltic countries to obtain improved production quotas for several agricultural products.[179] In addition, the final Copenhagen "package deal"

[175] X, "Baltic countries urge better farm production quotas in enlarged EU", *Uniting Europe* (2002) 187, pp. 6–7.

[176] X, "EU to take specific Baltic agricultural situation into account, Verheugen says", *Uniting Europe* (2002) 195, p. 4.

[177] Council Enlargement Group, "Preparation of the next Accession Conference with Estonia: Chapter 7 Agriculture", Brussels, 30 October 2002, 13495/02, p. 21.

[178] Act of Accession, *OJ* (2003) L 236/357.

[179] For Estonia, for instance, the national milk quota was raised from 562,633 to 624,485 tonnes together with the establishment of a special restructuring reserve to be released from 1 April 2006 to the extent that the on-farm consumption of milk and milk products has decreased since 1998. See: Act of Accession, *OJ* (2003) L 236/353.

included additional budget compensation (€ 5,8 million for Estonia, € 6,8 million for Latvia and € 12,6 million for Lithuania), higher top up ceilings for direct agricultural aid through national payments up to 55 % in 2004, 60 % in 2005 and 65 % in 2006 and 30 % above the applicable phasing-in level from 2007 onwards.[180] Lithuania managed to obtain clear EU guarantees with regard to the financing of additional costs resulting from the EU-Russia transit agreement on Kaliningrad as well as for the closing down of the Ignalina nuclear reactor beyond 2006 (cf. *supra*). A comparative analysis of the Copenhagen financial package in per capita terms reveals that the Baltic States have come out best of the negotiations on this basis:

Table 8: The Copenhagen Financial Package for the Years 2004–2006 (1999 Prices)[181]

Country	Population (millions)	GDP (€ billion)	Allocated expenditure (€ million)	Own resources (€ million)	Net balance (€ million)	Average/ head of population per year (€)
Czech Rep.	10.2	78	3,350	−2,573	777	25.4
Estonia	*1.3*	*7*	*735*	*−231*	*504*	*129.2*
Cyprus	0.7	11	516	−428	88	41.9
Latvia	*2.3*	*9*	*1,117*	*−287*	*830*	*120.3*
Lithuania	*3.4*	*15*	*1,863*	*−510*	*1,353*	*132.7*
Hungary	10.1	69	3,653	−2,280	1,373	45.3
Malta	0.4	4	310	−177	133	110.8
Poland	38.2	202	13,549	−6,552	6,997	61.1
Slovenia	2.0	23	1,014	−771	243	40.5
Slovakia	5.4	26	1,765	−934	831	51.2
TOTAL	74.2	444	27,875	−14,744	13,131	59.1

The interpretation of these figures requires some further information. First, in line with our conclusions on pre-accession assistance (cf. *supra*), smaller countries tend to receive proportionally more than larger countries. Second, the relatively high level of allocated expenditure to Lithuania is partly due to the special allowance made for the decommissioning of the Ignalina nuclear power plant and financial support

---

[180] X, "It's done: EU Membership deals concluded with first entrants at Copenhagen Summit", *Uniting Europe* (2002) 213, pp. 1–4.
[181] Figures based on Commission document "Net budgetary position after enlargement of the N-10", available at: www.landnet.at/filemanager/download/5548/.

for the solution of the Kaliningrad transit problem. Moreover, the Baltic States are relatively poor in comparison to other acceding countries, which implies that their contribution to the own resources is somewhat lower. Finally, the Baltic States all have external borders with Russia (and in the case of Lithuania also with Belarus) and are, therefore, eligible for Schengen money. This combination of factors explains why, for instance, Lithuania receives three times more money per capita than the Czech Republic. The latter country receives less than any other acceding State for the obvious reasons that it is relatively wealthy in terms of GDP, it does not have an external frontier and only a small agricultural sector. The Temilin nuclear power system was, in spite of frequent problems with Austria and in contrast to the Ignalina NPP, not regarded by the EU as in need of immediate closure.

Whereas the Copenhagen financial deal can be assessed as "at least satisfactory" for the Baltic States in comparison to the other acceding countries, the overall financial package for enlargement is rather modest in relation to the entire EU budget. The European Commission calculated that the total enlargement related expenditures between 1990 and 2006 amount to less than 1 % of the EU's GNP in 1999 and the average annual expenditures to around 0.05 %.[182] The acceding countries' full contribution to the budget from the date of accession and the reduced financial allocations in the field of CAP in combination with the principle of budgetary discipline supported by the EU's net contributors and frozen in the Berlin financial framework, explain why the overall budgetary cost of enlargement is rather limited in comparison to original estimates.[183] It also has to be taken into account that the calculation of a country's net position with regard to the EU budget is only one side of the story. The actual absorption of EU funds requires some amount of national co-financing and involves the mobilisation of a Member States' national administration. Meeting the rules for the

---

[182] European Commission, "Enlargement: Frequently Asked Questions: Costs of Enlargement", available at: http://europa.eu.int/comm/enlargement/faq/.

[183] The first serious economic studies of eastern enlargement estimated the total annual net cost of enlargement at € 58.1 billion (R. Baldwin, "Towards an integrated Europe", London, CEPR, 1994, p. 170.). After the 2002 Copenhagen European Council, the Commission calculated that the net cost of enlargement in the first three years (2004–2006) would not be more than € 10.3 billion (X, "Enlargement to cost EU citizens less than 10 euro a year", *Uniting Europe* (2002) 213, p. 6).

adoption of EU funds, therefore, constitutes a significant burden for the state budget of new Member States[184] and could lead to a situation where potential EU assistance is not fully exploited. Recent reports from Lithuania, for instance, indicate that almost 1 billion litas (€ 290 million) of financial support may be left unspent.[185]

---

[184] In this regard, Rasa Spokeveciute calculated that "during the period of 2004–2006 the additional co-financing which needs to be raised by the Lithuanian State will amount to around € 287 million". On the budgetary implications of EU accession for Lithuania, see: R. Spokeveciute, "The impact of EU Membership on the Lithuanian budget", SEI Working Paper (2003) 63, available at: http://www.sussex.ac.uk/sei/documents/wp63.pdf.

[185] X, "Only 21 percent of available EU Funds have been used in Lithuania", *The Baltic Times*, 13 October 2006.

CHAPTER THREE

DRAFTING THE TREATY OF ACCESSION

§ 1. *Structure and Legal Nature of the Accession Treaty*

Pursuant to Article 49 (2) EU, the results of the accession negotiations are embodied in an agreement between the Member States and the acceding state(s). The drafting of the fifth Accession Treaty in the history of the E(E)C/EU formally started in March 2002 and was finalised six weeks after the end of the negotiations so that it could be signed in Athens on 16 April 2003 with a view of accession of ten new Member States on 1 May 2004. Following previous practice, the 2003 Accession Treaty or "Treaty of Athens" includes the conditions of accession and adjustments to the Treaties for all acceding countries. This practice has important legal consequences because it denies the Member States' Parliaments and the European Parliament the right to approve or refuse individual applicant countries. A failure of ratification, therefore, means a veto of the entire enlargement process. If, however, an acceding country fails to ratify the Treaty of Accession, the Council could decide unanimously upon the necessary adjustments to allow its entry into force for those states that had deposited their instruments of ratification.[186]

The term 'Accession Treaty' is somewhat confusing because, in fact, it entails a single series of documents comprising three complementary elements: the Treaty itself (TA), the Act of Accession (AA) and a Final Act (FA). The TA is very short (three articles) and basically provides that the Czech Republic, Estonia, Cyprus, Latvia, Lithuania, Hungary, Malta, Poland, Slovenia and Slovakia become members of the European Union and thereby parties to the Treaties on which the Union is founded on the basis of the conditions of admission and adjustments to the Treaties as set out in the AA.[187] Such 'conditions' are basically the transitional arrangements agreed during the negotiations, while

---

[186] This so-called "Norwegian clause" is included in Art. 2 (2) TA.
[187] As set out in Art. 1 (2) TA, the provisions of the AA form an integral part of the TA.

the 'adjustments' are limited to technical adaptations in so far as they do not alter the fundamental principles of the integration process.[188] Changes to the Treaties that go beyond mere adjustments need to follow the Treaty amendment procedure of Article 48 EU. The ECJ confirmed the limits of changes to the Treaties on the basis of Article 49 EU in *Hauptzollambt* v. *OHG Koenig*. In this case of 1974 the Court spelled out that: "no provision in the Treaty of Accession or in the Act accompanying can be construed as validating measures, whatever their form, which are incompatible with the Treaties establishing the Communities".[189] In this respect, the introduction of a unanimity requirement for changes to the transit of persons regime between Kaliningrad and other parts of Russia in Article 3 of Protocol No. 5 to the Accession Treaty is remarkable because, in fact, it creates an exception to the Treaty provisions of Articles 62 EC and 67 EC (cf. *supra*).

On the relationship with the founding Treaties, Article 1 (3) TA reveals that the provisions concerning the rights and obligations of the Member States and the powers and jurisdiction of the Union apply in respect to the Accession Treaty. This provision has also been included in all previous Accession Treaties and illustrates—together with the obligation for the acceding countries to accept the *acquis communautaire*—the continuity of the Community legal order after the accession of new Member States.[190] The Court's judgment in a case concerning the accession of Greece that "the provisions of the Act of Accession must be interpreted with reference to the foundations of the Community, as established by the Treaty, [and that] derogations permitted by the Act of Accession from the rules laid down in the Treaty must be interpreted in such a way as to facilitate the achievement of the objectives of the Treaty and the application of all of its rules" confirms this view.[191]

---

[188] C. Hillion, "The European Union in dead. Long live the European Union...A commentary on the Treaty of Accession 2003", 29 *European Law Review* (2004), p. 584.

[189] ECJ, Case 185/73, *Hauptzollamt Bielefeld* v. *OHG Koenig* [1974] ECR 607 at para. 3.

[190] J.P. Puissochet, *L'élargissement des Communautés européennes*, Paris, Editions techniques et économiques, 1974, p. 50. In this respect, the ECJ proclaimed the principle that "the provisions of Community law apply *ab initio* and *in toto* to new Member States, derogations being allowed only in so far as they are expressly laid down by transitional provisions". Case 258/81 *Metallurgiki Halyps A.E.* v. *Commission* ECR [1982] 4261 at para. 8; Case C-233/97 *KappAhl Oy* [1998] ECR I-8069 at para. 15.

[191] ECJ, Joint Cases 194/85 and 241/85, *Commission v. Greece* [1988] ECR 1037 at para. 20.

The Treaty of Accession as conceived under Article 49 EU has a hybrid legal character.[192] On the one hand, it is an international agreement between Member States and acceding state(s), which has the status of primary Community law.[193] As such, it is not an "act of the institutions" in the sense of Article 230 EC.[194] Accordingly, the Court has no jurisdiction to consider the legality of its provisions, which can only be repealed, suspended or amended in accordance with the procedure of Article 48 EU.[195] On the other hand, numerous provisions concern transitional arrangements and technical adjustments to secondary legislation. The Act of Accession, therefore, clarifies that the acts adopted by the institutions to which the transitional measures or amendments apply retain their status in law and can be repealed or amended on the basis of the procedures for amending those acts.[196] The details of the permanent and temporary adaptations to the acts of the institutions are included in 18 annexes and 10 protocols to the AA.[197] The FA, containing no less than 44 declarations from the acceding countries and/or the old Member States, supplements the TA and AA. The ECJ has generally concluded that such declarations do not have binding legal force but must nevertheless be taken into consideration for the purpose of interpreting the Accession Treaty.[198]

The legal difference between binding protocols and interpretative declarations is important for the assessment of the accession negotiations

---

[192] Puissochet, *op. cit.*, footnote 190, p. 48.

[193] The primary law nature of Accession Treaties is clearly illustrated in the Treaty establishing a Constitution for Europe. Article IV-437 (2) repealed the Treaties of Accession but, given the continued relevance of various provisions, two specific Protocols (one joint Protocol for the first four Treaties of Accession and one specific Protocol on the fifth Accession Treaty) have been annexed to the Constitutional Treaty. *OJ* (2004) C 310/186.

[194] ECJ, Joint Cases 31/86 and 35/86, *LAISA* v. *Council* [1988] ECR 2285 at para. 17.

[195] *Ibid.*, para. 12. Case C-259/95, *Parliament* v. Council [1997] ECR I-5303 at para. 27. Case C-445/00, *Austria* v. *Council* [2003] ECR 8549 at para. 62. Yet, the European Court of Human Rights considered the legality of the exclusion of Gibraltar from certain parts of the EC Treaty by virtue of the 1972 Treaty of Accession in order to conclude that there had been a breach of Article 3 of Protocol No. 1 to the European Convention on Human Rights and Fundamental Freedoms. ECtHR, *Matthews* v. *The United Kingdom*, Application No. 24833/94, 18 February 1999, at para. 12.

[196] Articles 7–9 AA.

[197] As the Court declared in *Austria* v. *Council*, protocols and annexes to an Act of Accession have the status of primary law. Case C-445/00, *Austria* v. *Council* [2003] ECR 8549 at para. 62.

[198] ECJ, Case C-192/99, *Kaur* [2001] ECR 1237 at para. 23–24.

with the Baltic States. With regard to the energy chapter, for instance, Lithuania obtained a binding guarantee that it can invoke the general economic safeguard clause (cf. *infra*) until 31 December 2012 in cases of serious disturbances to its energy market as a result of the closure of the Ignalina NPP.[199] In relation to Estonia's energy market, on the other hand, the EU15 only issued a joint declaration recognizing that the restructuring of the oil shale sector requires particular efforts until the end of 2012.[200] This statement, however, does not constitute a legal basis for the granting of further derogations from the *acquis*.[201]

The observation that the guarantees for Lithuania included in the Kaliningrad compromise of November 2002 (cf. *supra*) have been implemented on the basis of a protocol to the AA is also very important from a legal point of view.[202] It implies that the ECJ can declare acts of the institutions concerning the transit of persons between Kaliningrad and other parts of the Russian Federation invalid if they are adopted without the approval of Lithuania and if the scope and the content of those measures fall under Article 3 of the Accession Protocol. It also gives Lithuania a legal basis to claim Community assistance for any costs relating to the implementation of the *acquis* in this field. Finally, the Protocol lays down that the Kaliningrad question may not delay or prevent Lithuania's full participation in the Schengen *acquis*. On this question, a declaration of the EU15 reveals that even though the objective is to include Lithuania in the first group of new Member States to participate fully in Schengen, this decision depends on an objective evaluation of the situation.[203] In other words, Lithuania did not have a legal guarantee to be admitted into the Schengen area at any particular date. There was only a political commitment on the part of the EU to assist Lithuania with the implementation of the required legislation.

---

[199] Article 4 of Protocol No. 4 on the Ignalina Nuclear Power Plant, *OJ* (2003) L 236/945. On the interpretation of this provision, see *infra* Part V, Chapter 3, § 2.

[200] Declaration 8 on oil shale, the internal electricity market and Directive 96/92/EC of the European Parliament and the Council of 19 December 1996 concerning rules for the internal market in electricity, *OJ* (2003) L 236/975.

[201] ECJ, Case C-413/04, *op. cit.*, footnote 91, para. 58. See *supra* Chapter 2, § 4.1.

[202] Protocol No. 5 on the transit of persons by land between the region of Kaliningrad and other parts of the Russian Federation, *OJ* (2003) L 236/945.

[203] Declaration No. 12 on the transit of persons by land between the region of Kaliningrad and other parts of the Russian Federation, *OJ* (2003) L 236/976.

§ 2. Safeguard Measures and the Role of the Commission in the Post-accession Period

2.1. The Commission Opinion and Comprehensive Monitoring Reports

The adoption of the final Commission Opinion on 19 February 2003 formed a crucial step in the formal enlargement procedure under Article 49 EU. Importantly, this favourable Opinion did not end the monitoring role of the European Commission in the pre-accession period. As envisaged in its 2002 Strategy Paper and endorsed by the 2002 Copenhagen European Council, the Commission produced comprehensive monitoring reports for the Council and the European Parliament six months before the envisaged date of accession.[204] This final assessment on the state of preparedness for EU membership of the ten acceding countries filled a gap between the signature of the Treaty of Athens (16 April 2003) and the actual date of accession (1 May 2004). This interim period is interesting from a legal point of view. On the one hand, acceding states are obliged to refrain from any action contrary to the substance of Community law. On the other hand, they are only legally bound by Community law and the jurisdiction of the Court of Justice from the date of accession.[205] Confronted with this legal dilemma, the ECJ referred to the principle of good faith in international relations[206] and legitimate expectations of private individuals[207] to assert its jurisdiction over pre-accession actions with post-accession consequences.[208]

---

[204] The 'composite' comprehensive monitoring report as well as the comprehensive country monitoring reports are available at: http://www.europa.eu.int/comm/enlargement/report_2003/index.htm#comprehensive.

[205] Article 2 AA. On the possibility to introduce new transitional arrangements in this period, see comments on case C-413/04 in Chapter 2, § 4.1. of this Part.

[206] In *Opel Austria* v. *Council* the Court of First Instance ruled that the principle of good faith is a rule of customary international law and, therefore, binding on the Community. CFI, Case T-115/94, *Opel Austria* v. *Council* [1997] ECR II-39 at para. 90.

[207] In this regard, the interim period between the signature of a treaty and its entry into force is comparable to the period between the adoption and the deadline for the implementation of directives. Concerning the application of the principle of legitimate expectations to the latter situation, see: ECJ, Case C-129/96, *Inter-Environnement Wallonie* [1997] ECR I-7411.

[208] ECJ, Case C-27/96, *Danisco Sugar* [1997] ECR I-6653. For comments on the intertemporal application of EC law relating to the accession of new Member States, see: S.L. Kaleda, "The interim obligations of a state acceding to the European Union in the light of the inter-temporal jurisprudence of the Court of Justice", 26 *European Law Review* 7 (2001), pp. 599–604; S.L. Kaleda, "Immediate Effect of Community Law in the new Member States: Is there a Place for a Consistent Doctrine?", in: F. Snyder, (ed.), *The European Union and Governance*, Brussels, Bruylant, 2003, pp. 131–157;

Arguably, the Commission's comprehensive monitoring reports aimed to prevent an inflation of infringement procedures after the accession of ten new Member States.

In comparison to the enhanced pre-accession strategy regular reports, the comprehensive monitoring reports did not follow the structure of the Copenhagen criteria but rather focused on the commitments and requirements arising from the accession negotiations. Accordingly, the final Commission reports virtually ignored issues such as the status of Russian-speaking minorities in Estonia or Latvia but mainly assessed for each of the 29 chapters of the *acquis* the state of preparedness of the respective countries in terms of transposition of legislation, implementing structures, administrative capacity and enforcement procedures. In its conclusion for each chapter, the Commission indicated which issues required "enhanced efforts" to ensure that they would be resolved by the time of accession. So-called "issues of serious concern" implied a request of "immediate and decisive action" to be taken by the country in question. A comparative analysis of the individual comprehensive monitoring reports reveals that the three Baltic countries faced serious problems with regard to preparations for the general system of mutual recognition of qualifications and the mutual recognition and training of certain professions.[209] This problem, however, seemed to be typical for most CEECs.[210] In general, Estonia, Latvia and Lithuania had to address respectively three, two and four issues of serious concern in various chapters of the *acquis*. With this record, the Baltic States approached an average level of preparation in comparison to the other acceding countries.[211]

In spite of the identified issues of concern, the Commission confirmed that all acceding countries demonstrated their commitment and ability to apply the *acquis* from 1 May 2004 onwards. In view of its role as guardian of the Treaties, the Commission promised continuous moni-

---

R. Hernu, "Contribution à l'étude de l'application du droit communautaire en cas d'adhésion à l'Union européenne de nouveaux états members", in: T. Cao-Huy, (ed.), *Etudes sur l'élargissement de l'Union européenne*, Paris, PUF, 2003, pp. 173–194; I. Van Der Steen, "Toetreding van nieuwe lidstaten: temporele capriolen voor burgers en buitenlui", 9 *NTER* 1–2 (2003), pp. 26–33.

[209] The comprehensive country monitoring reports are available at: http://www.europa.eu.int/comm/enlargement/report_2003/index.htm#comprehensive.

[210] Only Hungary and the Slovak Republic did not receive a similar warning from the Commission.

[211] The record of the acceding countries ranged from only one issue of serious concern (Slovenia) to nine issues of serious concern (Poland).

toring of the required efforts in the transposition and implementation of the acquis "so that all remaining gaps may be closed by the time of accession". Importantly, the Commission also insisted on the inclusion of safeguard clauses in the Treaty of Accession.[212]

2.2. *The General Economic Safeguard Clause*

The practice of safeguard clauses is nothing new in the EU's enlargement history. Article 152 of the Act of Accession for Austria, Finland and Sweden, for instance, entailed a general economic safeguard clause which has been used as a model for the drafting of Article 37 of the Act of Accession for the fifth enlargement. The only difference concerns the duration of the validity of the safeguard clause. Taking into account the different economic and legal position of the ten acceding countries in comparison to the three former EFTA Member States, the general economic safeguard clause now lasts for three years instead of one year.[213] This clause enables both old and new Member States to request the Commission to institute temporary emergency measures protecting a sector of the economy or to protect against serious deterioration in the economic situation of a given area. Upon request of the state concerned, the Commission determines, on the basis of an emergency procedure, the protective measures which it considers necessary and specifies the conditions and modalities of their application.[214] The measures envisaged may involve derogations from the rules of the EC Treaty and the Act of Accession but cannot include the establishment of border controls. They apply as long as strictly necessary for

---

[212] For an analysis of the safeguard clauses, see: E. Lannon, "Le traité d'adhésion d'Athènes. Les négociations, les conditions de l'admission et les principales adaptations des traités résultant de l'élargissement de l'UE à vingt-cinq Etats membres", 40 *Cahiers de droit européen* 1–2 (2004), pp. 64–72; P. Garcia, "Le traité d'Athènes, un traité d'adhésion comme les autres?", *Revue du Marché commun et de l'Union européenne* 478 (2004), pp. 290–292; K. Inglis, "The Union's fifth Accession Treaty: new means to make enlargement possible" 41 *Common Market Law Review* (2004), pp. 953–960.

[213] Remarkably, in its 2002 Strategy Paper the Commission envisaged that the duration of the validity of the general economic safeguard clause should be two years instead of three years as was later included in Article 37 of the Act of Accession (European Commission, 2002 Strategy Paper, p. 25).

[214] As the ECJ concluded with regard to a similar clause in the Act of Accession of Greece, the Commission has a wide discretion in determining whether the conditions justifying the adoption of protective measures are fulfilled. See: Case 11/82, *SA Piraiki-Patraiki* [1985] ECR 207 at para. 40.

the attainment of its objectives. Priority is given to measures that least disturb the functioning of the internal market.[215]

This general economic safeguard clause gives the new Member States a possibility to react to potential economic shocks that certain regions or economic sectors might encounter as a result of accession. Significantly, Protocol No. 4 explicitly refers to this option in case of problems as a result of the closure of the Ignalina NPP.[216] For the old Member States, on the other hand, this clause could be invoked in case of serious disturbances of transnational competition.[217] Given the limited impact of the small Baltic States on intra-Community competition, this application of the general economic safeguard clause has never been contemplated.

In addition to the traditional general economic safeguard clause, the Commission also suggested in its 2002 Strategy Paper a special internal market related safeguard mechanism as well as a *sui generis* safeguard clause to address any serious breach or a threat of a serious breach in the area of criminal law under Title VI of the EU Treaty and Directives and Regulations relating to mutual recognition in civil matters under Title IV of the EC Treaty (also called the "Justice and Home Affairs safeguard clause").

2.3. The Internal Market Safeguard Clause

The internal market safeguard clause, included in Article 38 Act of Accession, empowers the Commission to act "if a new Member State has failed to implement commitments undertaken in the context of the accession negotiations" and causes "a serious breach of the functioning of the internal market". It is noteworthy that reference is made to the negotiation process and not to the commitments enshrined in the Act of Accession itself, considering that the Act of Accession reflects the outcome of the negotiations and contains all essential commit-

---

[215] Art. 37 (3) AA.

[216] Importantly, Article 4 of Protocol No. 4 extends the application of the general economic safeguard clause until 2012 whereas Art. 37 AA only covers a period of three years after accession. On the interpretation of this provision, see *infra* Part V, Chapter 3, § 2.

[217] In Declaration 43 to the Final Act, the Commission makes clear that the general economic safeguard clause "also covers agriculture". Apparently, this declaration was inspired by the specific problems of the agricultural sector in Poland because the Commission made clear that the measures envisaged a monitoring of trade flows between Poland and other Member States.

ments undertaken during these negotiations.[218] The ambiguity of the formulation of Article 38 AA has forced six new Member States to issue a joint declaration on the application of this Article. According to the Czech Republic, Estonia, Lithuania, Poland, Slovenia and the Slovak Republic, "the notion has failed to implement commitments undertaken in the accession negotiations only covers the obligations that are arising from the original Treaties [...] under the conditions laid down in the Act of Accession, and the obligations defined in this Act".[219] Accordingly, these six new Member States understand that the use of the internal market safeguard clause is restricted to failures to fulfil Treaty obligations, in the same way as under Article 226 EC. The Commission does not accept this point of view. In its own declaration on the safeguard clauses, the Commission only promised to hear the view(s) and positions of the Member State(s) concerned before deciding to apply the safeguard measures.[220]

Remarkably, Article 38 AA defines the scope of the internal market safeguard clause broadly, including "any commitments in all sectoral policies which concern economic activities with cross-border effect". An "imminent risk" of a breach of the functioning of the internal market is sufficient to trigger the application of the safeguard clause. Here the distinction with Article 226 EC, the Treaty basis for pursuing a Member State that has failed to meet its obligations, becomes obvious. Article 38 AA can be used as a tool of prevention anticipating potential problems of compliance and implementation.[221] In this respect, it reflects somewhere the Commission's rapid intervention mechanism for the free movement of goods under Regulation 2679/98, which allows for information exchange "when an obstacle occurs or when there is a threat thereof".[222] Article 226 EC, on the other hand, can only be applied after a breach of Community rules occurred and the

---

[218] Hillion, "Treaty of Accession 2003", *op. cit.*, footnote 188, p. 603.

[219] Declaration No. 22 by the Czech Republic, the Republic of Estonia, the Republic of Lithuania, the Republic of Poland, the Republic of Slovenia and the Slovak Republic on Article 38 of the Act of Accession, *OJ* (2003) L 236/978.

[220] Declaration No. 43 by the Commission of the European Communities on the general economic safeguard clause, the internal market safeguard clause and the justice and home affairs safeguard clause, *OJ* (2003) L 236/985.

[221] K. Inglis, "The Union's fifth Accession Treaty: new means to make enlargement possible" 41 *Common Market Law Review* (2004), p. 958.

[222] Article 3 of Council Regulation (EC) No. 2679/98 of December 1998 on the functioning of the Internal Market in relation to the free movement of goods among the Member States, *OJ* (1998) L 337/8. This rapid reaction mechanism is a direct

Commission decided to start a procedure against the Member State in question.[223] As under Article 226 EC, the Commission has a wide discretion to apply the internal market safeguard clause. The Commission may act on the request of a Member State or on its own initiative. Safeguard measures may be imposed up to three years after accession.[224] They can apply as long as the relevant commitments are not implemented.

Whereas the internal market safeguard clause is a specific legal instrument ensuring the implementation of the *acquis*, the different levels of economic development and social protection among the Member States also raise questions as regards the functioning of the internal market after enlargement. Of particular significance are two recent judgments of the ECJ.[225] Both cases, which are not linked to the application of the internal market safeguard clause, reveal the tension between the economic freedoms of the internal market, the protection of workers and the respect for fundamental social rights. It is no coincidence that this challenge is most visible in the Baltic Sea region, which links the richest and poorest Member States of the EU.

The first case concerns a conflict between Swedish trade unions and a Latvian construction company employing its own 'posted' Latvian workers in Sweden. The company refused to pay Swedish minimum wages or to conclude a Swedish collective agreement. The Swedish Building Workers' Union, therefore, launched a blockade of the construction site, ultimately leading to the withdrawal of the Latvian company from Sweden. The latter claimed the illegality of the trade union's actions on the basis of Article 49 EC and Directive 96/71/EC on the posting of workers before the Swedish Labour Court, which

---

result of the ECJ's judgment in the so-called 'strawberries' case. ECJ, Case C-265/95, *Commission* v. *France* [1997] ECR I-6959.

[223] A procedure under Regulation 2679/98 is not a precondition for starting a procedure under Article 226. See: ECJ, Case C-320/03, *Commission* v. *Austria* [2005] ECR I-9871, at para. 35.

[224] Again, it is remarkable that the time span of the safeguard clause has been extended to three years instead of two years as originally suggested by the Commission in its 2002 Strategy Paper.

[225] Case C-438/05, *The International Transport Workers' Federation and The Finnish Seamen's Union* v. *Viking Line*, judgment of 11 December 2007 and Case C-341/05, *Laval un Partneri* v. *Svenska Byggnadsarbetareförbundet*, judgment of 18 December 2007. For preliminary comments on both cases, see: N. Reich, "Free Movement v. Social Rights in an Enlarged Union—The Laval and Viking Cases before the ECJ", *Juridica International* (2007), pp. 100–115.

referred the question to the ECJ on 15 September 2005.[226] The main issue is whether the obstacles to the activities of the Latvian company and, therefore, to the freedom of services, could be justified on the basis of the right of collective action. The Court explicitly acknowledged that the right to take collective action must be recognized as "a fundamental right which forms an integral part of the general principles of Community law".[227] The exercise of this right may none the less be subject to certain restrictions. In the case of the Swedish Trade Unions, the Court observed that the pressure asserted on the Latvian company in order to sign a collective agreement constituted an inappropriate restriction on the freedom to provide services.

A similar question on the compatibility of trade union action with the internal market rules was at stake in the case of a Finnish shipping company (Viking Line) that decided to 'reflag' its vessel in order to employ an Estonian crew. The Finnish trade unions, competent to negotiate collective agreements with Finnish vessels contested this decision by going on strike. Moreover, they informed the International Transport Workers' Federation, which prohibited all its affiliates—including the Estonian trade unions—from entering into negotiations with Viking Line. The shipping company alleged a breach of the freedom of establishment under Article 43 EC and Regulation 4055/86 on maritime transports.[228] The Court pointed out that the restrictions to the freedom of establishment resulting from the trade union's action could not be objectively justified when they prevent ship owners from registering their vessels in a State other than that of which the owners of the vessels are nationals.

2.4. *The Justice and Home Affairs Safeguard Clause*

The dynamic development of the *acquis communautaire* in the field of Justice and Home Affairs after the Treaty of Amsterdam entered into

---

[226] Reference for a preliminary ruling from the Arbetsdomstolen by order of that court of 15 September 2005 in Laval un Parteneri Ltd v Svenska Byggnadsarbetareförbundet, Avdelning 1 of the Svenska Byggnadsarbetarefördbundet, Svenska Elektrikerförbundet, Case C-341/05, *OJ* (2005) C-281/10.

[227] Case C-341/05, *Laval*, judgment of 18 December 2007, at para. 91.

[228] Reference for a preliminary ruling from the Court of Appeal by Order of that Court of 23 November 2005 in 1) The International Transport Workers' Federation, 2) The Finnish Seamen's Union v. 1) Viking Line ABP 2) OÜ Viking Line Eesti, Case C-438/05, *OJ* (2006) C 60/16.

force in May 1999 has triggered the inclusion of a new and specific safeguard clause on "framework decisions or any other relevant commitments, instruments of co-operation and decisions relating to mutual recognition in the area of criminal law under Title VI of the EU Treaty and Directives and Regulations relating to mutual recognition in civil matters under Title IV of the EC Treaty" in Article 39 of the Act of Accession. On the basis of this Article, the Commission has a wide discretion to take 'appropriate measures'—either on its own initiative or upon a motivated request of a Member State and after consulting the Member States—to address serious shortcomings or any imminent risks of such shortcomings in transposition, implementation or application of the legal instruments in question.[229] The requirement of consultation of the Member States derives from the fact that the Act of Accession gives the Commission a power to adopt safeguard measures to Title VI EU, whereas the Commission does not have such far-reaching power under the Treaty on European Union.[230] Hence, it can be argued that the safeguard mechanism installed under the Act of Accession significantly increases the Commission's monitoring powers *vis-à-vis* the new Member States during the first three years after accession. As with the internal market safeguard clause, the possibility of safeguard measures is targeted exclusively for shortcomings of the new Member States.

The potential applicability of the JHA safeguard clause to the Baltic States could be derived from the 2003 comprehensive monitoring reports, which insisted on enhanced efforts from the three countries to tackle issues such as data protection, corruption, money laundering and the fight against organized crime.[231] Reports from the Open Society Institute on anti-corruption policy and judicial capacity in the acceding countries confirmed problems of law enforcement in the three Baltic States.[232] Latvia seemed to be the weakest link as the United States placed this country in 2005 on the list of "major money laundering

---

[229] Article 39 explicitly refers to "the temporary suspension of the application of relevant provisions and decisions in the relations between a new Member State and any other Member State or Member States" as a possible remedy.

[230] Hillion, "Treaty of Accession 2003", *op. cit.*, footnote 188, p. 606.

[231] The comprehensive country monitoring reports are available at: http://www .europa.eu.int/comm/enlargement/report_2003/index.htm#comprehensive.

[232] Those reports can be found at: http://www.eumap.org.

countries".[233] In spite of these concerns, the Commission has never taken any initiative to apply the safeguard mechanism of Article 39 AA. Consequently, it might be concluded that specific safeguard clauses have to be seen as instruments to put pressure on the acceding countries to continue their efforts after the end of accession negotiations rather than as effective tools of coercion.

2.5. *Additional Transitional Arrangements*

In addition to the pre-determined transitional measures and the potential application of the safeguard clauses, Article 41 and 42 AA allowed for the introduction of specific transitional measures in the field of agriculture and with regard to the application of the Community veterinary and phytosanitary rules during the first three years after accession.[234] The Commission could adopt these new arrangements in accordance with the relevant comitology procedures on the common organization of the markets in the CAP. A good example concerns the new Member States' obligation to ensure that there is no speculative stockpiling of agricultural products. In line with previous enlargement practice, the European Commission therefore adopted two Regulations including the rule that stocks of sugar and other foodstuffs in the first year(s) after accession may not exceed the average of the previous years.[235] Of particular significance is Article 6 of Regulation 60/2004 on the sugar sector, which obliges the Member States to establish a system for the identification of surplus quantities. Moreover, the Member States were expected to guarantee that the operators eliminate this surplus from

---

[233] This report of the Bureau for International Narcotics and Law Enforcement Affairs of the US State Department is available at: http://www.state.gov/p/inl/rls/nrcrpt/2005/vol2/html/42388.htm.

[234] This period can be extended on the basis of a unanimous decision of the Council, on a proposal from the Commission and after consultation of the European Parliament.

[235] Commission Regulation (EC) No. 1972/2003 of 10 November 2003 on transitional measures to be adopted in respect of trade in agricultural products on account of the accession of the Czech Republic, Estonia, Cyprus, Latvia, Lithuania, Hungary, Malta, Poland, Slovenia and Slovakia, *OJ* (2003) L 293/3. This Regulation entered into force on 1 May 2004 and applies until 30 April 2007. Given the particularities of the sugar sector, the Commission adopted a special Regulation (EC) No. 60/2004 on 14 January 2004, *OJ* (2004) L 9/8. This Regulation deals with excessive stocks of sugar during the period of 1 May 2004 and 30 April 2005. The legal basis of both Regulations is Article 41 of the Act of Accession, which provides for the opportunity to adopt specific transitional arrangements in the area of the common agricultural policy.

the market or, if this had not been done, to "charge an amount equal to the quantity in question multiplied by the highest import charges applicable to the product concerned".[236]

The Estonian *Riigikogu* adopted the necessary legislation only few weeks before the date of accession. The so-called Overstock Charge Act was published on 27 April 2004 and entered into force three days later.[237] This legislation included the imposition of charges on companies whose sugar stocks exceeded the permissible amount. At the time of writing, no less than twenty-nine companies challenged the constitutionality of such charges on the grounds of the right to property, legal certainty, legitimate expectations and proportionality. Whereas the applicants have a strong case in the light of the previous jurisprudence of the Estonian Supreme Court on those principles,[238] the question arises to what extent the Commission Regulations affect the claims of the companies concerned. In this respect, the *Weidacher* case of the ECJ dealing with a similar problem at the time of Austria's accession to the EU is highly significant.[239] This case concerned an Austrian company that went bankrupt due to high charges imposed on olive oil imported from Tunisia, exceeding the normal stocks as provided under Commission Regulation 3108/94, which also included the obligation for the new Member States to tax the holders of surplus stocks.[240] The ECJ rejected the claim that the fundamental right to protection of legitimate expectations or the principle of proportionality had been violated, mainly because of the Commission's wide margin of discretion in the Common Agricultural Policy (CAP) and the observation that any normally diligent economic actor must have known, since the official publication of the Act of Accession, that the Commission was empowered to adopt such transitional measures with repercussions on surplus stocks built up before the publication of the Regulation.[241] Obvi-

---

[236] Commission Regulation 60/2004, *OJ* (2004) L 9/11.

[237] *Riigi Teataja* 2004, I, 30, 203.

[238] A. Albi, "Supremacy of EC Law in the New Member States: Bringing Parliaments into the Equation of Co-operative Constitutionalism", 3 *European Constitutional Law Review* 1 (2007), p. 50.

[239] ECJ, Case C-179/00, *Weidacher* [2002] ECR I-501.

[240] Commission Regulation (EC) No. 3108/94 of 19 December 1994 on transitional measures to be adopted on account of the accession of Austria, Finland and Sweden in respect of trade in agricultural products, *OJ* (1994) L 328/42.

[241] ECJ, Case C-179/00, *Weidacher* [2002] ECR I-501, at para. 33.

ously, this judgment has important repercussions for the cases pending before the Estonian courts.[242]

The issue of sugar stocks is a very sensitive question in Estonia, mainly because the European Commission has issued a fine of € 45.7 million to the Estonian government for its failure to prevent the build-up of surplus sugar stocks amounting to 91,000 tons.[243] Estonia contests the rules for the determination of the surplus quantities in a pending case before the Court of First Instance.[244] The main argument of the Estonian government concerns the inclusion of sugar accumulated by private households equivalent to an amount of 63,000 tons in the calculation of the fine. According to the Estonian reasoning this excessive number can be explained by the general fear for increasing sugar prices after EU accession, which stimulated private individuals to purchase large quantities of sugar for the production of home made jams and syrups. Hence, the Estonian government argues that the non-speculative nature of the sugar stockpiling in private households excludes those numbers from the application of Regulation 60/2004, which only aims at preventing companies from stocking up and selling subsidised sugar that was imported before accession to the EU. The Commission, however, maintains that it is impossible to separate the amount of sugar meant for private consumption from the amount destined for commercial purposes.

Whereas the dispute concerning the inclusion of the amount of sugar in private households does not directly affect the proceedings before the Estonian national courts, it is noteworthy that the Estonian government also claims that Regulation 832/2005 discriminates against Estonian undertakings in comparison to undertakings in the so-called old Member States. Moreover, it also invokes the right to property of undertakings,

---

[242] For comments on the cases before the Estonian courts, see: Albi, "Supremacy of EC law", *op. cit.*, footnote 238, pp. 50–53.

[243] "Commission charges five Member States for failure to prevent build-up of surplus sugar stocks", Brussels, 13 November 2006, IP/06/1551. The fines imposed on the other Member States are significantly lower: € 19 m on Cyprus, € 4.4 m on Latvia, € 1.2 m on Malta and € 4.2 on Slovakia. The legal basis for the Commission's charges is Art. 7 (2) of Regulation 60/2004, providing that "in case the proof of elimination from the market is not provided [...] the new Member State is charged with an amount equal to the quantity not eliminated multiplied by the highest export refunds applicable to white sugar [...] during the period from 1 May 2004 and 30 April 2005".

[244] Action brought on 25 August 2005, *Republic of Estonia* v. *Commission of the European Communities* Case T-324/05, *OJ* (2005) C 271/24.

which is one of the arguments used in the Estonian national context. Hence, there is a certain interaction between the Estonian national procedures and the procedure before the CFI.

§ 3. *The Final Step: Ratification of the Accession Treaty*

3.1. *The Legal Framework: Constitutional Requirements and Laws on Referendum*

Pursuant to Article 49 (2) EU and Article 2 (1) TA, the Treaty of Athens could only enter into force after ratification by all contracting parties "in accordance with their respective constitutional requirements". In each of the 15 EU Member States, ratification was based on a parliamentary procedure, which revealed a broad consensus on the question of enlargement.[245] With the exception of Cyprus, ratification of the Accession Treaty in the acceding countries was linked to the outcome of a popular referendum.

In principle, the Constitutions of Estonia, Latvia and Lithuania entrust the task of international treaty ratification to their respective parliaments. The legal impact of EU accession on fundamental and, taking into account the historic development of the Baltic States, very sensitive issues such as national sovereignty and national identity implied that national referendums on this question were unavoidable. Table 9 gives an overview of the basic legal provisions surrounding the organization of the referendums regarding accession to the European Union as well as of the final results.

3.1.1. *Estonia*
The Estonian Constitution explicitly states that "the *Riigikogu* shall ratify and denounce treaties by which the Republic of Estonia joins international organizations or unions" (Art. 121 (3)). Moreover, issues regarding the ratification and denunciation of international treaties are explicitly excluded from referendums (Art. 106). In spite of these basic

---

[245] The figures of the Parliamentary votes on Treaty of Athens reveal an overwhelming majority in favour of enlargement in all 15 EU Member States.

See: http://www.europa.eu.int/comm/enlargement/negotiations/pdf/treaty_ratification_130204.pdf. The regular Eurobarometer surveys, however, reveal that popular support to EU enlargement in the EU 15 was around 50 per cent with 30 per cent against. See: http://europa.eu.int/comm/public_opinion/index_en.htm.

Table 9: EU Accession Referendums in the Baltic States:
The Legal Framework

	Estonia	**Latvia**	**Lithuania**
Legal basis (constitution)	Art. 105 on "issues of national concern" and Art. 162 on "constitutional amendments"	Art. 68 (3): new provision on "EU Membership"	Art. 9 (1) on "issues of national concern"
Requirements for positive outcome	Simple majority of voters participating in the referendum	Turnout requirement of at least 50 % of the number of voters who participated in the previous elections. Simple majority of voters participating in the referendum	Turnout requirement of at least 50 % of the electorate. Simple majority of voters participating in the referendum
Eligible voters	Citizens older than 18	Citizens older than 18	Citizens older than 18
Legal Nature	Binding	Binding	Binding
Date	14 September 2003	20 September 2003	10–11 May 2003
Outcome:	Turnout: 64 % 'yes': 66.9 % 'no': 33 %	Turnout: 72.5 % 'yes': 67 % 'no': 32.2 %	Turnout: 63.4 % 'yes': 91 % 'no': 8.9 %

provisions, a referendum on accession to the EU was deemed necessary because it involved "an extremely important state choice".[246] In this respect, Estonia's Constitutional Expert Committee referred to the *travaux préparatoires* of the Constitutional Assembly, which revealed that accession to a political, economic or military union of states requires a constitutional amendment of Article 1 of the Estonian Constitution.[247] The latter provision lays down the eternity and inalienability of

[246] According to Article 105 of the Estonian Constitution, "[t]he Riigikogu has the right to submit a bill or *other national issue* to a referendum". [emphasis added]

[247] The Constitutional Expert Committee was established in May 1996 in order to carry out a thorough analysis of potential problems of the Estonian Constitution in

Estonia's sovereignty and independence and can, pursuant to Article 162 of the Constitution, only be amended by referendum. Given the impact of EU membership on Estonia's traditional understanding of national sovereignty, the Expert Committee as well as the Council of Europe's Venice Commission[248] proposed to amend Article 1 in order to introduce an explicit legal basis for Estonia's participation in the EU.[249] In spite of these clear recommendations, the political sensitivity of amendments to the 'holy provision' of Estonia's Constitution and the high level of euroscepticism among the Estonian population[250] put the entire idea of a constitutional referendum on ice. In this context, Prime Minister Mart Laar expressed his doubts whether an amendment of the Constitution was necessary at all whereas President Lennart Meri suggested a referendum on withdrawal from the EU some years after accession instead of a popular vote in anticipation of this step.[251]

Confronted with the obvious legal and political difficulties surrounding the question of a referendum on the Treaty of Accession, the Ministry of Justice finally developed the idea of 'supplementing' rather than 'amending' the Estonian Constitution on the basis of the so-called 'Third Constitutional Act'.[252] Article 1 of this document, which has a rather ambiguous legal status,[253] lays down that "Estonia may belong to

---

the light of accession to the EU. The final report of the Expert Committee is available on http://just.ee/juridica2.html.

[248] Council of Europe Venice Commission Opinion on Constitutional Issues Involved in Estonia's Accession to the European Union, CDL-INF (1998) 010e, Strasbourg, 18 June 1998, available at: http://www.venice.coe.int/docs/1998/CDL-INF(1998)010–e.asp.

[249] The proposed amendment, to be added to Article 1 (1) of the Estonian Constitution provided that "Estonia may, on the basis of a referendum, participate to the European Union, which is an association of states created by its Member States on the basis of the Treaties".

[250] Together with Latvia, Estonia has always had the most eurosceptic public opinion, with more than 50 per cent against EU Membership in May 2001.
See: Eurobarometer reports (http://europa.eu.int/comm/public_opinion/index_en.htm).

[251] A. Albi, "Revision of the Baltic Constitutions for EU Accession", in: R. Lindahl, (ed.), *Transition and EU Enlargement. Economic, Legal, Political and Social Change in Eastern Europe*, Göteborg, CERGU, 2005, p. 186.

[252] With the Constitution itself as the first and the Constitution Implementation Act of 1992 as the second Constitutional Act. The Text of the Third Constitutional Act, officially called "The Constitution of the Republic of Estonia Amendment Act", is available at: http://www.legaltext.ee/en/andmebaas/ava.asp?m=026.

[253] In contrast to other countries with a tradition of constitutional laws, the Estonian constitution does not contain explicit references concerning the legal status of constitutional acts.

the European Union, proceeding from the fundamental principles of the Constitution of the Republic of Estonia". Obviously, the last part, which seems to be inspired by Article 23 (1) of the German Constitution and the case law of the German Constitutional Court, has been included to reduce the sensitivity of the issue of national sovereignty. It is, however, not entirely clear as to what constitute "the fundamental principles of the Estonian Constitution". Dr. Eerik Kergandberg, judge of Estonia's Supreme Court, referred to principles of human dignity, the rule of law and the obligation to preserve the Estonian nation and culture.[254] A constitutional working group preparing the ratification of the Treaty establishing a Constitution for Europe concluded that the fundamental principles constitute "an open catalogue" based upon Estonia's national sovereignty; the state's foundations of liberty, justice and law; national security; preservation of the Estonian nation and culture; human dignity; social statehood; democracy; the rule of law; respect for fundamental rights and freedoms and proportionate exercise of state authority.[255] In any event, this provision does not challenge the principle of supremacy of EU law because Article 2 of the Third Constitutional Act reveals that "[i]n case Estonia belongs to the European Union, the Constitution of the Republic of Estonia will be applied, taking into consideration the rights and obligations deriving from the Accession Treaty". It rather has to be understood as a kind of safeguard clause against future modifications of the Union, foreclosing ratification of Treaty amendments contrary to the fundamental principles of Estonia's Constitution.

The Third Constitutional Act passed three parliamentary readings without many deliberations and was approved in a referendum on 14 September 2003. This date was strategically chosen at the end of the referendum series in Central and Eastern Europe, with only Latvia still on the list.[256] The organization of the referendum entailed important

---

[254] E. Kergandberg, "Role of the Constitutional Review Chamber of the Supreme Court of Estonia in the European Union", 60 *Zeitschrift für Öffentliches Recht* 3 (2005), p. 472.

[255] J. Laffranque, "A Glance at the Estonian Legal Landscape in View of the Constitution Amendment Act", 12 *Juridica International* (2007), p. 57.

[256] Initially, Estonian President Arnold Rüütel, proposed to organize the referendum on the same day as the EU accession referendums in Latvia and Lithuania. The date of 23 August, i.e. the anniversary of the Molotov-Ribbentrop Pact, had been suggested. M. Ruuda, "Rüütel: EU Referendum on the same day in Baltics", EU Observer, 18 December 2001 (http://www.euobserver.com).

legal difficulties. From a strictly legal point of view, the question concerning ratification of the Accession Treaty could not in itself be brought to a referendum because Article 106 of the Constitution prohibits the ratification of international treaties on the basis of a referendum. Accordingly, a prior amendment of the Constitution seemed necessary. Given the legal and political constraints of such an undertaking, the question of accession to the EU, as an issue of national concern (on the basis of Art. 105), coincided with the adoption of the Third Constitutional Act (on the basis of Art. 162). In order to avoid the risk of a constitutional deadlock in case voters would accept EU accession and reject the Third Constitutional Act or the other way round, the referendum question combined the two issues into one question which could only be approved or rejected: "Are you in favour of accession to the European Union and passage of the Act on Amendments to the Constitution of the Republic of Estonia?".

This example of legal creativity raises many questions and remarks. First, although both issues were closely related, the question about EU accession and the modifications of the Constitution were based on a different legal basis with different legal consequences.[257] From a strict legal point of view, a prior referendum on constitutional amendments or at least two separate questions would, therefore, have been more appropriate.[258] Second, the adoption of constitutional acts does not fit well within Estonia's legal traditions.[259] In combination with the observation that the basic text of the Constitution remains the same but has to be interpreted in line with EU law as a result of the supplementary Constitutional Act, this mechanism raises problems of legal certainty

---

[257] As an issue of national concern, the question on EU accession was put to referendum on the basis of Article 105, which prescribes that the outcome "shall enter into force on the date on which the results of the referendum are announced". The question on the adoption of the Constitutional Amendment Act, on the other hand, was based on Article 162, which implies that constitutional amendments accepted by referendum cannot enter into force before three months after their proclamation by the President of the Republic.

[258] J. Laffranque, "The Constitution of Estonia and Estonia's Accession to the European Union", 4 *Baltic Yearbook of International Law* (2004), p. 15.

[259] In contrast to the constitutions of other countries (e.g. Austria, Sweden, the Czech Republic), the Estonian Constitution does not provide for the adoption of constitutional acts. The only other Constitutional Act adopted next to the Constitution, i.e. the "Constitution of the Republic Implementation Act", essentially includes transitional arrangements which are incomparable to the fundamental rules on exercising power resulting from the Third Constitutional Act. See: A. Albi, "Estonia's Constitution and the EU: How and to What Extent to Amend It?", *Juridica International* 7 (2002), p. 43.

particularly because the interpretation possibilities are undetermined.[260] Third, the combination of the Third Constitutional Act with the question on accession to the EU apparently formed a way to avoid the explicit and rigid amendment procedures included in the Constitution. Arguably, this procedural manoeuvring undermines to a certain extent the clarity and consistency of the Estonian Constitution. To use the words of Anneli Albi, "[t]he Third [Constitutional] Act creates unnecessary legal chaos and destroys the clear and coherent constitutional basis of Estonia's statehood".[261] It is, therefore, no surprise that the Constitutional Chamber of Estonia's Supreme Court was confronted with numerous complaints concerning the legality of the referendum and the compatibility of the Estonian Constitution and accession to the EU. The Court rejected all applications on procedural grounds[262] and did not tackle these fundamental issues. The question of the relationship between the Third Constitutional Act and the substantial provisions of the Estonian Constitution can, however, no longer be avoided after Estonia's accession to the EU (see *infra* Part VI).[263]

Pursuant to the Constitution (Art. 105) and the Referendum Act[264] (Art. 4), the result of a referendum is binding for all state institutions. A negative outcome would, therefore, have had important legal consequences. First, the Parliament could not have ratified the Accession Treaty, also because Article 123 (1) of the Constitution prohibits the ratification of international treaties that are in conflict with the Constitution, which would have been the case without the adoption of the Third Constitutional Act. Second, according to Article 168 of the Constitution, an unsuccessful referendum on constitutional amendments may not be re-iterated within one year. The latter provision clearly enhanced the stakes of the referendum and has important consequences for future

---

[260] *Ibid.*

[261] *Ibid.*, p. 44.

[262] In most cases the deadline for submitting an application was exceeded; the Supreme Court also stated that constitutional review of the EU Accession Treaty could only be initiated by Courts and by the Legal Chancellor but not by individuals. See: Laffranque, "The Constitution of Estonia", *op. cit.*, footnote 258, pp. 18–19; A. Albi, *EU Enlargement and the Constitutions of Central and Eastern Europe*, Cambridge, Cambridge University Press, 2005, pp. 92–93.

[263] Of particular importance in this respect is the Opinion of the Constitutional Review Chamber of the Supreme Court on the conformity of amendments to the Eesti Pact Act with Article 111 of the Constitution concerning the issuing of banknotes after the adoption of the euro. See *infra* Part VI, Chapter 1, § 1.3.

[264] An English version of the Referendum Act is available at: http://www.legaltext.ee.

EU Treaty amendments on the basis of Article 48 EU.[265] Finally, in case of a negative outcome, the President has to announce extraordinary elections to the *Riigikogu* (Art. 105 (4) Constitution).

In contrast to referendum legislation in Latvia and Lithuania, Estonia's Referendum Act does not provide for minimum turnout requirements. A simple majority is sufficient for a valid referendum. Importantly, the Referendum Act only allows Estonian citizens from the age of eighteen years to take part in the popular vote (Art. 2 (2)). As a result, 198,813 persons without Estonian citizenship (18 per cent of the total population older than eighteen)[266] could not decide on the question of EU accession, which raises questions of democratic legitimacy. Arguably, this restriction of eligible voters also had important consequences for the referendum campaign. High level politicians such as Prime Minister Juhan Parts and his predecessor Siim Kallas almost exclusively focused on the argument that EU accession would put Estonia in a better position to respond Russian demands on citizenship, language policy and visa regime.[267] Understandably, this position influenced the attitude of the Russian-speaking population. The difference in support for accession between ethnic Estonians and Russian-speakers increased spectacularly in the month before the referendum.[268] It was, therefore, not a surprise that the least amount of 'yes' votes was cast in Ida-Viru (57 per cent in favour and 43 per cent against), the region with the highest number of Russian-speaking citizens.[269] In general, 66.83 per cent of participating voters supported accession and 33.17 per cent were against. The turnout rate of 64.06 per cent was relatively high in

---

[265] On this point, see: A. Albi, "Referendums in the CEE Candidate Countries: Implications for the EU Treaty Amendment Procedure", in: C. Hillion, (ed.), *EU Enlargement: A Legal Approach*, Hart, Oxford, 2004, pp. 57–76.

[266] Personal calculations on the basis of information available at the website of the Statistical Office of Estonia, http://www.stat.ee.

[267] X, "Kallas Talk of 'Russian Card' Triggers Debate", *The Baltic Times*, 21 August 2003; C. Deloy, "The Estonians approve their country's entry into the European Union", available at: http://www.robert-schuman.org/anglais/oee/estonie/referendum/resultats.htm.

[268] In August 2003 the difference in support for accession between ethnic Estonians and the non-titular population was 7 per cent (respectively 62 per cent and 55 per cent). In September 2003 this was as much as 21 per cent (respectively 66 per cent and 45 per cent). See: E. Mikkel, G. Pridham, "Clinching the 'Return to Europe': The Referendums on EU Accession in Estonia and Latvia", in: A. Szczerbiak, P. Taggart, (eds.), *EU Enlargement and Referendums*, London, Routledge, 2005, p. 185.

[269] The results of the EU Accession referendum in Estonia are available on the website of the Estonian National Electoral Committee: http://www.vvk.ee.

comparison to previous general elections and implies that those voting in favour represented 42.60 per cent of the total electorate and 34.76 per cent of the population older than eighteen.[270]

3.1.2. *Latvia*

In March 2001, a high-level Working Group under the chairmanship of the Minister of Justice concluded that:

> Regarding the fundamental changes that will be generated by the accession to the EU, it is important that this process has the highest level of legitimacy that nowadays democratic countries may provide, i.e., that granted by a popular referendum.[271]

Importantly, the Latvian Constitution did not provide for such a possibility.[272] Article 68 (1) entrusts the task of international treaty ratification to the Parliament (*Saiema*) whereas Article 73 prohibits the organization of national referendums on this issue. Moreover, in contrast to the regulation in Estonia, the Latvian Constitution does not allow for referendums on "issues of national concern". Hence, the organization of a referendum on the question of EU accession required a prior constitutional amendment on the basis of the procedure provided in Article 76 of the Constitution.[273] Accordingly, the Parliament adopted a number of EU-oriented amendments to Article 68 on 8 May 2003. First, a new provision allows for the delegation of state institution competences to international organizations. Ratification of agreements providing for such a delegation requires a two-third majority of votes within the Parliament in which at least two-thirds of the members participate. Secondly and most importantly, another new paragraph to Article 68 explicitly states that "Membership of Latvia in the European Union shall be decided by a national referendum, which is proposed by the *Saeima*". Arguably, this provision does not only constitute a legal basis for a referendum on joining the EU but also, potentially, on withdrawal

---

[270] Personal calculations.

[271] X, "The Theoretical Foundations of the Amendments to Satversme proposed by the Working Group", received by e-mail from the *Saiema* European Union Information Centre (eiroinfo4@saeima.lv) on 25 February 2005.

[272] The amended version of the Latvian Constitution is available in English at: http://www.saeima.lv/LapasEnglish/Constitution_Visa.htm.

[273] Article 76 proclaims that "[t]he *Saeima* may amend the Constitution in sittings at which at least two-thirds of the members of the *Saeima* participate. The amendments shall be passed in three readings by a majority of not less than two-thirds of the members present".

from the EU.[274] In addition, the amended Article 68 provides for referendums on "substantial changes in the terms regarding the membership of Latvia in the European Union [...] if such referendum is requested by at least one-half of the members of the *Saiema*", which makes Latvia a potentially problematic state in case of future EU Treaty amendments on the basis of Article 48 EU.

The introduction of an explicit legal basis for the organization of EU membership referendum(s) coincided with discussions on the necessity of further amendments to the Constitution. In particular, similar to the debates in Estonia, the question arose to what extent EU membership affects the independence and sovereignty of Latvia as expressed in Articles 1 and 2 of the Constitution. It has, for instance, been argued that the transfer of competences to the EU institutions partly qualifies the statement that "the sovereign power of the State of Latvia is vested in the people of Latvia" (Art. 2).[275] The Working Group on constitutional amendments, however, did not accept such an interpretation and proceeded from the idea that only the exercise of delimited sovereign powers are entrusted to the EU level whereas sovereignty continues to reside in the people and is, therefore, not alienated.[276] From this perspective, a modification of Articles 1 and 2 of the Latvian Constitution was not deemed necessary.

This assessment has important legal consequences because under Article 77 amendments to the first articles of the Constitution have to be approved by a national referendum in which at least half of the electorate votes in favour whereas other referendums only need a majority of half of the number of voters who participated in previous elections (Art. 79). In other words, the fact that the referendum on EU accession did not require amendments to Latvia's independence and sovereignty provisions implied that the procedural requirements could

---

[274] X, "Constitutional Watch: Latvia", 10 *East European Constitutional Review* 2/3 (2001), p. 24.

[275] A. Usacka, "The Impact of the European Integration Process on the Constitution of Latvia", in: A. Kellermann, J. De Zwaan, J. Czuczai, (eds.), *EU Enlargement: The Constitutional Impact at EU and National Level*, The Hague, Asser, 2001, p. 340.

[276] As such, the Working Group followed a conceptual interpretation of sovereignty as it has been developed in the constitutions of the original Member States. See: B. De Witte, "Constitutional Aspects in the Original Six Member States: Model Solutions for the Applicant Countries?", in: A. Kellermann, J. De Zwaan, J. Czuczai, (eds.), *EU Enlargement: The Constitutional Impact at EU and National Level*, The Hague, Asser, 2001, pp. 77–79.

be significantly reduced.[277] Because the turnout rate was 72 per cent in the 2002 Parliamentary elections, the minimum turnout for the EU accession referendum constituted 36 per cent. Given the rule that only Latvian citizens older than 18 years were entitled to vote, which implied the exclusion of 22 per cent of the population, the Central Election Committee calculated that Latvia only needed 248,772 positive votes and at least 497,543 registered voters.[278]

With a turnout of 1,010,467 voters (72.53 %) of which 676,7000 voted in favour of accession (66.97 %), the outcome was better than expected.[279] This can partly be explained because Latvia closed the series of EU accession referendums, which allowed the pro-EU campaign to focus on fears of international isolation. President Vaira Vika-Freiberga, for instance, declared that "when the moment to take a decision comes, the Latvian electors will look at the other candidate countries and will ask themselves whether they shall remain the only one to stay behind".[280] The correlated argument that if Latvia would be the only Baltic State not to join the EU, it would be more vulnerable to Russian pressure further explains the significant gap in voting behaviour between the ethnic Latvian and non-Latvian citizens.[281] In combination with the absence of voting rights for non-citizens, the question of democratic legitimacy has been raised.[282] As in Estonia, the Latvian Constitutional Court also faced numerous complaints on the legality of the referendum.[283] All of them, however, failed to satisfy the procedural conditions under the Constitutional Court Law.[284]

---

[277] Albi, "Revision of the Baltic Constitutions", *op. cit.*, footnote 251, pp. 188–189.

[278] Central Election Commission of Latvia. "Referendum on Latvia Joining the European Union", at: http://web.cvk.lv/pub/.

[279] The results of the EU Accession referendum in Latvia are available at: http://www.tn2003.cvk.lv.

[280] Cited in: Mikkel, Pridham, *op. cit.*, footnote 268, p. 175.

[281] 63 per cent of ethnic Latvians supported Latvia's EU accession compared to only 30.3 per cent of non-Latvians. For a tentative analysis, see: I. Supule, "The Referendum on Latvia's accession to the European Union: Analysis and Conclusions", in: N. Kasatkina, (ed.), *Ethnicity Studies 2004*, Vilnius, Eugrimas, 2004, pp. 59–68.

[282] D. Auers, "How Democratic was the 2003 Latvian Referendum?", available at: http://www.policy.lv/index.php?id=102774&lang=en, 14 October 2003.

[283] A. Endzins, "The Position of the Constitutional Court of the Republic of Latvia following Integration into the European Union", 60 *Zeitschrift Öffentliches Recht* 3 (2005), p. 512.

[284] The conditions for submitting an application are laid down in Article 17 of the Constitutinal Court Law. The applications of several private individuals have been dismissed because their fundamental rights established by the Constitution had not

3.1.3. *Lithuania*

Article 136 of the Lithuanian Constitution provides that "the Republic of Lithuania can participate in international organizations provided that this does not conflict with the interests and independence of the State".[285] According to Article 138, the Lithuanian Parliament (*Seimas*) is constitutionally endowed with the ratification and denunciation of treaties concerning Lithuania's participation in such universal or regional international organizations. Already in 1998, the Constitutional Working Group of the *Seimas* discussed whether both provisions constituted a sufficient legal basis for Lithuania's accession to the EU.[286] In this respect, the specific nature of the EU in comparison to other international organizations, most notably its well-established principles of direct effect and supremacy as a result of a transfer of sovereign rights,[287] raised questions on the compatibility of EU membership with the numerous constitutional safeguards protecting Lithuania's sovereignty and independence.[288] Apart from the reference to Lithuania's interests and independence in Article 136 itself, other safeguards are included in the first articles of the Constitution, which proclaim the independence (Art. 1) and popular sovereignty (Art. 2) of the Lithuanian Republic. Moreover, Article 3 lays down that "no one may limit or restrict the sovereignty of the People or make claims to the sovereign powers of the People" whereas Articles 4 and 5 define that these powers shall be exercised directly or through democratically elected representatives, by the *Seimas*, the President, the Government and the Judiciary according to the limits established by the Constitution.

---

been violated. The Constitutional Court Law is available at: http://www.satv.tiesa.gov.lv/ENG/STlikums.htm.

[285] Noteworthy, this openness to international organizations is rather selective because a special Constitutional Act adopted on 8 June 1992 prohibits the Republic of Lithuania to join "any new political, military, economic or any other unions and commonwealths of states formed on the basis of the former USSR". This provision can only be changed when at least 75 per cent of the Lithuanian electorate approves it in a national referendum (Art. 7 (2) Law on Referendums).

[286] For comments on the work of the working group, see e.g. V. Vadapalas, "Independence and Integration—Constitutional Reform in Lithuania Preparing its Accession to the European Union", in: X, *Verfassungsrechtliche Reformen zur Erweiterung der Europäischen Union*, Baden-Baden, Nomos, 2000, pp. 9–22.

[287] Case 26/62, *Van Gent en Loos v. Nederlandse Administratie der Belastingen*, [1963], ECR 1; Case 6/64, *Flaminio Costa v. Enel* [1964] ECR 585; Case 106/77, *Simmenthal SpA v. Adminstrazione delle Finanze dello Stato*, [1978] ECR 629.

[288] See: P. Van Elsuwege, "The Process of Constitutional Revision in the light of Lithuania's accession to the European Union", 44 *Jurisprudencija* 36 (2003), pp. 59–69.

Significantly, amendments to any of the provisions included in the first Chapter of the Constitution (Arts. 1 to 17) require approval by more than half of Lithuania's electorate in a national referendum. For amending the independent, democratic status of the Lithuanian Republic as laid down in Article 1, a majority of no less than 75 per cent of the electorate is required.[289] Taking into account these important thresholds for amending the sovereignty provisions, the Constitutional Working Group proposed the introduction of so-called 'Community clauses' to Articles 136 and 138 of the Constitution, providing for the transfer of sovereign rights to the EU, direct effect and supremacy of EU law as well as the involvement of the *Seimas* in the process of European integration.[290] Such provisions could be introduced through the Parliamentary procedure laid down in Article 148 (3) of the Constitution[291] and did not require the organization of a constitutional referendum. Whereas this scenario excluded a legal obligation to organize a referendum on EU membership, it could not rule out this option because Article 9 (1) of the Constitution provides that "the most significant issues concerning the life of the State and the People shall be decided by referendum". Lithuania's Law on Referendums required that more than 50 per cent of the electorate approved the issue raised by the referendum. In other words, the threshold for a positive outcome was the same as for amendments to Chapter I of the Constitution. The chairman of the Constitutional Working Group concluded in 2001 that "it would be difficult to expect that such a majority of Lithuanian citizens would vote in a referendum for accession to the European Union".[292]

Taking into account the conclusions of the Constitutional Working Group, the Commission on Constitutional Amendments of the *Seimas*[293]

---

[289] Article 148 of the Constitution.

[290] Vadapalas, "Independence and Integration", *op. cit.*, footnote 286, pp. 9–22.

[291] According to Article 148 (3) of the Constitution, constitutional amendments of other chapters than the first Chapter "The State of Lithuania" and the Fourteenth Chapter "Alteration of the Constitution", which both require approval by national referendum, "must be considered and voted upon in the Seimas twice. There must be a period of not less than three months between these votes. The draft law on the alteration of the Constitution shall be deemed adopted by the Seimas if, in each of the votes, not less than 2/3 of all the members of the Seimas vote in favour thereof".

[292] V. Vadapalas, "Lithuania: Constitutional Impact of the Enlargement at National Level", in: A. Kellermann, J. De Zwaan, J. Czuczai, (eds.), *EU Enlargement: The Constitutional Impact at EU and National Level*, The Hague, Asser, 2001, p. 5.

[293] This Commission was established in March 2001 to submit, if necessary, draft amendments to the Parliament.

decided at the beginning of 2002 that no constitutional amendments were needed at all because the EU, as an international organization, did not infringe Lithuania's independence. Proceeding from the perception of the EU as a classical international organization, which constitutionally implies that accession to the EU does not differ from participation in the United Nations or the Council of Europe, the entire idea of organizing a popular referendum was put into question. This option, however, turned out to be politically unbearable. For this reason, the *Seimas* decided to go ahead with the organization of a referendum under Article 9 (1) of the Constitution, but not without changing the rules of the game.[294] On 4 June 2002, a new Referendum Law was adopted, which introduced the mandatory organization of a referendum "regarding participation by the Republic of Lithuania in international organizations, should this participation be linked with the partial transfer of the scope of competence of Government bodies to the institutions of international organizations or the jurisdiction thereof".[295] A positive outcome required a 50 per cent turnout and at least one third of the total electorate voting in favour. Still, these requirements were deemed to be too restrictive, particularly in comparison to the referendum laws in other candidate countries. After further discussions, the *Seimas* decided to abolish the qualified majority of one third of the electorate. Another proposal to give the Parliament a possibility to continue the process of EU accession in case the 50 per cent turnout requirement would not have been satisfied was rejected because this would basically downgrade the exercise into an advisory referendum.[296] Hence, on 27 February 2003, the *Seimas* passed a resolution on the announcement of a binding referendum on Lithuania's membership of the European Union requiring (i) a turnout of at least 50 per cent of all eligible voters and (ii) a simple majority of participating voters.[297]

---

[294] This is what Gediminas Vitkus called "the smart option"; see: G. Vitkus, "Referendums on the Membership in the European Union: The History, Issues and Lessons for Lithuania", available at: http://www.leidykla.vu.lt/inetleid/politol/25/sl.html.

[295] Art. 4 (5) Law on Referendum, No. IX-929, 4 June 2002, available at the website of the Seimas (http://www.lrs.lt/).

[296] L. Mazylis, I. Unikaite, "Referendum Briefing No. 8: The Lithuanian EU Accession Referendum, 10–11 May 2003", available at: http://www.sussex.ac.uk/sei/documents/epernbreflith.pdf.

[297] Seimas of the Republic of Lithuania Resolution on the Announcement of a Referendum on Lithuania's Membership of the European Union, No. IX-1350, 27 February 2003, available at the website of the Seimas (http://www.lrs.lt/). See

Even though the hurdle for a positive outcome in the referendum was significantly lower in comparison to the old Law on Referendums, the turnout requirement of 50 per cent continued to be a very tricky issue. For this reason, various measures were included in the legislation to facilitate a higher turnout. Voting time was extended (from 6 am to 10 pm instead of from 7 am to 8 pm for other elections) and the referendum was held on two days (10–11 May 2003). Voters were given a possibility to vote in a "territory of temporary presence" instead of their official place of residence. Finally, the possibility of postal voting was extended to 11 days prior to the referendum, replacing the old period of five days. Besides these procedural changes to increase the turnout, high level politicians, businessmen as well as the Catholic Church actively promoted participation to the referendum up to the final moment even though the Referendum Law prohibits campaigning within less than 30 hours before the start of the voting and on the day of voting (Art. 16 (5)).[298] The persuasion proved to be effective because, notwithstanding a rather low participation rate on the first day (23 per cent), as many as 63.37 per cent of the electorate turned out to vote, with an overwhelming majority of 91.07 per cent in favour of EU accession.[299]

In spite of the convincing figures, the procedural changes to the Referendum Law and the one-sided referendum campaign raised questions about the democratic legitimacy of Lithuania's EU accession.[300] Partly in response to these critical voices and against the background of discussions surrounding the Convention on the Future of the Union, the *Seimas*

---

also Article 7 (1) and 7 (2) of the Law on Referendum as amended by the Seimas on 25 February 2003, No. IX-1349.

[298] When it appeared that the voter turnout on the first day remained relatively low—approximately 23 per cent—the President and the Prime Minister made a dramatic appeal broadcasted on television to encourage people to vote. Catholic priests summoned those present in the Sunday mass to go straight to the polls. Finally, a supermarket chain gave a free bottle of beer, lemonade or chocolate to everyone who had voted. Reported in: A. Albi, "EU Accession Referendums in the Baltic States", 11 *Tilburg Foreign Law Review* (2003) 3, p. 658.

[299] The official results of the EU accession referendum are available at the website of Lithuania's Central Electoral Committee, at: http://www.vrk.lt/2003/referendumas/index.eng.html.

[300] See e.g. Lithuanian Free Market Institute, "Debates on the Referendum on Lithuania's Membership in the EU", available at: http://www.freema.org/Projects/Referendum.phtml; G. Sharkanas, "The Actual Mission of the European Union: Destroying Democracy", available at: http://counter-propaganda.w3.lt/euruni/eumils/eneumils.php.

re-opened the debate on constitutional amendments. On 23 December 2003, it started the procedure for adopting a separate Constitutional Act covering the transfer of competences, the relationship between EU and national law and the interaction between the Government and the Parliament on the implementation of EU legislation.

The choice of a Constitutional Act supplementing the Constitution rather than including specific Community clauses in the text of the Constitution was preferred because it underlines the unique characteristics of the EU.[301] According to Irmantas Jarukaitis, the real explanation for the preference of a separate Constitutional Act has been the intention "to emphasize the independence of the national constitutional system from that of the EU".[302] Such an interpretation conceals the real impact of EU membership on Lithuania's legal system. Hence, it could be concluded that clear-cut amendments to the text of the Constitution, in the form of clauses guaranteeing the transfer of sovereign rights, would better reflect the true nature of a pluralistic legal order.[303] In comparison to the situation in Estonia (cf. *supra*), on the other hand, Constitutional Acts fit better within the legal tradition of the country because Article 150 of the Lithuanian Constitution explicitly declares constitutional laws to be a constituent part of the Constitution. Moreover, the preamble to the Constitutional Act has clearly been drafted in the light of other constitutional provisions. The reference to the *Seimas* as the representative and communicator of the nation, executing the will of the citizens as expressed in the referendum of 10–11 May 2003, relates to Articles 2, 3, 4 and 5 of the Constitution. The statement that the EU respects human rights and fundamental freedoms and that Lithuania's membership of the EU will contribute to a more efficient securing of human rights and freedoms fits with Chapter 2 of the Constitution (Arts. 18–37) on "the human being and the state". Finally, the remark that "the European Union respects the national identity and constitutional traditions of its Member States" and the fact that EU membership seeks to ensure "the security of the Republic

---

[301] Motion to Supplement the Constitution with the Constitutional Act on the Participation of Lithuania in the European Union, *Lithuanian Parliamentary Monitor* 12 (2003), p. 34.

[302] I. Jarukaitis, "Ratification of the European Constitution in Lithuania and its Impact on the National Constitutional System", in: A. Albi, J. Ziller, (eds.), *European Constitution and National Constitutions: Ratification and Beyond*, The Hague, Kluwer Law International, 2007, p. 20.

[303] *Ibid.*

of Lithuania and welfare of its citizens", is clearly related to the constitutional safeguard that participation in international organizations may not contradict the interests and independence of the State (Art. 136) and echoes the basic guidelines of Lithuania's foreign policy as laid down in Article 135 of the Constitution.[304]

The first article of the Constitutional Act[305] includes a transfer of sovereignty provision which reflects the traditional understanding that sovereignty can be limited, shared or pooled without being lost.[306] From this perspective, participation in the EU is seen as another mode of applying national sovereignty and is, as such, in conformity with Articles 2 and 3 of the Lithuanian Constitution. This interpretation is not unique and seems to be inspired by the French Constitution, which also contains a similar provision on popular sovereignty (Art. 3)[307] and a specific clause on European integration (Art. 88 (1)),[308] introduced in response to the French Constitutional Court's decision on the Maastricht Treaty.[309] The spirit of the French Constitution is also present in Article 3 of the Constitutional Act, which regulates the participation

---

[304] Article 135 proclaims that "In implementing its foreign policy, the Republic of Lithuania shall follow the universally recognised principles and norms of international law, *shall strive to safeguard national security and independence as well as the welfare, basic rights, and freedoms of its citizens*, and shall contribute to the creation of the international order based on law and justice. In Lithuania, war propaganda shall be prohibited". [Emphasis added].

[305] Article 1 of the Constitutional Act states that "The Republic of Lithuania, being a Member State of the European Union, *shares or entrusts the competence of state institutions to the European Union* in the areas specified by treaties, upon which the European Union is based, and the extent that it would, *together with other Member States of the European Union*, commonly fulfil the membership obligations in these areas and enjoy the membership rights". [Emphasis added].

[306] See e.g. D. Obradovic, "Community Law and the Doctrine of Divisible Sovereignty", 20 *Legal Issues of Economic Integration* (1993), pp. 1–20.

[307] Article 3 of the French Constitution proclaims that "National sovereignty shall belong to the people, who shall exercise it through their representatives and by means of referendum. No section of the people nor any individual may arrogate to itself, or to himself, the exercise thereof [...]." Official English translation of the French Constitution, available at: http://www.assemblee-nationale.fr/english/8ab.asp.

[308] According to Article 88(1) of the French Constitution "The Republic shall participate in the European Communities and in the European Union constituted by States that have freely chosen, by virtue of the treaties that established them, *to exercise some of their powers in common*." [Emphasis added].

[309] Décision No. 92–308 DC, 9 April 1992, http://www.conseil-constitutionel.fr/decision/1992/92308dc.htm. For comments, see e.g. B. Mathieu, "Droit constitutionel français et construction européenne", in: K. Mavrias, D. Maus, (ed.) *Défense nationale— Intégration européenne. Les réponses constitutionelles*, Athens, Sakkoulas, 2002, pp. 47–70.

of the *Seimas* in European affairs.[310] Interesting enough, Lithuania's Constitutional Act also contains an explicit provision on the direct effect and supremacy of EU law:

> The norms of the European Union law are a constituent part of the legal system of the Republic of Lithuania. If it concerns the treaties upon which the European Union is based, the norms of European Union law shall be applied directly, while in case of collision of legal norms, the former shall enjoy supremacy over the laws and other legal acts of the Republic of Lithuania.[311]

Such a blunt constitutional statement is quite exceptional. Only the Irish Constitution contains a more or less comparable provision on the domestic effect of EU law (Art. 29.4.10).[312] It seems no coincidence that Lithuania followed the Irish example because in Ireland constitutional provisions on the exclusive law-making powers of the Parliament (Art. 15.2.1) and the exclusive judicial powers of the judiciary (Art. 34) were found to be incompatible with the law-making powers of the Community institutions and the judicial powers of the European Court of Justice and Court of First Instance.[313] Taking into account that Articles 4 and 5 of the Lithuanian Constitution are very similar to the above-mentioned Articles 15.2.1 and 34 of the Irish Constitution, the introduction of a clause on the domestic consequences of EU law seems logical.

Whereas the explicit recognition of the supremacy of EU law may avoid important constitutional difficulties, which appeared in several old

---

[310] This provision resonates somewhere Article 88 (4) of the French Constitution even though it has to be noted that the right of control of national parliaments on EU affairs is included in other constitutions as well (e.g. Germany, Finland, Portugal, Austria, Sweden, Belgium and Greece).

[311] Article 2 Constitutional Act.

[312] Article 29.4.10 of the Irish constitution lays down that "[n]o provision of this Constitution invalidates laws enacted, acts done or measures adopted by the State which are necessitated by the obligations of membership of the European Union or of the Communities, or prevents laws enacted, acts done or measures adopted by the European Union or by the Communities or by institutions thereof, or by bodies competent under the Treaties establishing the Communities, from having the force of law in the State". The Irish Constitution in available at: http://www.taoiseach.gov.ie/upload/publications/297.htm (Before the introduction of constitutional amendments related to the ratification of the Nice Treaty, this provision was numbered 29.4.7.)

[313] G. Hogan, "Ireland and the European Union: Constitutional Law and Practice", in: A. Kellermann, J. De Zwaan, J. Czuczai, (eds.), *EU Enlargement: The Constitutional Impact at EU and National Level*, The Hague, Asser, 2001, pp. 89–108.

Member States,[314] a number of small remarks have to be made. First, Article 7 (1) of the Lithuanian Constitution still provides that "any law or statute that is in conflict with the Constitution shall be invalid", which seems to contradict the ECJ's judgment in *Internationale Handelsgesellschaft* that even a fundamental rule of national constitutional law cannot challenge the supremacy of a directly applicable Community law.[315] Hence, in light of the ECJ case law the term "supremacy over the laws and other legal acts of the Republic of Lithuania" in Article 2 of the Constitutional Act on Lithuania's membership in the EU also includes constitutional provisions. Egidijus Küris, President of Lithuania's Constitutional Court, argues that Article 7 (1) of the Constitution has to be amended in this sense.[316] Importantly, such an amendment requires approval of at least 50 per cent of the electorate in a constitutional referendum. An amendment or at least a clarification of the relationship between EU law and the text of the Lithuanian Constitution seems indeed recommended in the light of the Constitutional Court ruling of 14 March 2006, which proclaims that Article 2 of the Constitutional Act "consolidates the priority of application of European Union legal acts in the cases where the provisions of the European Union arising from the founding Treaties of the European Union compete with the legal regulation established in the Lithuanian national legal acts (regardless of what their legal power is), *save the Constitution itself*".[317] It is not very clear how this statement can be linked to the ECJ's ruling in *Internationale Handesgesellschaft*.

Moreover, Article 7 (2) proclaims that "only laws which are promulgated shall be valid". This might create problems as regards the direct application of regulations which have been adopted before Lithuania's EU accession and which have not been published in Lithuanian.[318] Finally, the fact that the Constitutional Act on Lithuania's EU

---

[314] De Witte, *op. cit.*, footnote 276, pp. 73–79.

[315] Case 11/70, *Internationale Handelsgesellschaft GmbH v. Einfuhr- und Vorratstelle für Getreide und Futtermittel*, [1970] ECR 1125.

[316] E. Küris, "Role of the Constitutional Court of Lithuania in the European Union", 60 *Zeitschrift für Öffentliches Recht* 3 (2005), p. 591.

[317] Emphasis added. The Constitutional Court of the Republic of Lithuania, Case No. 17/02–24/02–06/03–22/04 of 14 March 2006, "On the limitation of the rights of ownership in areas of particular value and in forest land", at para. 9.7. Available in English at: http://www.lrkt.lt/dokumentai/2006/r060314.htm.

[318] I. Jarukaitis, "Lithuania", in: A. Kellermann, J. Czuczai, S. Blockmans, *et al.* (eds.), *The Impact of EU Accession on the Legal Orders of the New EU Member States and (Pre-)Candidate Countries*, The Hague, Asser, 2006, p. 394.

membership has been adopted after the date of accession might raise questions on the constitutionality of the transfer of competences. Arguably, Articles 136 and 138 of the Constitution provide a sufficient legal basis but this clearly undermines the importance of the Constitutional Act as the constitutional basis for Lithuania's accession to the EU.[319]

3.2. *Interpretation of the Referendum Experience*

A comparative analysis of the referendum experience in the Baltic States reveals a number of common characteristics. First, in all three countries a debate took place whether accession to the European Union, and its subsequent transfer of sovereignty, was in conformity with the applicable constitutional provisions on the 'independence' and 'sovereignty' of the state. Understandably, the history of the Baltic States resulted in very 'sovereinist' and protective constitutions.[320] As a result, amendments to the sovereignty provisions are subject to a lengthy procedure, including a positive outcome in a popular referendum. Importantly, the requirements of such a constitutional amendment referendum are often much stricter than those of regular referendums on 'issues on national concern'. This is the case in Latvia, where a constitutional amendment of the sovereignty and independence provisions requires a positive vote of at least half of the electorate. In Lithuania, amendments to Chapter I of the Constitution also have to be approved by 50 per cent of the electorate and for amendments to the independence provision of Article 1 even by 75 per cent. Even though in Estonia the procedural requirements for a positive outcome are the same for all types of referendums, a clear-cut amendment to Article 1 of the Constitution was ruled out for pragmatic reasons.

Taking into account the legal and political costs for organizing a constitutional amendment referendum, high-level politicians in the three Baltic countries downplayed the impact of EU accession on national sovereignty. In Latvia and Lithuania, a perception of the EU

---

[319] *Ibid.*, pp. 395–396.

[320] The term "souverainist" has been borrowed from Anneli Albi. She distinguishes four characteristics to define the "souverainist character" of a constitution: (i) the absence of provisions with regard to a transfer of competences to international organizations; (ii) a distinction between 'sovereignty' and 'independence'; (iii) constitutional safeguards protecting sovereignty and independence and (iv) safeguards for constitutional revision of the sovereignty provisions. See: A. Albi, "Post-Modern Versus Retrospective Sovereignty: Two Different Sovereignty Discourses in the EU and Candidate Countries", in: N. Walker, (ed.), *Sovereignty in Transition*, Oxford, Hart, 2003, pp. 401–421.

as a classical international organization implied that the EU accession referendum was regarded as 'an issue of national concern' but not as a step within the process of constitutional amendments to the sovereignty provisions. Only in Estonia, the referendum on EU accession coincided with the adoption of the Third Constitutional Act, which supplemented rather than amended the Constitution. In other words, the referendums focused essentially on the question of EU accession whereas the connected constitutional authorisation for a transfer of sovereign rights was largely kept outside the sphere of public debate. In Latvia, a general provision on the delegation of competences to international institutions was included on the basis of a parliamentary procedure. In Lithuania, a more straightforward Constitutional Act on the consequences of EU membership was adopted only after the successful referendum whereas in Estonia the transfer of sovereign powers was only indirectly included on the basis of the Third Constitutional Act and in the rather ambiguous provision that "as of Estonia's accession to the European Union, the Constitution of the Republic of Estonia applies taking account of the rights and obligations arising from the Accession Treaty". These minimal constitutional amendments contrast with the more forthright European clauses in the constitutions of other Central and Eastern European countries.[321] Arguably, the historically conditioned sensitivity to the concepts of national sovereignty and independence in combination with the low public support for joining a new Union might explain this position.[322]

Related to the low public support, the organization of the EU accession referendums coincided with important procedural manoeuvring in order to facilitate the achievement of a positive result. In Latvia, the *Saiema* introduced a specific type of referendum with a low turnout requirement. In Estonia, the *Riigikogu* adopted a legislative amendment to the Law on Referendums permitting the fusion of two issues—on EU

---

[321] See: A. Albi, "Europe Articles in the Constitutions of Central and Eastern European Countries", 42 *Common Market Law Review* 2 (2005), pp. 399–423; S. Biernat, "Are the Acceding States Constitutionally Prepared to Become Members of the European Union?", in: N. Neuwahl, (ed.), *European Union Enlargement. Law and Socio-Economic Changes*, Montréal, Thémis, 2004, pp. 63–85.

[322] The high level of euroscepticsm, on its turn, is closely linked to these countries' recent history as part of the Soviet Union. The consequences of this period are more visible in Estonia and Latvia than in Lithuania, which explains the comparatively more positive attitude of the Lithuanian population *vis-à-vis* accession to the European Union.

accession and on 'supplementing' the Constitution—into one referendum with a single question. In Lithuania, the *Seimas* significantly reduced the threshold majority and adopted several amendments facilitating a higher voter turnout. In addition, the date of the referendum was strategically chosen, with Estonia and Latvia—not coincidentally the countries with the most eurosceptic population—at the end of the row.

Importantly, the procedural changes to the constitutional framework and to the referendum laws may have significant consequences for future EU Treaty amendments on the basis of Article 48 EU. Each of the Baltic constitutions contains a kind of safeguard against further steps in the process of European integration. This is most obvious in Latvia, where the Constitution explicitly provides for a national referendum in case of substantial changes to the terms of EU membership (Art. 68 (4)). In Estonia, Article 1 of the Constitutional Act refers somewhat ambiguously to respect for "the fundamental principles of the Constitution" as a condition for participation in the EU whereas in Lithuania the classical safeguard included in Article 136 of the Constitution remains valid. Within this legal context, EU Treaty amendments can be expected to revive the debate on the consequences of EU membership, even though such a discussion has been largely avoided with regard to the 'Treaty establishing a Constitution for Europe' and the 'Treaty of Lisbon' (cf. *infra*).

Finally, the EU accession experience revealed an important cleavage between the titular and non-titular population. In Estonia and Latvia, where a significant number of non-citizens were excluded from participation in the referendum, regions with a large proportion of Russian-speaking citizens reported the lowest number of positive votes. Notwithstanding the absence of ethnic tensions comparable to the situation in Estonia and Latvia, an analysis of the Lithuanian referendum results reveals similar patterns as regards the voting behaviour of ethnic minorities. The lowest turnout (37.2 per cent) and the highest percentage of 'No'-votes (21.56 per cent) were cast in Visaginas, an area with a majority of Russian-speaking citizens working in the Ignalina nuclear power station. In Salcininkai, a region with a large number of Polish inhabitants the percentage of votes against EU membership was approximately the same (20.6 per cent) but with a higher turnout (56.13 per cent).[323]

---

[323] L. Mazylis, I. Unikaite, "Referendum Briefing No. 8: The Lithuanian EU Accession Referendum, 10–11 May 2003", available at: http://www.sussex.ac.uk/sei/documents/epernbreflith.pdf.

The highly nationalistic campaigns, focusing on security, sovereignty and independence, partly explain these results. Another important element is that the ethnic minorities, even those with EU citizenship, appeared to be more sceptical about their future economic and social opportunities after accession to the EU.[324] In other words, the referendum results reveal that the integration of minorities remains an important challenge after EU enlargement.

---

[324] See e.g. survey results of the Latvian European Integration Bureau, "Attitude in Society Toward Latvia's European Union Membership", at: http://www.eib.gov.lv/latvija-eiropa/eng/eu_report_july.doc.

THE TREATY OF ACCESSION AND DIFFERENTIATION IN THE EU

According to the conclusions of the 1993 Copenhagen European Council, candidates were expected to incorporate the entire *acquis communautaire* before their accession to the EU. Accordingly, acceptance of the *acquis* has been a key element of the pre-accession strategy with a tight monitoring on the part of the European Commission on the incorporation of the 31 negotiating chapters. In this context, the EU accession negotiations essentially aimed at sorting out specific problems concerning the application of the *acquis*. This has been done through temporary derogations, (financial) Community assistance, technical adjustments to the Community legislation and/or the inclusion of safeguard clauses in the Act of Accession. These safeguard clauses are to be conceived as instruments of post-accession conditionality.[325] As such, they operate as a kind of stick behind the door for the Commission in addition to Article 226 EC. The transitional arrangements in general and the safeguard clauses in particular thus provide the means for differentiation between the new Member States and the EU15 in terms of application of the *acquis*.[326]

Whereas differentiation among the candidate countries was promoted as one of the key principles of the enhanced pre-accession strategy—and notwithstanding the bilateral nature of the negotiations—the EU's negotiating practice revealed a tendency towards a more or less uniform treatment of the countries involved. This was particularly the case with regard to the core principles of the internal market. As such, results of negotiations with one country provoked a kind of spill-over effect on the negotiations with other countries. The competitive nature of the accession process prevented a co-ordination of positions among the candidate countries, which only enhanced the asymmetrical relationship between

---

[325] Inglis, "The Union's fifth Accession Treaty", *op. cit.*, footnote 221, p. 953.

[326] A. Ott, "The Principle of Differentiation in an Enlarged European Union", in: A. Ott, K. Inglis, (eds.), *The Constitution for Europe and an Enlarging Union: Unity in Diversity*, Groningen, Europa Law Publishing, 2005, pp. 105–131.

the negotiating parties. Only at the very end of the negotiations, when it was clear that a joint accession of ten countries would take place on 1 May 2004, the Baltic States formed a common front on the issue of direct payments for farmers and on production quotas for agricultural products. A similar co-operation among the three Baltic States proved impossible during the early stages of the negotiations. With regard to the external relations chapter, Estonia never insisted on the continuation of the Baltic Free Trade Area in case of a differentiated accession whereas Latvia and Lithuania asked for a transitional arrangement on this point. The divergent negotiating positions of the three countries aroused political tensions, which clearly illustrated the paradoxes of the EU enlargement process. In particular, it became obvious that a strict legal and individual approach, which fails to take into account the wider geopolitical consequences of enlargement, potentially undermines the general objective of regional co-operation. The problems with regard to the extension of the Partnership and Co-operation Agreement with Russia and the compromise on Kaliningrad transit further revealed the limits of an enlargement methodology that nearly exclusively focused on the relationship between the EU and the candidate countries and largely excluded the countries left outside the enlargement framework. From this perspective, EU enlargement in general and the EU accession negotiations in particular increased the legal and transactional boundaries between new EU Member States and outsider states.[327] The forced termination of the free trade arrangements with Ukraine and the introduction of visa regimes for Russian borderland residents illustrate this point.

In general, the Baltic States secured important and specific transitional arrangements or technical adjustments in the fields of fisheries, taxation, energy and environment. In combination with the general transitional measures on the free movement of workers, the free movement of capital and agriculture—and taking into account some minor transitional arrangements in other areas as well as the postponed entry of the new Member States in the eurozone and the Schengen area[328]—the

---

[327] In this respect, reference can be made to the theory of Michael Smith, who identifies geopolitical, legal, cultural and transactional boundaries to determine the EU's relations with outsider states. See: M. Smith, "The European Union and a Changing Europe: The Boundaries of Order", 34 *Journal of Common Market Studies* 1 (1996), pp. 5–28.

[328] The Baltic States joined the Schengen area on 21 December 2007 together with the Czech Republic, Hungary, Poland, Malta, Slovenia and Slovakia. Full participation

Baltic States will only fully apply the entire *acquis communautaire* several years after the date of accession. In other words, the Treaty of Athens introduced a complicated structure for the Union characterised by legal differentiation between the Member States.[329] It is obvious that this new structure has important legal implications. The discussions surrounding the necessity of constitutional amendments allowing for accession to the EU demonstrated the sensitivity of notions such as 'independence' and 'national sovereignty'. Whereas this is definitely not an exclusive phenomenon for the Baltic States, the historic development of these countries as well as the inclusion of numerous constitutional safeguards protecting the sovereignty and independence of the state, only reinforces the importance of this debate. In addition, the EU accession referendums revealed a significant gap between the perceptions of the titular and non-titular populations of these countries. For the EU, the accession of new Member States thus involves the challenge of finding a balance within the increased economic, political and cultural diversity, not only inside the Union but also in its relations with third countries.

---

in the European Monetary Union (EMU) is subject to an evaluation procedure and a decision of the Council; see *infra* Part VI, Chapter 1, § 1.3.

[329] In this context, the term 'legal differentiation' means that by excluding or delaying the participation of new Member States in some policy areas the Treaty of Athens provides for difference in treatment between the new and old Member States with regard to implementation of and compliance with the *acquis communautaire*.

PART FIVE

THE IMPACT OF EU ENLARGEMENT ON THE TRIANGULAR RELATIONSHIP BETWEEN THE EU, RUSSIA AND THE BALTIC STATES

One of the main criticisms on EU enlargement has been the lack of a parallel policy towards Russia.[1] Notwithstanding the remark in Agenda 2000 that particular attention must be paid to the "legitimate security and economic concerns" of those countries who were not included in the enlargement strategy,[2] the EU clearly preferred a continuation of the 'wait and see approach' that characterised its policy *vis-à-vis* the former Soviet Union. A perfect example concerns the long-lasting reluctance on the part of the EU to discuss the question of Kaliningrad transit in the framework of the PCA structures. Despite the fact that the European Parliament already in 1994 called for a special treatment of the Kaliningrad region,[3] the European Commission issued its first Communication on Kaliningrad only in January 2001.[4] In this document, the Commission acknowledged for the first time that EU enlargement raises specific issues for the development of this Russian exclave and suggested ideas and options to be discussed in the PCA context. Compared to the previous situation this meant a lot of progress. Unfortunately, the lack of substance in EU-Russia relations became clear once the most sensitive issues were under discussion. Russia and the EU only managed to reach common ground on the transit of persons at the very final moment on the basis of a political package deal (cf. *supra*). A similar process could be observed with regard to the extension of the PCA to the new Member States (cf. *supra*).

---

[1] M. Maresceau, "The EU Pre-Accession Strategies: A Political and Legal Analysis", in: M. Maresceau, E. Lannon, (eds.), *The EU's Enlargement and Mediterranean Strategies: A Comparative Analysis*, London, Palgrave, 2001, pp. 20–24.

[2] Agenda 2000. The Challenge of Enlargement (Vol. II), COM (97) 2000 final, p. 14.

[3] Resolution on Kaliningrad (Königsberg), a Russian exclave in the Baltic region: situation and outlook from a European viewpoint, *OJ* (1994) C 61/74.

[4] The EU and Kaliningrad: Communication from the Commission to the Council, COM (2001) 26 final, 17 January 2001.

Whereas the last-minute compromises did not affect the time schedule of enlargement, a number of pre-enlargement challenges have been transferred to the post-enlargement period. The integration of Russian-speaking minorities in Estonia and Latvia, the question of border delimitation between the latter countries and Russia as well as the transit of goods between Kaliningrad and mainland Russia are still on the agenda of the EU-Russia Strategic Partnership. It is, in other words, obvious that the EU accession of the Baltic States significantly affects the context of EU-Russia relations. Hence, the question is to what extent this new situation changes the EU's traditional approach towards Russia? In addition, particular attention is devoted to the impact of the EU on the outstanding political and legal problems between Russia and each of the Baltic republics.

CHAPTER ONE

TOWARDS A NEW APPROACH IN EU-RUSSIA RELATIONS?

§ 1. *From Common Strategy to Common Spaces*

1.1. *The Limits of a 'Wait and See' Approach*

It was clear from the outset that the bilateral Partnership and Co-opera-tion Agreement (PCA), to be conceived as an alternative to the Europe Agreements, was inadequate as an instrument to handle the external consequences of enlargement. Already in May 1998, the European Parliament considered that the Union should develop special links with Russia "going beyond the Partnership and Co-operation Agree-ment".[5] The Amsterdam Treaty, which entered into force 1 May 1999, provided for a new instrument to strengthen the EU's relations with Russia. According to the new Article 13 TEU, "the European Council can decide on Common Strategies to be implemented by the Union in areas where the Member States have important interests in common". In the aftermath of the massive devaluation of the rouble in August 1998, there was an understanding that the first Common Strategy would be on Russia.[6] The latter document, which was adopted by the June 1999 Cologne European Council and expired in June 2004, aimed at the development of a "Strategic Partnership based on common values".[7] This ill-defined concept scarcely concealed the lack of strategic vision on the part of the Union. Perhaps the most astonishing feature of the EU's external relations *vis-à-vis* Russia has been the virtual absence of the enlargement dimension.[8] The position of the EU has always

---

[5] European Parliament Resolution on the Commission Communication "The Future of Relations between the European Union and Russia" and the Action Plan "The European Union and Russia: the Future Relationship", *OJ* (1998) C 138/172.

[6] H. Timmermann, S. Gänzle, "The European Union's Policy towards Russia", in: H. Hubel, *EU Enlargement and Beyond: The Baltic States and Russia*, Berlin, Berlin Verlag, 2002, p. 158.

[7] Common Strategy of the European Union on Russia, *OJ* (1999) L 157/8.

[8] See e.g. M. Maresceau, "EU Enlargement and EU Common Strategies on Russia and Ukraine: An Ambiguous yet Unavoidable Connection", in: C. Hillion, (ed.), *EU Enlargement. A Legal Approach*, Oxford, Hart, 2004, pp. 181–219.

been that enlargement is an internal matter between the Member States and the candidate countries and that Russia had no power or right to interfere in that process. Accordingly, Russian attempts to start consultations on the possible negative impact of the Union's eastward expansion have always been dispelled by the axiomatic statement that both Russia and the EU would benefit from enlargement.[9] Accordingly, the Russian Federation has largely been confronted with a *fait accompli*. Only at the final moment, i.e. few months before the conclusion of the accession negotiations or the date of accession, discussions on unavoidable questions such as Kaliningrad transit or PCA extension entered a more substantial phase.

In order to avoid a complete deadlock in the bilateral relationship, which would be detrimental to both EU and Russian interests, the institutional framework established by the PCA turned out to be instrumental. In particular, the biannual EU-Russia summit meetings, bringing together the highest political representatives of both parties,[10] and meetings at ministerial level within the Co-operation Council—turned into the Permanent Partnership Council in 2003—allowed Russia to raise its enlargement related concerns. The legal basis for discussing these issues is provided in Article 102 of the PCA, which stipulates that "the Parties agree to consult promptly through appropriate channels at the requests of either Party to discuss any matter concerning the interpretation or implementation of this agreement and *other relevant aspects of relations between the Parties*".[11]

Significantly, the PCA does not allow for the adoption of legally binding decisions.[12] As a result, the agreements reached within the PCA framework take the form of 'Joint Statements', which have a political rather than a legal significance. The transformation of the political compromises into binding legal acts requires the conclusion of bilateral agreements or, with respect to the EC internal legal order, the adoption of directives or regulations. The conclusion of the Protocol on

---

[9] See: P. Van Elsuwege, "EU Enlargement and its Consequences for EU-Russia Relations: The Limits of a Fair Weather Strategy", Working Paper Chair Interbrew-Baillet Latour, Leuven, 2002, pp. 10–11.

[10] At the biannual EU-Russia Summits, the EU is represented by the Head of Government of the Member State holding the EU Presidency, the President of the European Commission, the Commissioner for External Relations and the High Representative for CFSP. Russia is represented by its President and Minister of Foreign Affairs.

[11] Emphasis added.

[12] Art. 90 PCA.

PCA extension is an example of a bilateral agreement complementing the "Joint Statement on EU enlargement and EU-Russia relations" whereas the Kaliningrad compromise of November 2002 resulted in a Protocol to the Treaty of Accession and Council Regulations on the Facilitated (Rail) Travel Document. Remarkably, no bilateral agreement on Kaliningrad has been concluded between the EC and Russia. As a result, Russian citizens cannot invoke provisions of the Joint Statement in case of potential problems with the Lithuanian authorities.[13] The partial incorporation of the Kaliningrad compromise into the legally binding Protocol No. 5 to the Act of Accession does not seem to change this situation because this Protocol exclusively deals with Lithuania's guarantees under the compromise and does not include any references to rights of Russian citizens. The situation is different with regard to the Council Regulations introducing the F(R)TD, which contain clear and precise provisions on the issuing and scope of the transit documents. As regards the PCA extension Protocol, it is legally significant that this document does not make any reference to the EU's commitments included in the Joint Statement on EU enlargement and EU-Russia relations. The Protocol only provides for the accession of the new Member States to the PCA. Hence, the Joint Statement remains a purely political document without any binding legal force.

The outcome of the Kaliningrad and PCA extension dilemmas clearly illustrates the rather pragmatic nature of EU-Russia relations. Various issues have often been directly or indirectly linked together in order to facilitate the finding of a political compromise. The EU's recognition of Russia's market economy status, announced at the May 2002 EU-Russia summit and effectively granted on 7 November 2002,[14] could, for instance, be interpreted as an attempt to create a more favourable climate for the discussion of the Kaliningrad issue at the 11 November 2002 EU-Russia summit. A similar striking parallel between Russia's WTO accession process, on the one hand, and progress in bilateral EU-Russia relations, on the other hand, appeared with

---

[13] M. Maresceau, "Bilateral Agreements Concluded by the European Community", 309 *Recueil des Cours The Hague Academy of International Law* (2004), p. 434.

[14] "EU announces formal recognition of Russia as 'market economy' in major milestone on road to WTO membership", IP/02/775, Brussels, 29 May 2002; "La Russie reconnue formellement comme economie de marché", *Agence Europe*, 8 November 2002, p. 10. Council Regulation (EC) No. 1972/2002 of 5 November 2002 amending Regulation (EC) No. 984/96 on the protection against dumped imports from countries not members of the European Community, *OJ* (2002) L 305/1.

regard to the conclusion of the PCA extension protocol. In the context of the latter discussions, President Putin severely criticized the EU's 'artificial support' for Russia's WTO entry.[15] In particular, the relatively limited practical benefits of the market economy status in terms of anti-dumping procedures, a result of the inclusion of a specific provision in the amended anti-dumping Regulation,[16] as well as the EU's objections to Russia's energy pricing explained Moscow's frustration. Whereas these issues were not directly related to EU enlargement and no direct reference to Russia's WTO accession was included in the Joint Statement on PCA extension, it is remarkable that the EU changed its position on the question of energy prices in May 2004, i.e. only few weeks after the PCA extension deal.[17] In this respect, the question has been raised "whether the EU diverged from its original position to secure something else".[18] At the least, the impression of large political package deals and last minute solutions reveal a lack of strategic planning on the part of the EU.

1.2. *The Legal and Political Consequences of the PCA Extension Deal*

The last minute compromise on the extension of the PCA to the new Member States avoided a legal deadlock after enlargement. Pursuant to Article 6 (2) of the Act of Accession, the accession of new Member States to mixed agreements requires the conclusion of protocols between the

---

[15] K. Barysch, *The EU and Russia. Strategic Partners or Squabbling Neighbours?*, London, Centre for European Reform, 2004, p. 20.

[16] The amended regulation provides that in particular market situations "when prices are artificially low, when there is significant barter trade, or when there are non-commercial processing arrangements", the normal value of the product shall be calculated on the basis of the cost of production or on the basis of representative export prices and information from other markets. Accordingly, as long as the EU regards Russian energy, transportation and raw materials costs as being "artificially low", the impact of Russia's market economy status remains limited. See: Article 1 (2) of Council Regulation (EC) No. 1972/2002, *OJ* (2002) L 305/2. On anti-dumping law and Russia, see: E. Borovikov, B. Evtimov, "EC's treatment of non-market economies in anti-dumping law: its history, an evolving disregard of international trade rules, its state of play: inconsistent with GATT/WTO?", *Revue des Affaires Européennes* 7 (2001–2002), pp. 875–896.

[17] "Russia-WTO: EU-Russia deal brings Russia a step closer to WTO membership", IP/04/673, Brussels, 21 May 2004.

[18] P. Sutela, "EU, Russia and Common Economic Space", *BOFIT Online Working Papers* 3 (2005), p. 26. Available at: http://www.bof.fi/bofit. It has to be mentioned that the EU's flexible position on the conclusion of the bilateral negotiations concerning Russia's WTO accession has often been connected with Russia's ratification of the Kyoto protocol.

Council, acting unanimously on behalf of the Member States, and the third country concerned. Article 6 (6) further provides that "should the protocols not have been concluded by the date of accession, the Community and the Member States shall take, in the framework of their respective competences, the necessary measures to deal with that situation upon accession".[19] The option of unilateral trade sanctions could in theory be contemplated but, in practice, the interdependence of EU-Russia trade relations made such a scenario highly undesirable. Russia's reluctance to accept a quasi-automatic extension of the PCA, therefore, brought the EU—but also the Baltic States—in a difficult situation, mainly because Russia *inter alia* insisted on firm commitments regarding the 'social integration' of the Russian-speaking minorities in Estonia and Latvia as well as on the future development of Kaliningrad.[20] Baltic representatives warned that any concessions to Russia in this respect would give rise to further Russian demands after enlargement. In order to counterbalance potential Russian attempts to raise the minorities issue, the Latvian government insisted on the inclusion of a specific note to the minutes of the 26 April 2004 Foreign Affairs Council, stating that the EU confirms that Latvia meets the Copenhagen political criteria.[21] In addition, the avoidance of explicit references to the Russian-speaking minorities in Estonia and Latvia was considered as a priority. Arguably, this issue formed a first test case of the Baltic States' ability to defend their interests in the EU.[22]

The final compromise, included in the Joint Statement on EU Enlargement and EU-Russia relations, does not name any countries and proclaims in rather general terms that:

> The EU and the Russian Federation welcome EU membership as a firm guarantee for the protection of human rights and the protection of

---

[19] Act concerning the conditions of accession of the Czech Republic, the Republic of Estonia, the Republic of Cyprus, the Republic of Latvia, the Republic of Lithuania, the Republic of Hungary, the Republic of Malta, the Republic of Poland, the Republic of Slovenia and the Slovak Republic and the adjustments to the Treaties on which the European Union is founded, *OJ* (2003) L 236/35.

[20] X, "Le cas des minorités russes dans les pays baltes serait le dernier problème à règler pour permettre l'extension de l'APC", *Agence Europe*, 23 April 2004, p. 8.

[21] A. Lobjakas, "EU/Russia: Landmark Enlargement Deal Signed, But Loose Ends Remain", *RFE-RL* 27 April 2004, available at: http://www.rferl.org/featuresarticle/2004/04/0f543104–8e81–492f-9def-0cfbdc9aa47c.html.

[22] K. Raik, T. Palosaari, "Its the Taking Part that Counts. The New Member States adapt to EU Foreign and Security Policy", *FIIA Report* 10 (2004), p. 33; available at: http://www.upi-fiia.fi/doc/FIIA_report_10.pdf.

persons belonging to minorities. Both sides underline their commitment to the protection of human rights and the protection of persons belonging to minorities.[23]

A concrete consequence of this commitment has been the establishment of a regular EU-Russia human rights dialogue after the November 2004 EU-Russia summit in The Hague and the recognition that respect for human rights, including the rights of persons belonging to minorities, constitutes a basic principle of EU-Russia co-operation in the field of freedom, security and justice.[24] Whereas the EU has not accepted any explicit references to the situation of the Russian-speaking minorities in Estonia and Latvia, it is obvious that the increased attention to 'persons belonging to minorities' in the EU-Russia Strategic Partnership is primarily related to the situation in those countries. Accordingly, the integration of the Russian-speaking minorities remains on the agenda after enlargement.

Whereas the PCA does not directly affect the legal position of the Russian-speaking minorities without Russian citizenship,[25] the extension of the PCA is not without consequences for this part of the Baltic States' population. The preamble to the PCA, for instance, explicitly refers to respect for minority rights as an important value of the bilateral relationship. Although the body of the agreement remains silent on the minority issue, Article 2 of the PCA identifies "respect for democratic principles and human rights *as defined in particular in the Helsinki Final Act and the Charter of Paris for a New Europe* [as] an essential element of partnership and of this Agreement".[26] Both CSCE documents contain references to minorities and, thus, indirectly confirm the parties' commitment to minority protection.[27] The Joint Statement on EU Enlargement and EU-Russia relations only increased the importance

---

[23] "Joint Statement on EU Enlargement and EU-Russia Relations", Brussels, 27 April 2004, available at: http://europa.eu.int/comm/external_relations/russia/russia_docs/js_elarg_270404.htm.

[24] Presidency Statement on EU-Russia Human Rights Consultations, Brussels, 1 March 2005, 6198/05.

[25] The provisions of the PCA on labour conditions (Art. 23), co-ordination of social security (Art. 24) or the establishment and operation of companies (Art. 28) only apply to Russian and EU citizens but not to the stateless Russian-speaking communities in Estonia and Latvia.

[26] Emphasis added.

[27] A Joint Declaration on Articles 2 and 107 further clarifies that the references to "respect for human rights" are inspired by the CSCE Helsinki Final Act and the Charter of Paris for a New Europe.

of this issue after the accession of the new Member States. Proceeding from this legal and political basis, the Russian Federation consistently raises the protection of the Russian-speaking minorities in Estonia and Latvia during the EU-Russia human rights consultations, mainly in response to EU concerns about Chechnya. In this context, the EU almost mechanically recalls the Member States' full compliance with the Copenhagen criteria, which closes the door to any potential discussion on the domestic situation in the Baltic States.[28]

Apart from the increased attention to minorities within the EU-Russia Strategic Partnership, the extension of the PCA has direct legal consequences for Russian citizens living and working in the Baltic States. Based upon the ECJ's case law, they can directly invoke the PCA's non-discrimination provision as far as their conditions of employment, remuneration or dismissal are concerned.[29] In general terms, the application of the PCA complements the relatively limited bilateral treaty relations between Russia and the Baltic countries.[30] The PCA, therefore, creates a more solid legal basis for economic relations between Russia and each of the Baltic republics.[31] The application of double customs tariffs, for instance, a common practice during the 1990s, is no longer possible under the PCA's 'most-favoured-nation' treatment.[32] Other unilateral trade sanctions, such as the suspension of wine imports from Georgia and Moldova or milk and meat from Ukraine in the spring of 2006, are in principle also excluded in Russia's trade relations with the Baltic States.[33] Of particular interest is Article

---

[28] See e.g. Presidency Statements on EU-Russia Human Rights consultations, Luxembourg, 1 March 2005, 6198/05 and 8 September 2005, 12081/05.

[29] See: ECJ, Case C-265/03 *Simutenkov* [2005] ECR 2579, at para. 29.

[30] For an overview of the bilateral treaties between Russia and each of the Baltic States, see: http://www1.urm.lt/data/30/l_rus.htm for Lithuania; http://www.mfa.gov.lv/en/policy/bilateral-relations/bilateral/ for Latvia and http://www.vm.ee/eng/kat_176/1430.html for Estonia.

[31] In this respect, it is remarkable that the bilateral trade between the three Baltic States and Russia has increased exponentially in comparison to the pre-accession period, see: "EU 25 and Member States trade with Russia", at: http://epp.eurostat.ec.europa.eu.

[32] Article 10 (1) PCA. A double customs tariff on Estonian and Latvian was introduced by the Russian Federation in the early 1990s. See: L. Kappila, *Russia's Policy Towards Estonia and Latvia 1992–1997*, available at: http://ethesis.helsinki.fi/julkaisut/val/yhtei/pg/kauppila/thebalti.pdf.

[33] Allegedly, pesticide residues found in the composition of the productions endangering the health of Russian citizens justified this decision. However, no evidence of this claim has been provided, which contradicts the provisions of the WTO Agreement on the Application of Sanitary and Phytosanitary Measures. Given the close link

19 PCA, which states that import restrictions on the grounds of *inter alia* health protection should not constitute "a means of arbitrary discrimination or a disguised restriction of trade between the Parties". As a result, the extension of the PCA has decreased Russia's instruments to put direct political or economic pressure on the Baltic countries. On the other hand, however, the Russian ban on imports of Polish meat, introduced in November 2005 in response to irregularities with Polish veterinary certificates, reveals that unilateral trade sanctions towards individual EU Member States cannot be excluded. The Polish government repeatedly raised an infringement of Article 19 PCA at the EU level but it was only after vetoing the start of negotiations on a new EU-Russia framework agreement that the European Commission started to undertake real action.[34]

Against the background of the Polish meat dispute, the Russian Federation also introduced a ban on fish stocks transported through the Estonian border checkpoints, allegedly on the basis of problems with the certification of the marine products.[35] In combination with Russia's threat to block all EU food imports after the accession of Bulgaria and Romania, it is clear that the extension of the PCA could not prevent the emergence of serious trade disputes after enlargement. On the one hand, this illustrates the weaknesses of the PCA as a legal instrument determining the bilateral relations between the EC and Russia.[36] On the other hand, it demonstrates the results of the EU's passive response *vis-à-vis* Russia's economic concerns as formulated in

---

between the interpretation of the PCA and the WTO agreement, it can be argued that similar unilateral trade sanctions are no longer allowed in Russia's trade relations with the EU Member States, even before Russia's formal accession to the WTO. For commentaries on Russia's trade sanctions against Georgia, Moldova and Ukraine, see: CEPS Neighbourhood Watch, April 2006, pp. 13–14, available at: http://www.ceps.be/files/NW/NWatch15.pdf.

[34] See: Council of the EU, "Problems in exports of meat, meat products and plant products to the Russian Federation", Brussels, 16 November 2005, 14533/05 and "Ban imposed by the Russian Federation on imports of animal and plant products from Poland", 20 November 2006, 15453/06. See also: A. Rettman, "Poland threatening to veto new EU-Russia Pact", *EUObserver*, 10 November 2006.

[35] J. Alas, "Russia bans EU fish imports", *The Baltic Times*, 29 November 2006.

[36] One of the problems is, for instance, the absence of a more straightforward dispute settlement procedure. Article 101 PCA only provides for the settlement of disputes on the basis of "recommendations". Conciliators may be appointed but their recommendations are not binding upon the Parties. This is an important difference with the old Europe Agreements, which endowed the Association Council with a power to adopt binding decisions and provided for arbitration in the event no settlement of the dispute was possible through the Association Council. See: M. Maresceau, E. Montaguti,

the pre-accession period.[37] The Joint Statement on EU enlargement and EU-Russia relations, i.e. the political complement of the legal extension protocol, addressed those questions *in extremis* but can hardly be seen as an illustration of a proactive policy.

Apart from the minority issue, the Joint Statement mainly addresses economic issues. In this respect, it is noteworthy that Russia, as a non-WTO member, was not entitled to any compensation for loss of market access on the basis of Article XXIV (6) GATT 1994.[38] The Joint Statement, however, indirectly applies this WTO principle as the EU confirmed that "compensatory tariff adjustments accorded in the context of EU enlargement through modifications of the EU tariff schedule will be applied on an MFN basis to the advantage of Russian exporters". Both parties also acknowledged that, in general, "the level of tariffs for imports of goods of Russian origin to the new Member States will decrease from an average of 9 % to around 4 % due to the application by the enlarged EU of the Common Customs Tariff to imports from Russia".[39] In addition, the Joint Statement takes account of specific derogations included in the Treaty of Accession and, to a certain extent, even complements the results of the bilateral accession negotiations. A good example is the agreement to increase the quota for the imports of Russian steel, which responds to Estonia's declaration to the Treaty of Accession calling to take into account the foreseeable expansion of the Estonian steel industry when negotiating the necessary adjustments to the quantitative restrictions included in the EC's bilateral steel agreements. Accordingly, the Joint Statement on EU enlargement can be regarded as a vehicle to overcome the paradox between the exclusively bilateral nature of the accession negotiations and the undeniable consequences of this process for Russia.

The Joint Statement has to be understood as a priority list of future actions, highlighting the most important aspects of the EU-Russia

---

"The relations between the European Union and Central and Eastern Europe: a legal appraisal", 32 *Common Market Law Review* (1995), pp. 1342–1343.

[37] It is, for instance, significant that Russia already in 1999 submitted a list of mainly economic concerns about EU enlargement (cf. *supra* Part IV, Chapter 2, § 2).

[38] On the application of this Article in the context of EU enlargement, see: M. Cremona, "The Impact of Enlargement: External Policy and External Relations", in: M. Cremona, (ed.), *The Enlargement of the European Union*, Oxford, Oxford University Press, 2003, pp. 186–196.

[39] Joint Statement on EU Enlargement and EU-Russia Relations', Brussels, 27 April 2004, available at: http://europa.eu.int/comm/external_relations/russia/russia_docs/js_elarg_270404.htm.

Strategic Partnership after enlargement. The Protocol on the extension of the PCA, on the other hand, constitutes a formal bilateral agreement, which essentially provides that the ten new Member States become parties to the agreement.[40] Significantly, the Protocol provisionally entered into force on 1 May 2004 in anticipation of ratification by the parties, in accordance with their own procedures.[41] On the EU side, the Council has signed and ratified on behalf of the EC and on behalf of the Member States[42] whereas the European Commission ratified on behalf of the European Atomic Energy Community.[43] Taking into account the statement of Russia's Foreign Minister, Sergei Lavrov, that "further EU action on minorities is needed before the PCA extension deal can be ratified by the Russian Duma",[44] Russia's ratification of this Protocol in October 2004 can be considered as surprisingly quick. Obviously, the better atmosphere as a result of the deal on Russia's WTO accession (cf. *supra*) in combination with the legal importance

---

[40] Maresceau, "Bilateral Agreements", *op. cit.*, footnote 13, p. 436.

[41] Council Decision 2006/456/EC of 26 April 2004 on the signing and provisional application of a Protocol to the Partnership and Cooperation Agreement establishing a partnership between the European Communities and their Member States, of the one part, and the Russian Federation, of the other part, to take account of the accession of the Czech Republic, the Republic of Estonia, the Republic of Cyprus, the Republic of Latvia, the Republic of Lithuania, the Republic of Hungary, the Republic of Malta, the Republic of Poland, the Republic of Slovenia, and the Slovak Republic to the European Union, *OJ* (2006) L 185/16.

[42] This is an application of Art. 6 (2) of the 2003 Act of Accession, which explicitly provides that the Council is competent to conclude enlargement protocols to mixed agreements after negotiations by the Commission. Significantly, Art. 6 (2) also explicitly states that "this procedure is without prejudice to the Community's own competences and does not affect the allocation of powers between the Community and the Member States as regards the conclusion of such agreements in the future or any other amendments not related to accession". *OJ* (2003) L 236/34. A similar procedure has been included in the Act concerning the accession of Romania and Bulgaria, *OJ* (2005) L 157/204.

[43] The Commission's ratification is based on Art. 101 of the Euratom Treaty. See: Council and Commission Decision 2006/457/EC, Euratom of 21 February 2005 on the conclusion of the Protocol to the Partnership and Cooperation Agreement establishing a partnership between the European Communities and their Member States, of the one part, and the Russian Federation, of the other part, to take account of the accession of the Czech Republic, the Republic of Estonia, the Republic of Cyprus, the Republic of Latvia, the Republic of Lithuania, the Republic of Hungary, the Republic of Malta, the Republic of Poland, the Republic of Slovenia, and the Slovak Republic to the European Union, *OJ* (2006) L 185/21.

[44] A. Lobjakas, "EU-Russia: Landmark Enlargement Deal Signed, But Loose Ends Remain", http://www.rferl.org, 27 April 2004; *Agence Europe*, 28 April 2004, p. 7.

of the PCA for raising the Kaliningrad transit problem (cf. *infra*) might explain the swift ratification.

Apart from the legal implications of PCA extension, the final solution of this question has also an important political dimension. Most importantly, the Russian Federation now formally came to terms with the EU accession of the Baltic States and acknowledged that the latter countries no longer belong to its post-Soviet sphere of influence.[45] Accordingly, the subordination of Baltic-Russian relations within the wider EU-Russia Strategic Partnership creates a new political context for dealing with the historic sensitivities. It also enhances the importance of Russia as a strategic partner of the EU. The problems regarding the conclusion of the Protocol on PCA enlargement confirmed the deficiencies of the Common Strategy and illustrated the need for new mechanisms to deal with Russia.

Proceeding from the ambition to create a Common European Economic Space, launched in May 2001,[46] a Franco-German 'non-paper'—discussed with Russian officials in the context of the Iraq crisis—suggested an extension of this model to other areas.[47] The proposal *inter alia* included a path to visa free travel and increased Russian participation in ESDP affairs. The preliminary discussions paved the way for the introduction of the aim to create four Common Spaces, namely a Common Economic Space; a Common Space on Freedom, Security and Justice; a Common Space of External Security and a Common Space on Research and Education, including Cultural aspects at the May 2003 Saint-Petersburg EU-Russia Summit.[48] The Council and the Commission later confirmed the EU's intention to develop the Common Spaces concept as "an extensive basis" for strengthening the

---

[45] P. Ehin, A. Kasekamp, "Estonian-Russian Relations in the Context of EU Enlargement", in: O. Antonenko, K. Pinnick, (eds.), *Russia and the European Union*, London, Routledge, 2005, p. 212.

[46] Joint Statement Moscow EU-Russia Summit, 17 May 2001, at para. 14, available at: http://ec.europa.eu/comm/external_relations/russia/summit17_05_01/statement.htm.

[47] See: "Franco-German plan sees visa free travel for Russians", EUObserver.com, 16 March 2003; T. Gomart, "Le Partenariat entre l'Union Européenne et la Russie à l'épreuve de l'elargissement", *Revue du Marché commun et de l'Union européenne* (2004) 479, p. 351.

[48] "Eleventh EU-Russia Summit. Saint Petersburg", IP/03/768, Brussels, 28 May 2002. Available at: http://ec.europa.eu/comm/external_relations/russia/sum05_03/ip03_768.htm.

EU-Russia Strategic Partnership.[49] The subsequent adoption of road maps with some concrete action points for the implementation of the Common Spaces programme at the 2005 Moscow EU-Russia Summit signalled a new approach to EU-Russia relations.

1.3. *The Common Spaces: A New Framework for the Development of a 'Genuine Strategic Partnership' after Enlargement?*

In comparison to the Common Strategy, which was only common among the EU Member States, the development of the Common Spaces concept within the context of joint EU-Russia institutions better reflects the idea of 'equal partnership'. This is also the main reason why the Common Spaces programme forms an alternative to the European Neighbourhood Policy (ENP). Russia did not want to be involved in the latter programme, mainly because of the dominant role of the Commission in terms of drafting and monitoring of the ENP Action Plans.[50] Hence, the road maps have been carefully drafted in order to avoid any impression that the EU is imposing its norms on Russia. It is, for instance, remarkable that the Common Strategy stressed the unilateral approximation of Russian legislation to EU standards[51] whereas the Common Spaces road maps use more neutral terms such as "regulatory convergence" or "the elaboration of common approaches".[52] Moreover, the Common Strategy listed numerous areas for possible co-operation but lacked any real proposals for concrete action. The task of transforming the broadly defined objectives into operational action

---

[49] Commission Communication on relations with Russia, COM (2004) 106, 9 February 2004; Council Report on the implementation of the Common Strategy of the European Union on Russia, 10601/04, 16 June 2004.

[50] The Common Spaces alternative, however, does not imply that the ENP has become completely irrelevant for EU-Russia relations. The issues discussed within the Common Spaces framework are largely similar to those dealt with in the ENP context. For this reason, the European Neighbourhood and Partnership Instrument (ENPI), which will replace the old TACIS financial instrument from 2007 onwards, also covers Community assistance to Russia.

[51] In this respect, the CSR reflects Article 55 PCA, which states that "Russia shall endeavour to ensure that its legislation will be gradually made compatible with that of the Community".

[52] In practice, however, it seems unlikely that the EU will depart from the *acquis* as the basis for co-operation. Accordingly, also within the Common Spaces concept the burden of adaptation essentially falls on Russia. See: C. Hillion, "Russian Federation", in: S. Blockmans, A. Lazowski, (eds.), *The European Union and its Neighbours. A Legal Appraisal of the EU's Policies of Stabilisation, Partnership and Integration*, The Hague, Asser, 2006, p. 494.

points was attributed to each incoming Council Presidency. In practice, however, the six-months Presidency work plans became 'routine
exercises' without many practical effects.[53] The Common Spaces road
maps intend to address the perceived lack of substance and coherence
in EU-Russia relations on the basis of a long-term and issues-based
agenda with some concrete action points.

Another remarkable difference between the Common Strategy and
the four Common Spaces is related to the legal basis of the strategic
agenda. The Common Strategy formed a Treaty-based instrument of
the EU's external relations (Art. 13 EU) whereas the Common Spaces
emerged as a *sui generis* solution for the lack of progress in bilateral
relations. Accordingly, the possibility provided by Article 23 EU to
adopt CFSP instruments by qualified majority such as joint actions,
common positions and any other decisions on the basis of the Common Strategy does no longer apply. Similar to the Common Strategy,
however, the institutional and legal framework of the PCA is the
primary instrument for the implementation of the Common Spaces
road maps. The question is whether the PCA provides an appropriate
framework given the absence of a possibility to adopt legally binding
decisions and the observation that several provisions of the PCA have
become outdated.[54]

Finally, the Common Spaces road maps do not entail spectacular new
domains or ambitions for bilateral co-operation but mainly reorganize
existing objectives in a new, common framework. It is significant that
the relations between Russia and the Baltic States are not mentioned
as such. The objective to "demarcate borders between the EU Member
States and Russia [...] following signing and ratification of pending
border agreements", however, clearly relates to Russia's borders with
Estonia and Latvia whereas the multiple references to minority protection are undeniably connected to the Russian-speaking population in
both countries. Somewhat surprisingly, Kaliningrad is not mentioned in
the road maps but numerous provisions on transit and free movement
cannot be disconnected from this specific area. Moreover, a further

---

[53] Council of the European Union, "Common Strategies: Report by the Secretary-
General/High Representative", 14871/00, 21 December 2000, p. 4.
[54] On the relation between the PCA and the Common Spaces, see: P. Van Elsuwege,
"The Four Common Spaces: New Impetus to the EU-Russia Strategic Partnership?",
in: M. Maresceau, A., Dashwood, (eds.), *Law and Practice of EU External Relations. Salient
Features of a Changing Landscape*, Cambridge University Press, 2008, pp. 326–351.

expansion of the bilateral legal framework between Russia and the EC/EU is envisaged on the basis of the Common Spaces agenda (see Table 10). It is obvious that this has important consequences for the stabilisation of Baltic-Russian relations.

Table 10: Bilateral Agreements between the EC/EU and Russia as Provided in the Common Spaces Road Maps[55]

Agreement on investment related issues Agreement on veterinary certification * Agreement on fisheries Agreement on Galileo/GLONASS cooperation Agreement on customs co-operation Agreement on trade in nuclear materials	*Common Economic Space*
Agreement on readmission * Agreement on visa facilitation * Agreement on mutual legal assistance Agreement on co-operation between the European Police Office (EUROPOL) and the Russian Federation * Agreement between Eurojust and the Russian Federation Agreement on judicial co-operation in criminal matters Agreement on information protection	*Common Space of Freedom, Security and Justice*
Agreement on science and technology co-operation *	*Common Space on Research and Education, including Cultural Aspects*

* means that this agreement has already been concluded

It is significant that the new dynamic created after the adoption of the Common Spaces road maps does not only allow for a further extension of the bilateral legal relationship between the EU and Russia but also stimulates the further improvement of bilateral relations between the Baltic States and Russia. On 13 October 2006, for instance, the Latvian Minister of Economy, Aigars Stokenbergs, and his Russian counterpart, German Gref, signed an intergovernmental agreement on economic co-operation and agreed on the formation of

---

[55] Based upon the Common Spaces road maps, availble at: http://ec.europa.eu/comm/external_relations/russia/summit_05_05/finalroadmaps.pdf#ces.

an intergovernmental committee on co-operation in spheres of economy, science and technology and culture.[56] In December 2007, a new set of bilateral agreements, most notably on the Russian-Latvian State border (cf. *infra*), has been concluded.[57] The further development of close bilateral relations is also on the agenda of the Russian-Estonian and Russian-Lithuanian intergovernmental committees, which have been established in 1998 and 1996 respectively.[58]

Obviously, the new context of EU-Russia relations offers increased opportunities for pragmatic co-operation between the Baltic States and Russia. The road map for a Common Economic Space, for instance, *inter alia* refers to the intention of closer co-operation on infrastructure projects. A practical consequence of activities in this area could be the extension of the 'Rail Baltica' project to Saint Petersburg.[59] Of particular significance is also the Common Space on Research and Education, including Cultural Aspects. The Baltic States could play a constructive role on the road to Russia's integration within a 'European Higher Education Area'. Between 1993 and 2005, the Council of the Baltic Sea States (CBSS) Eurofaculty project supported the curriculum development and training of local academic staff in the main universities of Estonia, Latvia and Lithuania.[60] As a pilot project for similar work in the Russian Federation, a EuroFaculty has already been established at the Immanuel Kant State University of Russia in Kaliningrad. The law faculty of this university now offers specific courses on the law of the European Union. This is completely in line with the objective identified in the Common Spaces' road map on "investigating means of promoting studies and training in Russia in the field of EU law". Accordingly, the EuroFaculty experience might be used for other

---

[56] Ministry of Foreign Affairs of the Republic of Latvia, Press Release 13 October 2006, available at: http://www.am.gov.lv/en/news/press-releases/2006/october/13-3/.

[57] Ministry of Foreign Affairs of the Republic of Latvia, Press Release 18 December 2007, available at: http://www.mfa.gov.lv/en/news/press-releases/2007/december/18-1/.

[58] On the work of the intergovernmental committees, see the websites of the Estonian and Lithuanian Ministries of Foreign Affairs (www.vm.ee and www.urm.lt).

[59] The "Rail Baltica" project aims at the modernisation of the railway line between Finland, the three Baltic States and Poland. See: http://www.transport-report.com/Content/Rail/TEN-T/Baltics.htm. See also: Parliamentary question No. 69 by Justas Vincas Paleckis (H-1065/05) on the implementation of the Rail Baltica project.

[60] The final report of the CBSS programme in the Baltic States, operating from 1993 to 2005, is available at: http://www.cbss.st/documents/cbsspresidencies/14icelandic/finalef-balticreport1993-2005.pdf.

Russian universities as well. Reciprocally, enhanced co-operation with Russian universities could provide new opportunities for setting up joint educational projects in the Baltic Sea area. The Northern Dimension framework, potentially in the form of a ND Research and Education Partnership, could certainly be a facilitating factor in this respect.[61]

§ 2. *A Reorientation of the Northern Dimension*

The Common Spaces agenda does not only create a new context for the EU's unilateral and bilateral policy *vis-à-vis* the Russian Federation but also significantly affects the multilateral Northern Dimension (ND). This Finnish-inspired policy framework entered the EU's institutional framework in 1999 in an attempt to create "better co-operation" and "synergies" between existing co-operation programmes in the North of Europe.[62] It introduced some important innovations in comparison to the EU's classical foreign policy instruments. First, the ND is based on a *'partner-oriented approach'*, which encourages active participation of the non-EU Member States Russia, Norway, Iceland and, initially, the candidate countries Poland, Estonia, Latvia and Lithuania. The fact that these partner countries have become involved in the process from the very beginning and participated in the Foreign Ministers' conferences on the Northern Dimension is rather unusual in the EU context.[63] Second, the ND entails a *'multilevel approach'*, including co-operation between governments, EU institutions and regional bodies such as the Council of the Baltic Sea States (CBSS), the Barents Euro-Arctic Council (BEAC), the Nordic Council of Ministers (NCM) and the Arctic Council (AC). Clearly, a division of labour between, on the one hand, the EU (responsible for the development of general policy guidelines) and, on the other hand, the (sub-)regional organizations (responsible for policy implementation and bottom-up communication)

---

[61] P. Van Elsuwege, "The Common Spaces in EU-Russia Relations and the Future of the Northern Dimension", in: C. Archer, (ed.), *The Northern Dimension of the European Union: Glancing Back, Looking Forward. Proceedings from the Northern Dimension Network*, Kaunas, Kaunas University of Technology, 2007, p. 43.

[62] Communication from the Commission, "A Northern Dimension for the Policies of the Union", COM (1998) 589 final, 25 November 1998.

[63] L. Heininen, "Ideas and Outcomes: Finding a Concrete Form for the Northern Dimension Initiative", in: H. Ojanen, (ed.), *The Northern Dimension: Fuel for the EU?*, Helsinki, FIIA, 2001, p. 42.

can be identified.[64] In addition, the ND aims at horizontal co-ordination among various EU instruments and institutions. This implies, on the one hand, synchronisation of the EU's financial programmes and, on the other hand, enhanced co-operation between the European Commission's Directorates-General. Accordingly, the ND formed a first worthwhile attempt to overcome the severe distinction between the enlargement and external relations policy of the EU. Last but not least, the ND cuts across the Union's pillar structure: the instruments stem from the first, the objectives from the second and the problems from the third.[65]

The innovative aspects of the ND essentially aimed at facilitating the EU enlargement process through the active engagement of Russia in regional co-operation with the Nordic countries and the other Baltic Sea States. Russia's initial reaction to this initiative has been largely positive. Noteworthy in this respect was the so-called Nida-initiative, a Joint Statement between Russia and Lithuania concerning common proposals for regional co-operation to be included in the first Northern Dimension Action Plan.[66] This first example of co-operation between an applicant country and the Russian Federation on issues related to EU enlargement was very significant because it showed Russia's willingness to discuss the future of Kaliningrad within the EU framework. In spite of this promising start, the initial enthusiasm quickly faded away mainly because of a lack of concrete proposals for the realisation of the ambitious goals. In addition, the perception that the ND agenda only marginally reflected Russia's interests contributed to a growing frustration on the Russian side. In this respect, it is interesting to notice the parallels between the old Common Strategy and the first years of the Northern Dimension. Both policy instruments took off in 1999 and

---

[64] Nicola Catellani speaks about a three-level structure. At the highest level, the EU's Northern Dimension lays down the general framework for co-operation in Northern Europe, including priorities, target areas and policy instruments. Regional organizations such as the CBSS, BEAC and the Arctic Council operate as an interface between the EU level, where instruments are shaped, and the sub-regional level, where instruments are applied. See: N. Catellani, "The Emergence of Multilevel Institutional Structures at the Borders of the European Union", Paper for the Conference of Multilevel Governance, University of Sheffield, June 2001, available at: http://www.shef.ac.uk/~perc/mlgc/papers/catellani.pdf.

[65] H. Ojanen, "The EU and its Northern Dimension: An Actor in Search of a Policy or a Policy in Search of an Actor?", 5 *European Foreign Affairs Review* 3 (2000), p. 374.

[66] Nida Joint Statement, published in: 6 *Lithuanian Foreign Policy Review* 2 (2000), pp. 227–228 and http://www.lfpr.lt/uploads/File/2000–6/Nida.pdf.

have been subject to similar criticisms such as the gap between major political declarations but limited progress on concrete issues and, most importantly, the absence of a joint EU-Russia agenda.

Notwithstanding its self-declared 'partner-oriented' approach, Russia has been largely excluded from decision-making in the context of the Northern Dimension initiative.[67] This lack of ownership of the ND policy by Russia clearly formed one of the main reasons for Moscow's decreasing enthusiasm for the ND concept after 1999 and arguably also for the failure of the EU's unilateral Common Strategy (cf. *supra*). In addition, the implementation of the ND Action Plans faced a number of practical and institutional burdens.

A first challenge has been to link money from different sources: PHARE for the candidate countries, INTERREG for the EU Member States and TACIS for Russia. The co-ordination between these funding mechanisms and the different contractual relations with the partner countries interfered with the organizational structure of the EU. Whereas TACIS and PHARE have been administered by the Commission's Directorates-General for External Relations and Enlargement, the INTERREG initiative has been conceived in the framework of the structural funds within the responsibility of the DG for Regional Policy. This bureaucratic division of labour, with different units responsible for different parts of the relevant ND instruments, often obstructed the smooth implementation of specific cross-border programmes. Differences in terms of the programming period, stated objectives, administrative structures, budget lines and the absence of cross-funding opportunities all inhibited an efficient co-ordination of the different instruments and initiatives.[68]

Second, the system of rotating EU presidencies reflects a varying attention to the Northern Dimension, depending on the strategic priorities of the Member State holding the Presidency. Whereas the Northern

---

[67] The Helsinki European Council in December 1999 invited the Commission to prepare, in cooperation with the Council and in consultation with the partner countries, an Action Plan for the Northern Dimension. The Feira European Council in June 2000 adopted the first ND Action Plan for the period 2000–2003. A second ND Action plan has been adopted on the basis of the same procedure by the October 2003 Brussels European Council for the period 2004–2006. See: http://ec.europa.eu/comm/external_relations/north_dim/ndap/index.htm.

[68] N. Catellani, "The Multilevel Implementation of the Northern Dimension", in: H. Ojanen, (ed.), *The Northern Dimension: Fuel for the EU?*, Helsinki, FIIA, 2001, pp. 61–63.

Dimension was high on the agenda of the Finnish (1999), Swedish (2001) and Danish (2002) presidencies, the Northern Dimension was not even mentioned in the 2003 programme of the Greek and Italian presidencies.[69] There is, in other words, a problem of continuity with regard to the implementation of the ND policy.

Third, the envisaged 'partner-oriented' and 'multilevel' approach appeared to be watered-down in practice. Whereas the Council guidelines initially defined the regional bodies as implementing actors, the first Action Plan reduced their role to that of advisors or consultants.[70] The Commission's unclear legal mandate in regional organizations such as the CBSS and BEAC (cf. *supra*) might explain this perceived reluctance to delegate responsibilities to the (sub-)regional level. The rather limited impact of non-EU actors brought Cattelani to the conclusion that "there seems little difference between the way the ND is implemented and the rather distinct top-down approach permeating most of the EU's policies".[71] At least, it can be concluded that the ND missed the opportunity to deal with the consequences of enlargement in a pro-active way and rather developed into just another element of EU-Russia relations. The new political and legal context after 1 May 2004 has only reinforced this tendency. Due to the EU accession of Poland, Estonia, Latvia and Lithuania, only three external partners remain (Russia, Iceland and Norway). Taking into account the highly developed relationship between the EU and the EEA-members Iceland and Norway, the ND is more than ever oriented towards Russia.

At the fourth ND Ministerial Meeting of 21 November 2005, the Foreign Affairs Ministers of the EU Member States, Russia, Iceland and Norway, and the European Commissioner for External Relations and Neighbourhood Policy agreed to reshape the ND into the "political and operational framework for promoting the implementation of the EU-Russia Common Spaces at regional/sub-regional/local level".[72] For

---

[69] The European Parliament expressed its concern to the absence of references to the Northern Dimension in the programmes of the Greek and Italian presidencies and called on both presidencies "to give full support to the ND process". European Parliament resolution on the Northern Dimension—New Action Plan 2004–2006, *OJ* (2004) C 38E/312.

[70] H. Haukkala, "The Northern Dimension of EU Foreign Policy", in: O. Antonenko K. Pinnick (eds.), *Russia and the European Union*, London, Routledge, 2005, p. 39.

[71] N. Catellani, *Short and Long-Term Dynamics in the EU's Northern Dimension*, COPRI Working Papers, 2001, 41, p. 16.

[72] Guidelines for the Northern Dimension Policy from 2007, 14358/1/05, 18 November 2005.

this purpose, the partners agreed to draft a joint political declaration and a framework policy document, which has been adopted against the background of the November 2006 Helsinki EU-Russia summit.[73] The active involvement of Russia in the preparation of the new ND basic texts as well as the explicit recognition that the ND is based on an equal partnership between the EU, Russia, Norway and Iceland forms another illustration of the new approach to EU-Russia relations.

EU enlargement had another interesting side effect in terms of the ND co-ordination objectives: due to the termination of the Europe Agreements and the PHARE assistance programme in the Baltic Sea region, a simplification of the complex legal framework has taken place. Estonia, Latvia, Lithuania and Poland have now become eligible for INTERREG funding. Consequently, co-ordination efforts are limited to two financial instruments. From 2007 onwards, more effective co-ordination is possible through the establishment of a single European Neighbourhood and Partnership Instrument (ENPI).[74] This option reflects the call for "a single common fund within which INTERREG, PHARE, TACIS and their CBC components would operate", made in a 1999 European Parliament resolution on the Northern Dimension.[75] In addition to the EU's funding mechanisms, ND projects are co-financed by various sources such as the World Bank, the European Bank for Development and Reconstruction, the Nordic Investment Bank and from contributions of individual countries. The compilation of the various resources under the umbrella of operational ND partnerships has turned out to be a pragmatic solution to the identified political and institutional obstacles.[76] An extension of this model beyond the existing Northern Dimension Environmental Partnership (NDEP) and the Northern Dimension Partnership on Health and Social Well-Being (NDPHS) forms a priority for the future. In this respect, Finnish Foreign

---

[73] The new ND Policy Framework Document and the Political Declaration on the Northern Dimension Policy are available at: http://ec.europa.eu/comm/external_relations/north_dim/doc/frame_pol_1106.pdf.

[74] Regulation (EC) No. 1638/2006 of the European Parliament and the Council of 24 October 2006 laying down general provisions establishing a European Neighbourhood and Partnership Instrument, *OJ* (2006) L 310/1.

[75] European Parliament resolution on the Communication from the Commission—A Northern Dimension for the policies of the Union, *OJ* (1999) C 279/32.

[76] P. Van Elsuwege, "The Northern Dimension Partnerships: A Model for Co-operation with the EU's Neighbours?", in: S. Liekis, R. Trimakas, (eds.), *The European Union and its New Neighbourhood: Addressing Challenges and Opportunities*, Vilnius, Mykolas Romeris University, 2006, pp. 26–45.

Affairs Minister, Erkki Tuomioja, proposed a ND Transport and Logistics Partnership and enhanced cooperation in the field of education, research and cultural exchange.[77]

It seems no coincidence that the two proposed new priority areas for the future ND are to be situated within the Common Economic Space and the Common Space on Research and Education, including Cultural Aspects. Both Spaces perfectly fit within the ND's ambition to promote co-operation and positive interdependence on the basis of concrete projects where all parties have a common interest. The more politically sensitive Spaces on external and internal security are somewhat more difficult to reconcile with the soft security approach of the ND. Accordingly, it can be concluded that the ND offers a framework for pragmatic co-operation between Russia and the Baltic States. Whereas the potential of this platform has not been fully exploited in the pre-accession period, partly because of institutional complexities and divergent interests of the parties involved, the new context after enlargement and after the adoption of the Common Spaces' road maps opens a window of opportunity to raise the profile of the ND, particularly because Russia has indicated an interest in the further development of this concept.

Several factors can explain Russia's renewed enthusiasm for the ND.[78] First, the Common Spaces logic echoes the idea of equal partnership and joint ownership. The reorientation of the ND along these lines is, therefore, a further confirmation of the new approach to EU-Russia relations. Second, the ND forms an alternative to the EU's more unilateral and conditionality based ENP. The more explicit focus on values and norms in the latter contrasts with the rather pragmatic co-operation in the ND framework. Finally, the reorientation of the ND as the regional pillar of the EU-Russia Strategic Partnership denotes Russia's special status in comparison to the other neighbouring countries included in the broad ENP concept. The EU accession of the Baltic States only increased the importance of Russia as the EU's strategic

---

[77] E. Tuomioja, "The Northern Dimension after 2006", available at: http://www. tuomioja.org/index.php. The suggestion of a ND Partnership on Transport and Logistics has also been included in the political declaration on the Northern Dimension Policy, adopted against the background of the November 2006 EU-Russia Summit, see: http://ec.europa.eu/comm/external_relations/north_dim/doc/pol_dec_1106.pdf

[78] T. Romanova, "Northwest Russian Perspective on the Northern Dimension", available at: http://www.baltic.org/mp/db/file_library/x/IMG/12850/file/Romanova_final291105.pdf.

neighbour. In particular, the EU's dependency on Russia's energy supplies and Russia's role in the so-called 'shared neighbourhood' of former Soviet republics illustrate the significance of the EU-Russia Strategic Partnership. Hence, the question is to what extent the EU accession of the Baltic States affects the EU's position on Russia, taking into account the continued existence of numerous problems in the bilateral relations between Russia and the Baltic republics after enlargement. In this respect, the integration of Russian-speaking minorities in Estonia and Latvia, the question of border delimitation and the Kaliningrad transit issue deserve particular attention.

CHAPTER TWO

REMAINING CHALLENGES IN BALTIC-RUSSIAN RELATIONS

§ 1. *The Integration of Russian-speaking Minorities*

1.1. *The Impact of Enlargement: Myths and Reality*

In considering the protection of the rights and interests of the Russian-speaking population as its responsibility,[79] Russia has consistently pushed to have this issue put on the agenda of the European Union. In the beginning of 2003, Igor Ivanov, the Russian Minister of Foreign Affairs, issued a letter to the Greek EU Presidency and the European Commission demanding for additional pressure on Estonia and Latvia in order to enforce further steps towards improving the rights of the Russian-speaking minorities before these countries' EU accession on 1 May 2004.[80] The Commission spokesman replied that "there is ample evidence the Baltic States are ensuring better treatment for ethnic Russians as part of their preparations for EU membership".[81] Additionally, he argued that "the situation should further improve after enlargement when even higher minority protection standards will apply to those two new member countries".[82] This statement seems to disregard the absence of a comprehensive minority rights policy in the EU. Due to a lack of specific legislative competences in this area, the *acquis* is almost exclusively based on a non-discrimination approach rather than on the protection or promotion of special minority rights (cf. *supra*). Hence, there remains a conceptual discrepancy between the rather restrictive significance of minority protection in the EU's internal legal order

---

[79] The "medium-term strategy for the development of relations between the Russian Federation and the European Union (2000–2010)" identified this issue as one of Russia's primary interests in the framework of EU enlargement.

[80] D. Cronin, "Ethnic Russian status must improve", *European Voice*, 27 February 2003.

[81] *Ibid.*

[82] X., "EU dismisses Russian claims for further EU action on minority rights in the Baltics", *Uniting Europe* 217 (2003), p. 4.

and its wider interpretation as part of the Copenhagen pre-accession criteria.[83]

Apparently, the EU proceeded from the assumption that the process of EU accession *as such* would automatically solve the problems of integration of the Russian-speaking population. In this regard, Jekaterina Dorodnova argued that "with the entry of Estonia and Latvia into the EU, the discriminatory treatment of the Russian-speaking minorities by the Estonian and Latvian governments is likely to become less pronounced".[84] Dmitri Trenin was even more optimistic:

> Hundreds of thousand of ethnic Russians will be quickly integrated into the new interethnic communities of the Baltic countries. The Baltic Sea coasts will see new 'Euro-Russians'. Because of this, the non-titular population of the Baltic States react to the prospect of joining the European Union with greater enthusiasm than the indigenous population.[85]

The latter assumption did not become reality. Statistical research conducted ahead of the accession referenda revealed that the attitudes of Baltic Russians did not differ significantly from those of the titular population.[86] An analysis of the referendum results (cf. *supra* Part IV) even suggests that Russian-speakers tend to be more Euroskepic. It can, therefore, be concluded that the Russian-speaking minorities do not regard the EU as a guardian of their rights.

Despite the efforts to accelerate the naturalisation process in the framework of the pre-accession strategy, a significant part of the Estonian and Latvian population, 8.3 and 17.2 per cent respectively, remains without citizenship.[87] The United Nations Human Rights Committee concluded in its 2003 observations on Latvia and Estonia that

---

[83] See e.g. C. Hillion, "Enlargement of the European Union: The Discrepancy between Membership Obligations and Accession Conditions as regards the Protection of Minorities", 27 *Fordham International Law Journal* 2 (2003), pp. 715–740; G. Schwellnus, "Double Standards? Minority Protection as a Condition for Membership", in: H. Sjursen, (ed.), *Questioning Enlargement. Europe in Search of Identity*, London—New York, Routledge, 2006, pp. 186–200.

[84] J. Dorodnova, "EU Concerns in Estonia and Latvia: Implications of Enlargement for Russia's Behaviour Towards the Russian-speaking Minorities", *EUI Working Papers* (2000) 40, p. 37.

[85] D. Trenin, *Baltic Chance. The Baltic States, Russia and the West in the Emerging Greater Europe*, Washington, Carnegie Endowment for International Peace, 1997, p. 37.

[86] P. Ehin, "Determinants of public support for EU membership: Data from the Baltic countries", 40 *European Journal of Political Research* 5 (2001), p. 51.

[87] On the impact of the pre-accession strategy on the naturalisation process in Estonia and Latvia, see *supra* Part III, Chapter 4 § 3.1.

this situation has adverse consequences in terms of the enjoyment of the rights and freedoms included in the International Convent on Civil and Political Rights.[88] EU enlargement did not solve the problems of political participation and representation of the stateless population. Whereas Estonia had to extend the right of belonging to political parties to EU citizens and Latvia had to introduce voting rights for EU citizens at local and European Parliamentary elections as a result of EU citizenship legislation, those rights have not been granted to non-citizens (cf. *infra* Part VI).

The limited possibilities of political participation contribute to a further alienation from the state institutions. The result is a vicious circle of self-segregation and the establishment of a serious and long-term democratic deficit. This is, for instance, clearly illustrated in Riga, where approximately 35 per cent of the inhabitants are non-citizens. There is a widespread fear that the participation of these persons would lead to a profound political change in the Latvian capital.[89] In combination with the socio-economic consequences of statelessness,[90] it is obvious that EU enlargement only reinforced the feelings of disappointment and discrimination amongst this part of the population.

Apart from the citizenship question, language remains the main—and perhaps the most important—distinctive criterion among the population of Estonia and Latvia. Whereas the ECJ's case law on language requirements in respect of the EC's fundamental freedoms provides a framework for interpretation of the notion 'public interest' in Estonia's and Latvia's language legislation (cf. *supra* Part III), significant hurdles for the large Russian-speaking minorities remain in place. Both in Estonia and Latvia, a State Language Inspectorate monitors compliance with

---

[88] Concluding observations of the Human Rights Committee: Latvia, CCPR/CO/79/LVA, dated 6 November 2003 [Latvia]; Concluding observations of the Human Rights Committee: Estonia, CCPR/CO/77/EST, dated 15 April 2003 [hereafter: 2003 UN Human Rights Report Estonia].

[89] See: V. Kalnins, *Latvia: Regional and Municipal System*, at: http://www.balticdata.info/latvia/politics/latvia_politics_administration_basic_information.htm.

[90] On the socio-economic problems of Russian-speakers in general and non-citizens in particular, see: P. Van Elsuwege, "Russian-speaking minorities in Estonia and Latvia: Problems of Integration at the Threshold of the European Union", *ECMI Working Paper* 20 (2004), pp. 29–32. A recent report of the European Commission against Racism and Intolerance confirmed the inferior socio-economic position of the Russians-speaking and stateless community. See: Council of Europe, European Commission against Racism and Intolerance, Third Report on Estonia, adopted on 24 June 2005, CRI (2006) 1, pp. 27–28.

the language laws in the public and private sector. This *inter alia* implies that language inspectors carry out announced and unannounced visits to work places in order to find out whether persons in employment have the required language certificates and linguistic proficiency required by law to be employed in the position they hold. In *Podkolzina* v. *Latvia*, the European Court of Human Rights pointed at the procedural weaknesses of such language inspections in Latvia.[91] Recently, the Council of Europe's Commission against Racism and Intolerance reported complaints about the State language inspectors' 'over-zealous' way of imposing fines.[92] In Estonia, a 2006 report of Amnesty International criticized the undefined powers of the Language Inspectorate.[93] In a response to this criticism, the Estonian Parliament amended the Language Act in February 2007.[94] The new provisions grant the Language Inspectors the right to make a proposal to an employer to fire a person due to insufficient language proficiency or to send a person to re-examination. When this person fails to pass a re-examination, his or her language certificate may be claimed invalid. Even though the Language Inspectorate has in recent years adopted an increasingly lenient and pragmatic approach towards the implementation of the language laws, Russian-speakers fear losing their jobs if their language skills are found to be insufficient.[95] This problem is particularly pertinent in Ida-Virumaa, a region in northeast Estonia with a majority of Russian-speakers. In this area, persons belonging to the Russian-speaking community rarely have a chance to practice the Estonian language in their everyday lives. The Language Inspectorate, however, does not appear to take into account regional specificities when applying the language

---

[91] ECtHR, Judgment of 9 April 2002, *Podkolzina* v. *Latvia*, 46726/99, para. 36. The Court *inter alia* referred to the fact that in this case the assessment of the applicant's linguistic knowledge was left to a single civil servant and the examination procedure "lacked the fundamental guarantees of fairness".

[92] Council of Europe, European Commission against Racism and Intolerance, Third Report on Latvia, adopted on 29 June 2007, CRI (2008) 2, at para. 120.

[93] Amnesty International, "Linguistic Minorities in Estonia: Discrimination must Stop", December 2006, p. 12, at: http://web.amnesty.org/library/Index/ENGEUR510022006.

[94] The Law on Amendments to the Law on Language (adopted 8 February 2007; valid since 1 March 2007), *Riigi Teataja* I (2007) 17, 82.

[95] Information from Vadim Poleshtshuk, Legal Information Centre for Human Rights, Estonia.

law.[96] It seems obvious that a strict application of the new provisions raises questions as to the protection of linguistic minorities.[97]

In Latvia, the main problem concerns the use of the Russian language in relations with the official institutions. There is no legislation regulating oral communication with the state or municipal authorities whereas in written communication the use of foreign languages—i.e. any language but Latvian and the traditional Liv language—is explicitly prohibited unless there is an official translation into the Latvian language.[98] This regulation opposes Article 10 (2) of the Framework Convention on the Protection of National Minorities[99] and, therefore, explains why Latvia has issued a reservation to the application of this provision. A similar remark can be made as regards the right of minorities to display traditional names, street names and other topographical indications in the minority language under Article 11 (3) of the FCNM. Whereas Latvia has a legitimate right to formulate such reservations, it is nevertheless problematic to present this Convention as part of the EU Member States' common constitutional traditions in the framework of the EU's pre-accession policy to countries with substantial minority populations such as Turkey or (the former Yugoslav Republic of) Macedonia.[100]

In Estonia, the language legislation is more complex and ambiguous. Article 51 of the Estonian Constitution provides a right to receive responses from state agencies, local governments and their officials in the minority language in places where at least one-half of the permanent residents belong to a national minority whereas Article 52 states that in

---

[96] Council of Europe, European Commission against Racism and Intolerance, Third Report on Estonia, adopted on 24 June 2005, CRI (2006) 1, at para. 18. The text of the Employment Contracts Act is available at: http://www.legaltext.ee/en/andmebaas/ava.asp?m=022.

[97] It is noteworthy that with regard to the alleged problems with language inspections in Latvia, the OSCE High Commissioner on National Minorities has published a "Practical Guide for the State Language Inspectors on the Implementation of the Latvian State Language Law". A similar guide might be useful for Estonia as well.

[98] Art. 10 (2) of the Latvian Official Language Law, available at: http://www.ttc.lv. Only for submissions to police and medical institutions, rescue services and other institutions in case of urgent calls for medical aid, commission of crimes or other violations of law, or calls for emergency in cases of fire, accident or other emergences, the state language requirement does not apply.

[99] Art. 10 (2) of the FCNM provides that "[i]n areas inhabited by persons belonging to national minorities traditionally or in substantial numbers, if those persons so request and where such a request corresponds to a real need, the Parties shall endeavour to ensure, as far as possible, the conditions which would make it possible to use the minority language in relations between those persons and the administrative authorities".

[100] see *supra* Part III, Chapter 1, § 2.2.1.

the latter situation the minority language can even be used as an internal working language in local governments. Article 11 of the Language Act specifies that the application of the right included in Article 52 of the Constitution requires a proposal from the local government in question and an affirmative decision of the Estonian government. In practice, the government has not yet granted such permission, despite requests from the Sillamäe and Narva local government councils.[101] As regards the application of Article 51 of the Constitution, specified in Article 10 of the Language Act, the Advisory Committee of the FCNM has pointed out that the requirement that at least half of the permanent residents of a locality belong to a national minority is very high, in particular in the light of the legal uncertainty surrounding the term 'national minority' in Estonia.[102] The condition of citizenship as one of the factors for identifying the formal application of the respective provisions remains a point of discussion. This is also the case for the "National Minority Cultural Autonomy Act", which includes a similar condition.[103]

The condition of citizenship also affects the non-citizen's opportunities to apply for certain jobs in the public and the private sector. Whereas EU accession reduces the possibility of the Baltic States to reserve certain professions exclusively to their own nationals,[104] this has

---

[101] K. Albi, "The Right to Use Minority Languages in the Public Sphere. Evaluation of Estonian Legislation in Light of the International Standards", 8 *Juridica International* (2003), p. 157.

[102] Council of Europe, Advisory Committee on the Framework Convention for the Protection of National Minorities, ACFC/INF/OP/II(2005)001, Strasbourg, 22 July 2005, p. 23 at para. 97.

[103] The UN Committee on the Elimination of Racial Discrimination, therefore, recommends that the definition of a minority under the 1993 Law on Cultural Autonomy of National Minorities be amended to include non-citizens, in particular, stateless persons of long-term residence in Estonia. See: UN Report of the Committee on the Elimination of Racial Discrimination, New York, 2006, A/61/18, p. 57, at para. 271.

[104] In this respect, the ECJ's restrictive interpretation of the exceptions to the free movement of persons is of particular significance. The public service exception of Art. 39 (4) EC, for instance, presumes "the existence of a special relationship of allegiance to the State and reciprocity of rights and duties which form the foundation of the bond of nationality" (ECJ, Case 149/79, *Commission v. Belgium* [1980] ECR 3381, para. 10). Other posts cannot be reserved for a Member States' own nationals, not even for considerations relating to the preservation of national identity (ECJ, Case C-473/93, *Commission v. Luxembourg* [1996] ECR I-3207, para. 35). The exception of "exercise of public authority" (Art. 45 EC) only applies to activities which "taken on their own, constitute a direct and specific connection with the exercise of official authority" (ECJ, Case 2/74 *Reyners* [1975] ECR 631, para. 45–46). For comments on the restrictions to

not fundamentally changed the position of those countries' minority population without EU citizenship. A striking example is the fact that non-citizens cannot work as sworn advocates or advocate's assistants in Latvia.[105] On 27 May 2004, access to the profession of advocate has been extended to EU citizens who have obtained the qualification of an advocate in one of the EU Member States. Other foreign advocates may practice in Latvia on the basis of binding international agreements. Accordingly, Latvia fulfilled its obligations under EC law.[106] Latvia's 'non-citizens', however, continue to be barred from becoming sworn advocates.

Obviously, EU membership does not automatically solve the citizenship and language dilemmas in Estonia and Latvia and even tends to increase the gap between the population groups. On the other hand, it cannot be denied that the EU accession of both countries also has a number of positive side effects for the Russian-speaking minorities in general and the non-citizens in particular. First, minority protection has become one of the key elements of the EU-Russia Strategic Partnership, which implies that this question remains in the spotlight after the end of the Commission's pre-accession monitoring activities. Second, despite the absence of a well-designed internal EU policy in the field of minority protection—mainly due to a lack of normative competences—the EU is not totally irrelevant with regard to minority issues. Of particular importance are Council Directives 2000/43 EC of 29 June 2000 implementing the principle of equal treatment between persons irrespective of racial or ethnic origin and Directive 2003/109 EC of 25 November 2003 concerning the status of third-country nationals who are long-term residents.[107] Directive 2003/86/EC of 22 September 2003 on the right of family reunification[108] also applies to the Russian-speaking minorities without Estonian or Latvian

---

the EC free movement of persons, see: K. Lenaerts, P. Van Nuffel, *Constitutional Law of the European Union*, London, Sweet & Maxwell, 2005, pp. 191–198.

[105] See: Article 14 (1) and 83 of the Latvian "law on advocacy", at: http://www.ttc.lv/.

[106] Of particular importance are Council Directive 77/249/EEC of 22 March 1977 to facilitate the effective exercise by lawyers of freedom to provide services [*OJ* (1977) L 78/17] and Directive 98/5/EC of the European Parliament and of the Council of 16 February 1998 to facilitate practice of the profession of lawyer on a permanent basis in a Member State other than that in which the qualification was obtained [*OJ* (1998) L 77/36].

[107] On Directive 2003/109, see *infra* at § 1.3.1.

[108] *OJ* (2003) L 251/12.

citizenship. However, given the long-term residence of entire families in the countries concerned, the question of family reunification is not a specific problem in comparison to the situation of the newly established migrants in other EU Member States.

1.2. *Towards a More Effective Anti-discrimination Legislation?*

In its 2003 comprehensive monitoring reports on Estonia and Latvia, the European Commission observed that in the field of anti-discrimination legislation "important shortcomings subsist with regard to the full transposition of the *acquis*".[109] Notwithstanding the fact that the Estonian and Latvian Constitutions as well as a number of specific laws contain provisions prohibiting discrimination on the basis of race or nationality,[110] legal experts came to the conclusion that this is insufficient to comply with the so-called Race Equality Directive.[111] This Directive, adopted on the basis of Article 13 EC,[112] has a far-reaching scope of application, covering not only direct and indirect discrimination but also "harassment".[113] The prohibition of discrimination applies to a

---

[109] European Commission, Comprehensive Report on Latvia's Preparations for Membership, p. 35. A similar observation can be found in the Comprehensive Report on Estonia's Preparations for Membership, p. 35.

[110] Article 12 of the Estonian Constitution establishes an explicit ban of discrimination: "Everyone is equal before the law. No one shall be discriminated against on the basis of nationality, race, colour, sex, language, origin, religion, political or other opinion, property or social status, or on other grounds. The incitement of national, racial, religious or political hatred, violence or discrimination shall, by law, be prohibited and punishable. The incitement of hatred, violence or discrimination between social strata shall, by law, also be prohibited and punishable". Article 91 of the Latvian Constitution states that "All human beings in Latvia shall be equal before the law and the courts. Human rights shall be realised without discrimination of any kind".

[111] Council Directive 2000/43/EC of 29 June 2000 implementing the principle of equal treatment between persons irrespective of racial or ethnic origin, *OJ* (2000) L 180/22.
For a legal analysis of the implementation of this Directive in Estonia and Latvia, see: V. Poleshchuk, *Report on Measures to Combat Discrimination. Country Report Estonia*, February 2005; G. Feldhune, *Report on Measures to Combat Discrimination. Country Report Latvia*, December 2004, both reports are available at http://www.migpolgroup.com.

[112] This provision has been introduced by the Treaty of Amsterdam and grants to the Community the power "to take appropriate action to combat discrimination based on sex, *racial or ethnic origin*, religion or belief, disability, age or sexual orientation" [emphasis added]. Notwithstanding the limits of this Article, such as the requirement of unanimity in the Council and the absence of direct effect or specific references to national minorities, it offers a basis for adopting measures which help to protect the rights of minorities.

[113] According to Article 2 (3) harassment shall be deemed to be discrimination when "an unwanted conduct related to racial or ethnic origin takes place with purpose or

wide range of areas, including employment, vocational training, social protection, education and access to goods and services.[114] A specific Directive has been adopted for equal treatment in employment and occupation.[115] Significantly, both Directives also apply to third-country nationals. However, they do not cover difference of treatment based on nationality and are without prejudice to provisions and conditions relating to the entry into and residence of third-country nationals or stateless persons on the territory of Member States. In addition, the Directives do not apply to "any treatment which arises from the legal status of the third-country nationals and stateless persons".[116] In other words, the differences between citizens and non-citizens are not perceived as discrimination on the basis of race and ethnic origin. For the specific case of the Russian-speaking minorities it is also noteworthy that 'language' is not included as one of the grounds for discrimination.[117] This observation, however, does not imply that language is totally excluded from the application of the Directives. It could, for instance, be argued that unreasonable or disproportionate language proficiency requirements can constitute an indirect discrimination on the grounds of ethnic origin as prohibited under Directive 2000/43.[118]

Notwithstanding the limitations of the EC anti-discrimination directives, they lay down minimum requirements aiming at combating discrimination against persons belonging to minorities. Member States are under an obligation to ensure effective protection of individual rights.[119] Victims of discrimination must have the right of redress through an administrative or judicial procedure. Once a plaintiff has established facts on the basis of which it can be presumed that there has been

---

effect of violating the dignity of a person and of creating an intimidating, hostile, degrading, humiliating or offensive environment".

[114] Art. 3 (1) of Directive 2000/43.

[115] Council Directive 2000/78/EC of 27 November 2000 establishing a general framework for equal treatment in employment and occupation, *OJ* (2000) L 303/16. This Directive tackles discrimination on the grounds of religion or belief, disability, age or sexual orientation (Art. 1).

[116] Art. 3 (2) of Directive 2000/43 and Directive 2000/78.

[117] The obvious explanation is the scope of Article 13 EC, which is limited to discrimination based on sex, racial or ethnic origin, religion or belief, disability, age or sexual orientation.

[118] The EU Network of Independent Experts on Fundamental Rights, *The Protection of Minorities in the European Union*, Thematic comment No. 3, 25 April 2005, available at: http://ec.europa.eu/justice_home/cfr_cdf/doc/thematic_comments_2005_en.pdf, p. 19.

[119] Art. 7 of Directive 2000/43 and Art. 9 of Directive 2000/78.

discrimination, the burden of proof shifts to the respondent.[120] Plain-
tiffs are to be protected against victimisation and in particular against
dismissal.[121] Finally, Member States have the obligation to disseminate
information on the anti-discrimination legislation in co-operation with
non-governmental organizations,[122] they have to establish a specialised
body for the promotion of equal treatment[123] and should provide for
"effective, proportionate and dissuasive sanctions" in case of breaches
of the anti-discrimination legislation.[124]

In the framework of the EU pre-accession process, the Baltic States
have introduced new legislation in accordance with the EC non-
discrimination directives. The Lithuanian Parliament, for instance,
adopted a general "law on equal treatment" on 18 November 2003.[125]
In Latvia, the labour law includes a general non-discrimination clause
prohibiting differential treatment based on "race, skin colour, age, disability, religious, political or other conviction, national or social origin,
property or marital status or other circumstances of an employee".[126]
In Estonia, the criminal code has been amended to prohibit incitement
to hatred and discrimination and provisions against discrimination in
the employment sector have been introduced in the Law on Employment Contracts.[127] A general law on equality and equal treatment was
drafted in October 2002 but has been withdrawn at the beginning of
2003, officially because this law would overlap with the constitutional
provisions concerning anti-discrimination and equality. The European
Commission against Racism and Intolerance of the Council of Europe,
however, considered this decision to be "a set-back in the fight against

---

[120] Art. 8 of Directive 2000/43 and Art. 10 of Directive 2000/78.
[121] Art. 9 of Directive 2000/43 and Art. 11 of Directive 2000/78.
[122] Art. 10–12 of Directive 2000/43 and Art. 12–14 of Directive 2000/78.
[123] Art. 13 of Directive 2000/43.
[124] Art. 15 of Directive 2000/43 and Art. 17 of Directive 2000/78.
[125] Republic of Lithuania "law on equal treatment", Vilnius, 18 November 2003,
IX-1826, official translation available at: http://www3.lrs.lt/pls/inter3/dokpaieska
.showdoc_e?p_id=245120.
[126] Art. 7 and 29 of the Labour Law, adopted 20 June 2001 and entered into force
on 1 July 2002. The text of this law is available at http://www.ttc.lv. On 21 June 2006
President Vike-Freiberga returned a controversial Labour Law amendment, which
would have deleted sexual orientation from its anti-discrimination provisions, back to
the *Saeima* because it clearly violated EC Directive 2000/78.
[127] Council of Europe, European Commission against Racism and Intolerance,
Third Report on Estonia, adopted on 24 June 2005, CRI (2006) 1, at para. 41. The
text of the Employment Contracts Act is available at: http://www.legaltext.ee/en/
andmebaas/ava.asp?m=022.

discrimination in Estonia" and recommended the Estonian authorities to adopt a comprehensive anti-discrimination law ensuring equality in areas such as housing, access to public services, education and health care, etc.[128] The European Commission of the EU also informed the Estonian authorities about deficiencies in the implementation of the EC anti-discrimination directives and threatened to start a procedure before the ECJ on the basis of Article 226 EC. This pressure seemed to produce effect as the Estonian Ministry of Justice presented a new draft law on equal treatment in November 2006. The draft law, which passed a first reading in the *Riigikogu* on 14 February 2007, addresses several 'grey areas' of Estonia's anti-discrimination legislation and provides for more detailed non-discrimination provisions *inter alia* in the areas of education, social protection or access to publicly available goods or services.[129]

In addition to the drafting of new legislation, governmental bodies have been designed with tasks in the field of anti-discrimination. The Legal Chancellor of Estonia—an independent official, provided by the Constitution,[130] who is responsible for ensuring that legal acts adopted by the parliament and the local councils are in conformity with the Constitution and the state laws—has been empowered to fulfil certain functions of an ombudsman, including the capacity to receive and examine residents' complaints.[131] A similar function has been given to the Latvian National Human Rights Office (LNHRO). Both institutions do not have the power to enforce their recommendations or to levy any fines but can submit a constitutional complaint to the Constitutional Court.

---

[128] *Ibid.*, at para. 39–42.

[129] Equal Treatment Bill no. 1101 SE, at: http://www.riigikogu.ee.

[130] Chapter XII of the Constitution. The Legal Chancellor is a government official responsible for supervising the lawfulness of government actions. This institution is common in Nordic countries. For comments on the role of the Legal Chancellor in Estonia, see: R. Maruste, "Democracy and the Rule of Law in Estonia: Progress Achieved and the Problems Remaining", 26 *Review of Central and East European Law* (2000) 3, pp. 321–324.

[131] His duties concerning the promotion and application of the principle of equal treatment are clearly written down in Article 35 of the Legal Chancellor Act, which entered into force from 1 January 2004 onwards. It is noteworthy that Estonia's 2006 draft law on equal treatment (cf. *supra*) foresees the creation of a new specialised equality body—an "*equal treatment and equality commissioner*"—who will advise and provide independent assistance to people pursuing their complaints about non-discrimination. The mandate of the Legal Chancellor will remained unchanged.

Whereas the bones of a comprehensive anti-discrimination legislation exist in both Estonia and Latvia, only a limited number of cases have been brought to justice. A 2005 sociological study in Tallinn revealed that up to 40 per cent of non-Estonians experienced feelings of discrimination but in the same year the Legal Chancellor reported only one complaint regarding discrimination on the basis of ethnicity.[132] In Latvia, it was only in May 2006 that a Court for the first time since Latvia's independence in 1991 recognized ethnic discrimination in hiring an employee.[133] This observation indicates that further action to disseminate information and public awareness on anti-discrimination legislation is necessary. In this respect, training of judges, prosecutors and lawyers on the implementation of the non-discrimination provisions has been recommended.[134]

Finally, the classical problem of strengthened administrative capacity can be mentioned as one of the problems regarding the effective enforcement of non-discrimination provisions. The LNHRO, for instance, has been coping with problems of funding and excessive workload.[135] It can therefore be concluded that, notwithstanding the direct impact of Directive 2000/43 on the establishment of institutional structures and legal provisions dealing with the prohibition of discrimination, the main challenge is to improve the effective implementation of this legal framework. In this respect, it is noteworthy that the European Parliament Committee on Civil Liberties, Justice and Home Affairs requested the Commission to examine "the quality and content of laws implement-

---

[132] V. Poleshchuk, A. Semjonov, "Interethnic Relations and Unequal Treatment", in: A. Hallik, V. Poleshchuk, A. Saar, *et al.*, *Estonia: Interethnic Relations and the Issue of Discrimination in Tallinn*, Tallinn, LICHR, 2006, p. 38.

[133] The case concerned a woman of Roma origin, Sanita Kozlovsko, who applied for a job in a Jelgava clothing shop. Before even questioned about her qualifications, she was denied the position because of "her accent when speaking Latvian". The employer also made negative comments on her appearance and obviously held negative stereotypes against Roma. On 25 May 2006, the Jelgava City Court ruled that the owner of the clothing shop must pay 1,000 LVL (€ 1,422) in compensation to the plaintiff. For comments, see: E. Celms, "Roma woman breaks legal barrier for minorities", *Baltic Times*, 31 May 2006.

[134] European Commission against Racism and Intolerance, Third Report on Estonia adopted on 24 June 2005, CRI (2006) 1, Strasbourg, 21 February 2006, para. 44–45; Concluding Observations of the Committee on the Elimination of Racial Discrimination on Estonia, CERD/C/EST/CO/7, 15 August 2006, at para. 19.

[135] Feldhune, *op. cit.*, footnote 111, p. 38; See also: Expert Review Mission on Latvian Human Rights Office and Ombudsman Functions in Latvia: Considerations and Recommendations, Final Report, 22 May 2001, at: http://www.un.lv/down/undp_publ/omb/omb_e.pdf.

ing the anti-discrimination directives [...] and to bring, as a matter of urgency, an action before the Court of Justice against those Member States that have not correctly transposed them".[136] Significantly, the final resolution underlines that "the new Member States which have not transposed the anti-discrimination directives must be subject to infringement procedures for violating EC law in the same way as the old Member States".[137] It seems that Estonia and Latvia were amongst the target countries of this specific provision. With regard to Estonia, it is significant that the UN Committee on the Elimination of Racial Discrimination explicitly referred to the deficient transposition of Directive 2000/43/EC when it expressed its concern about the absence of a comprehensive anti-discrimination legislation in civil and administrative affairs in August 2006.[138]

Whereas the anti-discrimination directives are important landmarks for the protection of ethnic minorities within the EU, their narrow scope of application implies that they are insufficient to ensure a comprehensive protection of the large Russian-speaking and stateless population in Estonia and Latvia. In this specific context, legal safeguards against discrimination on the basis of language or nationality—grounds of discrimination not included in the respective directives—are highly relevant. It is noteworthy that Article 10 of the Estonian Employment Contracts Act includes discrimination on the basis of the level of language proficiency unless this is "an essential and determinative professional requirement arising from the nature of the professional activity or related conditions".[139] It is important that the latter provision, which in itself pursues a legitimate aim, is not interpreted too broadly. The lack of clear provisions on language discrimination in the EC directives

---

[136] European Parliament, Committee on Civil Liberties, Justice and Home Affairs, Report on non-discrimination and equal opportunities for all (rapporteur: Tatjana Zdanoka), A6–189/2006, 18 May 2006. The impact of rapporteur Zdanoka, a representative of Latvia's Russian-speaking minority in the EP, is visible in the report. The explicit references to the term "non-citizens" and, in particular, the proposal to grant migrants of Roma origin and non-citizens an active and passive voting right "at all levels" raised heavy debates in the European Parliament [See: Debates of 13 June 2006, P6_CRE (2006) 06–13]. It is noteworthy that no references to "non-citizens" or "voting rights" are retained in the final resolution.

[137] European Parliament Resolution on non-discrimination and equal opportunities for all, 14 June 2006, P6_TA-PROV (2006) 0261, at para. 26.

[138] Concluding Observations of the Committee on the Elimination of Racial Discrimination on Estonia, CERD/C/EST/CO/7, 15 August 2006, at para. 11.

[139] The English language version of the Estonian Employment Contracts Act is available at: http://www.legaltext.ee.

limits the role of the ECJ to a check of potential indirect discrimination on the basis of ethnic origin. A similar remark can be made with regard to citizenship conditions determining access to employment or in the areas included in Directive 2000/43.[140] Of course, the granting of citizenship belongs to the exclusive competence of the Member States and differences in treatment between citizens and non-citizens are inherent to the national state system.[141] A situation where up to almost 10 or 20 per cent of the population does not have the citizenship of the state of residence requires, however, adequate legal instruments to define the rights and obligations of the non-citizen population. The often-amended Estonian "Law on Aliens" and the Latvian "Law on the Status of Former USSR citizens who are not citizens of Latvia or any other State" address this question (cf. *supra* Part I). At the EU level, the adoption of Council Directive 2003/109 concerning the status of third-country nationals who are long-term residents forms an additional point of reference.

1.3. *The Legal Status of Estonia's and Latvia's Non-Citizens in the EU*

1.3.1. *The Opportunities and Limits of Directive 2003/109*
The EU accession of Estonia and Latvia has introduced a new differentiation between Estonian and Latvian citizens, on the one hand, and the non-citizen population on the other. Whereas the former can rely on the rights connected to their status of EU citizens and the extensive case law of the European Court of Justice in this respect, non-citizens are treated as third country nationals under EU law. This difference in legal status has important consequences in terms of free movement rights. According to the ECJ's established case law, third country nationals—including stateless persons—cannot autonomously rely on the EC Treaty provisions concerning free movement of persons.[142] All rights they have in this area depend on a family relationship with a migrant

---

[140] The EU Network of Independent Experts on Fundamental Rights, *The Protection of Minorities in the European Union*, Thematic comment No. 3, 25 April 2005, available at: http://ec.europa.eu/justice_home/cfr_cdf/doc/thematic_comments_2005_en.pdf, pp. 21–22.

[141] Under international law, citizenship is generally accepted as a basis for providing distinctions in civil rights. See e.g. Art. 1 (2) of the International Covenant on the Elimination of All Forms of Racial Discrimination.

[142] ECJ, case 238/83, *Meade*, judgment of 5 July 1984, [1984] ECR 2631, para. 7.

national of an EU Member State[143] or an employment contract with
an in an EU Member State established enterprise providing services in
another Member State.[144] On the other hand, third-country nationals
and stateless persons are explicitly included in the personal scope of
most EC legislation on social security rights.[145] The ECJ confirmed
the lawfulness of this situation on the basis of the international obligations of the Member States and the objectives of the social security
regulations.[146]

The Treaty of Amsterdam, which entered into force 1 May 1999,
introduced important provisions for the development of the legal status
of third-country nationals. On the basis of Article 63 (4) EC the Council
is entitled to adopt "measures defining the rights and conditions under
which nationals of third countries who are legally resident in a Member
State may reside in other Member States". The October 1999 Tampere
European Council, which was completely devoted to the new provisions
of the Amsterdam Treaty, laid down important guidelines for developing the legal status of third-country nationals.[147] It maintained that the
EU "must ensure fair treatment of third country nationals who reside
legally on the territory of its Member States" and "should aim at granting them rights and obligations comparable to those of EU citizens".
The European Council clearly acknowledged that "the legal status of
third country nationals should be approximated to that of Member
States' nationals."[148] The Heads of State or Government decided to
pay special attention to the situation of third-country nationals settled
on a long-term basis:

---

[143] Directive 2004/38/EC of the European Parliament and of the Council of 29
April 2004 on the right of citizens of the Union and their family members to move
and reside freely within the territory of the Member States amending Regulation (EEC)
No. 1612/68 and repealing Directives 64/221/EEC, 68/360/EEC, 72/194/EEC,
75/34/EEC, 75/35/EEC, 90/364 EEC, 90/965/EEC and 93/96/EEC, *OJ* (2004)
L 158/77.

[144] ECJ, case C-113/89, *Rush Portuguesa*, judgment of 27 March 1990, [1990] ECR
I-1417, para. 12; ECJ, case C-43/93, *Vander Elst*, judgment of 9 August 1994, [1994]
ECR I-3803, para. 21.

[145] Regulation (EC) No. 883/2004 of the European Parliament and of the Council
of 29 April 2004 on the coordination of social security systems replacing Council
Regulation (EEC) No. 1408/71, *OJ* (2004) L 166/1.

[146] ECJ, cases C-95/99 to C98/99 and C-180/99, *Khalil and others*, judgment of
11 October 2001, [2001] ECR I-7413, para. 49 and 55.

[147] Presidency Conclusions of the Tampere European Council (15–16 October
1999), *Bull. EU* 10, 1999, I-2.

[148] *Ibid.*, I-6.20.

> A person who has resided legally in a Member State for a period of time to be determined and who holds a long-term residence permit, should be granted in that Member State a set of uniform rights which are as near as possible to those enjoyed by EU citizens.

Finally and significantly, the European Council endorsed "the objective that long-term legally resident third-country nationals be offered the opportunity to obtain the nationality of the Member State in which they are resident."[149] Although not exclusively devised for their specific case, these conclusions of the Tampere European Council, drafted at a time when accession negotiations had already begun with Estonia but not with Latvia, are of particular significance for the legal status of these countries' stateless population.

The Tampere conclusions led to an important European Commission proposal for a Council Directive concerning the status of third-country nationals who are long-term residents.[150] This document explicitly declares that the concept of third-country nationals also applies to stateless persons.[151] The scope of the Directive is defined in broad terms, applying to "all third-country nationals residing legally in a Member State, irrespective of the grounds on which they were originally admitted". Significantly, it also covers "third-country nationals born in the territory of a Member State and residing there without having acquired its nationality."[152] The combination of these elements implies that this Directive, formally adopted by the Council on 25 November 2003[153] is an essential element for defining the legal status of the large stateless communities in Estonia and Latvia. The EU Member States, with the exception of the United Kingdom, Ireland and Denmark,[154]

---

[149] *Ibid.*, I-6.21.

[150] European Commission, Proposal for a Council Directive concerning the status of third-country nationals who are long-term residents, COM (2001), 127 final, 13 March 2001.

[151] *Ibid.*, p. 11.

[152] *Ibid.*, p. 12.

[153] Council Directive 2003/109/EC of 25 November 2003 concerning the status of third-country nationals who are long-term residents, *OJ* (2004), L 16/44.

[154] In accordance with Articles 1 and 2 of the Protocol on the position of the United Kingdom and Ireland and Articles 1 and 2 of the Protocol on the position of Denmark, annexed to the Treaty on European Union and the Treaty establishing the European Community, these countries do not take part in the adoption of measures pursuant to Title IV of the Treaty establishing the European Community and are not bound by or subject to its application.

had to adopt the necessary implementation measures by 23 January 2006 at the latest.[155]

In order to guarantee fair treatment of third country nationals— including stateless persons—and promote their full integration, Directive 2003/109 lays down criteria for the acquisition of a long-term resident status, certified by an EC long-term residence permit,[156] and determines its connected rights. In comparison to the ambitions of the Tampere European Council and the Commission proposal, the European Parliament and the Council have seriously watered down the scope of the rights connected to the EC long-term resident status.[157] An analysis of the long-term resident Directive in the light of Directive 2004/38/EC on the right of citizens of the Union and their family members to move and reside freely within the territory of the Member States reveals significant disparities. With regard to the right of equal treatment, for instance, Article 24 of Directive 2004/38 provides that Union citizens residing in the territory of another Member State "enjoy equal treatment with the nationals of that Member State *within the scope of the Treaty*".[158] Article 11 of Directive 2003/109, on the other hand, restricts the equal treatment to a prescribed number of areas. There is, in other words, no general rule of equality for third-country nationals.[159] Moreover, in contravention to equal treatment as regards access to employment and self-employed activities, Member States may retain restrictions "in cases where, in accordance with existing national

---

[155] Council Directive 2003/109, Art. 26.

[156] Article 2 (g) defines the EC long-term residence permit as "a residence permit issued by the Member State concerned upon the acquisition of long-term resident status". Article 8 lays down the technical modalities of the long-term resident's EC residence permit.

[157] For a more detailed overview concerning the adoption of Directive 2003/109 and the role of the different institutional actors in this process, see: P. Van Elsuwege, "Russian-speaking minorities in Estonia and Latvia: Problems of Integration at the Threshold of the European Union", *ECMI Working Paper* 20 (2004), pp. 41–49 and S. Boelaert-Suominen, "Non-EU Nationals and Council Directive 2003/109/EC on the Status of Third-Country Nationals who are long-term residents: five paces forward and possibly three paces back", 42 *Common Market Law Review* 4 (2005), pp. 1011–1052.

[158] Directive 2004/38/EC of the European Parliament and the Council of 29 April 2004 on the right of citizens of the Union and their family members to move and reside freely within the territory of the Member States amending Regulation (EEC) No. 1612/68 and repealing Directives 64/221/EEC, 68/360/EEC, 72/194/EEC, 75/34/EEC, 75/35/EEC, 90/364/EEC, 90/365/EEC and 93/96/EEC, *OJ* (2004) L 158/77. [emphasis added].

[159] J. Handoll, "The Long-Term Residents Directive", 4 *European Yearbook of Minority Issues* (2004/5), p. 403.

or Community legislation, these activities are reserved to nationals, EU or EEA citizens" (Art. 11 (3)). Given the large number of such reservations in the Latvian and Estonian legislation,[160] this sentence clearly limits the potential benefits of the EC long-term resident status for the stateless population of those countries. A similar remark can be made in connection to the fact that "Member States may require proof of appropriate language proficiency for access to education and training" and the possible limitation of social assistance and social protection to core benefits.[161]

Apart from the qualified right of equal treatment in a wide area of economic and social matters, Directive 2003/109 provides for a right of residence in other Member States. This right refers to any stay in another Member State for a period exceeding three months.[162] It is noteworthy that also the family members of moving long-term residents have the right of residence in another Member State, even if they do not have a long-term resident permit themselves (Art. 16). The interpretation of the family members' rights are, however, based upon the conditions included in the family reunification Directive rather than on the more generous provisions of Directive 2004/38.[163] Article 14 of Directive 2003/109 distinguishes three possible cases in which long-

---

[160] In Latvia, this list includes not less than 38 professions mainly in the public sphere but also including jobs in the private sector such as advocates, heads of detective agencies or internal auditors. For the entire list, see: M. Mitrofanovs, A. Gamajejevs, V. Jolkins, *et al.*, "The Stateless People of Latvia. The Last Prisoners of the Cold War", Riga, 2006, pp. 79–80; also available at: http://www.pctvl.lv/i/doc/last_prisoners.pdf. For comments on Estonia's and Latvia's language and citizenship legislation, see *supra* Part III, Chapter 4, § 3.

[161] Council Directive 2003/109, Art. 11 (3) b and Art. 11 (4). With regard to the situation in Estonia, see: http://www.lichr.ee/eng/researchers.analysis/diff.htm.

[162] Of particular importance for Estonia's and Latvia's non-citizens is Article 21 of the Schengen Convention, which states that aliens holding a valid residence permit and valid travel documents can move freely within the Schengen area for *up to three months* (Convention implementing the Schengen agreement of 14 June 1985, *OJ* (2000) L 239/19). It is noteworthy that, pursuant to Article 3 (2) of the Act of Accession, this provision only applied after Estonia's and Latvia's full entry to the Schengen area. On the paradoxical effects of the EC visa legislation for Estonia's and Latvia's stateless population, see *infra* at 1.3.2.

[163] Council Directive 2003/86/EC of 22 September 2003 on the right to family reunification, *OJ* (2003) L 251/12. For comments, see: K. Groenendijk, "Family Reunification as a Right under Community Law", 8 *European Journal of Migration and Law* 2 (2006), pp. 215–230; H. Schneider, A. Wiesbrock, "The Council Directive on Family Reunification: Establishing Proper Rights for Third Country Nationals?", in: H. Schneider, (ed.), *Migration, Integration and Citizenship. A Challenge for Europe's Future. (Vol. II)*, Maastricht, Forum Maastricht, 2005, pp. 35–69.

term residents may exercise the right of residence: (i) as workers in an employed or self-employed capacity, (ii) as persons pursuing studies or vocational training or (iii) without exercising an economic activity but in possession of adequate resources to reside in the second Member State. Importantly, the Council introduced the possibility of additional restrictions to the right of residence in another Member State. According to Article 15 (3) "Member States may require third-country nationals to comply with integration measures, in accordance with national law" and "the persons concerned may be required to attend language courses".[164] Another important derogation from the principle of free residence is contained in Article 14 (4). According to this provision "Member States may limit the total number of persons entitled to be granted right of residence, provided that such limitations are already set out for the admission of third-country nationals in the existing legislation at the time of the adoption of this Directive". Finally, restrictions to the right of residence are possible on the basis of public policy and domestic security (Art. 17), as well as public health (Art. 18).

A third important aspect of the long-term resident status is related to significant safeguards against expulsion of long-term residents (Art. 12). This protection entails that a decision to expel a long-term resident can only be taken when he/she constitutes an "actual and sufficiently serious threat to public order or domestic security". Furthermore, this decision cannot be founded on economic considerations. Member States also have to take into account several aspects before taking a decision to expel a long-term resident, including his duration of residence in the territory of the Member State, the age of the person concerned, the consequences of this decision for the person and his family members as well as the links with the country of residence or the absence of links with the country of origin. Finally, this article contains provisions of judicial protection such as the guarantee of a judicial redress procedure and legal assistance to long-term residents lacking adequate resources. Obviously inspired by the ECJ case-law on free movement of persons, the initial Commission proposal went even further. The Commission document explicitly referred to the "personal conduct" of a long-term resident as a condition for expulsion. In line

---

[164] It has to be mentioned, however, that in order to avoid excessive requirements, these conditions cannot be applied when the third-country nationals already passed an integration test when obtaining the long-term resident status.

with the ECJ judgment *Adoui and Cornuaille* personal conduct cannot be considered a sufficiently serious threat if a Member State does not take severe enforcement measures against its own nationals who commit similar offences.[165] Furthermore, criminal convictions as such do not automatically justify an expulsion decision. Explicit references to these effects have been deleted on the instigation of Germany and Spain.[166] In addition, supplementary judicial protection measures such as the prohibition of emergency expulsion procedures and the requirement that judicial redress procedures have suspensory effect have been dropped in the final version of the Directive. Together with the introduction of limitations to the principle of equal treatment and the right of residence in other Member States, it can be concluded that the initial Commission proposal contained much more safeguards protecting the rights of long-term residents lacking EU citizenship. The most problematic amendment, however, might be the inclusion of additional conditions for acquiring the long-term resident status.

Directive 2003/109 introduces the possibility for non-citizens to acquire an EC residence permit after five years of legal residence and on the condition that they have a sickness insurance as well as stable and sufficient resources in order not to become a burden on the social security system of their Member State of residence. Importantly, Article 5 (2) of the Directive further states that "Member States may require third-country nationals to comply with integration conditions, in accordance with national law". This provision, which was not included in the Commission proposal, seems to undermine the requirement contained in the initial document that "for the sake of legal certainty, it is essential that the acquisition of the status should not be left to Member States' discretion where the conditions are actually met".[167] The Directive does not contain any specifications concerning the permissible national integration conditions. Consequently, it seems that the Member States retain a large freedom of appraisal. In this respect, Sonja Boelaert-Suominen concludes that:

> The spectre of Member States placing and continuously moving the bar
> of integration requirements so high that certain third-country nationals

---

[165] ECJ, Joint cases 115 and 116/81, *Adoui and Cornuaille*, judgment of 18 May 1982, [1982] ECR I-1665, para. 8.

[166] Council of the European Union, 9636/02 MIGR 50, Brussels, 18 July 2002, p. 9 and 15483/02 MIGR 133, Brussels, 20 Dec. 2002, 18.

[167] COM (2001) 127 final, p. 7.

may simply be unable to obtain the desired secure legal status, may not be far-fetched. The Commission and the ECJ will have to be vigilant to ensure that Article 5 (2) is not used as a vehicle to erode the basic rationale of the Directive: to promote the integration of third-country nationals who have been long-term residents in EU Member States.[168]

In Latvia, applicants for the EC long-term resident status have to pass a test in order to prove a basic knowledge of the Latvian language. The required knowledge corresponds to stage B of the first level, which is the second lowest level of state language knowledge.[169] The Estonian Parliament decided to introduce a similar language requirement only from June 2007 onwards. Accordingly, this condition is primarily targeted at new immigrants whereas non-citizens who had lived in Estonia for a long time and already held an Estonian long-term resident permit were able to apply for an EC long-term resident permit without additional integration requirements.[170]

The introduction of a language test is in line with a recent trend in many old Member States to link the granting or extension of residence permits to the successful completion of compulsory integration courses, containing both language instruction and civic orientation.[171] Such requirements are legitimate under Directive 2003/109 as long as they are applied without any discrimination.[172] Hence, it does not seem that the Baltic States intend to introduce extraordinary hurdles for the acquisition of the long-term resident status even though the

---

[168] S. Boelaert-Suominen, "Non-EU Nationals and Council Directive 2003/109/EC on the Status of Third-Country Nationals who are long-term residents: five paces forward and possibly three paces back", 42 *Common Market Law Review* 4 (2005), p. 1023.

[169] See: The Latvian Office of Citizenship and Migration Affairs, 'The Long-Term Resident Status of the European Community in Latvia, at: http://www.ocma.gov.lv/?_p=454&menu__id=124.

[170] Estonian Ministry of the Interior, "Permanent residence permit-holders not affected by long-term resident language requirements", Press release No. 59, 7 April 2006, at: http://www.sisemin.gov.ee/atp/?id=17509.

[171] Austria, Luxembourg, Germany, Belgium, the Netherlands, Greece, Finland, Spain and France introduced or are planning to introduce such integration courses. See: European Commission Staff Working Document, *Second Annual Report on Migration and Integration*, SEC (2006) 892, Brussels, 30 June 2006, p. 16.

[172] Recital 5 of Council Directive 2003/109 states that "Member States should give effect to the provisions of the Directive without discrimination on the basis of sex, race, colour, ethnic or social origin, genetic characteristics, language, religion or beliefs, political or other opinions, membership of a national minority, fortune, birth, disabilities, age or sexual orientation", *OJ* (2004) L 16/44.

language test forms an additional condition not foreseen in the initial Commission proposal.

The procedure for acquiring the long-term resident status might further hamper the potential effects of this new legislation upon the legal situation of non-citizens in Estonia and Latvia. To acquire this status, the long-term resident has to take the initiative. He/she should lodge an application to the competent authorities of the Member State of residence accompanied by documentary evidence that the necessary conditions of residence duration, stable and regular income, sickness insurance and, possibly, integration into the local community are met (Art. 7). The applicant has to pay a State duty for the examination of the documents up to € 50 (750 EEK) in Estonia and between € 30 and € 100 (20 and 70 Ls) in Latvia.[173] It is striking that Directive 2003/109 remains silent on this administrative requirement whereas Article 25 (2) of Directive 2004/38 explicitly provides that all documents for the registration of the right of permanent residence of EU citizens and their family members "shall be issued free of charge or for a charge not exceeding that imposed on nationals for the issuing of similar documents".[174] In Estonia, the state duty for the issuing of a residence permit for EU citizens and their family members is, therefore, the same as for the issuing of an Estonian ID card (150 EEK or € 10).[175] The cost for a non-citizen EC long-term resident permit is, in other words, up to five times higher. Accordingly, the State duty forms an additional hurdle for the acquisition of the EC permanent resident status. Taking into account the existing problems in the process of naturalisation in Estonia and Latvia, which are partly due to a lack of information and motivation, it seems rather unlikely that the new Directive will seriously affect the situation of the non-citizen population. Only a small group

---

[173] Information from http://www.mig.ee/eng/state_fees/ and http://www.ocma.gov. lv/?_p=503&menu__id=135. With regard to the situation in Latvia, it is noteworthy that the State duty depends upon the period of examination and on the legal status of the person concerned. Non-citizens of the Republic of Latvia pay less than other foreigners with a valid residence permit. The latter have to pay a fee ranging between € 100 and € 240 (70 and 170 Ls). The basis for this differentiation is, however, not very clear and raises questions about proportionality.

[174] Directive 2004/38, *OJ* (2004) L 158/113. In case C-344/95, the ECJ clarified that the sum of all the charges paid during each step in the adminstrative procedure cannot exceed the amount payable when an ID card is issued even if the individual charges are lower. See: ECJ, Case C-344/95, *Commission* v. *Belgium* [1997] ECR I-01035, at para. 26.

[175] http://www.mig.ee/eng/state_fees/

of well-informed non-citizens can be expected to apply for this status whereas a large majority of stateless residents might remain outside the new framework.[176]

Notwithstanding the contribution of Directive 2003/109 to the judicial protection of Estonia's and Latvia's non-citizens—particularly because the core provisions concerning the acquisition of the long-term residence status and its connected rights to equal treatment qualify for direct effect[177]—the conditions for acquiring this status as well as the limitations in scope of the directive clearly reduce its value as an instrument ensuring equality between the long-term resident non-citizens and EU citizens as provided under the Tampere European Council conclusions.

1.3.2. *The Paradoxical Effects of Council Regulation 539/2001*

Directive 2003/109 does not regulate the movement of long-term resident third country nationals. Accordingly, third country nationals—including stateless persons—fall within the scope of the Community visa legislation. The final indent of Article 3 of Council Regulation 539/2001 listing the third countries whose nationals must be in possession of visas when crossing the external borders and those nationals who are exempt from that requirement provides that "stateless persons may be exempted from the visa requirement if the third country where they reside and which issued their travel document is one of the third countries listed in Annex II".[178] Pursuant to Article 1 (1) of the same Directive, Annex II includes countries whose nationals are automatically exempted from the visa requirement for stays not exceeding a period of three months. Before accession, all EU candidates figured on this list. Hence, it was up to each individual Member State to decide whether or not to apply a visa requirement for Estonia's and Latvia's

---

[176] In 2006, the Estonian Citizenship and Migration Board registered 7,378 applications for long-term residence and 7,090 were issued. Information from the Estonian Ministry of Internal Affairs (http://www.sisemin.gov.ee). For Latvia, no data were yet available at the time of writing—information requested from the Latvian Office of Citizenship and Migration Affairs (http://www.ocma.gov.lv).

[177] S. Peers, "Implementing Equality? The Directive on long-term resident third-country nationals", 29 *European Law Review* 4 (2004), p. 443.

[178] Council Regulation (EC) No. 539/2001 of 15 March 2001 listing the third countries whose nationals must be in possession of visas when crossing the external borders and those whose nationals are exempt from that requirement, *OJ* (2001) L 81/1.

non-citizen population.[179] In practice, all Schengen countries required visas from Estonia's and Latvia's non-citizens. Only Denmark, Lithuania and Estonia/Latvia applied a visa-free regime for those persons on the basis of bilateral agreements.[180]

As a result of their accession to the EU, the new Member States have been removed from Annex II.[181] This created a legal loophole as far as the application of Article 3 of Regulation 539/2001 concerned the stateless population in Estonia and Latvia. On the one hand, they no longer met the condition of residence in a third country to benefit from the potential visa exemption under this Regulation. On the other hand, the partial application of the Schengen *acquis* to the new Member States, as provided under Article 3 of the Act of Accession, implied that they could not enjoy the right to visa-free movement within the Schengen area for a period of less than three months as guaranteed by Article 21 of the Schengen Convention.[182] Hence, the EU accession of the Baltic States paradoxically reduced the scope of the possibility of granting a visa exemption for those countries' stateless population. Moreover, stateless persons resident in a third country could be granted a more flexible regime than those in a Member State that does not yet fully applies the Schengen rules.

In order to remedy this anomalous situation, the Parliament and the Council jointly requested the Commission to table proposals "to exempt holders of aliens' and non-citizens' passports residing in a Member State from the visa obligation".[183] Accordingly, the Commission suggested an

---

[179] Recital 7 to Council Regulation 539/2001 stipulates that "given the differences in the national legislation applicable to stateless persons and to recognised refugees, Member States may decide whether these categories of persons shall be subject to the visa requirement, where the third county in which these persons reside and which issued their travel documents is a third country whose nationals are exempt from the visa requirement".

[180] Information from e-mail correspondence with representatives from the Estonian and Latvian Ministries of Foreign Affairs, on file with the author.

[181] The removal of the new Member States from Annex II of Council Regulation 539/2001 is based on Article 20 of the Act of Accession, *OJ* (2003), L 236/39 as specified in Annex II to the Act of Accession, *OJ* (2003) L 236/725.

[182] Article 21 of the Schengen Convention provides that aliens holding a valid residence permit and valid travel documents can move freely within the Schengen area for up to three months (Convention implementing the Schengen agreement of 14 June 1985, *OJ* (2000) L 239/19). Pursuant to Article 3 (2) of the Act of Accession, this provision could only apply in the new Member States after a unanimous Council decision. This decision (2007/801/EC) was adopted on 6 December 2007, *OJ* (2007) L 323/24.

[183] Declaration on holders of aliens' and non-citizens' passports, included in: Council Secretariat, "Proposal for a Regulation of the European Parliament and of the Coun-

amendment of Council Regulation 539/2001 granting an automatic visa exemption for recognized refugees and stateless persons who are permanently resident in an EU Member State and who have a valid travel document issued by that particular Member State.[184] It is noteworthy that the final version of the amendment Regulation, adopted on 21 December 2006, refers to "stateless persons and other persons who do not hold the nationality of any country" rather than to "stateless persons" as such.[185] This peculiar formulation stems from the somewhat ambiguous differentiation in Latvia's domestic legislation between stateless persons falling within the scope of the 1954 Convention relating to the Status of Stateless Persons, and the category of non-citizens, which do not fall within the scope of this Convention because, in contrast to stateless persons, they do have a specific link with Latvia.[186] Whereas this distinction is hard to defend from an international law perspective,[187] the drafting of Council Regulation 1932/2006 amending Regulation 539/2001 avoids any misunderstanding as regards the application of the automatic visa exemption for persons falling within the scope of the Estonian law on aliens and Latvia's non-citizen legislation.[188] As a result, the amendment ends the odd situation that a large part of the lawfully resident population of two new Member States were not only excluded from free movement within the EU[189] but were even obliged

---

cil establishing a Community Code on the rules governing the movement of persons across borders (Schengen Borders code)—outcome of the European Parliament's first reading", Brussels, 18 July 2005, 10588/05, p. 15.

[184] European Commission, "Proposal for a Council Regulation amending Regulation (EC) No. 539/2001 listing the third countries whose nationals must be in possession of visas when crossing the external borders and those whose nationals are exempt from that requirement", Brussels, 13 July 2006, COM (2006) 84 final.

[185] Art. 1 (1) (b) of Council Regulation (EC) No. 1932/2006 of 21 December 2006 amending Regulation (EC) No. 539/2001 listing the third countries whose nationals must be in possession of visas when crossing the external borders and those whose nationals are exempt from that requirement, *OJ* (2006), L 405/23.

[186] On the distinction between non-citizens and stateless persons in Latvia, see *supra* Part I, Chapter 6, § 3.2.

[187] International law does not envisage any other categories besides citizens, foreigners and stateless persons.

[188] This is also clearly expressed in the European Parliament Report on the proposal for a Council Regulation amending Regulation (EC) No. 539/2001 listing the third countries whose nationals must be in possession of visas when crossing the external borders of Member States and those whose nationals are exempt from that requirement (rapporteur: I. Varvitsiotis), A6–0431/2006, 29 November 2006.

[189] The right to move and reside freely within the territory of the Member States embodied in Article 18 of the EC Treaty concerns only the citizens of the Union.

to apply for a visa before travelling within the Schengen area.[190] The fact that this anomaly has only been abolished from 19 January 2007 onwards, i.e. more than two and a half years after the date of accession, is astonishing and clearly illustrates the total lack of a pro-active policy on the part of the EU as regards the post-enlargement legal status of the Russian-speaking minorities in Estonia and Latvia.

It seems obvious that the amendment to Regulation 539/2001 significantly improves the legal status of the stateless Russian-speaking minorities in the EU. It does not only open the gates to visa-free travelling to the Schengen countries but also makes the rights connected to the EC long-term resident status more attractive. On the other hand, some important differences between Estonian or Latvian citizens and non-citizens continue to exist. For travels to the United Kingdom or Ireland, the visa requirement for non-citizens still applies. Moreover, the non-citizens cannot automatically enjoy the right of visa-free travel with countries that unilaterally established the visa-free regime for citizens of the European Union.

1.3.3. *'Civic Citizenship' as a Solution to the Remaining Problems?*
Apart from the differences concerning movement rights, non-citizens cannot take part in European Parliament elections and, in the case of Latvia, they are also barred from participation in municipal elections. They have to pass the naturalisation procedures to acquire EU citizenship, which is, in the words of the ECJ, "destined to be the fundamental status of nationals of the Member States".[191] Notwithstanding the recognized importance of voting rights and access to nationality as important instruments of integration, the Commission did not address these elements in its proposal on the EC long-term resident status because "the EC Treaty provides no specific legal basis for it".[192] In a later Communication on immigration, integration and

---

[190] Regulation 539/2001 does not bind the United Kingdom and Ireland. In the light of their respective association with the implementation, application and development of the Schengen *acquis*, Iceland and Norway decided to lift the visa regime for the non-citizens whereas Switzerland continues to require a visa from holders of an aliens or non-citizen passport. [Information from the embassies or consulates of the respective countries in Estonia and Latvia].

[191] See e.g. ECJ, Case C-184/99, *Grzelczyk* [2001] ECR I-6193, at para. 31; Case C-224/98, *D'Hoop* [2002] ECR I-6191, at para. 28; Case C-148/02, *Garcia Avello* [2003] ECR I-11613, at para. 22; Case C-209/03, *Bidar* [2005] ECR I-2119, at para. 31.

[192] COM (2001) 127 final, p. 8.

employment, however, the Commission expressed the opinion "that granting long-term resident immigrants political rights is important for the integration process and that the Treaty should provide the basis for so doing."[193] Moreover, the Commission re-introduced[194] the concept of 'civic citizenship', defined as "guaranteeing certain core rights and obligations to immigrants which they would acquire over a period of years, so that they are treated in the same way as nationals of their host state, even if they are not naturalised".[195] The European Parliament expressly welcomed the inclusion of this concept, conferring on long-term resident third-country nationals "economic, social and political rights and duties, *including a right to vote in local and European elections*".[196] The European Economic and Social Committee (EESC) shared this view.[197] In the current state of Community law, however, the extension of voting rights to non EU-citizens is the exclusive competence of the Member States.[198]

It is noteworthy that the idea of granting voting rights on the basis of stable residence rather than on the basis of nationality is a long-standing issue within the Council of Europe. Already in 1977, the Parliamentary Assembly referred to this suggestion in a recommendation "on the political rights and position of aliens".[199] The 1992 "Convention on the Participation of Foreigners in Public Life at Local Level" includes the obligation for the contracting parties to grant to every foreign resident the right to vote and to stand for election in local authority

---

[193] Communication from the Commission to the Council, the European Parliament, the European Economic and Social Committee and the Committee of the Regions on immigration, integration and employment, COM (2003) 336 final, Brussels, 3 June 2002, p. 2.

[194] This concept has been introduced for the first time in the Communication from the Commission to the Council and the European Parliament on a Community immigration policy, COM (2000) 757 final, Brussels, 22 November 2000.

[195] COM (2003) 336 final, p. 2.

[196] Emphasis added. European Parliament, Report on the Communication from the Commission on immigration, integration and employment, A5–445/2003, 1 December 2003, para. 32.

[197] Opinion of the European Economic and Social Committee on the Communication from the Commission on immigration, integration and employment, SOC/138, Brussels, 10 December 2003.

[198] ECJ, Case C-300/04, *Eman and Sevinger*, [2006] ECR I-8055 at para. 45.

[199] Council of Europe Parliamentary Assembly, Recommendation 799 (1997) on the political rights and position of aliens, para. 10 (b), at: http://assembly.coe.int/Main. asp?link=/Documents/AdoptedText/ta77/EREC799.htm.

elections after 5 years of legal residence.[200] A Parliamentary Assembly Recommendation of 2001 even urges the governments to grant those rights after a period of three years[201] whereas a more recent report of the Venice Commission stipulates that "residency could be a criterion for allowing non-citizens the right to vote not only in local elections, but in regional, national and presidential elections as well".[202] There is, in other words, a clear tendency within the Council of Europe framework in the direction of a new interpretation of citizenship, including political rights on the basis of common criteria of residence.

At the EU level, the European Economic and Social Committee actively promoted the suggestion of a residence-based citizenship in the framework of the Convention on the Future of Europe.[203] Several members of the Convention subscribed to the vision that EU citizenship should not only be linked to nationality of a Member State but also to stable residence in the Union.[204] Such an amendment of Article 17 EC, which now defines EU citizenship as the exclusive privilege of nationals of EU Member States, would solve the existing democratic deficit in Estonia and Latvia where approximately one fifth of the population is excluded from participation in the European Parliament elections and, only in the case of Latvia, also in municipal elections. As a Union citizen, the stateless population would also have a right of diplomatic protection from any Member State authority in third countries in which Estonia or Latvia are not represented.

The scope of the freedom of movement and residence, which is another basic right connected to EU citizenship, would not necessarily change as this provision is subject to the limits and conditions as laid

---

[200] Convention on the Participation of Foreigners in Public Life at Local Level, Strasbourg, 5 February 1992, ECT 144, at: http://conventions.coe.int/treaty/en/Treaties/Html/144.htm.

[201] Council of Europe Parliamentary Assembly, Recommendation 1500 (2001) on the Participation of Immigrants and Foreign Residents in Political Life in the Council of Europe Member States, para. iv. (a), at: http://assembly.coe.int/Main.asp?link=/Documents/AdoptedText/ta01/EREC1500.htm.

[202] European Commission for Democracy through Law, Report on the abolition of restrictions on the right to vote in general elections, CDL_AD (2005) 011, Strasbourg, 4 April 2005, at para. 24.

[203] In an own-initiative opinion, addressed to the European Convention, the EESC recommended the granting of EU citizenship to third-country nationals with long-term resident status. See: Opinion of the European Economic and Social Committee on Access to European Union citizenship, Brussels, 14 May 2003, SOC/141.

[204] For an overview of the proposed amendments, see: http://european-convention.eu.int.

down in the treaties and secondary legislation, in this case Directive 2003/109. Other rights enjoyed by Union citizens, such as the right to address a petition to the European Parliament and the right to make complains to the Community Ombudsman are already extended to resident third country-nationals.[205] It can, therefore, be concluded that an extension of EU citizenship to long-residing third-country nationals is essentially related to the granting of voting rights to this category of persons. Taking into account the political sensitivity of this issue in many Member States, the proposal to link the rights of EU citizenship to stable residence in the Union rather than to the nationality of a Member State has not been withheld in the Constitutional Treaty nor in the Lisbon Treaty but nevertheless remains an interesting mindset.[206]

§ 2. *The Question of Border Delimitation*

Together with the fate of the Russian-speaking communities in Estonia and Latvia, the relations between both countries and Russia remained strained after enlargement due to the absence of formal border agreements. During the pre-accession period, the EU had always been very reluctant to play an active role on this issue (cf. *supra*). It is also noteworthy that this problem was not mentioned in the Joint Statement on EU enlargement and EU-Russia relations. Only after the accession of the Baltic States, the border question formally entered the agenda of the EU-Russia Strategic Partnership. On the occasion of the 14th EU-Russia summit of November 2004, the EU leaders called on Russia to sign and ratify the outstanding border agreements with Estonia and Latvia as a condition for progress towards the establishment of a Common Space of Freedom, Security and Justice in general and visa-free travel between the EU and Russia in particular.[207] This active engagement on the part of the EU immediately seemed to produce effect. Russian President Putin principally agreed to resolve the outstanding border issues and proposed to sign border agreements with Latvia and Estonia on 10 May 2005, in the framework of the 15th EU-Russia Summit and against the background of the celebrations of the 60th anniversary

---

[205] According to Article 194 EC and Article 195 EC respectively.
[206] See e.g. N. Reich, "The Constitutional Relevance of Citizenship and Free Movement in an Enlarged Union", 11 *European Law Journal* 6 (2005), pp. 675–698.
[207] 14th EU-Russia Summit, The Hague, 25 November 2004, http://europa.eu.int/comm/external_relations/russia/summit_11_04/index.htm.

of the allied victory over Nazi Germany. In addition, Putin suggested signing political declarations on the foundations of relations between the Russian Federation and the two Baltic republics.[208]

Putin's initiative presented the Baltic leaders with a political dilemma. Not attending the anniversary to protest against what was called a Russian "propaganda gimmick" and to remind the crimes of totalitarian communism—as was suggested in an open letter signed by 100 MEPs[209]—could give the impression that the Baltic States were not willing to overcome the difficulties of the past. It would also be an additional argument for Russia to portray Estonia and Latvia as supporters of the Nazi regime.[210] In the end, the Latvian President, Vaira Vike-Freiberga, attended the celebrations "to draw the world's attention to the reverse side of Victory Day",[211] whereas her Estonian and Lithuanian counterparts refused to go to Moscow. The heated discussions clearly illustrate the core problem of Baltic-Russian relations, i.e. the divergent visions on the consequences of the Molotov-Ribbentrop Pact for the legal status of the contemporary Baltic republics.[212]

On the question of border delimitation, the Baltic representatives did not want to enter into any arrangement that could undermine their claim of historic or legal continuity. Russia's original drafts remained completely silent on this issue. In a reaction, the Latvian Foreign Ministry presented its own proposal, which explicitly confirmed the importance of the 1920 Riga Peace Treaty as "a legally binding document [...which...] has not lost its validity also today".[213] Moscow immediately responded that "it is known that the 1920 Peace Treaty became invalid

---

[208] Political Declaration on the Foundations of Relations Between the Republic of Estonia [Latvia] and the Russian Federation, Press Release 6 February 2005, available at: http://www.russiaeu.org.

[209] X, "MEPs sharply criticise Russia over planned WWII victory celebration", *Helsingin Sanomat*, 26 November 2004.

[210] In this regard, see e.g. the publications of the Russian Foreign Ministry concerning the "Involvement of Estonian [Latvian] SS Legions in War Crimes in 1941–1945 and the Attempts to Revise the Verdict of the Nuremberg Tribunal in Estonia [Latvia]". Unofficial translations from Russian are available at: http://www.russiaeu.org/ss-est.htm and http://www.russiaeu.org/ss-lat.htm.

[211] Vaira Vike-Freiberga's statements raised controversy in Moscow: See: Russian MFA Information and Press Department Commentary Regarding a Media Question Concerning Latvian President Vaira Vike-Freiberga's Statements Explaining the Motives of her Decision to Visit Moscow on 9 October 2005 (http://www.ln.mid.ru).

[212] See Part I of this study.

[213] Political Declaration on the Foundations of Relations between the Republic of Latvia and the Russian Federation. Latvian Draft, presented at 10 February 2005, available at: http://www.am.gov.lv.

upon Latvia's joining the Soviet Union in August 1940".[214] Eventually, the divergent visions on the consequences of the state continuity principle prevented the conclusion of border agreements with Latvia.

With Estonia, which did not claim the inclusion of similar explicit statements, border agreements were finally signed on 18 May 2005.[215] Almost immediately, three Estonian citizens addressed the Supreme Court requesting that the border agreements would be declared unconstitutional, *inter alia* with reference to the principle of state continuity and the Tartu Peace Treaty of 2 February 1920.[216] The Supreme Court dismissed the petitions on procedural grounds.[217] The discussion, however, continued after a majority of Estonian MPs decided to add an introductory declaration to the treaties' act of ratification including clear references to the Tartu Peace Treaty and "the legal continuity of the Republic of Estonia proclaimed on 24 February 1918".[218] Russian government representatives immediately suspended the ratification process and demanded new negotiations.[219] In legal terms, the Russian

---

[214] Russian MFA Information and Press Department Commentary Regarding Publication of the Latvian Draft of a Declaration on the Foundations of Relations between our Countries, Press Release, 11 February 2005, available at: http://www.ln.mid.ru.

[215] On 18 May 2005 the Estonian Foreign Minister Urmas Paet and his Russian counterpart Sergei Lavrov signed the "Treaty between the Government of the Republic of Estonia and the Government of the Russian Federation on the Estonian-Russian Border" and the "Treaty between the Government of the Republic of Estonia and the Government of the Russian Federation on the delimitation of the maritime zones in the Gulf of Finland and the Gulf of Narva". The border treaties need to be ratified and come into force 30 days after the exchange of letters of ratification. Available at: http://www.vm.ee.

[216] Pursuant to Article 122 of the Estonian Constitution, the 1920 Tartu Peace Treaty determines the land borders of Estonia.

[217] Under the Constitutional Review Court Procedure Act individuals have to show how the contested Act violates their rights. It is not possible to submit petitions for the protection of the interests of other people or in a public interest, as was the case in this procedure. See: Supreme Court of Estonian Ruling 3–4–1–12–05 of 8 September 2005, available in English at: http://www.nc.ee.

[218] Act on the Ratification of the State Border Treaty between the Republic of Estonia and the Russian Federation and the Treaty on the Delimitation of Maritime Areas of Narva Bay and the Gulf of Finland between the Republic of Estonia and the Russian Federation [unofficial translation], available at: http://www.vm.ee.

[219] Statement by the Ministry of Foreign Affairs of the Russian Federation Concerning the Estonian Parliament's Ratification of Border Treaties with Russia, Press Release 126/05, available at: http://www.russiaeu.org/. For comments, see: K. Repson, "Border Treaty requires new negotiations", *Baltic Times*, 29 June 2005; X, "Moscou retire sa signature du traité frontalier avec l'Estonie", *Agence Europe*, 29 June 2005; L. Mälksoo, "Which Continuity: The Tartu Peace Treaty of 2 February 1920, the Estonian-Russian Border Treaties of 18 May 2005, and the Legal Debate about Estonia's Status in International Law", 10 *Juridica International* 1(2005), pp. 144–149.

government initiated a procedure of "withdrawal of signature" of the Estonian-Russian border treaty.[220] This rather unusual gesture under international law implies that a State which has signed but not yet ratified the treaty notifies that it does no longer intend to become a party to the treaty. As a result, the State in question is no longer bound by the international law obligation to refrain from acts that would defeat the object and purpose of the treaty.[221]

At the end of June 2006, the Russian Foreign Ministry transmitted a note to the Estonian Foreign Minister suggesting negotiations on a new border agreement, stating the invalidity of all the previous documents on the territorial question. On 4 September 2006, the Estonian Foreign Ministry responded that "the Government of Estonia has neither the authority nor the intention to hold new talks with Russia on the text of the border treaties".[222] In Latvia, the Parliament's foreign affairs committee put the issue back on the political agenda in January 2007.[223] After lengthy discussions, a draft law has been sent to Parliament for approval. The new proposal allowed the government to sign the border agreement with Russia without any explanatory declarations. Remarkably, the parliamentary law clearly states that this decision is based on the grounds of the Constitutional Law on the sovereignty of the Republic of Latvia adopted by the Latvian Supreme Council on August 21, 1991.[224] There is, in other words, an indirect, unilateral reference to the principle of state continuity. This did not prevent the signature of the border treaty between the Latvian and Russian Prime

---

[220] See: Russian MFA Information and Press Department Commentary Regarding a question from ITAR-TASS News Agency concerning "withdrawal of signature" from Russian-Estonian border treaties, Press-release 167/05, available at: http://www.russiaeu.org/pr167-05.htm.

[221] Pursuant to Article 18 of the Vienna Convention on the Law of Treaties, a State is under an obligation not to defeat the object and purpose of a treaty, until it makes clear its intention not to become a party to the treaty. For the text of the Vienna Convention on the Law of Treaties, see: http://untreaty.un.org/ilc/texts/instruments/english/conventions/1_1_1969.pdf; For comments, see: Council of Europe (ed.), *Treaty Making—Expression of Consent by States to be Bound by a Treaty*, The Hague, Kluwer Law International, 2001, pp. 9–10.

[222] See: http://www.ln/mid.ru, document 1486–06–09–2006.

[223] X, "Latvian Border Treaty with Russia moves forward", *The Baltic Times*, 18 January 2007.

[224] X, "Artis Pabriks familiarises ambassadors of EU and NATO countries with solution to concluding of Latvia-Russia Border Treaty", at: http://www.am.gov.lv/en/news/press-releases/2007/january/17-1/.

Ministers, Aigars Kalvitis and Mikhail Fradkov, on 27 March 2007.[225]
Despite discussions on the constitutionality of the new agreement,[226]
the Latvian parliament quickly ratified it on 17 May 2007. The Russian
State Duma followed on 5 September 2007 so that the treaty could
enter into force on 18 December 2007. The swift proceeding of the
ratification procedure is remarkable given the difficulties to conclude a
similar border agreement with Estonia. The improvement of Russian-
Latvian relations, reflected by perspectives of closer energy co-operation,
certainly facilitated the ratification process.[227]

After the significant progress in solving the border dispute between
Russia and Latvia, the formal demarcation of the Russian-Estonian border remains on the agenda. A political breakthrough is not in prospect
given the troubled bilateral relations after the relocation of a Soviet war
memorial in Tallinn in May 2007. In this context, the EU seems to
return to its strategy of the pre-accession period, i.e. to downplay the
importance of the border question. It is significant, for instance, that the
absence of a formal border agreement between Russia and Estonia did
not hinder the latter's full entry to the Schengen zone on 21 December
2007. Even though the practical consequences of the border dispute are
limited given the effective border controls at the *de facto* border lines, the
formalisation of this situation in the form of legally binding bilateral
agreements would help to overcome the remaining frictions between the
countries involved. Historic sensitivities, in combination with the legal
importance of the state continuity principle, form the main stumbling
block to further progress. A pragmatic solution avoiding those questions
seems the only possible solution. Inspiration could perhaps be found
in the 1994 Treaty on Friendly Relations and Good Neighbourly Co-
operation of the Republic of Lithuania and the Republic of Poland
in which both sides formally accepted "the integrity of their current

---

[225] The text of the treaty is available at: http://www.am.gov.lv/en/policy/signing-
of-Border-Treaty/.

[226] On 26 April 2007, the Latvian Constitutional Court opened a case on the border
treaty's compliance with the Latvian Constitution. On 29 November 2007, the Court
conformed the legality of the Latvian-Russian border treaty. See: Case 2007–14–01
of the Latvian Constitutional Court at: http://www.satv.tiesa.gov.lv.

[227] An important element is certainly the potential of *Gazprom* investments in
Latvia's underground gas storage facility of Dobele as an important branch-line of the
ambitious Nordstream project (cf. *infra*). At the beginning of 2008, however, Latvian-
Russian relations soured after Latvia's expulsion of a Russian diplomat on charges of
espionage. See: "Russia warns Latvia in diplomat expulsion row", 22 January 2008,
at: http://en.rian.ru/.

territories, with capitals in Vilnius and Warsaw, not taking into account how the borders were formed in the past".[228]

§ 3. *The Kaliningrad Transit Issue*

The most obvious example of how the Baltic States' EU accession influences EU-Russia relations concerns the question of transit between the Russian enclave Kaliningrad and mainland Russia. The Joint Statement adopted at the 11 November 2002 EU-Russia summit included a political compromise for the transit of persons (cf. *supra* Part IV, § 5) but left open the question of transit of goods. On this issue, the Joint Statement only observed that "the Russian Federation and the European Union agree to continue discussions within the PCA framework on the appropriate technical modalities".[229] As a result, the facilitation of Kaliningrad cargo transit remained high on the agenda and returned on the table in the discussions surrounding the extension of the PCA. Together with the question of transit of persons after Lithuania's accession to the Schengen agreement, it remains an important challenge for the future of EU-Russia relations.

3.1. *The Transit of Goods*

The dilemmas concerning the transit of goods from mainland Russia to Kaliningrad reflect to a large extent the visa question related to the movement of persons. In comparison to the latter issue, however, no specific facilitated transit procedures for Kaliningrad have been developed. Russia's insistence on a special arrangement without transit formalities was unacceptable for the EU because this would open the door to tax evasion and fraud.[230] The idea of establishing a free trade area (FTA) between the EC and Kaliningrad, as a testing ground for a more comprehensive EC-Russia FTA afterwards, also failed to materialise mainly due to a lack of political will and technical or legal

---

[228] Treaty on Friendly Relations and Good Neighborly Cooperation of the Republic of Lithuania and Republic of Poland, published in: *Lithuanian Foreign Policy Review* 2 (1998).

[229] Joint Statement on EU Enlargement and EU-Russia Relations, Brussels, 27 April 2004, available at: http://europa.eu.int/comm/external_relations/russia/russia_docs/js_elarg_270404.htm.

[230] Communication from the Commission to the Council, "Kaliningrad: Transit", COM (2002) 510 final, 18 September 2002, p. 5.

obstacles such as the need for adequate controls on the rules of origin, standards and certification procedures, etc.[231] Finally, the idea of a transit corridor was totally unacceptable for Lithuania.[232] As a result, the transit of Russian goods to Kaliningrad is treated in accordance to the rules on external Community transit, laid down in Articles 91 to 97 of the Community Customs Code,[233] and in the Convention on a Common E(E)C/EFTA Transit Procedure.[234]

The external transit procedure allows for the movement of non-Community goods to cross the territory of the Community without paying duties or taxes. During this procedure the goods are not in free circulation and are not to be released on the market. The procedure provides for guarantees to be given for the payment of duties and taxes if the goods are lost during the transit procedure. Pursuant to Article 27 (3) of the Common Transit Procedure, this financial guarantee has to be issued by an insurance company registered in the country in which the guarantee is provided, i.e. Lithuania. In combination with the fees for services rendered by Lithuanian customs brokers and tightened veterinary and phyto-sanitary controls, the harmonisation of Lithuania's legislation with the principles of the EC transit procedure involved increased costs for Russian carriers. The Kaliningrad Regional Administration calculated that the costs of transit of goods almost doubled as a result of enlargement.[235] This observation, together with concerns over a possibility of uncontrolled growth of tariffs in the future, explains the prominent position of the Kaliningrad transit issue in the Joint Statement on PCA extension. In this document, both parties confirm the principle of freedom of transit of goods and acknowledge that:

---

[231] E. Vinokurov, "Kaliningrad in the Framework of EU-Russia Relations: Moving Toward Common Spaces", *Chair Interbrew—Baillet Latour Working Papers* 20 (2004), pp. 27–29.

[232] Seimas of the Republic of Lithuania, Resolution on Cooperation with the Kaliningrad Region of the Russian Federation, Vilnius, 10 September 2004, available at: http://www3.lrs.lt.

[233] Council Regulation (EEC) No. 2912/92 of 12 October 1992 establishing the Community Customs Code, *OJ* (1992) L 302/1.

[234] Convention between the European Economic Community, the Republic of Austria, the Republic of Finland, the Republic of Iceland, the Republic of Norway, the Kingdom of Sweden and the Swiss Confederation, on a Common Transit Procedure, *OJ* (1987) L 229/2.

[235] A. Zernov, K. Shopin, *Kaliningrad Transit of Goods: In Need for a Strategic Approach to Problem-solving'*, available at: http://www.kaliningradexpert.org/stuff/pubs/transit_%20eng.pdf.

the goods in such transit shall not be subject to unnecessary delays or restrictions and shall be exempt from customs duties and transit duties or other charges related to transit, except charges for transportation or those commensurate with administrative expenses entailed by transit or with the costs of services rendered and [...] treatment no less favourable than that which would have been accorded to such goods had they been transported without transiting through the EU territory shall be accorded to goods in transit to and from Kaliningrad region.[236]

The provisions on Kaliningrad transit complement the rules on external Community transit, which fall within the scope of the jurisdiction of the European Court of Justice. A number of prejudicial procedures have been disputed before the ECJ concerning irregularities committed in the course of a Community transit operation. They essentially concern the determination of the State competent for the recovery of duties on entry.[237] It is not inconceivable that disputes concerning the application of the transit procedure in Lithuania, leading to higher costs for Russian products transferred to Kaliningrad, give rise to legal procedures. Given the fact that the Joint Statement cannot be regarded as a legally binding document, essentially because it has not been negotiated and concluded following the EC Treaty procedures, the provisions of the Joint Statement do not qualify for direct effect (cf. *supra*).[238] In order to solve this legal imperfection, a specific bilateral agreement on the interconnection of the EU and Russian customs transit regimes has been anticipated "as soon as both sides are ready from a legal and practical point of view".[239] Article 78 PCA, which envisages *inter alia* further facilitation of trade and transit, provides a basis for such an agreement. In addition, Article 12 PCA establishes the freedom of transit of goods in accordance to normal GATT practice and Article 19 lists the possible grounds for restrictions to this principle. The Joint Statement on EU Enlargement specifically links these basic provisions to the Kaliningrad region. From this perspective, the legal importance of the PCA for regulating the transit of goods to Kaliningrad forms a

---

[236] Joint Statement on EU Enlargement and EU-Russia Relations, Brussels, 27 April 2004, available at: http://europa.eu.int/comm/external_relations/russia/russia_docs/js_elarg_270404.htm.

[237] ECJ, Case C-233/98, Judgment of 21 October 1999, *Hauptzollambt Neubrandburg* v. *Lensing & Brockhausen GmbH* [1999] ECR, I-7365; Case C-66/99, Judgment of 1 February 2001, *D. Wandel GmbH* v. *Hauptzollambt Bremen* [2001] ECR, I-873.

[238] M. Maresceau, "Bilateral Agreements", *op. cit.*, footnote 13, p. 434.

[239] Joint Statement on EU Enlargement and EU-Russia Relations, *op. cit.*, footnote 236.

plausible explanation for Russia's swift ratification of the PCA extension protocol (cf. *supra*).

In anticipation of a specific bilateral agreement on customs transit, the introduction of a new computerised transit system at the end of 2005 formed an important step towards the reduction of transit costs. Moreover, Russian customs authorities are allowed to submit electronic transit declarations directly to Lithuanian offices of departure. It means that, instead of using services of Lithuanian customs brokers, Russian carriers can provide transit data to Russian customs offices, which are entering the data into the system and transmitting it to the point of entry into the Community customs territory. The rules of electronic data interchange between the Lithuanian and Russian customs authorities are laid down in a technical agreement, which was concluded in December 2005.[240]

Notwithstanding these technical adjustments, the Kaliningrad transit procedure remains unpopular among Russian carriers. Problems to get a guarantee valid in the EU and technical difficulties with electronic declarations not accepted at the office of departure, often due to the imprecise description of goods in Lithuanian, are the most common complaints.[241] The full interconnection of the EU and Russian transit regimes, as foreseen in the Joint Statement on EU Enlargement, could solve these issues. The main obstacle in this respect concerns the requirement for Russia to align its national transit rules to the standard of documentation applied in the EU. In particular, Russia would be required to ensure full compliance with the Single Administrative Document, i.e. the transit declaration form used for entry into the EU and EFTA.[242] Apart from the obvious technical problems connected to

---

[240] This agreement is in fact a purely technical arrangement concluded between the Federal Customs Service of the Russian Federation and the Customs Department of Lithuania. The European Commission (DG TAXUD) was informed about the idea to conclude this agreement and agreed that it could be concluded in this form because technical details of information exchange between customs authorities of third countries belong to the competence of the Member States. Information from Sarunas Avizienis, Head of Customs Legislation Division, Customs Department, Lithuania.

[241] E-mail correspondence with Sarunas Avizienis, Head of Customs Legislation Division, Customs Department, Lithuania (sarunas.avizienis@cust.lt). See also a letter of complaint of Nikolay P. Tulayev, Member of the Federation Council and Representative of the Kaliningrad Regional Duma of 26 January 2005, EP-PE_LTD(2006)301773, on file with the author.

[242] See: http://ec.europa.eu/taxation_customs/customs/procedural_aspects/general/sad/index_en.htm.

such operation, this question also has an important political dimension. Rather than unilaterally implementing the EC transit rules, Russia insists on a more balanced approach. Hence, negotiations on a bilateral EC-Russia customs agreement or, alternatively, Russia's accession to the Common Transit Procedure promise to be a difficult exercise.[243]

3.2. *The Transit of Persons*

Regarding the transit of persons, the EU and Russia welcomed "the smooth introduction and running of the FTD/FRTD scheme" in the Joint Statement on EU Enlargement and EU-Russia relations.[244] Less than three years after the introduction of the new procedures, more than one million FRTDs had already been issued and only a single accident had been reported.[245] The number of FTDs remained much lower, particularly because a lot of people preferred full-scale multi-entry Lithuanian visas, issued free of charge for Kaliningrad residents. The entry into force of the EC-Russia visa facilitation agreement, which sets the price at € 35 and does not include any exceptions for Kaliningrad, might change this situation in favour of the less expensive FTDs.[246] Moreover, frequent travellers appear to prefer the free FRTDs, which are valid for single return trips and are issued free of charge at the station, to the FTDs, which apply for multiple trips but should be applied for at the consular office at a cost of € 5. Because the Lithuanian authorities issue the FRTD on a separate sheet and not—as required by Regulation (EC) 693/2003—in the passport of the person travelling, the FRTD can be thrown away and requested again several times, without filling up the passport.[247] Arguably, the correct application of Regulation 693/2003 would enhance the requests for FTDs. Table 11 also reveals a decrease of FRTDs in 2005. Whereas no official explanations have been provided, this tendency could be related

---

[243] A. Nakou, *Harmonisation of the Law of Russia and European Union in the Sphere of Customs Regulation*, Moscow, 2005, RECEP, p. 8, available at: http://www.recep.ru/files/documents/harmonization_nakou_eng.pdf.

[244] Joint Statement on EU Enlargement and EU-Russia Relations, *op. cit.*, footnote 236.

[245] European Commission Report on the functioning of the facilitated transit for persons between the Kaliningrad region and the rest of the Russian Federation, COM (2006) 840 final, 22 December 2006, pp. 5–6.

[246] E. Vinokurov, "Kaliningrad Transit and Visa Issues Revisited", *CEPS Commentaries*, July 2006, available at: http://www.ceps.be/Article.php?article_id=531.

[247] COM (2006) 840 final, p. 5.

to the increase of passengers travelling by air and the requirement for FRTD travellers to have an international passport from 1 January 2005 onwards.[248]

Table 11: The Number of Travellers Making Use of the FTD/FRTD System (2003–2006)[249]

	2003 (1.7.–31.12)	2004	2005	2006
Passengers	293,719	613,101	412,711	584,359
FRTD	156,417	293,076	217,994	264,461
FTD	1,836	3,095	3,149	1,074

The general satisfaction with the FTD/FRTD transit procedure does not imply that this question has been resolved. The agreed regime is temporary and could, in principle, be abolished after Lithuania's full integration into the Schengen area on 21 December 2007.[250] In this respect, the EU fulfilled the ambition to include Lithuania in the first group of new Member States to participate fully in the Schengen *acquis*—as expressed in Declaration No. 12 to the Treaty of Accession.

Article 3 of Protocol No. 5 to the Treaty of Accession stipulates that any further decisions concerning the transit of persons between Kaliningrad and other parts of Russia can only be taken on the basis of a unanimous Council decision on a proposal from the Commission.[251] Clearly, changes to the current arrangement might provoke important

---

[248] Pursuant to the compromise reached in November 2002, an internal Russian passport was sufficient before 1 January 2005 (cf. *supra* Part IV, § 5.3.).

[249] Statistical data for the period between 2003–2005: European Commission Report on the functioning of the facilitated transit for persons between the Kaliningrad region and the rest of the Russian Federation, COM (2006) 840 final, 22 December 2006, p. 5. For the year 2006, the information has been obtained from Antanas Muralis, Lithuanian Ministry of Foreign Affairs (e-mail correspondance, on file with the author).

[250] Pursuant to Art. 3 (2) of the Act of Accession, Lithuania's full integration into the Schengen area depends upon a unanimous Council Decision of the participating Member States. This Decision was adopted on 6 December 2007 and provided for the abolition of all internal border controls at land and sea borders from 21 December 2007 onwards. See: Council Decision 2007/801 EC on the full application of the provisions of the Schengen *acquis* in the Czech Republic, the Republic of Estonia, the Republic of Latvia, the Republic of Lithuania, the Republic of Hungary, the Republic of Malta, the Republic of Poland, the Republic of Slovenia and the Slovak Republic, *OJ* (2007) L 323/34.

[251] Protocol No. 5 to the 2003 Treaty of Accession on the transit of persons by land between the region of Kaliningrad and other parts of the Russian Federation, *OJ* (2003) L 236/946.

legal and political discussions within the enlarged European Union. An additional problem concerns the prospect of visa free transit by high-speed non-stop trains. The feasibility study, which formed part of the Kaliningrad compromise, revealed that the cost of the necessary infrastructure works would hardly be justifiable from an economic point of view.[252] Accordingly, it seems that the idea to transform Kaliningrad into a 'pilot region' for visa-free movement is not a short-term option, particularly because the Common Spaces' road maps do not include any reference to such a scenario and no specific rules on Kaliningrad have been provided in the EC-Russia agreement on visa facilitation. The latter observation might indicate that, notwithstanding the ambitious statements in the 1999 Medium-Term Strategy, the Russian Federation is not very keen to give any special status to Kaliningrad in its relations with the EU, mainly because of a fear of secessionist trends. On the other hand, the Kaliningrad issue has been instrumental to trigger discussions on EU-Russia relations in general. The idea of reciprocal visa-free travel as a long-term perspective within the Common Space of Freedom, Security and Justice, has, for instance, entered the EU-Russia agenda in the context of the Kaliningrad discussions on transit of persons.[253] A similar remark can be made regarding the prospect of a free trade area (cf. *supra*). For the time being, however, visa-free travel does not appear to be a realistic solution to the transit question.

Given the absence of potential alternatives such as high-speed non-stop trains and the cumbersome procedure to change the existing rules, the continuation of the *status quo* is the only reasonable option. The Council Regulations establishing the FTD/FRTD scheme are part of the Schengen *acquis*.[254] Significantly, the Regulation on the uniform format for FTD/FRTD has been included in the list of provisions and acts covered by Article 3 (1) of the Act of Accession. This means that

---

[252] The estimated cost for upgrading the existing infrastructure or the construction of new lines would be between € 350 and 500 million. See: Feasibility Study on High-Speed Non-Stop Trains. Final Report, European Commission, DG Enlargement, 153 p. This high cost explains why the December 2006 Commission report remains silent on this option. See: COM (2006) 840 final.

[253] P. Joenniemi, "Responding to Russia's Kaliningrad Offensive", in: H.M. Bircken-bach, C. Wellmann, (eds.), *The Kaliningrad Challenge. Options and Recommendations*, Hamburg, Lit, 2003, p. 50.

[254] Recital 14 and 11 of Regulation 693/2003 and 694/2003 respectively, *OJ* (2003) L 99/9 and L 99/16. Denmark, the United Kingdom and Ireland are not bound by the Regulations whereas its provisions are applicable to the non-EU Schengen associates Iceland and Norway.

it is binding on and applicable in the new Member States as from the date of Accession. Regulation 693/2003 establishing the FTD/FRTD and amending the Common Consular Instructions and the Common Manual, on the other hand, has not been included in this list. While binding on all Member States, this implies that it only became applicable following Council Decision 2007/801 EC.[255] This Decision, however, does not require a revision of the existing Kaliningrad transit procedures because the FTD/FRTD have a legal status equivalent to Schengen transit visa[256] and, subject to the rules set out in Regulation 693/2003, the provisions of the Schengen *acquis* relating to visas also apply to the FTD/FRTD. Hence, Lithuania's full participation in the Schengen area, including the removal of internal border controls, does not necessarily require a revision of the existing procedures.[257] In other words, a continuation of the FTD/FRTD scheme is legally possible and politically advisable.

It is noteworthy that the prolongation of the facilitated travel mechanism requires a continued financial effort on the part of the EU, in line with the commitments included in Protocol No. 5 to the Act of Accession.[258] Apart from the € 12 million implemented under the PHARE programme in the period between December 2003 and April 2004, another € 40 million has been covered under a Special Kaliningrad Transit Programme between 1 May 2004 and 31 December 2006. In the framework of the 2007–2013 financial perspectives, a maximum amount of € 108 million has been earmarked under a specific "Kaliningrad Transit Scheme".[259] This is the price to be paid for the flexible solution at the EU's external border between Lithuania and Russia.

---

[255] *OJ* (2007) L 323/34.

[256] Article 3 Regulation 693/2003.

[257] This point of view is confirmed by the Commission in its December 2006 assessment report on Kaliningrad transit, COM (2006) 840 final, p. 6.

[258] According to this Protocol, the European Community bears "any additional costs" incurred by implementing the facilitated transit regime between Kaliningrad and mainland Russia (cf. *supra*).

[259] COM (2006) 840 final, p. 4.

CHAPTER THREE

THE ROLE OF THE BALTIC STATES IN THE EU'S RELATIONS WITH RUSSIA

The question of Kaliningrad transit clearly illustrates the particular role of Lithuania in the development of EU-Russia relations. In combination with the regular tensions between Moscow and Estonia and Latvia regarding the treatment of Russian-speaking minorities or the conclusion of border agreements, it is obvious that EU membership of the Baltic States adds a new dimension to the EU-Russia relationship. The fear exists that Estonia, Latvia and Lithuania will bring their frictions with Russia into the EU, which could negatively impact the entire EU-Russia Strategic Partnership. On the other hand, voices have been raised that EU enlargement forms a unique opportunity to resolve the outstanding issues because one of the root causes of distrust, i.e. the Baltic security dilemma, has largely been overcome.[260] Within the new political and legal context after enlargement, the main challenge for the Baltic States is, therefore, to find a balance between the deep-seated historical preoccupations *vis-à-vis* Russia, on the one hand, and the need for pragmatic co-operation on the other.

§ 1. *The Legacy of the Soviet Period*

1.1. *A Continuous Challenge for the Baltic States*

More than fifteen years after the restoration of their independence, the Soviet past remains a 'hot topic' with significant political and legal implications in each of the Baltic States. Apart from the demographic and geographic challenges, discussed above, the application of restrictions to former communist party members or secret service collaborators on the basis of so-called "lustration laws"[261] raises interesting legal

---

[260] A. Kasekamp, "Baltic EU Membership: A Stabilising Factor in Relations with Russia", in: Wilhelmsen, (ed.), *Putin's Russia. Strategic Westernisation?*, Oslo, Norwegian Institute of International Affairs, 2004, p. 55.

[261] Lustration in this context concerns the regulation of persons' activities because of their involvement with the Communist regime. For comments, see: N. Letki, "Lustration

questions. In Lithuania, for instance, the "law on the evaluation of the USSR State Security Committee and the present activities of former permanent employees of the organization", which was enacted on 16 July 1998, bans former KGB employees from being employed in a wide range of public and private sector institutions until 1 January 2009.[262] In 2004 and 2005, the European Court of Human Rights found that the employment restrictions in private institutions violate Article 14 (prohibition of discrimination) and 8 (right to respect to private life) of the European Convention on the Protection of Human Rights and Fundamental Freedoms.[263] Notwithstanding the legitimacy of the aims pursued by the law—i.e. the protection of the state's national security—the wide scope of the restrictions, together with the fact that the KGB Act only entered into force a decade after the restoration of Lithuania's independence and the applicants' departure from the KGB, contributed to the overall assessment of the measures as being disproportionate and thus discriminatory.[264] In 2007, the KGB Act still had to be amended in order to remove the restrictions on employment in the private sector. The Lithuanian legislation on this point is, in other words, not in compliance with the European Convention on the Protection of Human Rights and *mutatis mutandis* Article 6 (2) EU. The reluctance of the Lithuanian Parliament to rectify this situation illustrates the sensitivity of the debates.

A more or less comparable discussion is taking place in Latvia. In order to protect the state's democratic order, independence and national security, Article 5 (6) of the Parliamentary Election Law and Article 9 (5) of the Municipal Election Law prohibit the inclusion in the candidate lists of persons that "belong or have belonged to the

---

and Democratisation in East-Central Europe", 54 *East-Asia Studies* 4 (2002), pp. 529–552; D. Robertson, "A Problem of their Own, Solutions of their Own: CEE Jurisdictions and the Problems of Lustration and Retroactivity", in: W. Sadurski, A. Czarnota, M. Krygier, (eds.), *Spreading Democracy and the Rule of Law? The Impact of EU Enlargement on the Rule of Law, Democracy and Constitutionalism in Post-Communist Legal Orders*, Dordrecht, Springer, 2006, pp. 73–96.

[262] The list includes nearly all jobs in state institutions as well as posts in banks and credit unions, companies providing detective or security services, communication enterprises, schools, etc. The persons concerned can also not work as lawyers or notaries nor can they perform "a job requiring a weapon".

[263] ECtHR, Judgment of 27 July 2004, *Sidabras and Dziautas* v. *Lithuania*, 55480/00 and 59330/00; Judgment of 7 April 2005, *Rainys and Gasparavicius* v. *Lithuania*, 70665/01 and 74345/01.

[264] ECtHR *Sidabras and Dziautas* v. *Lithuania*, at para. 60; *Rainys and Gasparavicius* v. *Lithuania*, at para. 36.

salaried staff of the USSR, Latvian SSR or foreign state security, intelligence or counterintelligence services".[265] Those restrictions, introduced in 1995, significantly limited the political rights of Tatjana Zdanoka, a former member of the Latvian Communist Party. On the grounds of her participation in the Communist Party's activities, Zdanoka lost her seat in the Riga City Council and was barred from participation in the 1998 and 2002 parliamentary elections.[266] The Latvian Constitutional Court confirmed the legitimacy of the restrictions but also concluded that they "may only exist for a specific period".[267] Zdanoka then brought the case before the European Court of Human Rights.

The First Section of the ECtHR concluded in June 2004 that the strict application of the Latvian election law was not proportionate to the legitimate aims which it pursued and, therefore, infringed Article 3 of Protocol No. 1 (right to stand for election) as well as Article 11 (freedom of assembly) of the ECHR.[268] The Court *inter alia* stipulated that the "duty of loyalty to the state" imposed on parliamentarians cannot be similar to that required of members of the public service[269] and took into account the applicant's individual conduct as well as the observation that the disputed restriction was only inserted in 1995 but did not exist for previous elections.[270] Less than two years later, however, the Grand Chamber of the ECtHR came to an entirely different conclusion. Contrary to the arguments of the Court's First Section, the fact that the applicant was never prosecuted for a criminal offence and the late adoption of the impugned statutory measures were not deemed to be of fundamental importance for the proportionality test.[271]

---

[265] The English translation of these texts of these laws is available at http://www.minelres.lv/NationalLegislation/Latvia/latvia.htm.

[266] Significantly, Mrs. Zdanoka was also unable to take part in the Parliamentary elections of 1993 and 1995 as well in the municipal elections of 1994 because the Latvian authorities refused to include her on the residents' register as a Latvian citizen. Only in 1996, a Latvian Court recognised her as holding Latvian nationality on the ground of being a descendent of a person who had possessed Latvian nationality before 1940. See: ECtHR (Grand Chamber), Judgment of 16 March 2006, *Zdanoka* v. *Latvia*, Application No. 58278/00, at para. 30.

[267] Case No. 2000–03–01 of the Constitutional Court of the Republic of Latvia, Riga, 30 Aug. 2000, at http://www.satv.tiesa.gov.lv/Eng/spriedum.htm.

[268] ECtHR (First Section), Judgment of 17 June 2004, *Zdanoka* v. *Latvia*, Application No. 58278/00.

[269] *Ibid.* at para. 85.

[270] *Ibid.* at para. 95–96.

[271] ECtHR (Grand Chamber), Judgment of 16 March 2006, *Zdanoka* v. *Latvia*, Application No. 58278/00, at para. 129–131.

The Grand Chamber of the ECtHR rather referred to the historical and political circumstances which gave rise to the enactment of the law in Latvia to conclude that restrictions as applied to the applicant were not arbitrary nor disproportional.[272] In line with the judgment of the Latvian Constitutional Court, the Grand Chamber also observed that the restrictions cannot be applied indefinitely. It is up to the Latvian Parliament to "keep the statutory restriction under constant review, with a view to bringing it to an early end".[273] Arguably, Latvia's greater stability as a result of accession to the EU constitutes a factor to be reckoned with in the assessment of the election legislation.

In February 2004, with the Court case still pending, the Latvian Parliament decided not to impose restrictions on former members of the Communist Party in the 2004 European Parliament elections, allowing the participation and election of Tatjana Zdanoka. With regard to the municipal and parliamentary elections, however, the restrictions are still in force. It is noteworthy that already in August 2000 three judges of the Latvian Constitutional Court—out of seven—stressed in their dissenting opinion that the Latvian democratic system is sufficiently stable to allow the abolition of the political restrictions for taking part in the elections.[274] A similar view can be found in the conclusions of the OSCE Election Observation Missions to the October 2002 and 2006 parliamentary elections.[275] For the time being, however, the Latvian Parliament does not seem to revise the restrictions to the political activities of former Communist Party members at the municipal or national level. In June 2006, the Latvian Constitutional Court confirmed the legitimacy of the election legislation in general but clarified that the individual conduct of each person has to be taken into account.[276]

---

[272] *Ibid.* at para. 132–134.

[273] *Ibid.* at para. 135.

[274] Dissenting Opinions of the Constitutional Court Judges Aivars Endzins, Juris Jelagins and Anita Usacka in case No. 2000–03–01, at: http://www.satv.tiesa.gov.lv/Eng/spriedum.htm.

[275] The Conclusions of the Election Observation Missions in Latvia are available at: http://www.osce.org/odihr-elections/documents.html?lsi=true&limit=10&grp=2 15./.

[276] In particular, the Court refers to the violent events of January 1991, "when the people in Latvia made their choice about on what 'side of the barricades' to stand" to assess the situation of each individual. Case No. 2005–13–0106 of the Constitutional Court of the Republic of Latvia, Riga, 15 June 2006 at http://www.satv.tiesa.gov .lv/Eng/spriedum.htm, at para. 20. It is noteworthy that in April 2007, the vice mayor of Ludza, a small town in eastern Latvia, was found to be an active member of the Communist Party of the Soviet Union and the Latvian Communist Party after January

The examples of the Lithuanian and Latvian cases before the ECtHR clearly illustrate the continuous challenges related to the Baltic States' transition from Soviet republics to EU Member States. In this respect, it is striking that the European Commission's pre-accession monitoring reports remained completely silent on the restrictions imposed on former Communist Party members or secret service collaborators. Of course, the ECtHR only concluded its judgments after the date of accession but at least a reference to the Constitutional Court cases or an announcement of the procedures before the ECtHR could have been expected. Apparently, the EU did not want to become engaged in domestic issues related to the legacy of the Soviet past. It is, however, difficult if not impossible to avoid this topic. On the one hand, respect for the European Convention of Human Rights is one of the foundational values of the European Union (Art. 6 (2) EU). On the other hand, the Soviet past largely determines the Baltic States' relations with the EU's strategic partner, Russia.

Apart from the legal questions related to the principle of state continuity and its consequences (cf. *supra* Part I), political and symbolical issues such as the removal of Soviet era monuments often create bilateral tensions. The Estonian War Graves Protection Act, for instance, adopted on 10 January 2007,[277] raised fierce reactions in Russia.[278] On the basis of this Act, the government removed a Soviet war grave monument, known as "the Bronze Soldier", from a park in downtown Tallinn to a military cemetery. For Russia and the Estonian Russian-speaking population, this decision illustrates a lack of respect for the

---

1991. The vice mayor will now be banned from the candidate lists in the national parliamentary elections. See: X, "Vice mayor guilty of Communist cooperation", *The Baltic Times*, 13 April 2007.

[277] See: http://www.president.ee/en/duties/press_releases.php?gid=87267; RT I 2007, 4, 21 (available in English at: http://www.legaltext.ee).

[278] Some Russian politicians even demanded economic sanctions on Estonia. See: X, "Bronze Statue fight escalating in Estonia", *Baltic Times*, 25 January 2007. Whereas Foreign Minister Lavrov dismissed the option of economic sanctions, he nevertheless stated that "we must react to the attempt by the government of Estonia to push a law through parliament that would desecrate the memory of those who fought against fascism. Our reaction must be tough, firm, directed towards the mobilization of public opinion, the political position of the European countries in the first place in order to prevent such a blasphemous approach to the memory of the fighters against fascism". Transcript of replies to Russian Media Questions by Minister of Foreign Affais Sergey Lavrov, at: http://www.ln.mid.ru, 27 January 2007.

Red Army soldiers that fought against Nazi Germany[279] whereas the monument is a symbol of the Soviet occupation for the native Estonian population.[280] Whereas this example might appear somewhat artificial, the statue controversy symbolises the conflict between the Baltic States and Russia over the post-World War II history, which determines the relations between those countries. Hence, the question arises as to what extent the Soviet legacy influences the EU's relations with Russia after enlargement.

1.2. *A New Challenge on the EU-Russia Agenda*

Already in 2002, Toomas Hendrik Ilves—former Estonian Foreign Minister, Member of the European Parliament and currently President of Estonia—announced a "less naïve" policy in comparison to the old Member States.[281] In particular, the perception that economic interests formed the primary motivation for the EU's relations with Russia has been criticized. His successor in the Ministry of Foreign Affairs, Kristina Ojuland, also warned that "common values and democratic standards should not be sacrificed for economic gains".[282] Her Latvian counterpart, Sandra Kalniete, echoed a similar vision when she insisted that "values not trade are the cornerstone of [the EU's] relationship with Russia".[283] The preference for a strict, value-based approach opposing the often pragmatic and economically motivated position of the old

---

[279] The dispute concerning the removal of the Bronze Soldier comes after the discussions surrounding a monument in the Estonian town Lihula. The Lihula monument, depicting an Estonian soldier in a World War II German uniform, was unveiled on 20 August 2004 in tribute to "Estonian men who fought in 1940–1945 against Bolshevism and for the restoration of Estonian independence". After strong international protests, the Estonian government ordered the removal of the monument to a private museum in Lagedi, near Tallinn. M. Kolb, "Looking for the truth behind Lihula", *Baltic Times*, 27 April 2005.

[280] It is noteworthy that the Council of Europe Secretary General, Terry Davis, called upon the Estonian government to "treat fallen soldiers with dignity and respect". See: http://www.coe.int/T/dc/Press/NoteRedac2007/20070124_sg_memorialcont _en.asp.

[281] Kasekamp, Ehin, *op. cit.*, footnote 45, p. 218.

[282] Address by the Minister of Foreign Affairs Kristiina Ojuland at the event "Dialogue with a new Member State: Estonia" in Vienna, 28 September 2004, available at: http://www.vm.ee/eng/kat_140/4828.html.

[283] S. Kalniete, "EU Relations with Russia must focus on values, not trade", *Europe's World* 1 (2005), see: http://europesworld.link.be/europesworld/PDFs/EW1_1.3 _Kalniete_EU_Relations_with_Russia.pdf.

Member States is also reflected in the Estonian Government's EU policy document for 2004–2006.[284]

It is striking that Lithuanian official documents generally adopt a slightly different discourse. The Lithuanian governmental and parliamentary foreign policy papers do not include references to 'values' but mainly emphasize the necessity to protect Lithuania's national interests in the development of a "mutually beneficial partnership between the EU and Russia".[285] In this respect, President Adamkus underlined the importance of trade relations within an "open dialogue of equal partners".[286] The better atmosphere of Lithuanian-Russian relations, due to the absence of minority or border disputes, as well as the comparatively higher significance of bilateral trade,[287] could explain this differentiation among the Baltic States. In this context, it also has to be mentioned that Russia has always adopted a more favourable position towards Lithuania than to the other Baltic republics. As a 'political reward' for its more liberal citizenship policy, Moscow started the withdrawal of Russian troops from Lithuanian territory already in 1993, i.e. one year before an agreement on this question was achieved with Estonia and Latvia, and in October 1997 presidents Brazauskas and Yeltsin signed the first

---

[284] Whereas it is noteworthy that this almost 40 pages long document attributes only a single paragraph to relations with Russia, the clear statement that "the partnership between the European Union and Russia must be based on common values" and references to "the development of the rule of law and democracy in Russia" illustrate this position. http://www.riigikantselei.ee/failid/The_Government_s_European_Policy _for_2004_2006_FINAL.pdf.

[285] See: Programme of the Government of the Republic of Lithuania for 2004–2008 (Foreign Policy Chapter); Agreement between Political Parties of the Republic of Lithuania on the Main Foreign Policy Goals and Objectives for 2004–2008, 5 October 2004; *Seimas* Resolution on Directions in Foreign Policy of the Republic of Lithuania following Lithuania's accession to Nato and the European Union, 1 May 2004. All documents are available at the website of the Lithuanian Ministry of Foreign Affairs: http://www.urm.lt.

[286] Address by H.E. Mr. Valdas Adamkus, President of the Republic of Lithuania to the Heads of Foreign Diplomatic Missions in Lithuania, http://www.urm.lt/popup2 .php?item_id=8497.

[287] Lithuania has a higher volume of foreign trade with Russia than its Baltic neighbours. In 2003, Russia was responsible for 8.9 per cent of Lithuania's exports and 22.7 per cent of imports. With Latvia and Estonia these figures are significantly lower: 5.4 per cent of Latvian exports and 8.7 per cent of imports; 3.9 per cent of Estonian exports and 8.6 per cent of imports. See: A. Purju, "Foreign Trade Between the Baltic States and Russia: Trends, Institutional Settings and Impact of EU Enlargement", *Turku School of Economics and Business Administration Working Papers*, 2004, available at: http://www.tukkk.fi/pei.

border agreement between Russia and a former Soviet republic.[288] The relative stability of Lithuanian-Russian relations is further illustrated through Russia's moderate reaction to Lithuania's claims for compensation for the period of Soviet occupation or to the decision in 1999 to sell the Mazeikiai oil refinery to the American company Williams rather than to the Russian contender Lukoil on purely political grounds. According to Arkady Moshes, "it is quite probable that, had similar legislation been passed in Latvia or Estonia, Russia's reaction would have been much stronger".[289] Arguably, the general satisfaction regarding the implementation of the FTD/FRTD scheme on transit of persons between Kaliningrad and the rest of Russia only confirms Lithuania's status as Russia's preferential partner in the Baltic region.

Notwithstanding the differentiation of the Baltic States' relations with Russia, recognition of the so-called 'historical heritage issue'—i.e. the Soviet annexation of the Baltic republics and its socio-economic, political and legal consequences—forms a common interest of the three new Member States. The sensitivity of this question has been illustrated in the framework of the 60th anniversary of the allied victory over Nazi Germany on 9 May 2005 (cf. *supra*). On this occasion, Baltic representatives started a lobbying campaign to raise the issue of the occupation of the Baltic States by the Soviet Union inside the EU. Within the European Parliament, the 'Baltic Europe Intergroup' actively promoted the inclusion of specific references to this question in a resolution on the end of the Second World War.[290] The statement that "for some nations the end of World War II meant renewed tyranny inflicted by the Stalinist Soviet Union" as well as the provision that "there cannot be reconciliation without truth and remembrance" implicitly referred

---

[288] P. Ehin, P. Willerton, "Baltic Diversity and Russian Power Interests: Policy Differentiation in an era of Change", 25 *The Soviet and Post-Soviet Review* (1998) 3, p. 260.

[289] A. Moshes, "The Double Enlargement, Russia and the Baltic States", *DUPI Working Paper* 4 (2002), p. 6; available at: http://www.dupi.dk/webtxt/http://www.dupi.dk/webdocs/wp200204.pdf.

[290] The Baltic Europe Intergroup was established at the outset of the 2004–2009 Parliamentary term and includes some forty MEPs, representing five mainstream political groups and coming from Finland, Sweden, Denmark, Britain, Germany, Lithuania, Latvia and Estonia. The main aim of the Baltic Europe Intergroup is to raise the profile of the Baltic Sea Region within the enlarged EU. For this reason a "Strategy for the Baltic Sea Region" has been drafted. See: http://www.hanse-parlament.de/Downloads/EuropeStrategyBSR.pdf.

to the Baltic case.[291] It is remarkable that a US Senate resolution passed in the same period is much more explicit in the sense that it urged Russia to "issue a clear and unambiguous statement of admission and condemnation of the illegal occupation and annexation by the Soviet Union from 1940 to 1991 of the Baltic countries of Estonia, Latvia and Lithuania".[292] In combination with President Bush's public support for the Baltic case,[293] the straightforward position of the United States contrasts with the more reserved statements of the European Parliament, and in particular the European Commission and certain EU Member States. It is, for instance, a public secret that countries such as France, Germany and Italy oppose antagonizing Russia.

The different positions of the various EU actors became obvious in the discussions surrounding the general assessment of EU-Russia relations, which was instructed by the December 2003 Brussels European Council.[294] In this context, the European Parliament Committee on Foreign Affairs prepared a report which *inter alia* tackled "the occupation and subsequent annexation and tyranny of the Soviet Union" and considered the "full recognition of these facts by Russia as a basis for comprehensive reconciliation between Russia and all member countries of the EU".[295] During the parliamentary debates, several Baltic MEPs highlighted the importance of this issue. The response of Commissioner Ferrero-Waldner that it is up to historians to clarify the past and that the EU's priority must be to look to the future revealed a more pragmatic position of the European Commission.[296] This approach raised frustrations among prominent Baltic representatives. Vytautas Landsbergis, for instance, openly criticized the Commission's reluctance to raise the

---

[291] European Parliament resolution on the sixtieth anniversary of the end of the Second War in Europe on 8 May 1945, B6–0290/2005, 12 May 2005.

[292] Senate Concurrent Resolution 35, available at: http://www.govtrack.us/congress/bill.xpd?bill=sc109–35. [A concurrent resolution is a legislative proposal that must be passed by the House and Senate but does not require the signature of the President and does not have the force of law].

[293] In his speech delivered in Riga on 7 May 2005, President Bush explicitly referred to the Soviet occupation of the Baltic States, which raised criticisms in Russia. The text of the speech is available at: http://www.whitehouse.gov/news/releases/2005/05/20050507–8.html.

[294] Presidency Conclusions Brussels European Council (12 December 2003), *Bull. EU* 12 (2003), I.24.67.

[295] European Parliament Report on EU-Russia relations, Committee on Foreign Affairs (rapporteur: Cecilia Malmström), A6–0135/2005, 4 May 2005.

[296] Debates of the European Parliament, 25 May 2005.

Soviet history in relations with Russia.[297] It is indeed striking that the European Parliament adopts a much more straightforward position on this question.

The final European Parliament resolution on EU-Russia relations[298] can be considered to be completely in line with the foreign policy agenda of the Baltic countries. First, the preamble to the resolution equates the criminalities of the Nazi regime with that of the Soviet Union. Second, the resolution seeks Russia's recognition of the occupation of the Baltic States. Third, the text calls for a stronger EU position regarding the rule of law in Russia and concerning Russia's power politics in the former Soviet republics and in Chechnya. Fourth, the European Parliament calls upon the Commission and the Council to show solidarity and unity in the event of Russian attempts to drive a wedge between certain old and new Member States. Fifth, the European Parliament resolution touches upon specific problems in the relations between the Baltic States and Russia such as (i) the application of discriminatory tariffs favouring Russian ports in the Baltic Sea area, (ii) the request to delete the reference to the Baltic States in Russia's social security legislation as an area where the Russian military may be deployed and (iii) the ratification of border agreements with Estonia and Latvia, which was considered as a prerequisite for the signing of an EC-Russia visa facilitation agreement.

The Baltic pressure for a more value-based approach and the consistent references to the historical heritage of the Soviet period have clearly found their way into the European Parliament whereas the Commission and the Council appear to opt for a more pragmatic approach in EU-Russia relations, as is clearly illustrated by the parallel conclusion of the visa facilitation and readmission agreements[299] or the reluctance within the latter institutions to discuss the question of the Baltic States' occupation. Accordingly, the various positions on how to

---

[297] See e.g. the parliamentary question of Vytautas Landsbergis on the importance of Europe's past in a bid to live in the present and lay the foundations for our future by having recourse to truth, not 'opinions', H-0428/05, 9 June 2005.

[298] European Parliament Resolution on EU-Russia relations, 2004/2170(INI), 26 May 2005.

[299] Both agreements have been signed in the framework of the May 2006 Sochi EU-Russia summit and entered into force on 1 June 2007; *OJ* (2007) L 157/37 and L 173/34. It is noteworthy that the EC-Russia readmission agreement replaces the bilateral Lithuanian-Russian readmission agreement concluded in the framework of the Kaliningrad transit compromise (cf. *supra*).

deal with Russia form one of the major challenges for the enlarged EU. In particular, there is a risk of a new dividing line between the old and new Member States on this question. The French-German proposal to gradually establish a visa-free travel regime with Russia, for instance, inspired the Estonian government to include in its EU policy Action Plan that agreements on visa-free travel can only be based on the unconditional fulfilment of objective criteria including effective control of external borders, secure travel documents, existence of a readmission agreement and control over illegal immigration.[300]

Another example of the difference in attitudes between new and old Member States concerns the EU's relations *vis-à-vis* Russia's neighbours. In the aftermath of the coloured revolutions in Ukraine and Georgia, Baltic representatives felt disappointed about the cautious reaction of the old Member States in an attempt not to defy Russia. In this respect, Toomas Hendrik Ilves described the position of the EU15 as "a naïve appeasement policy [...], based on lack of knowledge or the pursuit of narrow national agendas rather than based on the interests of the Union as whole".[301] The agreement between Russia's state-owned gas company *Gazprom* and the German consortium BASF-E.ON-Ruhrgas on the construction of a gas pipeline bypassing the Baltic States and Poland only confirmed the perception that the old Member States pursue their own bilateral agenda. According to the Lithuanian President, Valdas Adamkus, the deal concluded between Russian President Putin and former German Chancellor Schroeder illustrated the lack of solidarity and consensus between EU Member States.[302] The Polish Defence Minister, Radek Sikorski, even referred to a new "Molotov-Ribbentrop Pact".[303] The Baltic and Polish representatives fear an increased dependency from Russia as well as the environmental consequences of the project for the Baltic Sea Region.[304] The EU, however, considers the construction of the Northern European gas pipeline, which is part of the Trans-European

---

[300] http://www.riigikantselei.ee/failid/The_Government_s_European_Policy_for _2004_2006_FINAL.pdf.

[301] T.H. Ilves, 'The Pleiades Join the Stars: Transatlanticism and Eastern Enlargement', 18 *Cambridge Review of International Affairs* 2 (2005), p. 197.

[302] X, "Lithuanian leader faults EU over new gas pipeline", *International Herald Tribune*, 27 October 2005.

[303] X, "Gas Pipeline Triggers New Backlash", *Baltic Times*, 3 May 2006.

[304] F. Cameron, "The Nord Stream Gas Pipeline Project and its Strategic Implications", European Parliament Briefing Note, http://www.europarl.europa.eu/meetdocs/ 2004_2009/documents/dv/703/703356/703356en.pdf.

Energy Networks,[305] as a private business project.[306] In this respect, it is noteworthy that the European Commission has announced inquiries concerning state aid offered by the German government.[307] Be that as it may, it is obvious that the pipeline project has aroused frustration in the Baltic countries.

Russia, for its part, seems not very satisfied with the Baltic States' contributions to the EU's policy and heavily criticizes the so-called "phantom pains of the past".[308] Whereas Baltic representatives tend to interpret Russia's reaction as a strategy to divide the old and new Member States, the Baltic countries—and Poland—are sometimes perceived as Russophobic troublemakers and unreliable partners.[309] As a result, there is a risk that EU-Russian relations will be essentially determined on the basis of special relations between Putin and the leaders of major EU Member States. The Common Spaces concept, which originates from a French-German non-paper discussed with Russia in the context of the Iraq crisis, clearly illustrates the importance of such informal decision-making outside the formal PCA or CFSP structures. On the other hand, the fear to become marginalized within the EU has inspired the Baltic States to adopt a rather low profile in shaping the EU's Russia policy.[310]

The adoption of the Common Spaces' road maps as well as the recent conclusion of bilateral agreements between the EC and Russia on various issues such as veterinary certification for the export of animal products, trade in steel products, readmission and visa facilitation

---

[305] Decision 1229/2003/EC of the European Parliament and the Council of 26 June 2003 laying down a series of guidelines for trans-European energy networks and repealing Decision No. 1254/96/EC, *OJ* (2003) L 176/11.

[306] See: Answer to parliamentary question H-0144/06 by Aloyzas Sakalas concerning the agreement between Germany and Russia on the construction of a gas pipeline under the Baltic Sea, available at: http://www.europarl.europa.eu. Commissioner Piebalgs also defended the Nord Stream project as a private undertaking in a public hearing taking place in the European Parliament on 29 January 2008. See: R. Goldirova, "EU defends controversial Baltic gas pipeline", www.euobserver.com, 30 January 2008.

[307] H. Spongenberg, "EU queries state aid in German-Russian gas deal", www.euobserver.com, 9 May 2006.

[308] G. Parker, "Russia says new Member States damaging EU relationship", *Financial Times*, 21 May 2006.

[309] V. Kononenko, "Normal neighbours or trouble-makers? The Baltic States in the Context of Russia-EU Relations", in: A. Kasekamp, (ed.), *Estonian Foreign Policy Yearbook 2006*, Tallinn, Estonian Foreign Policy Institute, 2006, p. 83.

[310] Raik, Palosaari, *op. cit.*, footnote 22, p. 34.

reveals that the EU accession of the Baltic States has not resulted in a legal deadlock of EU-Russia relations. It can, therefore, be concluded that the political tensions between the Baltic States and Russia do not seem to undermine the further deepening of the EU-Russia Strategic Partnership. Of course, the conclusion of a new framework agreement, replacing the PCA, will be a significant test case for the EU-Russia Strategic Partnership. The negotiations of such an agreement promise to be very difficult not only because of the issues under discussion but also because of the new political circumstances in both the EU and Russia. In comparison to the situation in the first half of the 1990s, the time of negotiations on the PCA, Russia has developed from a passive observer into an assertive partner actively defending its national interests in a pragmatic way. On the EU side, the enlargement to 27 Member States has obviously complicated the drafting of new agreements requiring unanimity in the Council. The delay in the opening of the negotiations as a result of a Polish veto in response to Russia's ban on the import of Polish meat (cf. *supra*) already formed a first illustration of the difficulties in finding a common EU position. Moreover, the ambition to include a wide range of issues exceeding the EC's exclusive competences implies that a new bilateral framework agreement with Russia will almost necessarily be a mixed agreement. This has important consequences for the ratification process, since all Member States' parliaments have to ratify such agreement before it can enter into force. In other words, the Baltic States have—at least formally—an important role to play in the establishment of a new contractual relationship with Russia. It is, therefore, not inconceivable that the 'historic heritage issue' will be brought up during the discussions. On the other hand, the interest in a stable legal framework for EU-Russia relations, as well as pragmatic considerations of an economic and political nature, seem to undermine the hypothesis to present Russia's recognition of the Soviet occupation of the Baltic States as a condition for further progress.

§ 2. *The Question of Energy Security*

Notwithstanding the undeniable importance of Russia's responsibility for the Soviet Union's Baltic policy, there seems to be a growing understanding that this question should not undermine the pragmatic development of EU-Russia relations. Kestutis Paulauskas, for instance, concludes that:

Building relations with Moscow on the condition that Russia will redeem historical grievances is a naïve and counter-effective approach. Tallinn, Riga and Vilnius should concentrate instead on more everyday and pressing challenges [...].[311]

One of the most obvious challenges concerns the Baltic dependency on Russian energy supplies. The oil and gas imports from Russia range between 90 and 100 per cent.[312] The mandatory closure of the Ignalina Nuclear Power Plant as well as the forced restructuring of Estonia's oil shale sector (cf. *supra*) and the liberalisation of the energy companies in line with EU requirements further increases the vulnerability of the Baltic energy sector. Moreover, the Baltic States' electricity network is fully compatible with the Russian system but only since the end of 2006 there is a direct connection between Estonia and Finland (Estlink) whereas an electricity link between Lithuania and Poland is still under construction as part of the EU's investment in trans-European energy networks (TENs).[313] Simultaneously, Russia pursues a twofold strategy to reduce its own dependency upon the transit facilities of the Baltic countries after the demise of the Soviet Union. On the one hand, the construction of the new oil terminal in Primorsk and the project of the Northern European gas pipeline are clearly designed to avoid negotiating transit fees with Estonia, Latvia and Lithuania.[314] On the other hand, Russia's state-owned oil and gas companies, *Transneft* and *Gazprom*, are dominant players on the Baltic energy markets, which use their market power to gain control over energy supply. The decision of *Transneft* to re-route the transport of crude oil from the Latvian port of Ventspils to the Russian port of Primorsk or the refusal to sign an agreement with *Kazmunaigaz* on the import of oil from Kazakhstan

---

[311] K. Paulauskas, "The Baltics: From Nation States to Member States", *Institute For Security Studies, Occasional Paper* 62 (2006), p. 39.

[312] "Baltic Sea Region", The Energy Information Administration of the US Department of Energy, available at: http://www.eia.doe.gov/emeu/cabs/baltics.htm.

[313] See: Proposal for a Decision of the European Parliament and of the Council laying down guidelines for trans-European energy networks, COM (2003) 742 final, Brussels, 10 December 2003. On TENs in general, see: http://ec.europa.eu/ten/energy/index_en.htm.

[314] It has been calculated that the undersea gas pipeline between Russia and Germany costs three to four times as much as the alternative of a parallel pipeline through Poland and the Baltic States. Accordingly, the geostrategic importance of energy supplies seems to balance pure economic considerations. See: K. Smith, *Russian Energy Politics in the Baltics, Poland and Ukraine: A New Stealth Imperialism*, Washington, Center for Strategic and International Studies, 2005, p. 17.

to Lithuania are generally regarded as politically motivated moves to increase Russia's grip on the Baltic energy sector.[315] The most recent example of Russia's geopolitical power has been the termination of oil supplies to Lithuania's Mazeikiu Nafta refinery, officially as a result of technical problems at the Druzhba pipeline but according to Lithuanian officials as a countermeasure for the sale of the oil refinery to Poland's PKN Orlen instead of a Russian contender.[316]

The reaction of the Baltic States is based on a combination of increased regional co-operation and the integration of the Baltic energy policy into a wider EU strategy. Already in 1998 the three Baltic Ministers of Energy signed an agreement on co-operation in the energy sector. In 1999, the Baltic Council of Ministers approved a Baltic Energy Strategy, including a Memorandum of Joint Intentions on the creation of a Common Baltic Energy Market (CBEM).[317] A concrete consequence of this regional co-operation has been the decision to construct a new nuclear reactor in Lithuania by 2015, financed by the three Baltic national energy-providing companies (Lietuvos Energija AD, Eesti Energia and Latvenergo). Lithuanian representatives are looking for possibilities to keep the Ignalina NPP open until this date in order to avoid an increased dependency on Russian gas imports.[318] The question is, however, whether this option is legally possible in the light of Lithuania's obligations under the Treaty of Accession. Pursuant to Article 1 of Protocol No. 4, the Ignalina NPP has to be closed by 31 December 2009 but Article 4 of the same Protocol provides that:

---

[315] L. Mauring, D. Schaer, "The Effects of the Russian Energy Sector on the Security of the Baltic States", 8 *Baltic Security and Defence Review* (2006), p. 70; K. Smith, "Security Implications of Russian Energy Policies", *CEPS Policy Brief* 90 (2006), p. 2; H. Elletson, *Baltic Independence and Russian Foreign Energy Policy*, London, GMB, 2006, pp. 15–16; A. Spruds, "Latvian-Russian Energy Relations: Between Economics and Politics", in: N. Muiznieks, (ed.), *Latvian-Russian Relations:Domestic and International Dimensions*, Riga, University of Latvia, 2006, pp. 110–118.

[316] A similar problem of oil supply took place in 1999 when the oil refinery was sold to the American Company Williams instead of Russian investor Lukoil. On the recent problems, see: X, "Russia Halts Oil Supplies to Lithuania after Major Pipeline Leaks", *Moscow News*, 3 August 2006 and X, "Lithuania accuses Russia of Delaying Pipeline Repairs", *Moscow News*, 8 August 2006. Following the Polish example, Lithuania has threatened to veto the start of negotiations on a new EU-Russia framework agreement as long as the oil supply to the Mazeikiu refinery remains disrupted. See: X, "Lithuania threathens to block EU-Russia agreement", *www.euractiv.com*, 26 February 2007.

[317] X, "The Baltic States Say 'Yes' to Nuclear Energy", available at: http://www.euronuclear.org/e-news/e-news-12/baltic-states-print.htm.

[318] A. Rettman, "Lithuania may ask EU to extend nuclear shutdown deadline", www.euobserver.com, 23 February 2007.

> Without any prejudice to the provisions of Article 1, the general safeguard clause referred to in Article 37 of the Act of Accession shall apply until 31 December 2012 if energy supply is disrupted in Lithuania.[319]

The scope of the latter provision is rather ambiguous. Paragraph 1 of Article 37 AA allows new Member States to apply for authorisation to take special measures "until the end of a period of up to three years after accession", i.e. 1 May 2007. Paragraph 3 clarifies that measures authorised on this legal basis may involve derogations from the rules of the EC Treaty and the Act of Accession "to such an extent and for such periods as strictly necessary" for the attainment of its objectives.[320] It is not very clear whether the date of 31 December 2012 mentioned in Article 4 of Protocol No. 4 refers to the deadline for requesting the safeguard measures, in contravention to paragraph 1 of Article 37 AA, or, to the deadline for the application of the safeguard measures, in contravention to paragraph 3 of Article 37 AA. Only the interpretation that the safeguard clause can be invoked until the end of 2012 and that the measures adopted in this respect can apply without any concrete deadline could justify the adoption of safeguard measures until the year 2015. Significantly, the Commission determines the conditions and modalities of the safeguard measures.[321] Given the Commission's insistence on the swift closure of the Chernobyl-type of nuclear reactors, it is far from certain that a request for the application of Article 37 AA will be accepted.[322] Moreover, the safeguard clause may only apply "without any prejudice to the provisions of Article 1", which means that the deadline of 31 December 2009 cannot be extended on the basis of Art. 37 AA. Given the primary legal status of the Accession Treaty, a renegotiation of this commitment would then require an agreement of all Member States in accordance to the procedure of Article 48 EU. In any event, it is obvious that the sensitive issue of energy

---

[319] *OJ* (2003) L 236/945.

[320] *OJ* (2003) L 236/45.

[321] Art. 37 (2) AA.

[322] See *supra*, Part IV, Chapter 2, § 4.2. Also after enlargement, the Commission confirmed its intention to support the swift closure of the old nuclear power plants. See e.g. the speech of Andris Piebalgs, Energy Commissioner, at the European Parliament Plenary Session, "20 years after Chernobyl: lessons for the future", Brussels, 26 April 2006, Speech/06/261. In a private correspondence with the author, the Commission services confirmed that Lithuania's obligation to close Unit 2 of the Ignalina NPP by 31 December 2009 "cannot be under negotiation any more". Letter of the European Commission, DG Energy and Transport, 3 May 2007. On file with the author.

supply and the mandatory closure of the Ignalina NPP remains a hot topic after the date of Lithuania's accession.

The Baltic countries agreed to adopt common positions in the EU and in particular with regard to the EU-Russia energy dialogue. In this respect, Estonia, Latvia and Lithuania pursue a legal approach based upon the principles of the European Energy Charter Treaty (ECT). This multilateral agreement, concluded among the 51 signatories of the 1991 European Energy Charter, establishes important rights and obligations in the energy field including rules on investments, transit, competition, taxation, environment, transfer of technology and access to capital markets.[323] Due to the broad scope of the agreement, both the European Communities and the Member States are parties.[324] Russia signed the ECT in December 1994 but the State Duma has not yet ratified the agreement.[325] Russian ratification would have important legal consequences for the EU in general and for the Baltic States in particular. It would subject the trade in Russian energy goods to GATT rules[326] and, most importantly, it would provide for the unimpeded transit of energy across Russian territory.[327] In practical terms, the ECT would give the EU access to oil and gas from Turkmenistan and Kazakhstan via the Russian pipeline network. This is a serious issue for Russia, which does not want to become an ordinary transit country. Russia's refusal to ratify the ECT has, in other words, a huge political

---

[323] The Energy Charter Treaty, *OJ* (1998) L 69/26. For comments, see: C. Bamberger, J. Linehan, T. Waelde, "The Energy Charter Treaty", in: M. Roggenkamp, (ed.), *Energy Law In Europe: National, EU and International Law and Institutions*, Oxford, Oxford University Press, 2001, pp. 171–212; E. Paasivirta, "The European Union and the Energy Sector: The Case of the Energy Charter Treaty", in: M. Koskenniemi, (ed.), *International Law Aspects of the European Union*, The Hague, Kluwer Law International, 1998, pp. 197–214; T. Waelde, (ed.), *The Energy Charter Treaty: An East-West Gateway for Investment and Trade*, London, Kluwer Law International, 1996, 700 p.

[324] The accession of the European Communities is based on a wide range of legal bases: Article 95 of the ECSC Treaty, Art. 54 (2), the last sentence of Art. 57 (2), Arts 66, 73c (2), 87, 99, 100a, 113, 130s (1) and 235, in conjunction with the second sentence of Art. 228 (2) and the second subparagraph of Art. 228 (3) EC Treaty [old numbering] and Art. 101 EAEC Treaty. See: Council and Commission Decision of 23 September 1997 on the conclusion, by the European Communities, of the Energy Charter Treaty and the Energy Charter Protocol on energy efficiency and related environmental aspects, *OJ* (1998) L 69/1.

[325] In accordance to Article 45 ECT, Russia provisionally applies the agreement "to the extent that such provisional application is not inconsistent with its constitution, laws or regulations".

[326] Art. 29 ECT.

[327] Art. 7 ECT.

significance because this could potentially affect the whole system of economic and political relations in the former Soviet territory.[328] The decision of *Gazprom* to disrupt the supply of gas to Ukraine in the beginning of 2006 clearly illustrated the geopolitical importance of the energy question. The latter dispute provided an opportunity for the Baltic countries to raise the need for a common EU energy policy. The March 2006 European Council, which launched an Energy Policy for Europe (EPE), formed an important step in this direction. On this occasion, the EU Member States agreed to develop "a common external policy approach in support of energy policy objectives".[329] From a legal point of view, the recognition of the external dimension of the EU's energy policy is highly significant as an example of the interconnection between the Community's competences under the first pillar[330] and the Common Foreign and Security Policy. Accordingly, the EPE requires the involvement of both the European Commission, the High Representative for the CFSP and the EU Member States.

Of particular importance for the Baltic States is the clear commitment to revitalise the EU-Russia energy dialogue in order to secure Russia's ratification of the ECT. At the May 2006 EU-Russia Sochi Summit meeting, President Putin clarified that Russia is seeking for amendments to the ECT in the form of a specific Transit Protocol. The October 2006 informal Lahti European Council, which was largely devoted to the EU's external energy relations and was also attended by Russian President Putin, revealed that a Russian ratification of the ECT is not a realistic option in the short term.[331] Hence, the EU aims to include the main principles of the ECT in the post-PCA "Strategic Partnership Agreement".[332] This strategy reveals a continuity of the pragmatic

---

[328] K. Westphal, "The EU-Russia Relationship and the Energy Factor: A European View", in: K. Westphal, (ed.), *A Focus on EU-Russia Relations*, Frankfurt am Main, Lang, 2005, pp. 21–24.

[329] Presidency Conclusions Brussels European Council (23–24 March 2006), *Bull. EU* 3 (2006), I.7.43.

[330] Notwithstanding the absence of a specific legal basis for a European energy policy, the EC Treaty provisions on the internal market, competition, common commercial policy, environment and transport all relate to the energy field. It is noteworthy that, in contrast to the current situation, the Treaty of Lisbon provides for a specific legal basis for the EU's energy policy (Art. 194 TFEU).

[331] X, "EU, Russia make slow progress on energy", *www.euractiv.com*, 23 October 2006.

[332] Communication from the Commission to the European Council, *External Energy Relations—From Principles to Action*, COM (2006) 590 final, Brussels, 12 October 2006, p. 3.

nature of EU-Russia relations after enlargement. In line with the package deals on Kaliningrad and PCA extension or the linkage between visa facilitation and readmission, it might be expected that a deal on EU-Russia energy co-operation will be linked to other items identified in the Common Spaces' road maps.

EU ENLARGEMENT AS A "DEUS EX MACHINA"?

The EU accession of the Baltic States does not automatically solve all problems with Russia. The absence of a formal border agreement with Estonia, the integration problems of Russian-speaking minorities as well as practical problems concerning the transit of goods to Kaliningrad are still on the agenda. The EU has always been rather hesitant to discuss these issues with Russia during the pre-accession period, particularly because it did not want to give Moscow a veto right on the question of enlargement. Moreover, the essential bilateral nature of the accession preparations largely ignored the historically burdened relationship between the Baltic States and Russia. Hence, the pre-accession challenges have to a large extent been transferred to the post-accession period.

An analysis of the developments during the first years after enlargement seems to indicate that the remaining tensions between the Baltic States and Russia do not necessarily have a negative impact on the evolution of the EU-Russia Strategic Partnership. The adoption of the Common Spaces' road maps, the conclusion of bilateral agreements on visa facilitation and readmission as well as the new start of the Northern Dimension policy did not pose major problems. This can be attributed to the low profile of the Baltic States in the Council and to the Commission's reluctance to link trade relations with political questions such as Russia's non-recognition of the Baltic thesis on state continuity. Only at the level of the European Parliament, the increased attention to the legacy of the Soviet period is striking. The rather straightforward Parliamentary resolutions do, however, not have any visible impact on the formal legal relationship with Russia.

There seems to be a clear understanding in the Baltic republics that only a subordination of their individual relations with Russia to a wider EU-Russia strategy can provide security and stability. For this reason, Estonia, Latvia and Lithuania support a further deepening of the EU-Russia Strategic Partnership on the basis of legally binding agreements. This explains the rather cautious position of the Baltic States on the Polish decision to veto the start of negotiations of a new

Strategic Partnership Agreement. In spite of their principled support to the Polish position, the Baltic leaders underlined the need for a new framework agreement as an instrument to solve problem issues between individual Member States and Russia.[333]

The negotiation of a Strategic Partnership Agreement will be a significant test case for the new approach to EU-Russia relations after enlargement. In comparison to the previous situation, the intention to come up with a more balanced approach is reflected in the Common Spaces' agenda and in the new Northern Dimensions concept. From a Russian point of view, a logical consequence of this evolution is the development of joint decision-making mechanisms, for instance in the area of the European Defence and Security Policy.[334] It remains to be seen whether the Baltic States will be prepared to discuss such far-reaching scenarios, particularly given the legal prerequisite that mixed agreements require unanimity in the Council and ratification of the Member States' national parliaments. Arguably, the domestic sensitivity of the 'historic legacy issue' in both the Baltic republics and Russia might reopen discussions on the outstanding problems in Baltic-Russian relations.

The impact of the EU on the remaining issues is not unambiguous. With regard to the situation of the Russian-speaking minorities in Estonia and Latvia, the Race Equality Directive forms an important anti-discrimination landmark but problems of implementation and the lack of provisions on language discrimination limit its significance. Moreover, the EU accession of Estonia and Latvia has resulted in an additional differentiation between the citizen and non-citizen population of those countries. Only in January 2007, the visa requirement for non-citizens travelling within the Schengen area has been abolished. Whereas Directive 2003/109 guarantees a number of important rights to long-term resident third country nationals, the cumbersome procedure for acquiring such status raises doubts about the practical effects of this legislation. The multiple qualifications added in the adoption

---

[333] This position is, for instance, clearly illustrated in a press release of the Latvian Ministry of Foreign Affairs of 16 November 2006, entitled "Latvia supports commencement of EU-Russia discussions on new co-operation agreement", at: http://www.am.gov.lv/en/news/press-releases/2006/november/16–12/.

[334] Remarks by Russian Minister of Foreign Affairs Sergey Lavrov after Roundtable Meeting in International Affairs Committee of the State Duma of the Russian Federation, Moscow, 28 November 2005, doc. 2533–29–11–2005, available at: http://www.ln/mid.ru.

process of this Directive further leads to the conclusion that it does not satisfy the ambition of the 1999 Tampere European Council to grant long-term resident third country nationals a set of rights comparable to those enjoyed by EU citizens. Finally, the establishment of an EU-Russia human rights dialogue forms an interesting 'confidence building measure' and a channel to discuss the fate of the Russian-speaking population on a regular basis. In practice, however, the discussions are largely confined to standard diplomatic statements.

On the question of border delimitation between Russia and Estonia, the EU has returned to a 'wait and see' approach after a short period of active diplomacy in the wake of enlargement. The fact that the conclusion of border agreements is part of the Member States' competence explains the EU's reluctance but it remains striking in the light of the importance attributed to good neighbourliness in other areas. Finally, the pragmatic solution to the Kaliningrad transit issue has avoided overt conflicts with Russia and even has a positive effect on the development of the Strategic Partnership. The general satisfaction with the facilitated transit mechanisms does, however, not avoid new challenges in a long-term perspective. It remains to be seen to what extent Kaliningrad can operate as a crowbar for opening discussions on issues such as free trade or visa free travel.

From the EU point of view, the EU accession of the Baltic States seems to be a success story in the light of its basic rationale to provide stability and security in the region. Of course, the remaining challenges of minority integration and good neighbourly relations with Russia cannot be underestimated. It would be a huge overstatement to suggest that the Russian-speaking minorities in Estonia and Latvia no longer face any form of discrimination as a result of enlargement or that the question of Kaliningrad transit has been solved indefinitely. Moreover, EU enlargement has brought a number of new challenges on the EU's agenda. Apart from the increased complexity of EU-Russia relations, the reform of the EU's institutional structures after the constitutional crisis resulting from the negative outcome of the Constitutional Treaty referendums in France and the Netherlands remains a clear priority. The next section analyses the position of the Baltic States on this internal reform process in order to draw some preliminary conclusions on the role of those countries in the EU.

PART SIX

THE CONSTITUTIONAL CONSEQUENCES OF EU ENLARGEMENT: DEVELOPMENTS AT THE NATIONAL AND EUROPEAN LEVEL

As demonstrated in the previous chapters, the prospect of enlargement operated as a catalyst for constitutional change in both the candidate countries and in the EU itself. This final section argues that the inter-connected processes of constitutional transition at the national and European level continue after the date of accession. In this respect, the changes to the Baltic States' legal systems are analysed from a constitutional and institutional perspective. In addition, specific atten-tion is devoted to the role of the Baltic States in the EU's internal reform process.

CHAPTER ONE

THE ADAPTATION OF THE BALTIC STATES' LEGAL SYSTEMS

§ 1. *A Continuous Revision of Constitutional Provisions*

Apart from the constitutional amendments related to the transfer of sovereign rights, discussed in the context of the EU accession referendums (cf. *supra*), EU membership also involved significant amendments to specific articles of the Baltic States' constitutions. A good example is the amendment to Article 47 of the Lithuanian Constitution regarding the acquisition of land ownership by foreigners. Already in 1996, in connection with the ratification of the Europe Agreement, a right to acquire non-agricultural land for the purpose of economic activities was extended to EU citizens and legal persons.[1] These activities had to be established and registered in accordance with Lithuanian legislation. Given the EC Treaty provisions and the ECJ's case law on the freedom of establishment for nationals of EU Member States and the free movement of capital,[2] the European Commission concluded in its 2002 monitoring report that "there is still a need to abolish the constitutional restrictions on the acquisition of agricultural land by foreigners and foreign legal persons and the authorisation procedures restricting the acquisition of non-agricultural land by foreigners".[3] Accordingly, the Lithuanian Parliament adopted further amendments to Article 47 on 23 January 2003, which now includes the provision that "[i]n the Republic of Lithuania foreign entities may acquire the ownership of land, internal waters, forests and parks under the constitutional law".[4] The relevant constitutional law, which basically amended the 1996 constitutional law on the application of Article 47 (2), was adopted on

---

[1] See *supra* Part II, Chapter 4, § 1.3.
[2] See in particular Case C-305/87, *Commission v. Greece* [1989] ECR 1461 and Case C-302/97, *Klaus Konle v. Republik Österreich* [1999] ECR 3099.
[3] European Commission, 2002 Regular Report on Lithuania's Progress Towards Accession, COM (2002) 700 final, p. 57.
[4] Law on amending Article 47 of the Constitution, IX-1305, 23 January 2003.

20 March 2003 and lays down a clear non-discrimination provision.[5] This law entered into force on 1 May 2004, with the exception of a 7-year transitional period concerning the acquisition of agricultural land and forestry land as defined in the Act of Accession to the EU (cf. *supra* Part IV).

1.1. *The Extension of Voting Rights to EU Citizens*

Another specific amendment to the Lithuanian Constitution concerns the right of EU citizens to participate in local elections. The original Article 119 granted this right exclusively to Lithuanian citizens, which clearly infringed the active and passive voting rights of resident EU citizens as laid down in Article 19 EC and Council Directive 94/80 of 19 December 1994.[6] Amendments ensuring compliance of the Lithuanian Constitution with the requirements of the EU citizenship legislation have been adopted in June 2002.[7] Significantly, the amended Article 119 (2) of the Lithuanian Constitution and the related amendment to the Law on Elections to Municipal Councils went further than strictly necessary as they extend the active and passive voting rights to all permanent residents of an administrative unit and not only to foreign EU citizens.[8]

Latvia, in contrast, adopted a very narrow approach to the required amendments. The wording of the original Article 101, laying down that "[e]very citizen of Latvia has the right, as provided for by law, to

---

[5] Pursuant to Article 6 (1) of the Constitutional Law, "Foreign subjects which meet the criteria established in Article 4 of this Law shall have the right in the Republic of Lithuania to acquire into ownership land, internal waters and forests under the same procedure and subject to the same terms and conditions as the citizens and legal persons of the Republic of Lithuania". The "foreign subjects which meet the criteria established in Article 4" include citizens and permanent residents or legal persons from (i) the EU and other parties to the Europe agreements or (ii) Member States of the OESO, NATO and the EEA, as well as permanent residents of the Republic of Lithuania without Lithuanian citizenship. All other foreign subjects are in principle prohibited to acquire into ownership land, internal waters and forests. Moreover, Article 16 (2) of the Constitutional Law explicitly prohibits the conclusion of international agreements that would extend the right of ownership of land plots to foreign subjects not meeting the criteria of Article 4.

[6] Council Directive 94/80/EC of 19 December 1994 laying down detailed arrangements for the exercise of the right to vote and to stand as a candidate in municipal elections by citizens of the Union residing in a Member State of which they are not nationals, *OJ* (1994) L 368/37.

[7] Law on the Amendment of Article 119 of the Constitution, LXV-2629, 20 June 2002.

[8] Law on Elections to Municipal Councils, IX-1080, 19 September 2002.

participate in the work of the State and of local government, and to hold a position in the civil service" was retained.[9] In addition, a new paragraph was adopted, which gives permanent resident EU citizens a right to vote in local elections and to participate in the work of local governments. Significantly, the new provision also explicitly states that "the working language of local governments is the Latvian language". Obviously, this sentence has been included as a gesture to the nationalist parties fearing the consequences of EU membership for the Latvian identity and language. It also has to be understood as a measure counterbalancing the abolition of the state language requirement for deputy candidates in local and parliamentary elections following a double conviction by the European Court of Human Rights and the UN Human Rights Committee and after persistent pressure from NATO Secretary-General George Robertson.[10] Finally, the restrictive position of the Latvian legislators provides a clear message to international observers calling for the granting of voting rights to all non-citizens in municipal elections.

In the framework of the 2002 elections to the Latvian Parliament, the International Election Observation Mission concluded that "involving non-citizens in local decision-making could represent a tangible step toward eliminating the current democratic deficit".[11] The absence of any progress in this area has been criticized on the occasion of the October 2006 Parliamentary elections.[12] The granting of voting rights to non-citizens has also been suggested in the concluding observations of the UN Human Rights Committee and in declarations of several high-level representatives of the Council of Europe and non-governmental organizations.[13] The amendments to the local election legislation

---

[9] It is noteworthy that the provision on work in public service has to be interpreted narrowly, in the light of the ECJ's case law in this respect. See e.g. ECJ, Case 149/79 *Commission* v. *Belgium* [1980] ECR 3881 at para. 10.

[10] See *supra* Part III, Chapter 4, § 3.1.

[11] The International Election Observation Mission is a joint effort between the OSCE Office for Democratic Institutions and Human Rights (ODIHR) and the Parliamentary Assembly of the Council of Europe (PACE). The Conclusions of the Mission are available at: http://www.osce.org/odihr/elections/field_activities/latvia2002/.

[12] OSCE Parliamentary Assembly, "Latvian election transparent and professional but issue of 'non-citizens' remains", at: http://www.oscepa.org/admin/getbinary. asp?fileid=1508.

[13] For an overview: Ministry of Foreign Affairs of the Russian Federation, "List of main claims and recommendations of international organizations and NGOs to Latvia as regards rights of national minorities", at: http://www.ln.mid.ru.

adopted in the framework of EU membership, therefore, formed a missed opportunity to tackle the problems of political participation and representation of the stateless Russian-speaking minorities. The result has only been a growing frustration among this part of the population because EU citizens have a right to vote in local elections—provided that they have registered residence on the administrative territory of the respective municipality at least 90 days prior to the date of election—and a right to stand as a candidate after 10 consecutive months before the date of election, whereas stateless Russian-speaking inhabitants born on Latvian territory during the Soviet period do not have any voting rights at all.[14]

In Estonia, Article 156 (2) of the Estonian Constitution already allowed permanent residents to vote in local elections under conditions prescribed by law. Accordingly, the introduction of specific references to the rights of resident EU citizens in the Local Government Council Election Act seemed sufficient to ensure compliance with EU law requirements.[15] A specific problem, however, concerns the second sentence of Article 48 (1) of the Constitution, which states that "only Estonian citizens may belong to political parties". Obviously, this provision restricts the passive voting rights of foreign EU citizens. Proceeding from Article 2 of the Third Constitutional Act,[16] the Legal Chancellor therefore proposed a teleological interpretation of the Constitution in the light of Estonia's obligations arising from the Treaty of Accession:

> To guarantee the fulfilment of Estonia's obligations I consider it possible to interpret the second sentence of § 48 (1) of the Constitution to the effect that citizens of the European Union are allowed to belong to political parties with the aim of participating in local elections.[17]

---

[14] The Election Law on City and Town Councils, District Councils and Pagast Councils, available at the website of the Central Election Commission of Latvia (www.cvk.lv). For an overview of Latvia's legislation on local elections, see also: http://europa.eu.int/youreurope/nav/nl/citizens/factsheets/lv/rightsinotherms/localelections/en.html.

[15] The amended version of the Local Government Council Act is available at the website of the Estonian Legal Language Centre (www.legaltext.ee).

[16] This Article proclaims that from the date of Estonia's accession to the European Union, "the Constitution of the Republic of Estonia applies taking account of the rights and obligations arising from the Accession Treaty".

[17] Interpretation proposed in Case No. 3–4–1–1–05 of 19 April 2005, Petition of the Chancellor of Justice to declare § 70 of the Local Government Election Act and

It is regrettable that the General Assembly of Estonia's Supreme Court did not express its appreciation on this interpretation in a case brought to the Court by the Legal Chancellor on the constitutionality of the first sentence of Article 5 (1) of the Political Parties Act, which restricted membership of political parties to Estonian citizens in line with Article 48 (1) of the Constitution. The General Assembly only observed that the Chancellor of Justice did not have a legal competence to request the Supreme Court to declare an Act unconstitutional on the ground that it is incompatible with EU law.[18] This position ignores the fact that the Legal Chancellor, as part of Estonia's judicial authorities, is held to take into account the supremacy of application of EU law.[19] In addition, the Legal Chancellor basically contested the conformity of Article 5 (1) of the Political Parties Act with the Estonian Constitution, which has—pursuant to Article 2 of the Third Constitutional Act—to be interpreted in the light of Estonia's EU membership obligations. The General Assembly of the Supreme Court, therefore, missed an opportunity to explain the meaning and implications of the Third Constitutional Act for the interpretation of the Constitution.[20]

Together with Judge Julia Laffranque, who issued a dissenting opinion in this case, it can be concluded that the reticence of the Supreme Court only promotes legal vagueness.[21] A clear-cut amendment of Article 48 (1) of the Constitution, extending the right of membership of political parties to all EU citizens seems recommendable for reasons of clarity and legal certainty. At least, a clear interpretation of the Constitution and its supplementary Amendment Act could have been expected. In the absence of such clarifications, the problem has been pragmatically solved after the Constitutional Committee of the *Riigikogu* initiated an amendment to the Political Parties Act enabling citizens of the European

---

§ 1(1), the first sentence of § 5(1) and § 6(2) of the Political Parties Act partly unconstitutional, available at: http://www.nc.ee/english/.

[18] Ibid., at para. IV-48–51.

[19] ECJ, Case 106/77 *Simmenthal* [1978] ECR 629, at para. 21.

[20] The issue of the relationship between the Third Constitutional Act and the substantial provisions of the Constitution has later been tackled in an Opinion of the Constitutional Review Chamber of the Supreme Court on the constitutionality of amendments to the Eesti Pank Act. (See infra § 1.3. of this Chapter).

[21] Dissenting Opinion of justice Julia Laffranque to the judgment of the General Assembly of the Supreme Court in case No. 3–4–1–1–05, at para. 6. (Available at: http://www.nc.ee/english/)

Union to belong to political parties.[22] As a result, the rights of foreign EU citizens are more extensive than those attributed to the so-called 'aliens', i.e. long-term resident inhabitants without Estonian (or EU) citizenship. Whereas citizens of other EU Member States can participate to local elections under the same conditions as Estonian citizens, aliens only have active but no passive voting rights. In addition, aliens have to satisfy more conditions to exercise their voting rights: they have to be in possession of a permanent residence permit and should have legally resided in a municipality or city for at least the last five years before the election day. For EU citizens, there is only a requirement of registration in the Estonian population register at the day of the elections. Thirdly, an EU citizen may be a member of a rural municipality or city electoral committee whereas aliens can only be a member of the division committee. Participation in both committees requires proficiency in Estonian. Finally, pursuant to the information obligation included in Article 11 of Directive 94/80 EC, the Local Government Council Election Act includes a subsection on "informing citizens of the European Union of their right to vote in council elections".[23] Such an information requirement is completely absent with regard to other non-Estonian residents. In the light of these observations, it can be concluded that Estonia and Latvia strictly implemented the legal requirements connected to EU citizenship whereas Lithuania, which has a much smaller non-EU population, decided to give equal voting rights to all permanent residents in local elections.

For European Parliament elections, participation is limited to EU citizens in the three Baltic countries. It is noteworthy that in Case C-145/04 concerning the voting rights of citizens of the British Commonwealth in Gibraltar, the ECJ concluded that the EC Treaty does not preclude the Member States from granting active and passive voting rights in European Parliament elections to "certain persons who have close links to them, other than their own nationals or citizens of the

---

[22] The amended version of the Political Parties Act is available at the website of the Estonian Legal Language Centre (www.legaltext.ee). For comments, see: C. Ginter, "Constitutional review and EC law in Estonia", 31 *European Law Review* (2006), pp. 912–923.

[23] The Local Government Election Act is available at the website of the Estonian Legal Translation Centre (www.legaltext.ee). For an overview of Estonia's legislation on local elections, see also:
http://europa.eu.int/youreurope/nav/nl/citizens/factsheets/ee/rightsinotherms/localelections/en.html.

Union resident in their territory".[24] It seems obvious that, on the basis of this judgment, the stateless Soviet era immigrants in Estonia and Latvia potentially qualify for participation in the European Parliament elections. Such decision belongs to the competence of the Member States concerned.[25] Given the reluctance of the Estonian and Latvian governments to grant far-reaching political rights to non-citizens, this remains a theoretical and hypothetical option.

1.2. *The Constitutional Consequences of the European Arrest Warrant*

Taking into account the dynamic nature of the European integration process, EU membership continues to affect the constitutional frame-work of the Baltic States after the date of accession. Latvia, for instance, amended Article 98 of the Constitution in June 2004 in order to satisfy the requirements of the Council framework decision on the European arrest warrant and the surrender procedures between Member States.[26] The old version of Article 98 provided that "*a citizen of Latvia may not be extradited to a foreign country*". This provision infringed the basic principle of the framework decision that an EU Member State can no longer refuse to surrender to another Member State their own citizens who have committed a serious crime or who are suspected of having com-mitted such a crime in another EU country, on the ground that they are nationals. Accordingly, the Latvian Parliament supplemented Article 98 of the Constitution enabling the extradition of Latvian citizens "in the cases provided for in international agreements ratified by the Saiema if by the extradition the basic human rights specified in the Constitution are not violated".[27] In Poland and Cyprus, two acceding countries which had not adopted constitutional amendments to the provision that Polish or Cypriote citizens cannot be extradited, the respective Constitutional Courts declared the European arrest warrant

---

[24] ECJ, C-145/04, *Spain* v. *United Kingdom*, Judgment of 12 September 2006, ECR [2006] I-7917, at para. 78.
[25] ECJ, Case C-300/04, *Eman and Sevinger*, Judgment of 12 September 2006, ECR [2006] I-8055, at para. 45.
[26] Council Framework Decision 2002/584/JHA of 13 June 2002 on the European arrest warrant and the surrender procedures between Member States, *OJ* (2002) L 190/1.
[27] See the amended version of the Latvian Constitution at: http://www.saeima.lv/LapasEnglish/Constitution_Visa.htm.

implementation measures unconstitutional.[28] Consequently, it can be concluded that amendments to Article 98 of the Latvian Constitution were indispensable to avoid similar problems.

The solution of qualifying the non-extradition of citizens in the light of international obligations and within the margins of fundamental constitutional principles reflects somewhere Article 16 (2) of the German Constitution, which in a first sentence also prohibits the extradition of German citizens but further states that "the law can provide otherwise for extraditions to a Member State of the European Union or to an International Court of Justice as long as the rule of law is upheld". In a case concerning the extradition of a German national suspected of links with *Al Qaida*, the German Constitutional Court concluded that the German Act implementing the European arrest warrant insufficiently guaranteed the basic constitutional principles ('*rechtstaatlichen Grundsätze*') and infringed Article 19 (4) of the German Constitution by excluding recourse to a court against the judicial decision granting extradition.[29] The Czech Constitutional Court, on the other hand, dismissed a claim that the Czech implementation law infringed the Constitution by authorising the surrender of Czech nationals abolishing the protection inherent in the double criminality rule. According to the Czech Constitutional Court, "there is no reason to assume that the current standard of protection of fundamental rights within the EU, through the application of the principles arising from these rights, offers a level of protection inferior to that which is provided in the Czech Republic".[30]

---

[28] An English summary of the Polish Constitutional Court case on the European Arrest Warrant of 27 April 2005 can be found at: http://www.ecln.net/elements/national_decisions/2005_POL_European_Arrest_Warrant.pdf. For comments, see: A. Lazowski, "Poland: Constitutional Tribunal on the Surrender of Polish Citizens under the European Arrest Warrant", 1 *European Constitutional Law Review* 3 (2005), pp.569–581. For the Decision of the Cypriote Supreme Court of 7 November 2005, see: http://www.kypros.org/PIO/cygov/judiciary.htm.

[29] BVerfG, 2BvR 2236/04 from 18 July 2005, available at the website of the German Constitutional Court (http://www.bverfg.de/). For comments, see: S. Molders, "The European Arrest Warrant Act is Void—The Decision of the German Federal Constitutional Court of 18 July 2005", 7 *German Law Journal* (2006) 1, pp. 45–57; C. Tomuschat, "Inconsistencies—The German Federal Constitutional Court on the European Arrest Warrant", 2 *European Constitutional Law Review* 2 (2006), pp. 209–226.

[30] Czech Constitutional Court, Case 66/04 on European Arrest Warrant, Judgment of 3 May 2006, available in English at: http://test.concourt.cz/angl_verze/doc/pl-66-04.html.

It is, in other words, obvious that the implementation of the European arrest warrant framework decision raises new questions concerning the relationship between the constitutions of the Member States and EU law. This discussion is reminiscent of the old *Solange* judgments of the German Bundesverfassungsgericht, which first called into question the competence of the Community institutions to protect fundamental rights (*Solange I*)[31] and later confirmed that the Communities ensured a level of protection comparable to the German Constitution (*Solange II*).[32] The judgment of the Czech Constitutional Court reflects the latter position whereas the recent judgment of the Bundesverfassungsgericht concerning the European arrest warrant is inspired by the old reticence about the capacity of the Community institutions to protect fundamental rights. This position can be seen as a reaction to the restrictions on judicial control in the third pillar.[33]

It seems obvious that the debate about the national constitutionality of European arrest warrant implementation measures is of particular significance for a country such as Latvia, which has included a constitutional safeguard on the extradition of its citizens. Of particular significance in this discussion is Case C-303/05 before the European Court of Justice. In this procedure, the Belgian *Cour d'Arbitrage* asked the ECJ—pursuant to Article 35 EU—to rule on the validity of the European arrest warrant framework decision in the light of the fundamental rights principles laid down in Article 6 (2) EU, in particular the principles of equality and legality in criminal proceedings.[34] Advocate-General Ruiz-Jarabo Colomer explicitly acknowledged the constitutional implications of this question.[35] Significantly, he does not accept the equation of the European arrest warrant with the procedure of extradition

---

[31] BVerfG 37, 271 (1974).

[32] BVerfG 73, 339 (1986).

[33] These restrictions include the optional nature of proceedings for a preliminary ruling, the limitation of legal standing to bring actions for annulment and the absence of an action for failure to fulfil obligations. For a critical comment on those restrictions, see the Opinion of Advocate-General Colomor in Case C-303/05, at footnote 81: "It is rather paradoxical that, in an area where the Union has an increased influence on the fundamental rights of individuals, the powers of the Court have been somewhat restricted".

[34] See: Case C-303/05, *Advocaten van de Wereld VZW* v. *Leden van de Ministerraad*, ECR [2007] I-3633.

[35] At para 8., the Advocate-General observes that "there is a far-reaching debate concerning the incompatibility between the constitutions of the Member States and European Union law; The Court of Justice must participate in that debate by embracing the prominent role assigned to it, with a view to situating the interpretation of the

between Member States.[36] This observation, in combination with the general recognition of fundamental rights in the EU—even without a formal legally binding Charter of Fundamental Rights[37]—allows the Advocate General to conclude that the framework decision does not infringe Article 6 (2) EU because it is consistent with the principle of equality and the principle of legality in criminal procedures. Arguably, this argumentation—upheld by the ECJ—solves potential questions concerning the constitutionality of surrendering Latvian citizens to other EU Member States on the basis of the European arrest warrant implementation measures.

Finally, the reference to "international treaties ratified by the *Saiema*" as a basis for extraditing Latvian citizens raises questions in the light of the application of the European arrest warrant. Its implementation in Latvia is not directly based on a ratified international treaty but on a law implementing an EU framework decision, which was adopted under Article 34 EU. In the *Pupino* case, the ECJ rejected the claim made by several Member States that acts adopted under Article 34 EU are purely international law and cannot create an obligation under Union law for national courts to interpret their laws in conformity with framework decisions.[38] Accordingly, potential claims on the constitutionality of the extradition of Latvian nationals will have to take into account Latvia's obligations under the EU Treaty.

The implementation of the framework decision concerning the European arrest warrant also gave rise to discussions in Estonia and Lithuania but neither country eventually decided on the introduction

---

values and principles which form the foundation of the Community legal system within parameters comparable to the ones which prevail in national systems".

[36] According to the Advocate General, the sole similarity between both models is their objective. The situation of a European arrest warrant, based upon the mutual recognition of judicial decisions in an area of freedom, security and justice is not comparable to the old situation where sovereign states cooperate in individual cases; *ibid.* at para. 45–46. Significantly, the Polish Constitutional Court argued in its European arrest warrant decision that despite the procedural differences between extradition and surrender, the two procedures are very similar when it comes to substance. See the English summary of the Polish arrest warrant case at: http://www.ecln.net/elements/national_decisions/2005_POL_European_Arrest_Warrant.pdf.

[37] According to the reasoning of the Advocate General, the Charter of Fundamental Rights reflects the common constitutional traditions of the Member States. Accordingly, the EU must respect those rights and the Court must protect them on the basis of Articles 6 and 46 (d) EU. *op. cit.* footnote 34, at para. 77.

[38] Case C-105/03, Judgment of 16 June 2005, *Pupino*, [2005] ECR, I-5285, at para. 43. For comments, see: M. Fletcher, M., "Analysis and Reflection—Extending Indirect Effect to the Third Pillar?", 30 *European Law Review* (2005) 3, pp. 862–877.

of a constitutional amendment. Article 36 of the Estonian Constitution allows for the extradition of citizens "under conditions prescribed by an international treaty and pursuant to a procedure prescribed by such treaty and by law". In spite of this opening to the implementation of the European arrest warrant, the subsequent provision that "extradition shall be decided by the Government of the Republic" seems hardly reconcilable with the idea that the surrender of requested persons between Member States has to be entirely judicial, as laid down in Article 1 (1) of the framework decision.[39] It has been argued that this apparently problematic constitutional provision has to be read in the light of the Third Constitutional Act, which in Article 2 ensures that the Estonian Constitution is applied according to the rights and obligations ensuing from the Accession Treaty.[40] Such an interpretative solution has also been proposed with regard to the political rights of EU citizens (cf. *supra*) and the competences of the European Central Bank (cf. *infra*). It seems, in other words, that Article 2 of the Third Constitutional Act forms a 'catch all' provision solving all existing and future constitutional issues arising in the context of Estonia's EU membership. This very flexible approach illustrates the already mentioned problems of legal clarity and consistency of the Estonian Constitution after Estonia's accession to the EU.

In Lithuania, Article 13 (2) of the Constitution allows for the extradition of citizens on the basis of an international agreement. Pursuant to Lithuania's monist system and general obligations under the EU Treaty and the Treaty of Accession, a constitutional amendment was not deemed necessary.[41] The Republic of Lithuania implemented the framework decision by amendments to the Criminal Code and the Criminal Procedure Code, which apply from 1 May 2004 onwards.[42]

---

[39] Report from the Commission based on Article 34 of the Council Framework Decision of 13 June 2002 on the European Arrest Warrant and the surrender procedures between Member States, COM (2005) 63 final, 23 February 2005, at p. 3.

[40] K. Raba, "Estonia", in: A. Moore, (ed.), *Police and Judicial Co-operation in the European Union: FIDE 2004 national reports*, Cambridge, Cambridge University Press, 2004, p. 90.

[41] V. Vadapalas, "Lithuania", in: A. Moore, (ed.), *Police and Judicial Co-operation in the European Union: FIDE 2004 national reports*, Cambridge, Cambridge University Press, 2004, p. 197.

[42] Information note from the Lithuanian Delegation to the Council Working Party on Cooperation in Criminal Matters, Brussels, 2 July 2004, 11097/04.

1.3. *The Constitutional Consequences of Participation in the Eurozone*

Apart from the European arrest warrant, participation in the European Monetary Union (EMU) also has important constitutional consequences. Pursuant to Article 4 of the Act of Accession, the new Member States take part in the EMU from the date of accession "with a derogation within the meaning of Article 122 EC".[43] This means that numerous EC Treaty provisions in the area of economic and monetary policy are not applicable to those countries.[44] In other words, upon accession, the new Member States did not transfer their monetary sovereignty.[45] This is clearly expressed in Article 43 (2) of the European System of Central Banks (ESCB) Statute, which explicitly states that the national banks of Member States with a derogation "retain their powers in the field of monetary policy according to their national law".[46]

This situation changes once the so-called convergence criteria, laid down in Article 121 (1) EC,[47] are fulfilled. Importantly, this provision stipulates that the assessment of a country's preparedness for introducing the euro *inter alia* includes an examination of legal compliance between a Member State's national legislation and the relevant EC Treaty provisions. This legal precondition reflects Article 109 EC, providing that each Member State shall ensure that its national legislation, including the statutes of its national central bank, is compatible with the EC Treaty and the Statute of the ESCB. The joint reading of both EC Treaty provisions implies that the introduction of the euro requires

---

[43] Article 4 of the Act concerning the conditions of accession of the Czech Republic, the Republic of Estonia, the Republic of Cyprus, the Republic of Latvia, the Republic of Lithuania, the Republic of Hungary, the Republic of Malta, the Republic of Poland, the Republic of Slovenia and the Slovak Republic and the adjustments to the Treaties on which the European Union is founded, *OJ* (2003) L 236/34.

[44] This concerns Art. 105 (1), (2), (3) and (5) EC on the objectives and basic tasks of the ESCB; Art. 106 EC on the issue of banknotes and coins; Art. 110 EC on legal acts of the ECB; Art. 111 EC on the exchange rate policy in respect of third currencies and Art. 112 (2) (b) EC on the appointment of members of the Executive Board of the ECB.

[45] B. Dziechciarz, "Impact of European Union Enlargement on EMU. Monetary Split-up into 'Ins' and 'Outs' as a Temporary or Permanent Phenomenon", in: K. Inglis, A. Ott, (eds.), *The Constitution for Europe and an Enlarging Union: Unity in Diversity?*, Groningen, Europa Law Publishing, 2005, p. 139.

[46] Protocol on the Statute of the European System of Central Banks and the European Central Bank, *OJ* (1992) C 191/68.

[47] The convergence criteria include (i) a high degree of price stability, (ii) the sustainability of the government financial position, (iii) exchange rates developments and (iv) stability of long-term interest rates.

the new Member States to accommodate their national laws and constitutions to the EC's exclusive competences in the field of economic and monetary policy. In particular, the national banks' exclusive right to issue bank notes—as laid down in Article 125 of the Lithuanian Constitution, Article 111 of the Estonian Constitution and Article 4 of the Latvian Bank Law[48]—conflicts with the provisions of Article 106 EC, which states that also the European Central Bank (ECB) may issue bank notes and grants the ECB an exclusive competence to authorise the issue of banknotes in the Community. The argumentation that the expression "to issue bank notes" in the national constitution only relates to the emission of national currency[49] and does, therefore, not preclude the emission of the euro by the ECB, has not been accepted by the European Commission.[50]

Given the political sensitivity of EU accession and due to the non-application of Article 106 EC for "countries with a derogation within the meaning of Article 122 EC", the necessary constitutional amendments have been postponed until after the date of accession. The preference for minimal changes to the Constitution became clear when the Lithuanian Parliament only proposed to delete the word "exclusively" from the wording of Article 125. The ECB, however, did not accept such a formulation because this would not recognize the fact that the power to issue euro banknotes is based on Community rather than national law. In addition, the suggested amendment failed to point at the conditions listed in the EC Treaty and the Statute of the ESCB. For these reasons, the ECB proposed the introduction of clear references to the Treaty and the Statute. In addition, further amendments to Articles 75, 84 and 126 turned out necessary in order to assure the personal independence of the Chair of Lithuania's national monetary board in accordance to Article 14 (2) of the ESCB Statute.[51]

On 25 April 2006, the *Seimas* adopted the law amending Article 125 of the Constitution, which repeals the provision concerning the

---

[48] The Latvian Constitution is silent on monetary issues. Accordingly, the "law on Latvijas Banka" forms the main legal act in this respect.

[49] This line of reasoning was developed by Prof. Vadapalas, see e.g. V. Vadapalas, "Lithuania", in: F. Kellermann, J. De Zwaan, J. Czuczai, (eds.), *EU Enlargement: The Constitutional Impact at EU and National Level*, The Hague, Asser, 2002, p. 358.

[50] European Commission, Convergence Report 2004, COM (2004) 690 final, p. 7.

[51] Opinion of the European Central Bank of 26 October 2005 at the request of Lietuvos Bankas on a draft law amending Article 125 of the Constitution of the Republic of Lithuania, CON/2005/38.

Bank of Lithuania's exclusive right to issue bank notes. In addition, Article 125 is supplemented with the provision that the legal status of the Chairman of the Board of the Bank of Lithuania and the grounds for dismissal are laid down in the Law on the Bank of Lithuania. The amendments to Article 125 and to the Law on the Bank of Lithuania are planned to enter into force on the day the Council of the European Union abrogates the derogation of Lithuania in line with the procedure of Article 122 (2) EC Treaty. This procedure implies that the Council decides, by qualified majority, after consulting the European Parliament and after discussions between the Heads of State or Government, on a proposal from the Commission whether or not a Member State fulfils the convergence criteria laid down in Article 121 (1) EC. On 16 May 2006, the European Central Bank and the European Commission assessed Lithuania's readiness for introducing the euro but concluded that there should be no change in its status as an EU Member State with a derogation.[52] According to the convergence reports, Lithuania met all criteria except the one on inflation.[53] Importantly, the legal amendments to the Constitution and the Law on the Bank of Lithuania have been assessed to be in conformity with the EC Treaty and the Statute of the ESCB.

The new target date for introducing the euro in Lithuania is set at 1 January 2010.[54] At least, the legal preparations for the adoption of the euro are already in place. The situation is more complicated in Estonia and Latvia. In its 2004 convergence report, the European Commission observed that the Estonian legislation, in particular the Eesti Pank Act, the Constitution as well as the currency law and the law on the security for Estonian Kroon, were not fully compatible with

---

[52] ECB, *Convergence Report May 2006*, available at: http://www.ecb.int/pub/pdf/conrep/cr2006en.pdf; European Commission, *2006 Convergence Report on Lithuania—Technical Annex*, SEC (2006) 614, Brussels, 16 May 2006, available at: http://ec.europa.eu/economy_finance/publications/convergence/report2006_lithuania_en.htm.

[53] The average inflation rate in Lithuania since April 2005 was 2.7 percent, i.e. 0.1 percentage above the reference value calculated on the basis of a 1.5 percentage margin to the average inflation rate in the three best-performing Member States. The Commission's negative recommendation was also inspired by the expectation of higher inflation rates in the near future as a result of labour cost developments and higher import prices, in particular for energy products.

[54] X, "EU sees 2010 as realistic date for Lithuanian euro entry", *The Baltic Times*, 5 October 2006.

Article 109 EC and the ESCB/ECB Statute.[55] In December 2005, the ECB reiterated that "for reasons of legal certainty, a change should be made to Article 111 of the Estonian Constitution".[56] Confronted with the constitutional dilemma between the exclusive right of the Estonian national bank to issue bank notes pursuant to Article 111 of the Constitution and the requirements under the EC Treaty, the *Riigikogu* enquired the Supreme Court to assess the compliance of amendments to the Eesti Pank Act with the Constitution.[57] In its Opinion, delivered on 11 May 2006, the Constitutional Review Chamber of the Supreme Court for the first time explicitly dealt with the question of the relationship between the Third Constitutional Act and the substantial provisions of the Estonian Constitution.

The point of departure of the judges' legal reasoning is that as a result of the adoption of the Third Constitutional Act, EU law has become one of the grounds for the interpretation and application of the Estonian Constitution. As a result, only that part of the Constitution is applicable, which is in conformity with the EU law requirements. The Constitutional Review Chamber, in other words, explicitly recognizes the supremacy of EU law in the Estonian legal order:

> The effect of those provisions of the Constitution that are not compatible with the European Union law and thus inapplicable, is suspended. This means that within the spheres, which are within the exclusive competence of the European Union or where there is a shared competence with the European Union, the European Union law shall apply in the case of a conflict between Estonian legislation, including the Constitution, with the European Union law.[58]

---

[55] European Commission, Convergence Report 2004, COM (2004) 690 final, p. 6.

[56] Opinion of the European Central Bank of 30 December 2005 at the request of the Estonian Parliament on a draft law amending the Eesti Pank Act, CON/2005/59, at para. 3.

[57] The legal basis for the Parliament's request is Article 7(1) of the Constitutional Review Court Procedure Act, which allows the *Riigikogu* to address the Supreme Court on the interpretation of the Constitution in conjunction with EU law "if the interpretation of the Constitution is decisive for the adoption of a draft Act necessary for the fulfilment of an obligation of a member of the European Union". This provision has been introduced in December 2005.

[58] Opinion of the Constitutional Review Chamber of the Supreme Court on the interpretation of the Constitution, 3–4–1–3–06, at para. 16. The English language version of this opinion is available at: http://www.nc.ee.

Applied to the concrete problem regarding the introduction of the euro, this line of reasoning implies that Article 111 of the Estonian Constitution will not be applied because of its incompatibility with Article 106 EC. While the ruling of the Supreme Court does not in itself remove the formal incompatibility between Article 111 with the EC Treaty and the ESCB Statute, the European Commission concluded in its 2006 convergence report that it provides legal clarity and, therefore, rules out the need for further amendment.[59] It is striking that the ECB, which also issues a convergence report on the basis of Article 122 (2) EC, is much more cautious. Whereas the ECB recognizes the contribution of the Supreme Court, it also concludes that "in a further revision of the Constitution, the text of Article 111 of the Constitution should be brought in line with the Treaty".[60] There are, indeed, good reasons to support a further clarification of this constitutional issue. One of the main problems is the ambiguous legal significance of the opinion of the Constitutional Review Chamber of the Supreme Court. Article 59 (1) of the Constitutional Review Court Procedure Act, introduced in December 2005, deals with the formal requirements of an opinion on the interpretation of the Constitution in conjunction with EU law but remains silent on its legal consequences for the legislator and the subsequent constitutional review practice.[61] It remains, for instance, unclear whether this opinion is binding to the Supreme Court itself, by analogy with its judgments.[62]

In Latvia, where the Constitution remains silent on monetary issues, the necessary amendments have been introduced to the Law on the Bank of Latvia. The ECB, however, also insists on a clear constitutional confirmation of Latvijas Banka's independence.[63] Article 108 EC and Article 7 of the ESCB Statute prohibit national central banks and the members of their decision-making bodies from seeking or taking instructions from the Community institutions or bodies, from any government

---

[59] European Commission, Convergence Report December 2006, COM (2006) 762, p. 6.

[60] ECB, Convergence Report December 2006, at: http://www.ecb.int/pub/pdf/conrep/cr200612en.pdf, p. 280.

[61] The English version of the Constitutional Review Procedure Act is available at: http://www.legaltext.ee.

[62] This problem has been raised by judges Kõve and Kergandberg in their dissenting opinions to this case.

[63] Opinion of the European Central Bank of 6 June 2006 at the request of the Latvian Ministry of Finance on a draft law amending the Latvian Constitution, CON/2006/27, at para. 3.

of a Member State or from any other body. The fact that the Latvian Constitution does not explicitly guarantee this requirement of independence, in contrast to the straightforward provision on the independent status of the State Audit Office in its Article 87, and the ambiguous wording of the Law on Latvijas Banka that "Latvijas Banka shall be supervised by the Parliament", explains the ECB's concerns.

In the margins of the constitutional debates on the issuing of banknotes and the independence of the monetary boards, an interesting discussion takes place on the spelling of the European currency. The governments of both Latvia and Lithuania requested the EU Presidency to respect the specificity of the Baltic languages in order to allow the Latvian form *eiro* and the Lithuanian form *euras* rather than the unified form *euro*. A similar position regarding the spelling of the single European currency in translated EU documents was maintained by Hungary, Slovenia and Malta. In this context, Latvia, Hungary and Malta submitted a declaration to the Lisbon Treaty proclaiming that "the spelling of the name of the single currency […] has no effect on the existing rules of the Latvian, Hungarian and Maltese languages".[64] Remarkably, no such declaration was added to the Treaty of Accession.

The reluctance on the part of the EU to accommodate the requests of the new Member States became obvious when the ECB rejected references to the '*euras*' in Lithuania's draft law on the adoption of the euro. The formulation of Article 2 of Regulation 974/98 EC that "the currency of the participating Member States shall be the euro" in combination with the December 1995 Madrid European Council conclusions that the "the name of the single currency must be the same in all the official languages of the European Union" formed the basic references for the ECB's position. Interestingly, the ECB developed the argument that "new Member States are under an unquestionable legal obligation to comply with political agreements concluded by the European Council pursuant to Article 5 (3) of the Act concerning the conditions of accession".[65] The latter provision states the equality of old

---

[64] Declaration No. 58 by the Republic of Latvia, the Republic of Hungary and the Republic of Malta on the spelling of the name of the single currency in the Treaties, *OJ* (2007) C 306/269. A similar declaration was made by Latvia and Hungary—but not Malta—to the Treaty establishing a Constitution for Europe.

[65] Opinion of the European Central Bank of 14 June 2005 at the request of Lietuvos Bankas on a draft law on the adoption of the euro, CON/2005/21, p. 4.

and new Member States with regard to the observation of European Council declarations.

Whereas conclusions of the European Council generally do not have any legal binding force, they can have direct consequences for the Member States in the light of subsequent Community legislation.[66] In this respect, the wording of Article 2 of Regulation 974/98 in combination with the exclusive competence of the Community in monetary matters strengthens the position of the ECB. It is noteworthy that Latvia insisted on a provision safeguarding "the sovereign right of Member States to spell the name of the single currency in accordance to their linguistic rules and usage traditions" in the discussions surrounding amendments to Regulation 974/98.[67] This suggestion was, however, not accepted by the Working Group of the Council nor by the Commission and the ECB. Proceeding from Latvia's strong linguistic reservation concerning the translation of this Regulation into the Latvian language,[68] the ECB proposed—for reasons of legal certainty—the inclusion of a specific reference to the uniform spelling of the name of the euro in the recitals and in Article 2 of the amended Regulation 974/98.[69] In the end, the new Council Regulation retained the old wording of Article 2.[70] In other words, the question on the spelling of the single currency has not explicitly been dealt with in the Regulation, which provoked a statement of the Latvian government that it would stick to the word '*eiro*' even if this would lead to a case before the European Court of Justice.[71] The ECB, on the other hand, considers the single spelling of the euro as

---

[66] K. Lenaerts, P. Van Nuffel, *Constitutional Law of the European Union*, London, Sweet & Maxwell, 2005, p. 387. On the consequences of the Madrid European Council conclusions, see: B. Martenczuk, "Der Europäische Rat und die Wirtschafts- und Währungsunion", (1998) *Europarecht*, pp. 151–177.

[67] Draft Council Regulation amending Regulation (EC) No. 974/98 on the introduction of the euro, 14886/05, Brussels, 19 December 2005.

[68] The Latvian delegation stated that it would object to the publication of the Regulation if no satisfactory solution was found.

[69] Opinion of the European Central Bank of 1 December 2005 on a proposal for a Council Regulation amending Regulation (EC) No. 974/98 on the introduction of the euro, *OJ* (2005) C 316/25.

[70] Council Regulation (EC) No. 2169/2005 of 21 December 2005 amending Regulation (EC) No. 974/98 on the introduction of the euro, *OJ* (2005) L 346/1.

[71] X, "Latvia prepared to fight spelling of 'eiro' in Court", EUObserver, 4 January 2006. The principle that the name of the single European currency in Latvia must be the masculine non-declinable form 'eiro' is laid down in Regulation No. 564 of the Latvian Cabinet of Ministers, *Latvijas Vestnesis*, No. 119, 29 July 2005.

a legal requirement under Article 109 EC.[72] Accordingly, the Court might be called to decide this discussion between, on the one hand, the ECB invoking the exclusive Community competence in monetary matters and, on the other hand, Latvia's point of view concerning the application of the subsidiarity principle on language issues, which do not fall within the Community's exclusive competences.

It is noteworthy that a similar linguistic row emerged after the EU accession of Bulgaria (and Romania) in January 2007. Taking into account that the Bulgarian language version of the Accession Treaty spells the word 'euro' the Bulgarian way ('*ebpo*'—pronounced as 'evro'), this country threatened to veto an association agreement with Montenegro if it was obliged to follow the EU's strict spelling rules on the single currency. In the end, a diplomatic solution was found by using the abbreviation "EUR" in the Bulgarian language version of the agreement. In the final discussions on the Lisbon Treaty, however, the EU Heads of State or Government accepted that the Bulgarian word '*ebpo*' can be used in the Bulgarian translation of all EU official documents. This creates an important precedent in contravention of the 1995 Madrid European Council conclusions.[73]

§ 2. *The Scrutiny Role of the Baltic States' National Parliaments*

The discussions on the introduction of the euro as well as the implementation of the European arrest warrant or the extension of voting rights to EU citizens all demonstrate the impact of EU accession on the constitutional framework of the Baltic States. The preference for minimal constitutional amendments, which characterised the position of the Baltic States before enlargement, implies that further interpretations and clarifications of the respective constitutional provisions are necessary. In addition, the role of national parliaments in preventing open conflicts between national constitutions and the requirements of EU membership cannot be underestimated.[74] In this respect, the

---

[72] In this respect, it is noteworthy that the ECB has included a specific chapter on "the single spelling of the euro" in its 2006 convergence reports (see: http://www.ecb.int/pub/convergence/html/index.en.html).

[73] *Agence Europe*, 20 October 2007, pp. 5–6.

[74] A. Albi, "Supremacy of EC Law in the New Member States: Bringing Parliaments into the Equation of Co-operative Constitutionalism", 2 *European Constitutional Law Review* 3 (2007) 1 pp. 25–67.

introduction of a specific provision in the Estonian Constitutional Review Court Procedure Act allowing the *Riigikogu* to address the Supreme Court on the interpretation of the Constitution in conjunction with EU law "if the interpretation of the Constitution is decisive for the adoption of a draft Act necessary for the fulfilment of an obligation of a member of the European Union" is highly relevant.[75] A similar specific procedure of *ex ante* judicial control does not exist in Latvia and Lithuania. On the other hand, the introduction of specific EU clauses in the constitutions of the latter countries implies that their national parliaments also have a right to address the Constitutional Court on questions regarding compliance of national laws with those new provisions and thus, indirectly, with the obligations of EU membership.[76] Moreover, the national parliaments play an indirect role in the process of law-making at the European level as a result of the parliamentary scrutiny mechanisms introduced after the accession to the EU.

In a situation where a large part of national legislation directly or indirectly derives from the European Union, it is obvious that EU membership has important implications for the institutional framework of national law-making. Already in the pre-accession period, the parliaments of the three Baltic States established European integration committees and specialised institutions dealing with the implementation of EU legislation.[77] These mechanisms and procedures have been further developed after the date of accession. In particular, new rules of procedure have been adopted to regulate government-parliament relations on EU issues. In Lithuania, the right of the *Seimas* to be informed about proposals for EU legal acts has even been constitutionally enshrined in Article 3 of the Constitutional Act on Lithuania's membership of the EU.[78] Under the Parliamentary rules of procedure, the sectoral committees of the *Seimas* are responsible for the initial examination of EU draft legislative acts and divide these proposals into three categories:

---

[75] Art. 7(1). The English language version of the Constitutional Review Court Procedure Act is available at: http://www.legaltext.ee. A first application of this provision has been the request of the *Riigikogu* concerning the compliance of amendments to the Eesti Pank Act with the Constitution (cf. *supra*).

[76] See: Arts 16–17 of the Latvian Constitutional Court Law, at http://www.satv.tiesa. gov.lv/ENG/STlikums.htm and Art. 65 of the Lithuanian Law on the Constitutional Court, at: http://www.lrkt.lt/Court_Law_New.pdf.

[77] See *supra* Part II, Chapter 4, § 2.

[78] Constitutional Act of the Republic of Lithuania on Membership of the Republic of Lithuania in the European Union, 13 July 2004, IX-2343.

'very relevant' (red), 'relevant' (yellow) and 'moderately relevant' (green). The government is obliged to submit its position on 'red' and 'yellow' issues to the *Seimas* within 15 days from the receipt of the proposals.[79] The parliamentary European Affairs Committee, or the Foreign Affairs Committee for CFSP matters, has the capacity to mandate the government's position on behalf of the *Seimas*. The mandate given to the government is based on a so-called 'scrutiny reserve mechanism', which implies that Lithuanian ministers should not agree to EU proposals in the Council until parliamentary scrutiny has been completed.

A comparable mandating arrangement has been introduced in Estonia through amendments to the *Riigikogu* rules of procedure in March 2004.[80] Accordingly, the European Affairs Committee examines all draft EU legislation, which after adoption would require the amendment of national legislation or would have significant economic or social consequences. The opinion of the Parliament is politically binding: if the Government fails to adhere to the position of the *Riigikogu* it must justify its behaviour to the European Affairs Committee or the Foreign Affairs Committee "at the earliest opportunity".[81] The European Affairs Committee of the Latvian Parliament has been attributed similar far-reaching powers. Pursuant to Article 185 of the *Saeima* Rules of Procedure, this Committee examines Latvia's official positions "*before* they are communicated to the EU institutions".[82] Regulation 286 of the Cabinet of Ministers further lays down that "the Ministry concerned *has to agree* on the national position with the Saeima European Affairs Committee".[83] The combined effect of both provisions implies that the Latvian parliamentary system of mandating the government on EU affairs is considered to be the strictest of all new Member States.[84]

---

[79] COSAC, Third Bi-annual Report: Developments in European Union Procedures and Practices Relevant to Parliamentary Scrutiny, May 2005, pp. 52–53, available at: http://www.cosac.org.

[80] Riigikogu Rules of Procedure Amendment Act, available at: http://www.riigikogu. ee. For comments, see: R. Laffranque, "Le controle parlementaire de la politique européenne du Gouvernement en République d'Estonie au regard des nouvelles dispositions du règlement intérieur du *Riigikogu*", *Juridica International* (2004), pp. 69–77.

[81] § 1524 (3) Riigikogu Rules of Procedure.

[82] Emphasis added. The Saeima Rules of Procedure are available at: http://www. saeima.lv/Likumdosana_eng/likumdosana_kart_rullis.html.

[83] Emphasis added. '*The Latvian Saiema and the European Union*', http://www.ecprd. org/ipex/latvia_more.asp.

[84] K. Szalay, *Scrutinty of EU Affairs in the National Parliaments of the New Member States. Comparative Analysis*, Budapest, Hungarian National Assembly, 2005, p. 54.

The constant monitoring of the government's positions in the three Baltic States has obviously been inspired by the parliamentary scrutiny mechanisms of the Nordic countries. The Finnish model has influenced the Estonian decentralised system, with important input from sectoral standing committees in the scrutiny work. Latvia's centralised scrutiny procedure is influenced more by the Danish system, which includes a quasi-legally binding instruction for the government to abide to the Parliament's mandate.[85] Finally, Lithuania's combination of a prior document-based approach and a politically binding mandating system reflects the Swedish model. The strong parliamentary control on the governments' policy formulation in the Council does not only reflect a Nordic culture of transparent governance but also has to be understood in the light of the Baltic States' sensitivity to the transfer of sovereign rights. The Statute of the Lithuanian *Seimas*, for instance, explicitly refers to the role of the European Affairs Committee in "the implementation of the sovereignty and the rights and duties of membership of the Republic of Lithuania in the European Union".[86] The Estonian Parliament presents the scrutiny mechanism as a "compensation for the transfer of legislative powers".[87] From this perspective, the Baltic States' representatives to the Convention on the future of Europe strongly defended an increasing role for the national parliaments within the EU's institutional structure.[88] Hence, a clear interconnection between internal constitutional developments in the accession countries and the wider process of constitutionalisation at the EU level can be observed.

---

[85] P. Kiiver, "The National Parliaments in an Enlarged Europe and the Constitutional Treaty", in: K. Inglis, A. Ott, (eds.), *The Constitution for Europe and an Enlarging Union: Unity in Diversity?*, Groningen, Europa Law Publishing, 2005, p. 94.

[86] Article 61 (1) of the Statute of the Seimas, available at: http://www.lrs.lt/.

[87] X, "Riigikogu and European Union", at: http://www.riigikogu.ee.

[88] Contribution from Peter Kreitzberg and Tunne Kelam on the role of National Parliaments, CONV 95/02, 13 June 2002; Speeches by Henrik Holelei (Estonian government representative) and Guntars Krasts (representative of the Latvian Parliament) on the role of National Parliaments; Contribution by Vytenis Andriukaitis and Dalia Kutraite-Giedraitiene, CONV 220/02, 1 August 2002.

CHAPTER TWO

THE ROLE OF THE BALTIC STATES IN THE PROCESS OF EUROPEAN CONSTITUTIONALISATION

§ 1. *The Positions of the Baltic States on the EU's Internal Reform Process*

Further reflection on "the role of national parliaments in the European architecture" formed one of the outstanding issues defined in the "Declaration on the future of the Union", annexed to the Treaty of Nice. This declaration paved the way for the adoption of the Laeken Declaration at the December 2001 Laeken European Council and the subsequent establishment of the "Convention on the future of Europe".[89] Significantly, the accession countries have been "fully involved" in the Convention's proceedings from the outset. They were presented in the same way as the Member States (one government representative and two national parliament members) and took part in the discussions without, however, being able to prevent any consensus among the Member States.[90] Moreover, the December 2002 Copenhagen European Council acknowledged that the acceding countries would "participate fully" in the IGC.[91]

An analysis of the positions adopted by the representatives of Estonia, Latvia and Lithuania within the Convention and the IGC gives an indication about the priorities of the latter countries within the EU. It is noteworthy that, in contrast to the Benelux countries for instance, the Baltic States did not present joint documents nor did they organize informal meetings to co-ordinate their positions. Nevertheless, it is possible to derive a number of common interests.

---

[89] See: The Future of the European Union—Laeken Declaration, available at: http://europa.eu.int/futurum/documents/offtext/doc151201_en.htm.

[90] *Ibid*. As regards Praesidium membership, the candidate States only had one representative, the Slovenian MP Aljozs Peterle, which was invited as 'guest' after pressure from all sections of the Convention. See: N. Walker, "Constitutionalising Enlargement, Enlarging Constitutionalism", 9 *European Law Journal* 3 (2003), p. 382.

[91] Presidency Conclusions Copenhagen European Council (12–13 December 2002), *Bull. EU* 12 (2002), I.3.8. Significantly, the invitation of the candidate countries that had concluded accession negotiations was already provided in the Declaration on the future of the Union, annexed to the Nice Treaty (cf. *supra*).

First, the three Baltic States firmly opposed any reference to federalism and considered the term 'Constitution' inappropriate to describe the Union's basic legal document.[92] This position reflects the deeply entrenched understanding that the notion of a constitution is inherently bound to the nation-state, which renders inappropriate its use in the context of the European Union.[93] Arguably, this conservative approach also marks the influence of the Soviet legacy. The parallels with the Soviet Constitution and its definition of the Soviet Union as "a federal, multinational state formed on the principle of socialist federalism"[94] explain the Baltic sensitivities.

Second, the Baltic debate on the future of the EU essentially focused on the preservation of national sovereignty and identity in an enlarged EU. Therefore, the Estonian, Latvian and Lithuanian representatives supported the inclusion of a so-called 'Member State protection clause' to the EU Treaty. This provision stipulates that the EU respects the national identities of the Member States, their political and constitutional structure as well as the essential state functions.[95] Another important novelty actively promoted by the Baltic States is the introduction of a clause on voluntary withdrawal from the Union.[96] Again, the

---

[92] See e.g. Contribution from Mr. Vytenis Povilas Andriukaitis, representative of the Lithuanian Parliament, "Draft of articles 1 to 16 of the Constitutional Treaty", CONV 578/03, Brussels, 26 Feb. 2003, pp. 4–5; Suggestion for amendment of Article 1, Title I by Mr. V.P. Andriukaitis, Mr. A.Gricius, Mr. O. Jusys, Mr. R. Martikonis, representatives of the Lithuanian Parliament and Government at: http://european-convention. eu.int/docs/treaty/pdf/1/Art1Andriukaitis.pdf; Suggestion for amendment of Article 1, Title I by Mrs. S. Kalniete, Mr. R. Zile, Mrs. L. Liepina, Mr. R. Piks, Mr. A. Karins and Mr. G. Krasts, representatives of the Latvian Government and Parliament, at: http://European-convention.eu.int/docs/treaty/pdf/1/Art%201%20Kalniete.pdf; Suggestion for amendment of Articles 3,5,6,7,8,9,10,12,16 by Mr. H. Hololei, alternate representative of the Estonian Government, at: http://european-convention. eu.int/docs/treaty/pdf/3/Art%203%20etc%20Hololei.pdf.

[93] This interpretation ignores the growing recognition that constitutions may also exist in non-state contexts. See: A. Albi, P. Van Elsuwege, "The EU Constitution, National Constitutions and Sovereignty: An Assessment of a European Constitutional Order", 29 *European Law Review* 6 (2004), p. 748.

[94] Article 70 (1) Soviet Constitution. See: R. Sharlet, *The New Soviet Constitution of 1977. Analysis and Text*, Brunswick, King's Court Communications, 1985, p. 99.

[95] Art. 3a of the Lisbon Treaty and Art. 4 in the new numbering of the Treaty on European Union.

[96] Art. 49a of the Lisbon Treaty and Art. 50 in the new numbering of the Treaty on European Union. For a legal analysis of this clause, see: J.-V. Louis, "Le droit de retrait de l'Union européenne", 42 *Cahiers de Droit Européen* 3–4 (2006), pp. 303–313.

Soviet heritage inspired the Baltic position.[97] Moreover, the insistence on a possibility of withdrawal reflects the traditional understanding of national sovereignty as laid down in the constitutions of Estonia, Latvia and Lithuania (cf. *supra*).[98]

Third, and related to the previous observations, the Baltic representatives actively promoted a reinforced and consistent application of the principle of subsidiarity. The Estonian government, *inter alia*, proposed that "the Commission should in every proposal phase explain the reasons why the measure envisaged should be adopted and why at the European level".[99] For monitoring the principle of subsidiarity an 'early warning system' involving the national Parliaments of the Member States has been proposed in combination with a right to refer to the European Court of Justice in case of an alleged breach of this rule. Lithuanian and Latvian representatives fully endorsed this mechanism of *ex ante* control and the possibility of *ex post* judicial review.[100] The importance attributed to the principle of subsidiarity is in line with the scrutiny role of the national parliaments and the preoccupation with retaining national sovereignty after accession to the EU.

Fourth, the equality of Member States is the core principle of the Baltic States' position on the reform of the Union's institutions. In this regard, the Baltic republics joined a coalition of small states, which basically subscribed to the principle of one Commissioner per Member State, promoted the preservation of the rotating Council Presidency and opposed the creation of new institutions that could upset the existing

---

[97] In his speech in favour of a withdrawal clause, Estonia's representative in the Convention, Henrik Hololei, argued that "such a clause formally existed even in the Soviet and Yugoslav constitutions [...] Not having this article makes it difficult to defend the new Constitutional Treaty in my country". Cited in: P. Aalto, *European Union and the Making of a Wider Northern Europe*, London-New York, Routledge, 2006, pp. 67–68.

[98] This is, for instance, clearly expressed in the following statement of Latvia's former Foreign Minister, Sandra Kalniete: "The European Union is made up of Member States who made up the Member States who voluntarily delegate a part of their sovereignty to the Union. Therefore, the citizens of the Union must have a guaranteed right to the return of the delegated part of their sovereignty". See: http://www.am.gov .lv/en/news/speeches/ (20 May 2005).

[99] Positions of the Estonian Government on the Future of Europe, available at: http://www.eib.ee.

[100] See e.g.: Contribution by Mr. V.P. Andriukaitis, representative of the Lithuanian Parliament, on "the positions discussed by the Committee on European Affairs of the Seimas of the Republic of Lithuania", CONV 338/02, p. 5; Speech by G. Krasts, Member of the Latvian Parliament and Alternate Member to the Convention, Brussels, 18 March 2003, at: http://european-convention.eu.int/docs/speeches/8318.pdf.

balances.[101] Generally speaking, the Baltic States essentially promoted a *status quo* on institutional affairs. Henrik Hololei, the alternate Estonian representative to the Convention, explicitly stated that "the imminent enlargement of the Union does not constitute a good excuse for a radical reform of so far served decision-making". He, therefore, argued that "the size and principles of the composition of the Commission, weighting of votes in the Council and the size of the European Parliament should be left untouched by the Convention".[102] Lithuanian representatives have expressed a similar preference for an institutional *status quo*.[103] Only Latvia has actively supported a reform of the system of QMV. The mechanism of double majority voting (states and population) has been promoted as an alternative because "such a system would facilitate decision-making and increase the influence of small countries in the Council".[104] This attitude reflects Latvia's dissatisfaction with the outcome of the Nice redistribution of votes.[105]

Fifth, the conservative approach towards the institutional reform process also implies a preference for the retention of a unanimity requirement in important fields of national sovereignty. Estonia, for instance, pleaded for unanimity voting in the areas of foreign and defence policy, social and regional policy and taxation.[106] Whereas the extension of QMV in other areas was supported in principle, decisions on this extension should be taken "on a case-by case basis taking into account the financial consequences and capabilities to implement the decisions taken by qualified majority",[107] and "recognizing that there are areas which are too sensitive for Member States to give up their

---

[101] Contribution submitted by Mr. M. Attalidis, Mr. P. Balazs, Mr. H. Christophersen, Mr. H. Farnleitner, Mr. L. Hjelm-Wallen, Ms. S. Kalniete, Mr. J. Kohout, Mr. I. Korcok, Ms. M. Kuneva, Mr. E. Lopes, Mr. R. Martikonis, Mr. L. Meri, Mr. D. Roche, Mr. D. Rupel, Mr. P. Serracino-Inglott, Mr. T. Tiikiakainen, members of the Convention, on "Reforming the Institutions: Principles and Premises", CONV 646/03, Brussels, 28 March 2003.

[102] Statement by Mr. Henrik Hololei, Alternate Member of the Convention representing the Government of Estonia, on articles 14–23 of the draft Constitutional Treaty, Brussels, 15–16 May 2003, at: http://european-convention.eu.int/docs/speeches/9157.pdf.

[103] See e.g. contribution by V.P. Andriukaitis, CONV 338/02.

[104] Latvia's position at the Intergovernmental Conference, available at: http://www.am.gov.lv.

[105] See *supra* Part III, Chapter 5, § 2.

[106] Tax harmonisation on the basis of QMV is seen as a threat to the very liberal features of the Estonian tax system.

[107] Contribution submitted by Mr. R. Martikonis: "Position of the Government of Lithuania on institutional reform", CONV 589/03, Brussels, 28 Feb. 2003.

powers".[108] The strong support for national vetoes in the fields of taxation and social policy aligned the Baltic States, and Estonia in particular, to the United Kingdom.[109] In other words, the Baltic States defended an intergovernmental rather than supranational vision on the future of the EU.

Of particular significance is the reluctance of the Baltic States to accept any form of supranational decision-making on second pillar issues. The main reason for this cautious approach is the fear that a further development of the EU's military capacities would undermine the role of NATO within the European security architecture. Moreover, the Baltic republics fear that old Member States might adopt a very soft approach towards Russia.[110] Finally, the most important argument against deepening integration in the area of foreign and security policy is that these policies affect the core of state sovereignty.[111] Whereas this position is understandable from the perspective of the Baltic States' recent history, it is somewhat paradoxical in the light of these countries' desire to have a strong Union that speaks with one voice in world affairs, in particular with regard to Russia. A similar paradox between the basic position of not transferring more sovereign rights and the interest in an efficient common policy at EU level can be found in the field of energy (cf. *supra*). Hence, the general perception of the Baltic countries as being the most eurosceptic new Member States does not necessarily correspond to the long-term interests of those countries.

---

[108] P. Ehin, V. Veebel, "National Report Estonia", in: C. Franck, D. Pyszna-Nigge, (eds.), *Positions of 10 Central and Eastern European Countries on EU Institutional Reforms*, Louvain-la-Neuve/Brussels, 2003, p. 45.

[109] It is, for instance, noteworthy that the Prime Ministers of Estonia and the UK, Juhan Parts and Tony Blair, published a joint letter in the Financial Times and the Estonian daily Postimees on 3 October 2003. In this respect, reference has been made to the "Britainisation" of Estonia's European policy. See: A. Lobjakas, "Estonia Adrift: Caught in the Crosswinds of the EU's Constitutional Debate", *Estonian Foreign Policy Yearbook* (2004), p. 92.

[110] A. Kasekamp, "The North-East", in: H. Mouritzen, A. Wivel, (eds.), *The Geopolitics of Euro-Atlantic Integration*, London—New York, Routledge, 2005, p. 156.

[111] K. Raik, "Does the European Union Still Matter for Estonia's Security? Positioning Estonia in CFSP and ESDP", *Estonian Foreign Policy Yearbook* (2003), p. 172.

§ 2. *The Stalled Ratification of the Constitutional Treaty and Prospects for the Future*

Pursuant to Article 48 EU, Treaty amendments in the EU require the approval of all Member States under "national constitutional procedures". The precedent of the discussions surrounding the organization of referendums on the Treaty of Accession illustrates the procedural and political complications of this notion (cf. *supra*). In particular, the tension between the constitutional provisions on the ratification of international agreements by the national parliaments and the organization of referendums on "issues of national concern" raises interesting legal questions. In principle, the constitutional systems of the three Baltic States provide for the possibility of constitutional review before the ratification of an international agreement.[112] This could solve the dilemma whether or not the ratification of an EC/EU Treaty amendment requires constitutional amendments and/or the organization of a national referendum. In practice, however, no constitutional review procedures were initiated with regard to the Europe Agreement, the Accession Treaty, the Treaty establishing a Constitution for Europe or the Lisbon Treaty. This implies that policy makers in the Baltic States had a certain margin of appraisal as regards the procedure for ratification of those important agreements.

Apparently, the accession referendum experience inspired high-level politicians in the three Baltic republics to downplay the significance of the EU's constitutional reform process as nothing more than a rationalisation of the existing treaties. The main argument that the rules applicable at the time of accession would not fundamentally change was particularly important in Latvia, given that the Latvian Constitution provides for the option of a binding national referendum in case of

---

[112] Pursuant to Arts 5–6 of the Estonian Constitutional Review Act, the Legal Chancellor and the President are competent to initiate constitutional review of an international agreement. Under Art. 106 of the Lithuanian Constitution, the Parliament and the President have a right to request an opinion of the Constitutional Court concerning the constitutionality of international agreements. Art. 17 of the Latvian Constitutional Court provides the right to initiate constitutional review of non-ratified international agreements to the President, at least 20 members of the Saeima, the Cabinet of Ministers, the Prosecutor General, the Council of the State Control, the Council of a Municipality, the State Human Rights Bureau, lower courts and private persons "whose fundamental rights established by the Constitution have been violated".

'substantial changes' to the terms of membership.[113] Of particular significance in the decision not to organize a referendum has been the statement of President Vike-Freiberga on 1 October 2003 that she did not see the need for a referendum as the new Treaty "would not fundamentally change the content of the Accession Treaty".[114] The option of organizing a referendum was also ruled out in Lithuania and Estonia, essentially because of the same reason.

Table 12: Ratification of the Treaty establishing a Constitution for Europe[115]

	Date	Parliamentary Approval	Public Support (Eurobarometer surveys)
Estonia	9 May 2006	71 %	32 %
Latvia	2 June 2005	73 %	41 %
Lithuania	11 November 2004	92 %	51 %

The parliaments of the three Baltic republics ratified the Constitutional Treaty with significant majorities. It is noteworthy that Lithuania was the first Member State to conclude the ratification procedure on 11 November 2004, i.e. less than two weeks after the document was formally signed, whereas Latvia and Estonia only ratified after the negative referendum outcomes in France and the Netherlands. The parliamentary support for the Constitutional Treaty is comparable to the outcome of the accession referendums (cf. *supra*) but does not necessarily reflect the level of public support as indicated in the official Eurobarometer reports. Only in Lithuania opinion polls conducted in November 2004 suggested that a majority of the population would vote in favour of the Constitution. Hence, the fear that the organization of referendums on future treaty revisions might complicate the ratification procedure at EU level seems justified. The question is whether it will be possible to

---

[113] Article 68 of the Latvian Constitution states that in this case a referendum has to be organized if this is requested by "at least one-half of the members of the Saeima". Only the biggest opposition party, the People's Party with 20 seats in the 100-seat Parliament, suggested the need of a referendum.

[114] See: http://www.unizar.es/euroconstitucion/Treaties/Treaty_Const_Rat_latvia .htm.

[115] Based upon the results of a special Eurobarometer report on the Constitutional Treaty, available at: http://ec.europa.eu/public_opinion/archives/ebs/ebs214_tables .pdf

avoid referendums in the future given the sensitivity of the transfer of sovereign powers and the countries' constitutional tradition of organizing referendums on issues of national concern. At least with regard to the ratification of the Lisbon Treaty no major problems can be expected given the ratified status of the more ambitious Constitutional Treaty in each of the Baltic States.[116]

---

[116] At the time of writing, ratification of the Lisbon Treaty was planned to take place through a parliamentary procedure in each of the Baltic States.

THE CONSTITUTIONAL CHALLENGES
AFTER ENLARGEMENT

The process of EU enlargement raises numerous constitutional questions, not only in the pre-accession period but also after the date of accession. Issues such as the extension of voting rights to EU citizens, the application of the European arrest warrant and the introduction of the euro clearly illustrate this point. The limited EU-related amendments in anticipation of the date of accession imply an almost constant revision of constitutional provisions during the first years of EU membership. In addition, further interpretations of the rather laconic constitutional provisions on the relationship between national law and EU law seem indispensable. This is particularly the case in Estonia. The inclusion of an all-embracing provision on the primacy of EU law in the Third Constitutional Act implies that parts of the Estonian Constitution are inapplicable, which raises problems of legal certainty and clarity. From this perspective, the alternative of clear-cut amendments to the text of the Constitution seems to be a better solution. It is noteworthy that the Estonian Legal Chancellor implicitly referred to this model when he proclaimed in the euro-related amendment discussions that "the best solution for ensuring the applicability of the Constitution, whereas proceeding from the principle of legal clarity, would be a Constitution wherein the amendments arising from the Accession Treaty and following from the transposition of EU law were introduced to".[117] It is also significant that in the legal debates about the ratification of the Constitutional Treaty in Estonia, the need to modernise or even entirely revise the Estonian Constitution has been brought to the fore.[118]

---

[117] Opinion of the Constitutional Review Chamber of the Supreme Court on the interpretation of the Constitution, 3–4–1–3–06, at para. 5.

[118] J. Laffranque, "Ratification of the European Constitution in Estonia: A New Constitution for Estonia?", in: A. Albi, J. Ziller, J. (eds.), *European Constitution and National Constitutions: Ratification and Beyond'*, The Hague, Kluwer Law International, 2007, p. 81.

A less far-reaching solution could be to include a reference to the Third Constitutional Act in the preamble or the general provisions of the Estonian Constitution.[119]

In contrast to the ambiguous Estonian constitutional framework, more straightforward amendments have been adopted to the Lithuanian and Latvian Constitutions. This does not mean, however, that all problems have been solved. Article 7 (1) of the Lithuanian Constitution, for instance, provides that any law or statute that is in conflict with the Constitution shall be invalid. Obviously, this provision has to be read in conjunction with the Constitutional Act ensuring the supremacy of EU law. Constitutional Court cases clarifying this relationship cannot be excluded.[120] In Latvia, the designation of the euro in the Latvian language raises interesting questions about the relationship between EU and Member State competences. Moreover, the constitutional provision that substantive changes to the terms of EU membership are subject to a binding national referendum promises to arouse discussions on the transfer of sovereign rights in case of future treaty amendments.

The ratification of the Treaty establishing a Constitution for Europe passed the parliamentary procedure in the Baltic States without many deliberations and a similar result can be expected with regard to the Lisbon Treaty. The timing of the EU's reform exercise, shortly after the referendums on EU accession, in combination with the strategy of high-level politicians to present the Constitutional Treaty as a document of simplification and rationalisation explain the absence of a profound public debate. Be that as it may, it seems obvious that a certain interaction between the national constitutional context of the Baltic States and the process of constitutionalisation at the EU level can be observed. The insistence of the Baltic representatives to include a clause on voluntary withdrawal in the EU Treaty, the importance attributed to the principle of 'subsidiarity' and the involvement of national parliaments in the EU's

---

[119] J. Laffranque, "A Glance at the Estonian Legal Landscape in View of the Constitution Amendment Act", 12 *Juridica International* (2007), p. 57.

[120] A Constitutional Court case of March 2006 "on the limitation of the rights of ownership in areas of particular value and in forest land" only contributed to the legal ambiguity surrounding the relationship between the supremacy clause of the Constitutional Act on Lithuania's EU Membership and Article 7 (1) of the Constitution. See *supra* Part IV, Chapter 3, § 3.1.3.

institutional structure all reflect the 'soverainist' nature of the Baltic constitutions, which is largely inspired by the Soviet heritage. The main challenge is, therefore, to further clarify the relationship between the national and European constitutional order without precluding further progress in the process of European integration.

GENERAL CONCLUSIONS

§ 1. *Understanding the EU Accession of the Baltic States: The Interaction between Law and Politics*

Estonia, Latvia and Lithuania regained their independence in August 1991 on the basis of the international law principle of state continuity. Whereas the E(E)C and its Member States explicitly recognized this reality, Russia has refused to accept the continued statehood of the Baltic States. The consequences of this different legal perspective cannot be underestimated. It explains, for instance, the divergent views on the validity of international agreements and determines the legal status of the large Soviet-era immigrants. In combination with the unpredictable domestic situation in Russia, the legal uncertainties after the restoration of the Baltic States' independence created an atmosphere with huge potential for conflict. The integration of the Baltic States in the EU enlargement process, on a par with the other countries from Central and Eastern Europe, can be regarded as the EU's response to this challenging environment. This does not imply that the EU accession of Estonia, Latvia and Lithuania was an evident or pre-determined option. The analysis of the EU's enlargement policy rather reveals a process of *ad hoc* reactions depending on the rapidly changing context in the EU, the candidate countries and Russia. Only after the retreat of the Russian troops and in the context of the EU accession of the Nordic countries Sweden and Finland, the EU formally acknowledged the membership perspectives of Estonia, Latvia and Lithuania.

Significantly, the three Baltic States followed a slightly different path to accession in comparison to the other new Member States from Central and Eastern Europe. Whereas the latter all signed Europe Agreements and then concluded Interim Agreements on trade and trade-related matters, the EC first concluded Free Trade Agreements with the three Baltic States and was only prepared to conclude fully-fledged association agreements afterwards. This differentiation might appear superficial but is important from a legal and political point of view. Association agreements are the most far-reaching type of bilateral agreements concluded between the EC and third countries. Whereas 'association' is neither a guarantee nor a formal prerequisite for accession to the EU, the conclusions of the 1993 Copenhagen European Council explicitly mentioned that the 'associated' countries from Central and Eastern Europe were destined to join the EU once they satisfied the criteria for accession. Accordingly, it was only with the conclusion of the Europe Agreements in June 1995 that the Baltic States were formally included in the EU's enlargement process to embrace the countries from Central and Eastern Europe.

In comparison to similar agreements concluded with the other Central and Eastern European countries, the focus on intra-Baltic co-operation formed a specific characteristic of the Europe Agreements with Estonia, Latvia and Lithuania. The condition of regional trade integration as a prerequisite for progress on the road to accession illustrated the EU's group approach towards the three Baltic republics at the beginning of the 1990s. The conclusion of a Baltic Free Trade Agreement as well as an additional agreement on the abolition of non-tariff barriers demonstrated the effectiveness of the EU's involvement. Whereas stimulating close regional co-operation continued to be an objective of the EU's pre-accession strategy, the publication of the European Commission's Opinions on the membership applications of Estonia, Latvia and Lithuania in June 1997 marked a significant turning point in the EU's approach in the direction of a more individual treatment of the three Baltic countries.

The recommendation to start accession negotiations with Estonia but not with Latvia and Lithuania revealed a first paradox of the EU enlargement methodology. The legal admission procedure, based upon the assessment of each individual candidate's progress towards meeting the formal accession criteria, sometimes interferes with the EU's insistence on close regional co-operation among the candidate countries. A clear example of this paradox is certainly the requirement to abandon free trade arrangements in case of differentiated accession to the EU. The legal and political consequences of differentiation explain, in other words, the preference for a joint accession of countries with close economic and legal connections. This observation is not without consequences for future enlargement waves, in particular towards the countries of the Western Balkans. An early accession of Croatia, for instance, will most probably imply that this country has to denounce agreements concluded in the framework of the regional trade integration programme of the Stabilisation and Association Process.

The paradoxical interplay between the legal and political dimensions of enlargement continued in the framework of the accession negotiations. Whereas the negotiations are conducted in bilateral IGCs and, in principle, proceed on an individual basis with each candidate country, the EU clearly applied a group approach by presenting equal solutions to all candidates. The competitive nature of the accession process forced the candidates to accept the EU's common positions as fast as possible, which illustrates the limits of differentiation between the countries concerned. This is particularly the case for core areas of the EU's internal market *acquis*. It is noteworthy, however, that the inclusion of flexible transitional arrangements in the Act of Accession allows for further differentiation after the date of accession.

In order to avoid the impression that (geo)political imperatives rather than objective criteria determine a country's progress towards accession, the EU has gradually developed an enhanced pre-accession strategy, including new financial instruments, Accession Partnerships and regular reports of the European Commission. The main problem is the absence of an independent monitoring mechanism or at least clear rules or guidelines for assessing the political criteria. As a result, the Commission's pre-accession monitoring reports sometimes suffer from a lack of transparency and consistency as far as the political conditions for membership are concerned. The specific condition of "respect for and protection of minorities" forms a case in point. An analysis of the Commission regular reports reveals that, in the absence of a comprehensive internal EU policy on minority protection, the Council of Europe Framework Convention on the Protection of National Minorities constitutes the main reference document in this respect. The credibility of the EU's conditionality in this area is, however, undermined by the observation that certain Member States have not yet ratified or, in the case of France, not even signed this document. The precedent of Latvia further illustrates that ratification *as such* is no condition for accession to the EU whereas its restrictive interpretations to the application of core provisions of the Framework Convention raise questions as to the degree of flexibility of this document.

The application of the EU's pre-accession conditionality *vis-à-vis* the Baltic States reveals a balanced picture. In general, the *acquis communautaire* provided clear guidelines for the adoption of national legislation. In areas where there is no binding *acquis*, the conditionality approach only appeared effective when it was linked to concrete membership related incentives or, at least, when substantial carrots and sticks were at stake. For instance, the absence of internal rules on the safety of nuclear installations did not prevent the EU to insist on a clear deadline for the closure and decommissioning of Lithuania's Ignalina Nuclear Power Plant. The amendments to Estonia's law on aliens in anticipation of the 1997 Luxembourg European Council or the abolition of the discriminatory 'windows system' in Latvia's citizenship legislation before the 1999 Helsinki European Council had to decide on the start of accession negotiations are other illustrations of this point. In general, however, the rather cursory statements included in the pre-accession monitoring reports did not necessarily have a concrete impact on the policy choices of the candidate countries. With regard to the integration of the Russian-speaking minorities, the Commission essentially focused on formal amendments rather than on the effective implementation and the concrete consequences of the legislation in question. The direct impact of the EU on important areas of minority protection such as the right to education in the minority language or the effective participation of minorities in public affairs has, therefore, been rather limited. Accordingly, effective co-operation with other normative based international organizations such as the OSCE or the Council of Europe turned out to be instrumental to ensure compliance with the EU's political pre-accession criteria.

Significantly, a discrepancy between the EU's almost unlimited powers to interfere in the domestic affairs of the candidate countries during the pre-accession period and the more restricted options after the date of accession could be observed. This can be attributed to the vague formulation of Article 49 EU and the Copenhagen criteria, which do not confine the Commission's monitoring activities to issues of legal competence. The Commission's role in the 'post-accession period', on the other hand, is based upon the principles of Community competence as laid down in the Treaties. A good example concerns the citizenship legislation in Estonia and Latvia. Whereas the European Commission constantly referred to the rate of naturalisation and stimulated a facilitation of the conditions for citizenship in its annual pre-accession monitoring reports, the fact that citizenship questions belong to the exclusive competences of the Member States implies that the EU can no longer play a significant role in this respect.

The application of the *acquis communautaire* does not automatically solve the integration dilemmas of the Russian-speaking communities in Estonia and Latvia. The ECJ case law indicates how far Member States can go in demanding proficient knowledge of a language as a condition for access to employment and reduces the possibilities of the Baltic States to reserve certain professions to their own nationals.[1] However, this does not necessarily improve the position of the Russian-speaking minorities, as is clearly illustrated by the example of Latvia's law on advocacy or recent amendments to the Estonian language act.[2] The absence of clear provisions on language discrimination in the EC non-discrimination directives as well as the lack of a specific legal basis for developing a comprehensive policy on minority integration at the EU level further reduce the significance of the Union as an actor promoting the integration of the minority population.

§ 2. *The External and Internal Consequences of the Baltic States' Accession to the EU*

For obvious reasons, the EU accession of the Baltic States significantly affects the Union's relations with Russia. The situation of the Russian-speaking minorities, the question of border delimitation, Kaliningrad transit and the different perspectives on the legacy of the Soviet Union are the most significant challenges. In the pre-accession period, the Union has always been very reluctant to discuss enlargement related issues with Russia. Only in the final stages, when questions such as Kaliningrad transit or the extension of the Partnership and Co-operation Agreement (PCA) could no longer be avoided, discussions took place within the framework of the Partnership institutions. Taking into account the incapacity of the Partnership Council to adopt binding decisions on the basis of the PCA as well as the legal complexities surrounding the conclusion and ratification of binding bilateral agreements, the enlargement related dilemmas in EU-Russia relations have largely been overcome on the basis of Joint Statements with a purely political significance.

The adoption of the four Common Spaces road maps, the conclusion of bilateral agreements on visa facilitation and readmission as well as the reorientation of the Northern Dimension imply that the EU accession of the Baltic States does not necessarily have negative consequences for the development of EU-Russia relations. Moreover,

---

[1] See e.g. ECJ, Case C-379/87, *Groener* v. *Minister for Education*, [1989] ECR 3987; ECJ, Case 149/79 *Commission* v. *Belgium* [1980] ECR 3881.
[2] See Part V, Chapter 2, § 1.

the significant increase of trade, new initiatives to enhance economic and scientific co-operation and, most significantly, the long-awaited conclusion of the border treaty between Latvia and Russia illustrate the positive impact of enlargement on the bilateral relations between the Russian Federation and each of the Baltic republics. On the other hand, however, numerous problems continue to exist. Russia's refusal to recognize the continued statehood of the Baltic States remains a crucial challenge. Moreover, the different interpretation of historical facts sometimes has a paralysing effect. The controversy concerning Estonia's War Graves Protection Act, for instance, seriously deteriorates the atmosphere for discussing any opening towards the conclusion of a border agreement.

The accession of the Baltic States has increased Russia's strategic importance for the EU. The security of energy supply and the democ-ratisation of the so-called 'common neighbourhood' of former Soviet republics are new long-term priorities on the EU's agenda. In this respect, a kind of 'spill-over effect' between the EU's external challenges and its internal legal development can be observed. The question of energy security triggers the need for a common energy policy and the effective implementation of the European Neighbourhood Policy. It is remarkable that the Lisbon Treaty includes a specific legal basis for the development of both policy areas.[3] This evolution illustrates the dynamic nature of the European integration process.

A similar dynamic process can be observed in the new Member States. Accession to the EU required a revision of national constitutional provisions, leading to a so-called 'integration dilemma': i.e. the balance between integration benefits and losses in terms of sovereignty.[4] This dilemma has dominated the domestic discussions on EU accession in each of the Baltic republics. Their recent history inside the Soviet Union and the resulting constitutional safeguards protecting the principle of national sovereignty implied difficult and minimal amendment proce-dures providing for the transfer of sovereign rights. The most innovative but also the most questionable solution in terms of legal clarity has been applied in Estonia. Instead of amending the Constitution itself, a specific Constitutional Amendment Act has been adopted together with

---

[3] Art. 194 TFEU and Art. 8 TEU, Treaty of Lisbon, *OJ* (2007) C 306/1.

[4] G. Herd, "The Baltic States and EU Enlargement", in: K. Henderson, (ed.), *Back to Europe. Central and Eastern Europe and the European Union*, London, UCL Press, 1999, p. 270.

the referendum on accession to the EU. It is rather paradoxical that this solution, which is the result of political reluctance to introduce clear-cut constitutional amendments on the transfer of sovereign rights, has opened the gates to a very wide interpretation of EU law supremacy leading to the partial inapplicability of formal constitutional provisions. Obviously, this situation undermines the clarity and consistency of the Estonian constitutional system. In Lithuania, on the other hand, the adoption of a specific Constitutional Act on the country's relations with the EU is less problematic in the absence of open conflicts between constitutional provisions and the obligations of EU membership.[5] It is, however, striking that the interrelationship between the Lithuanian and the EU legal order has only been clarified after the date of accession. In Latvia, the only Baltic country that reintroduced its interwar Constitution after the restoration of independence, the process of EU accession formed an incentive for the modernisation of this Constitution. In the framework of the political conditions for accession, a new Chapter VIII on 'fundamental human rights' has been included in October 1998. Other EU related amendments concerning the transfer of sovereign rights and specific issues related to EU citizenship rights or the European arrest warrant have been included shortly before or after the date of accession.

The Soviet legacy largely explains the preference for minimal and last minute constitutional amendments and the cautious approach towards far-reaching changes to the EU's institutional framework. The common heritage of the Soviet period also affects the position of the Baltic States in the enlarged EU. The interest in a stable, values-based Strategic Partnership with Russia, questions of energy security as well as a more active engagement in the area of the former Soviet Union are clear priorities after accession. Following the example of the Nordic countries, Estonia, Latvia and Lithuania actively support the democratic transition in neighbouring countries. Hence, it can be concluded that the Baltic States gradually find their specific 'niche' within the EU.[6]

---

[5] Only the formulation of Article 7 (1) of the Constitution, proclaiming that any laws or acts contrary to the Constitution shall be invalid remains somewhat ambiguous in the light of the ECJ ruling in *Internationale Handelsgesellschaft* (cf. *supra*).

[6] M. Kremer, "Towards an EU Baltic Policy", in: M. Buhbe, I. Kempes, (eds.), *Russia, the EU and the Baltic States. Enhancing the Potential for Cooperation*, Moscow, 2005, p. 25. (available at: http://www.cap.lmu.de/download/2006/2006_Russia-EU-Baltic.pdf).

OVERVIEW OF NEGOTIATIONS AND TRANSITIONAL ARRANGEMENTS WITH ESTONIA[1]

Negotiating Chapter	Opened	Closed[2]	Transitional arrangements
1. Free Movement of Goods	June 1999	December 2000	None; but Estonia may apply for a transitional period until 31 December 2006 with respect to maximum levels of dioxin content in fish and fish products (to be granted by the Commission in accordance with the procedure of Article 8 of Regulation 315/93).
2. Freedom of Movement for Persons	May 2000	March 2002	2+3+2 flexible arrangement on free movement of workers: during the first two years the 15 old Member States (EU 15) apply national measures, after this period reviews will be held and on the basis of a Commission report the EU 15 decide on whether to apply the *acquis*.

---

[1] Information from: European Commission, "Enlargement of the European Union. Guide to the Negotiations. Chapter by Chapter", available at: http://www.europa. eu.int/comm/enlargement/negotiations/chapters/negotiationsguide.pdf; Report on the results of the negotiations on the accession of Cyprus, Malta, Hungary, Poland, the Slovak Republic, Latvia, Estonia, Lithuania, the Czech Republic and Slovenia to the European Union, available at: http://www.europa.eu.int/comm/enlargement/negotiations/pdf/negotiations_report_to_ep.pdf; and the Act concerning the conditions for accession of the Czech Republic, the Republic of Estonia, the Republic of Cyprus, the Republic of Latvia, the Republic of Lithuania, the Republic of Hungary, the Republic of Malta, the Republic of Poland, the Republic of Slovenia and the Slovak Republic and the adjustments to the Treaties on which the European Union is founded, in particular Annex VI to this Act, including the list of transitional measures for Latvia, *OJ* (2003) L 236/33.

[2] All negotiating chapters have been officially closed in December 2002. For that reason, the provisionally closing dates of the different chapters have been included in this table.

Annex I (*cont.*)

Negotiating Chapter	Opened	Closed	Transitional arrangements
			The transitional period should in principle come to an end after five years but may be prolonged for a further two years in those Member States where there would be serious disturbances of the labour market or a threat of such disruption. Safeguards may be applied by the EU 15 up to the end of the seventh year after accession. Estonia may apply to nationals from the EU 15 national measures equivalent to the measures applied by that Member State. As long as the EU 15 apply national measures, Estonia may also resort to safe-guard measures with regard to the new Member States. The flexible arrangement further includes a standstill clause, which implies that the EU 15 cannot apply more restrictive measures than those applicable at the time of the signature of the Accession Treaty, and a preferential clause, which means that the EU 15 should give preference to nation-als of new Member States over non-EU labour.
3. Freedom to Provide Services	August 1999	December 2000	Lower levels of bank deposit guarantee and investor compen-sation until 31 December 2007.
4. Free Move-ment of Capital	Autumn 1999	May 2000	7-year transitional period for the acquisition of agricultural and forestry land, excluding self-employed farmers who have been residing for 3 years and active in farming from the scope. Pos-sibility to extend this transitional period by three years if Estonia invokes safeguard clause.

Annex I (*cont.*)

Negotiating Chapter	Opened	Closed	Transitional arrangements
5. Company Law	Sep. 1998	Apr. 2000	None
6. Competition Policy	May 1999	November 2001	None
7. Agriculture	June 2000	December 2002	Gradual phasing in of agricultural direct payments between 2004 and 2013 with a possibility to top-up direct payments to a certain level with money from the national budget and rural development allocations; unlimited use of domestic peat in organic farming for a period of 18 months after accession; permitted use of potassium permanganate for a period of 18 months after accession; permitted use in organic farming of seed and vegetative propagating material not produced by the organic production method until 1 January 2006; until the end of 2006, Estonia may consider cows of the breeds listed in Annex I to Regulation 2342/99 as eligible for the suckler cow premium provided that they have been covered or inseminated by bulls of a meat breed; permission to grant national payments for milk cows up to the level granted in 2003 for the marketing year 2004/2005; possibility to adopt further transitional measures relating to the CAP or veterinary and phytosanitary rules until 1 May 2007; agreement has been reached upon production quotas, premiums and other supply management instruments.[3]

[3] A detailed overview of these arrangements is available at the website of the Estonian Ministry of Agriculture: http://www.agri.ee/eng/index.html.

Annex I (*cont.*)

Negotiating Chapter	Opened	Closed	Transitional arrangements
8. Fisheries	April 1999	April 2000	None. Through technical adaptations in the Accession Treaty, Estonia can maintain its traditional fishing of small size Baltic herring for human consumption, caught in traditional waters.
9. Transport Policy	November 1999	March 2002	2+2+1 flexible arrangement on access of non-resident hauliers to the national road transport market of other Member States: after a two-years transitional period during which undertakings established in Estonia are reciprocally excluded from operation of national road haulage services in other Member States, this period can be prolonged for another two years (after notification to the Commission) and after this period for one additional year in case of serious disturbances, or threat thereof, on the national road haulage market.
10. Taxation	November 1999	June 2002	Reduced VAT rate on heating until 30 June 2007; turnover threshold to exempt SMEs from VAT set at € 16,000; lower excise duty rates on cigarettes until 31 December 2009; full alignment to the parent-subsidiary directive until 31 December 2008; VAT exemption on international passenger transport until the condition set out in Article 28(4) of directive 77/388 EEC is fulfilled or for as long as the same exemption is applied by any of the present Member States.

Annex I (*cont.*)

Negotiating Chapter	Opened	Closed	Transitional arrangements
11. EMU	Fist half 1999	December 1999	None; Estonia participates in EMU from the date of accession as a Member State with a derogation in the meaning of Article 122 EC.
12. Statistics	March 1999	June 1999	None
13. Employment and Social Policy	Sept. 1999	October 2000	None
14. Energy	Second half 1999	July 2002	Build up of oil stocks to required level until the end of 2009; implementation of electricity directive until the end of 2008. Estonia and the EU Member States also agreed on a declaration on oil shale and the electricity directive, in which, on the one hand, Estonia reserves its position regarding future legislative developments in this area and, on the other hand, the Union recognises the specific situation related to the restructuring of the oil shale sector which will require particular efforts until the end of 2012 and the need for gradual opening of the Estonian electricity market for non-household customers until that date.
15. Industrial Policy	Second half 1998	June 1999	None
16. Small and Medium-Sized Enterprises	October 1998	November 1998	None
17. Science and Research	Second half 1998	October 1998	None
18. Education and Training	Second half 1998	October 1998	None

Annex I (*cont.*)

Negotiating Chapter	Opened	Closed	Transitional arrangements
19. Telecom, IT and postal services	October 1998	April 1999	None
20. Culture and Audiovisual Policy	October 1998	October 2000	None
21. Regional Policy and co-ordination of structural instruments	April 2000	June 2002	None. The whole territory of Estonia is covered by Objective 1 of the Structural Funds with an indicative allocation of € 328.6 million until the end of 2006; Estonia is also eligible for assistance from the Cohesion Fund with an indicative allocation of 2.88% to 4.39% of the total resources of the Cohesion Fund, which equals € 218.6 to 333.2 million until the end of 2006; the indicative allocation to Estonia of the commitment appropriations for the Community initiatives INTERREG and EQUAL amounts to € 9.5 and 3.6 million respectively until the end of 2006; it was decided not to implement the Community programmes LEADER+ and URBAN in the period up to 31 December 2006.
22. Environment	December 1999	June 2001	Requirements on emissions of volatile organic compounds from storage of petrol do not apply until the end of 2005/2006 (dependent on type of storage installation); requirements for loading and unloading of existing mobile containers at terminals do not apply until the end of 2005/2006 (dependent on type

Annex I (*cont.*)

Negotiating Chapter	Opened	Closed	Transitional arrangements
			of containers); requirements for liquid and corrosive waste do not apply to oil-shale ash put on existing landfills in Estonia until 16 July 2009; requirements for the renovation/construction of sewerage systems and urban waste water treatment facilities do not apply until 31 December 2010; directive 98/83 on the quality of water for human consumption does not apply until 31 December 2013; higher levels of air pollution from large combustion plants until the end of 2015; directive 91/676 on nitrate pollution from agricultural sources does not apply until 31 December 2008; the Estonian populations of wolf, lynx and beaver are excluded from annex IV of Directive 92/43/EEC (species in need of strict protection) and added to Annex V (species whose taking in wild and exploitation may be subject to management measures); concerning lynx, the Commission will provide the Council with a report on the further application of this geographical exception by 1 May 2009, the Council may on this basis decide to terminate its further application acting by QMV on a proposal from the Commission; Estonia can allow hunting of brown bears under specified circumstances and subject to specific procedures set out in Article 16(2) and (3) of directive 92/43/EEC.
23. Consumer Protection	April 1999	May 1999	None

Annex I *(cont.)*

Negotiating Chapter	Opened	Closed	Transitional arrangements
24. Justice and Home Affairs	May 2000	March 2002	None but safeguard clause as regards judicial co-operation in civil and criminal matters applicable until 1 May 2007; full implementation of Schengen *acquis* (including lifting of internal border controls) subject to a unanimous Council decision.
25. Customs Union	May 1999	March 2002	None
26. External Relations	First half 1999	April 2000	None; the Treaty of Accession includes a unilateral declaration of Estonia insisting on amendments to the EC's bilateral steel agreements with Russia, Ukraine and Kazakhstan to take into account Estonia's traditional steel import needs, as well as the dynamic character of the Estonian metalworking industry and its foreseeable increasing import demand.
27. CFSP	First half 1998	April 2000	None
28. Financial Control	First half 2000	March 2001	None
29. Finance and Budgetary Provisions	First half 2000	December 2002	Estonia receives € 15.8 in 2004 and € 2.9 in 2005 and 2006 under a special 'lump-sum cash-flow facility'; Estonia shall pay € 2.5 to the Research Fund for Coal and Steel in four instalments between 2006 and 2009 (this contribution is estimated on the basis of Estonia's production of oil shale); temporary financial

Annex I *(cont.)*

Negotiating Chapter	Opened	Closed	Transitional arrangements
			assistance under the 'Transition Facility' until the end of 2006; temporary financial assistance under the 'Schengen Facility' (€ 68.7 million) until the end of 2006. Estonia's estimated contribution to the EU's own resources amounts to € 229.5 million, its total allocations are estimated at € 1,020.5.
30. Institutions	First half 2002	December 2002	Transitional measures as laid down in the Treaty of Accession[4]
31. Other	November 2002	December 2002	Arrangements for the interim period between the end of accession negotiations and the entry into force of the Accession Treaty.

---

[4] For an analysis of these transitional measures, see: P. Van Elsuwege, A. Vermeersch, "Institutional Reform in the EU: A Difficult Balancing Act", in: K. Inglis, A. Ott, (eds.), *The Constitution for Europe and an Enlarging Union: Unity in Diversity?* Groningen, Europa Law Publishing, 2005, pp. 57–84.

OVERVIEW OF NEGOTIATIONS AND TRANSITIONAL ARRANGEMENTS WITH LATVIA[1]

Negotiating Chapter	Opened	Closed[2]	Transitional arrangements
1. Free Movement of Goods	March 2001	March 2001	None
2. Freedom of Movement for Persons	June 2001	June 2001	2+3+2 flexible arrangement on free movement of workers: during the first two years the 15 old Member States (EU 15) apply national measures, after this period reviews will be held and on the basis of a Commission report the EU 15 decide on whether to apply the *acquis*. The transitional period should in principle come to an end after five years but may be prolonged for a further two years in those Member States where there would be serious disturbances of the labour

---

[1] Information from: European Commission, "Enlargement of the European Union. Guide to the Negotiations. Chapter by Chapter", available at: http://www.europa. eu.int/comm/enlargement/negotiations/chapters/negotiationsguide.pdf; Report on the results of the negotiations on the accession of Cyprus, Malta, Hungary, Poland, the Slovak Republic, Latvia, Estonia, Lithuania, the Czech Republic and Slovenia to the European Union, available at: http://www.europa.eu.int/comm/enlargement/ negotiations/pdf/negotiations_report_to_ep.pdf; and the Act concerning the conditions for accession of the Czech Republic, the Republic of Estonia, the Republic of Cyprus, the Republic of Latvia, the Republic of Lithuania, the Republic of Hungary, the Republic of Malta, the Republic of Poland, the Republic of Slovenia and the Slovak Republic and the adjustments to the Treaties on which the European Union is founded, in particular Annex VI to this Act, including the list of transitional measures for Latvia, *OJ* (2003) L 236/33.

[2] All negotiating chapters have been officially closed in December 2002. For that reason, the provisionally closing dates of the different chapters have been included in this table.

Annex II (*cont.*)

Negotiating Chapter	Opened	Closed	Transitional arrangements
			market or a threat of such disruption. Safeguards may be applied by the EU 15 up to the end of the seventh year after accession. Latvia may apply to nationals from the EU 15 national measures equivalent to the measures applied by that Member State. As long as the EU 15 apply national measures, Latvia may also resort to safeguard measures with regard to the new Member States. The flexible arrangement further includes a standstill clause, which implies that the EU 15 cannot apply more restrictive measures than those applicable at the time of the signature of the Accession Treaty, and a preferential clause, which means that the EU 15 should give preference to nationals of new Member States over non-EU labour.
3. Freedom to Provide Services	November 2000	June 2001	Lower levels of bank deposit guarantee and investor compensation until 31 December 2007.
4. Free Movement of Capital	November 2000	May 2001	7-year transitional period for the acquisition of agricultural and forestry land, excluding self-employed farmers who have been residing for 3 years and active in farming from the scope. Possibility to extend this transitional period by three years if Latvia invokes safeguard clause.
5. Company Law	November 2000	May 2001	None
6. Competition Policy	Mar. 2000	Nov. 2001	None

Annex II (*cont.*)

Negotiating Chapter	Opened	Closed	Transitional arrangements
7. Agriculture	June 2001	December 2002	Gradual phasing in of agricultural direct payments between 2004 and 2013 with a possibility to top-up direct payments to a certain level with money from the national budget and rural development allocations; permitted use in organic farming of untreated seeds, planting material and propagating material not produced by the organic production method until 1 January 2006; permitted use of non-organic sugar not produced by the organic production method until 1 January 2006; permitted use of potassium permanganate preparation in organic farming for a period from the date of accession; the requirements relating to fat content do not apply to drinking milk produced in Latvia for a period of five years from the date of accession (milk which does not comply with the Community requirements related to fat content may only be marketed in Latvia or exported to a third country); until the end of 2006, Latvia may consider cows of the breeds listed in Annex I to Regulation 2342/99 as eligible for the suckler cow premium provided that they have been covered or inseminated by bulls of a meat breed; structural requirements relating to health conditions for the production and marketing of fresh meat, fishery products and milk-based products do not apply to 77 meat establishments (until January 2006), 29 fish processing establishments (until January

Annex II (*cont.*)

Negotiating Chapter	Opened	Closed	Transitional arrangements
			2005) and 11 milk establishments (until January 2005); structural requirements relating to health conditions for animal by-products not intended for human consumption do not apply to 2 animal waste establishments; Latvia may postpone for a period of five years following the date of accession the application of Directives 2002/53 and 2002/55 on quality requirements for vegetable seeds; agreement has been reached upon production quotas, premiums and other supply management instruments.[3]
8. Fisheries	October 2000	October 2001	None. Latvia has been granted a specific management regime for the entire Gulf of Riga; Baltic sprat has been included into the list of species that are subject to management measures under the Common Fisheries Policy.
9. Transport Policy	November 2000	December 2001	2+2+1 flexible arrangement on access of non-resident hauliers to the national road transport market of other Member States: after a two-years transitional period during which undertakings established in Latvia are reciprocally excluded from operation of national road haulage services in other Member States, this period can be prolonged for another two years (after notification to the Commission) and after this period for one additional year in case of serious disturbances, or threat thereof, on the national

---

[3] A detailed overview of these arrangements is available at the website of the Latvian Ministry of Agriculture: http://www. http://www.lvaei.lv/es/index.html.

Annex II (*cont.*)

Negotiating Chapter	Opened	Closed	Transitional arrangements
			road haulage market; the requirement of installation and use of recording equipment in vehicles registered for the carriage of passengers or goods by road does not apply in Latvia until 1 January 2005 to vehicles registered before 1 January 2001 and engaged exclusively in domestic transport operations; the financial standing criterion for domestic road transport operators does not apply until 31 December 2006.
10. Taxation	May 2001	June 2002	Exemption from VAT on the supply of heating sold to households until 31 December 2004; application of a simplified procedure for charging VAT on timber transactions until 1 May 2005; turnover threshold to exempt SMEs from VAT set at € 17,200; lower excise duty rates on cigarettes until 31 December 2009; VAT exemption on international passenger transport and on services supplied by authors, artists and performers until the condition set out in Article 28(4) of directive 77/388 EEC is fulfilled or for as long as the same exemption is applied by any of the present Member States.
11. EMU	October 2000	November 2000	None; Latvia participates in EMU from the date of accession as a Member State with a derogation in the meaning of Article 122 EC.
12. Statistics	March 2000	June 2000	None

Annex II *(cont.)*

Negotiating Chapter	Opened	Closed	Transitional arrangements
13. Employment and Social Policy	March 2001	June 2001	Directive 89/654 EEC on minimum safety and health requirements for the workplace does not apply until 31 December 2004 in respect of installations already in use on 27 March 2002; Directive 89/655 EEC on minimum safety and health requirements for the use of work equipment by workers at work does not apply until 1 July 2004 in respect of installations already in use on 13 December 2002; Directive 90/270 EEC on the minimum safety and health requirements for work with display equipment does not apply until 31 December 2004 in respect of equipment already in use on 1 June 2001.
14. Energy	March 2001	December 2001	Build up of oil stocks to required level until 31 December 2009.
15. Industrial Policy	October 2000	October 2000	None
16. Small and Medium-Sized Enterprises	March 2000	June 2000	None
17. Science and Research	March 2000	June 2000	None
18. Education and Training	March 2000	June 2000	None
19. Telecom IT and postal services	March 2001	April 2002	None
20. Culture and Audiovisual Policy	March 2000	March 2001	None

Annex II *(cont.)*

Negotiating Chapter	Opened	Closed	Transitional arrangements
21. Regional Policy and co-ordination of structural instruments	March 2001	June 2002	None. The whole territory of Latvia is covered by Objective 1 of the Structural Funds with an indicative allocation of € 554.2 million until the end of 2006; Latvia is also eligible for assistance from the Cohesion Fund with an indicative allocation of 5.07 % to 7.08 % of the total resources of the Cohesion Fund, which equals € 384.8 to 537.4 million until the end of 2006; the indicative allocation to Latvia of the commitment appropriations for the Community initiatives INTERREG and EQUAL amounts to € 13.5 and 7.1 million respectively until the end of 2006; it was decided not to implement the Community programmes LEADER+ and URBAN in the period up to 31 December 2006.
22. Environment	March 2001	November 2001	Requirements on emissions of volatile organic compounds from storage of petrol do not apply until the end of 2005/2006/2008 (dependent on type of storage installation); requirements for loading and unloading at terminals do not apply until the end of 2005/2006/2007/2008 (dependent on type of terminals); requirements for existing mobile containers at terminals do not apply until 31 December 2008 for 68 road tankers; requirements for loading into existing storage installations at service stations do not apply until the end of 2004/2008 (dependent on type of service station); all shipments of waste shall be notified to the

Annex II (*cont.*)

Negotiating Chapter	Opened	Closed	Transitional arrangements
			competent authorities until 31 December 2010; Latvia has time until 31 December 2007 to achieve the recovery and recycling targets for packaging waste; a permanent site which is used for temporary storage of hazardous waste generated within Latvia will not be considered as a landfill until 31 December 2004; requirements for collecting systems and treatment of urban waste water are not fully applicable until 31 December 2015; requirements on the quality of water intended for human consumption do not fully apply until 31 December 2015; requirements for waste containing asbestos fibres or dust which is landfill do not apply until 31 December 2004; as regards integrated pollution prevention and control, installations in Latvia will not comply with the 'best available techniques' up to the end of 2010 (specific dates for each installation); specific requirements concerning radiological equipment and special services do not apply until the end of 2005.
23. Consumer Protection	October 2000	October 2000	None
24. Justice and Home Affairs	June 2001	June 2002	None but safeguard clause as regards judicial co-operation in civil and criminal matters applicable until 1 May 2007; full implementation of Schengen *acquis* (including lifting of internal border controls) subject to a unanimous Council decision.

Annex II *(cont.)*

Negotiating Chapter	Opened	Closed	Transitional arrangements
25. Customs Union	March 2001	October 2001	None
26. External Relations	March 2000	November 2000	None
27. CFSP	March 2000	June 2000	None
28. Financial Control	May 2001	November 2001	None
29. Finance and Budgetary Provisions	March 2001	December 2002	Latvia receives € 19.5 million in 2004 and € 3.4 million in 2005 and 2006 under a special 'lump-sum cash-flow facility'; Latvia shall pay € 2.69 to the Research Fund for Coal and Steel in four instalments between 2006 and 2009; temporary financial assistance under the 'Transition Facility' until the end of 2006; temporary financial assistance under the 'Schengen Facility' (€ 71.1 million) until the end of 2006.
30. Institutions	April 2002	December 2002	Transitional measures as laid down in the Treaty of Accession.[4]
31. Other	November 2002	December 2002	Arrangements for the interim period between the end of accession negotiations and the entry into force of the Accession Treaty.

---

[4] For an analysis of these transitional measures, see: P. Van Elsuwege, A. Vermeersch, "Institutional Reform in the EU: A Difficult Balancing Act", in: K. Inglis, A. Ott, (eds.), *The Constitution for Europe and an Enlarging European Union: Unity in Diversity?* Groningen, Europa Law Publishing, 2005, pp. 57–84.

OVERVIEW OF NEGOTIATIONS AND TRANSITIONAL ARRANGEMENTS WITH LITHUANIA[1]

Negotiating Chapter	Opened	Closed[2]	Transitional arrangements
1. Free Movement of Goods	May 2001	May 2001	Transitional period until 1 January 2007 for the preparation of documentation for the re-registration of medicinal products according to the EU requirements.
2. Freedom of Movement for Persons	June 2001	November 2001	2+3+2 flexible arrangement on free movement of workers: during the first two years the 15 old Member States (EU 15) apply national measures, after this period reviews will be held and on the basis of a Commission report the EU 15 decide on whether to apply the *acquis*. The transitional period should in principle come to an end after five years but may

---

[1] Information from: European Commission, "Enlargement of the European Union. Guide to the Negotiations. Chapter by Chapter", available at: http://www.europa. eu.int/comm/enlargement/negotiations/chapters/negotiationsguide.pdf; Report on the results of the negotiations on the accession of Cyprus, Malta, Hungary, Poland, the Slovak Republic, Latvia, Estonia, Lithuania, the Czech Republic and Slovenia to the European Union, available at: http://www.europa.eu.int/comm/enlargement/ negotiations/pdf/negotiations_report_to_ep.pdf; "Overview of Results of Accession Negotiations", available at: http://www.euro.lt; and the Act concerning the conditions for accession of the Czech Republic, the Republic of Estonia, the Republic of Cyprus, the Republic of Latvia, the Republic of Lithuania, the Republic of Hungary, the Republic of Malta, the Republic of Poland, the Republic of Slovenia and the Slovak Republic and the adjustments to the Treaties on which the European Union is founded, in particular Annex VI to this Act, including the list of transitional measures for Lithuania, *OJ* (2003) L 236/33.

[2] All negotiating chapters have been officially closed in December 2002. For that reason, the provisionally closing dates of the different chapters have been included in this table.

Annex III (*cont.*)

Negotiating Chapter	Opened	Closed	Transitional arrangements
			be prolonged for a further two years in those Member States where there would be serious disturbances of the labour market or a threat of such disruption. Safeguards may be applied by the EU 15 up to the end of the seventh year after accession. Lithuania may apply to nationals from the EU 15 national measures equivalent to the measures applied by that Member State. As long as the EU 15 apply national measures, Lithuania may also resort to safeguard measures with regard to the new Member States. The flexible arrangement further includes a standstill clause, which implies that the EU 15 cannot apply more restrictive measures than those applicable at the time of the signature of the Accession Treaty, and a preferential clause, which means that the EU 15 should give preference to nationals of new Member States over non-EU labour.
3. Freedom to Provide Services	July 2000	June 2001	Lower levels of bank deposit guarantee and investor compensation until 31 December 2007.
4. Free Movement of Capital	November 2000	May 2001	7-year transitional period for the acquisition of agricultural and forestry land, excluding self-employed farmers who have been residing for 3 years and active in farming from the scope. Possibility to extend this transitional period by three years if Lithuania invokes safeguard clause.
5. Company Law	July 2000	June 2001	None

Annex III *(cont.)*

Negotiating Chapter	Opened	Closed	Transitional arrangements
6. Competition Policy	May 2000	November 2001	None
7. Agriculture	June 2001	December 2002	Gradual phasing in of agricultural direct payments between 2004 and 2013 with a possibility to top-up direct payments to a certain level with money from the national budget and rural development allocations; permitted use in organic farming of seed and propagating material not produced by the organic production method until 1 January 2006; permitted use of non-organic sugar for bee-feeding preparations in certified organic apiaries until 1 January 2006; the requirements relating to fat content do not apply to drinking milk produced in Lithuania until 1 January 2009 (milk which does not comply with the Community requirements related to fat content may only be marketed in Lithuania or exported to a third country); until the end of 2006, Lithuania may consider cows of the breeds listed in Annex I to Regulation 2342/99 as eligible for the suckler cow premium provided that they have been covered or inseminated by bulls of a meat breed; structural requirements relating to health conditions for the production and marketing of fresh meat, fishery products and milk-based products do not

Annex III (*cont.*)

Negotiating Chapter	Opened	Closed	Transitional arrangements
			apply to 14 meat establishments, 5 fish processing establishments and 1 milk establishment (until January 2007); Council directive 93/85/EEC on the control of potato ring rot is not fully applicable until 1 January 2006; until 31 December 2010, the requirement to pay an equitable remuneration to the holder of a Community plant variable is not applicable for Lithuanian farmers who were authorised to use that variety before the date of accession without payment of authorisation; agreement has been reached upon production quotas, premiums and other supply management instruments.[3]
8. Fisheries	March 2001	June 2001	None
9. Transport Policy	November 2000	December 2001	2+2+1 flexible arrangement on access of non-resident hauliers to the national road transport market of other Member States: after a two-years transitional period during which undertakings established in Lithuania are reciprocally excluded from operation of national road haulage services in other Member States, this period can be prolonged for another two years (after notification to the Commission) and after this period for one additional year in case of serious disturbances, or threat thereof, on the national road haulage market; the requirement

---

[3] A detailed overview of these arrangements is available at the website of the Lithuanian Ministry of Agriculture: http://www. http://www.zum.lt.

Annex III *(cont.)*

Negotiating Chapter	Opened	Closed	Transitional arrangements
			of installation and use of recording equipment in vehicles registered for the carriage of passengers or goods by road does not apply in Lithuania until 31 December 2005 to vehicles produced before 1987 and engaged exclusively in domestic transport operations; the financial standing criterion for domestic road transport operators does not apply until 31 December 2006; phasing out of noisy aircrafts from third countries at Kaunas International Airport until 31 December 2004.
10. Taxation	May 2001	March 2002	Turnover threshold to exempt SMEs from VAT set at € 28,962; lower excise duty rates on cigarettes until 31 December 2009; VAT exemption on international passenger transport until the condition set out in Article 28(4) of directive 77/388 EEC is fulfilled or for as long as the same exemption is applied by any of the present Member States.
11. EMU	March 2001	July 2001	None; Lithuania participates in EMU from the date of accession as a Member State with a derogation in the meaning of Article 122 EC.
12. Statistics	April 2000	June 2000	None
13. Employment and Social Policy	November 2000	March 2001	None
14. Energy	May 2001	June 2002	Build up of oil stocks to required level until 31 December 2009; commitment to close Unit 1 of the Ignalina Nuclear Power Plant before 2005 and Unit 2 by

Annex III *(cont.)*

Negotiating Chapter	Opened	Closed	Transitional arrangements
			31 December 2009 in exchange for adequate Community assistance; possible application of general economic safeguard clause until 31 December 2012 if energy supply is disrupted in Lithuania.
15. Industrial Policy	October 2000	October 2000	None
16. Small and Medium-Sized Enterprises	May 2000	May 2000	None
17. Science and Research	March 2000	May 2000	None
18. Education and Training	March 2000	May 2000	None
19. Telecom, IT and postal services	October 2000	March 2001	None
20. Culture and Audiovisual Policy	May 2000	December 2000	None
21. Regional Policy and co-ordination of structural instruments	March 2001	June 2002	None. The whole territory of Lithuania is covered by Objective 1 of the Structural Funds with an indicative allocation of € 792.1 million until the end of 2006; Lithuania is also eligible for assistance from the Cohesion Fund with an indicative allocation of 6.15% to 8.17% of the total resources of the Cohesion Fund, which equals € 466.8 to 620.14 million until the end of 2006; the indicative allocation to Lithuania of the commitment

Annex III *(cont.)*

Negotiating Chapter	Opened	Closed	Transitional arrangements
			appropriations for the Community initiatives INTERREG and EQUAL amounts to € 19.9 and 10.5 million respectively until the end of 2006; it was decided not to implement the Community programmes LEADER+ and URBAN in the period up to 31 December 2006.
22. Environment	November 2000	June 2001	Requirements for existing petrol storage installations at terminals do not apply until 31 December 2007 to 12 terminals with a throughput less than or equal to 50,000 tonnes/year; requirements for loading and unloading of existing mobile containers at terminals do not apply until 31 December 2007 to 12 terminals with a throughput less than or equal to 150,000 tonnes/year; requirements for existing mobile containers at terminals do not apply until 31 December 2005 to 140 road tankers and 1,900 rail tankers; requirements for loading into existing storage installations at service stations do not apply until 31 December 2007 to service stations with a throughput less than or equal to 1,000m³/year; Lithuania has time until 31 December 2006 to achieve the recovery and recycling targets for packaging waste; requirements for collecting systems and treatment of urban waste water are not fully applicable until 31 December 2009; the emission limit values

Annex III (*cont.*)

Negotiating Chapter	Opened	Closed	Transitional arrangements
			for sulphur dioxide and for nitrogen oxides do not apply until 31 December 2015 for Lithuania's large combustion plants in Vilnius, Kaunas and Mazeikiai.
23. Consumer Protection	February 2001	February 2001	None
24. Justice and Home Affairs	June 2001	April 2002	None but safeguard clause as regards judicial co-operation in civil and criminal matters applicable until 1 May 2007; full implementation of Schengen *acquis* (including lifting of internal border controls) subject to a unanimous Council decision; in the framework of the problems related to the transit of persons by land between Kaliningrad and other parts of the Russian Federation, the Community has promised to assist Lithuania in fulfilling the conditions in order to secure that Lithuania will be in the first group of new Member States to participate fully in the Schengen *acquis*.
25. Customs Union	March 2001	October 2001	None
26. External Relations	March 2000	November 2000	None
27. CFSP	March 2000	June 2000	None
28. Financial Control	May 2001	November 2001	None

Annex III (*cont.*)

Negotiating Chapter	Opened	Closed	Transitional arrangements
29. Finance and Budgetary Provisions	March 2001	December 2002	Lithuania receives € 34.8 million in 2004 and € 6.3 million in 2005 and 2006 under a special 'lump-sum cash-flow facility'; temporary financial assistance under the 'Transition Facility' until the end of 2006; temporary financial assistance under the 'Schengen Facility' (€ 135.7 million) until the end of 2006.
30. Institutions	April 2002	December 2002	Transitional measures as laid down in the Treaty of Accession[4]
31. Other	November 2002	December 2002	Arrangements for the interim period between the end of accession negotiations and the entry into force of the Accession Treaty; legal and financial guarantees to Lithuania as regards Kaliningrad (see chapter 24) and Ignalina (see chapter 14).

---

[4] For an analysis of these transitional measures, see: P. Van Elsuwege, A. Vermeersch, "Institutional Reform in the EU: A Difficult Balancing Act", in: K. Inglis, A. Ott, (eds.), *The Constitution for Europe and an Enlarging European Union: Unity in Diversity?* Groningen, Europa Law Publishing, 2005, pp. 57–84.

BIBLIOGRAPHY

Edited Volumes

Albi, A., Ziller, J., (eds.), *European Constitution and National Constitutions: Ratification and Beyond*, The Hague, Kluwer Law International, 2006.

Aleinikoff, T.A., Klusmeyer, D., (eds.), *From Migrants to Citizens: Membership in a Changing World*, New York, Carnegie, 2000.

Antonenko, O., Pinnick, K., (eds.), *Russia and the European Union*, London, Routledge, 2005.

Answald, S., Jopp, M., (eds.), *The European Union and the Baltic States. Visions, Interests and Strategies for the Baltic Sea Region*, Berlin, Institüt für Europäische Politik, 1998.

Apap, J., (ed.), *Justice and Home Affairs in the EU. Liberty and Security Issues after Enlargement*, Cheltenham, Elgar, 2004.

Arnull, A., Wincott, D., (eds.), *Accountability and Legitimacy in the European Union*, Oxford, Oxford University Press, 2002.

Berglund, S., Ekman, J., Aarebrot, F., (eds.), *The Handbook of Political Change in Eastern Europe*, Cheltenham, Elgar, 2004.

Bermann, G., Pistor, K., (eds.), *Law and Governance in an Enlarged European Union*, Oxford, Hart, 2004.

Birckenbach, H.M., Wellmann, C. (eds.), *The Kaliningrad Challenge. Options and Recommendations*, Hamburg, Lit, 2003.

Blockmans, S., Lazowski, A., (eds.), *The European Union and its Neighbours. A Legal Appraisal of the EU's Policies of Stabilisation, Partnership and Integration*, The Hague, Asser, 2006.

Bremmer, I., Taras, R., (eds.), *New States New Politics. Building the Post-Soviet Nations*, Cambridge, Cambridge University Press, 1997.

Buhbe, M., Kempe, I., (eds.), *Russia, the EU and the Baltic States. Enhancing the Potential for Cooperation*, Moscow, CAP, 2005.

Cao-Huy, T., (ed.), *Etudes sur l'élargissement de l'Union européenne*, Paris, PUF, 2003.

Carrafielo, L., Spaepen, L., Vertongen, N., (reds.), *De Balten op de tweesprong tussen Oost en West*, Leuven, Garant, 1999.

Clark, R., Feldbrugge, F., Pomorski, S., (eds.), *International and National Law in Russia and Eastern Europe*. The Hague, Nijhoff, 2001.

Corten, O., Delcourt, B., Klein, P., *et al.*, *Démembrements d'états et délimitations territoriales: l'uti possidetis en question(s)*. Bruxelles, Bruylant, 1999.

Cottey, A., (ed.), *Subregional Cooperation in the new Europe: building security, prosperity and solidarity from the Barents to the Black Sea*, Houndmills, Macmillan, 1999.

Cramer, P., (ed.), *The Process of Estonia's Integration into the Western Economic System: International Legal Issues*, Göteborg, CERGU, 2001.

Cremona, M., (ed.), *The Enlargement of the European Union*, Oxford, Oxford University Press, 2003.

Czarnota, A., Krygier, M., Sadurski, W., (eds.), *Rethinking the Rule of Law after Communism*, Budapest, Central University Press, 2005.

Demm, E., Noel, R., Urban, W., (eds.), *The Independence of the Baltic States: Origins, Causes and Consequences. A Comparison of the Crucial Years 1918–1919 and 1990–1991*, Chicago, Lithuanian Research and Studies Center, 1996.

Dimitrova, A., (ed.), *Driven to Change. The European Union's Enlargement Viewed from the East*, Manchester, Manchester University Press, 2004.

Elgstrom, O., Jonsson, C., (eds.), *European Union Negotiations: Processes, Networks and Institutions*, London, Routledge, 2005.

Emiliou, N, O'Keeffe, D., (eds.), *The European Union and World Trade Law After the GATT Uruguay Round*, Chichester, Wiley, 1996.

Forsberg, T., (ed.), *Contested Territory: Border Disputes at the Edge of the Former Soviet Empire*, Aldershot, Elgar, 1995.

Franck, C., Pyszna-Nigge, D., (eds.), *Positions of 10 Central and Eastern European Countries on EU Institutional Reforms*, Louvain-la-Neuve/Brussels, 2003.

Ganino, M., Venturini, G., (eds.), *Europe Tomorrow: Towards the Enlargement of the Union*, Milan, Giuffre, 2001.

Hallik, A., Poleshchuk, V., Saar, A., *et al.*, *Estonia: Interethnic Relations and the Issue of Discrimination in Tallinn*, Tallinn, LICHR, 2006.

Hansen, B., Heurlin, B., (eds.), *The Baltic States in World Politics*, London, Curzon, 1998.

Hasegawa, T., Pravda, A., (eds.), *Perestroika: Soviet Domestic and Foreign Policies*, London, Royal Institute of International Affairs, 1991.

Henderson, K., (ed.), *Back to Europe. Central and Eastern Europe and the European Union*, London, UCL Press, 1999.

Heusel, W., (ed.), *Eastern Enlargement of the European Union*, Köln, Bundesanzager, 2002.

Hiden, J., Lane, T., (eds.), *The Baltic and the Outbreak of the Second World War*, Cambridge, Cambridge University Press, 1992.

Hillion, C., (ed.), *EU Enlargement: A Legal Approach*, Oxford, Hart, 2004.

Hubel, H., (ed.), *EU Enlargement and Beyond: The Baltic States and Russia*, Berlin, Berlin Verlag, 2002.

Huttenbach, H.R., (ed.), *Soviet Nationality Policies. Ruling Ethnic Groups in the USSR*, London, Mansell, 1990.

Inglis, K., Ott, A., (eds.), *The Constitution for Europe and an Enlarging Union: Unity in Diversity?*, Groningen, Europa Law Publishing, 2005.

Joenniemi, P., (ed.), Neo-nationalism or Regionality: The Restructuring of Political Space around the Baltic Rim, Stockholm, NordREFO, 1997.

Joenniemi, P., Prikulis, J., (eds.), *The Foreign Policies of the Baltic Countries: Basic Issues*, Riga, Centre of Baltic-Nordic History and Political Studies, 1994.

Jundzis, T., (ed.), *The Baltic States at Historical Crossroads*, Latvian Academy of Sciences, Riga, 2001.

Kapustans, J., (ed.), *Baltic States and EU Accession Negotiations: An Assessment*, Riga, Latvian Institute of International Affairs, 2002.

Kasatkina, N., (ed.), *Ethnicity Studies 2004*, Vilnius, Eugrimas, 2004.

Kellerman, A., De Zwaan, J., Czuczai, J., (eds.), *EU Enlargement. The Constitutional Impact at EU and National Level*, The Hague, Asser, 2001.

———, Czuczai, J., Blockmans, S., *et al.* (eds.), *The Impact of EU Accession on the Legal Orders of the New EU Member States and (Pre-)Candidate Countries*, The Hague, Asser, 2006.

Klabbers, J., Koskenniemi, M., Ribbelink, O., *et al.*, State Practice Regarding State Succession and Issues of Recognition, The Hague, Kluwer Law International, 1999.

Konstadinidis, S.V., (ed.), *The Legal Regulation of the European Community's External Relations after the Completion of the Internal Market*, Aldershot, Darmouth, 1996.

Koskenniemi, M., (ed.), *International Law Aspects of the European Union*, The Hague, Kluwer Law International, 1998.

Kubicek, P., (ed.), *The European Union and Democratization*, London, Routledge, 2003.

Lähteenmäki, K., (ed.), *Dimensions of Cooperation and Conflict in the Baltic Sea Rim*, Tampere, Tampere Peace Research Institute, 1994.

Lehti, M., Smith, D.J., (eds.), *Post-Cold War Identity Politics. Nordic and Baltic Experiences*, London, Cass, 2003.

Lejins, A., (ed.), *Baltic Security Prospects at the Turn of the 21st Century*, Helsinki, Kikimora, 1999.

———, Bleiere, D., (eds.), *The Baltic States: Search for Security*, Riga, Latvian Institute of International Affairs, 1996.

——, Ozolina, Z., (eds.), *Small States in a Turbulent Environment: The Baltic Perspective*, Riga, Latvian Institute of International Affairs, 1997.

——, Trenin, D., (eds.), *Ambivalent Neighbors. The EU, NATO and the Price of Membership*, Washington, Carnegie Endowment for International Peace, 2003.

Lindahl, R., (ed.), *Transition and EU Enlargement. Economic, Legal, Political and Social Change in Eastern Europe*, Göteborg, CERGU, 2005.

Loeber, D., (ed.), *Regional Identity under Soviet Rule: The Case of the Baltic States'*, New York, AABS, 1989.

Machowski, H., Kaczurba, J., Adamis, M., e.a., *The Further Development of CEFTA: Institutionalization, Deepening, Widening?*, Warszawa, Friederich Ebert Foundation, 1997.

Madl, F., (ed.), *On the State of the EU Integration Process: Enlargement and Institutional Reforms*, Budapest, ELTE, 1997.

Malfliet, K., De Meyere, P., Franckx, E., *et al.*, *Oost-Europa in Europa: Eenheid en Verscheidenheid: Huldeboek opgedragen aan Frits Gorlé*, Brussels, VUB Press, 1996.

——, Keygnaert, W., (eds.), *The Baltic States in an Enlarging European Union: Towards a Partnership between Small States?*, Leuven, Institute for European Policy, 1999.

Maniokas, K., Vilpisauskas, R., Zeruolis, D., (eds.), *Lithuania's Road to the European Union: Unification of Europe and Lithuania's EU Accession Negotiations*, Vilnius, Eugrimas, 2005.

Mannin, M., (ed.), *Pushing Back the Boundaries. The European Union and Central and Eastern Europe*, Manchester, Manchester University Press, 1999.

Manzocchi, S., (ed.), *The Economics of Enlargement*, Houndmills, Palgrave, 2003.

Maresceau, M., (ed.), *The Political and Legal Framework of Trade Relations between the European Community and Eastern Europe*, Dordrecht, Martinus Nijhoff, 1989, pp. 3–20.

——, (ed.), *The European Community's Commercial Policy after 1992: The Legal Dimension*, Dordrecht, Martinus Nijhoff, 1993.

——, (ed.), *Enlarging the European Union. Relations between the EU and Central and Eastern Europe*, London, Longman, 1997.

——, Lannon, E., (eds.), *The EU's Enlargement and Mediterranean Strategies. A Comparative Analysis*, Houndmills, Palgrave, 2001.

Medijainen, E. Made, V. (eds.), *Estonian Foreign Policy at the Cross-roads*, Helsinki, Kikimara, 2002.

Metuzale-Kangere, B., (ed.), *The Ethnic Dimension in Politics and Culture in the Baltic Countries 1920–1945*, Stockholm, Södertörn, 2004, pp. 92–120.

Meyers, W.H., Kazlauskiene, N., Giudale, M., (eds.), *Lithuania's Accession to the European Union. Successes and Challenges for a Rural Economy in Transition*, Iowa, Iowa State University Press, 1999.

Mitrofanovs, M., Gamajejevs, A., Jolkins, V., *et al.*, 'The Stateless People of Latvia. The Last Prisoners of the Cold War', Riga, 2006.

Mouritzen, H., Wivel, A., (eds.), *The Geopolitics of Euro-Atlantic Integration*, London—New York, Routledge, 2005.

Mrak, M., (ed.), *Succession of States*, The Hague, Nijhoff, 1999.

Muiznieks, N., (ed.), *Latvian-Russian Relations: Domestic and International Dimensions*, Riga, University of Latvia, 2006.

Müller, J.W., *Memory and Power in Post-War Europe: Studies in the Presence of the Past*, Cambridge, Cambridge University Press, 2002.

Müller-Graff, P.C., (ed.), *East Central European States and the European Communities: Legal Adaptation to the Market Economy*, Baden-Baden, Nomos, 1993.

Murray, A.V., *Crusades and Conversion on the Baltic Frontier 1150–1500*, Aldershot, Ashgate, 2001.

Neuwahl, N., (ed.), *European Union Enlargement. Law and Socio-Economic Changes*, Montréal, Thémis, 2004.

Nicolaides, P., Boaean, S., Bollen, F., *et al.*, *A Guide to the Enlargement of the European Union. A Review of the Process, Negotiations, Policy Reforms and Enforcement Capacity*, Maastricht, EIPA, 1999.

Nikodem, A., (ed.), *Implications of the Enlargement of the European Union*, Budapest, Kiadja a Bibó Istvan Szakkolégium, 1998.

Norgaard, O., Johannsen, L., Skak, M., *et al.*, *The Baltic States after Independence*, Cheltenham, Elgar, 1999.

Ojanen, H. (ed.), *The Northern Dimension: Fuel for the EU?*, Helsinki, FIIA, 2001.

Ott, A., Inglis, K. (eds.), *Handbook on European Enlargement. A Commentary on the Enlargement Process*, The Hague, Asser, 2002.

Pettai, V., Zielonka, J., (eds.), *The Road to the European Union (Vol. 2). Estonia, Latvia and Lithuania*, Manchester, Manchester University Press, 2003.

Redmond, J., (ed.), *The External Relations of the European Community. The International Response to 1992*, New York, St. Martin's, 1992.

Rieber, A., (ed.), *Forced Migration in Central and Eastern Europe, 1939–1950*, London, Frank Cass Publishers, 2000, 197 p.

Sadurski, W., Czarnota, A., Krygier, M., (eds.), Spreading Democracy and the Rule of Law? The Impact of EU Enlargement on the Rule of Law, Democracy and Constitutionalism in Post-Communist Legal Orders, Dordrecht, Springer, 2006.

Scheinin, M., (ed.), *International Human Rights Norms in the Nordic and Baltic Countries*, The Hague, Martinus Nijhoff, 1996.

Schimmelfennig, F., Sedelmeier, U., (eds.), *The Europeanization of Central and Eastern Europe*, New York, Cornell Univerisity Press, 2005.

Shain, Y., (ed.), *Governments in Exile in Contemporary World Politics*, New York—London, Routledge, 1991.

Sjursen, H., *Questioning EU Enlargement. Europe in Search of Identity*, London—New York, Routledge, 2006.

Smith, D., (ed.), *The Baltic States and their Region. New Europe or Old?*, Amsterdam—New York, Rodopi, 2005.

Smith, G., (ed.), *The Baltic States. The National Self-Determination of Estonia, Latvia and Lithuania*, Macmillan, Basingstoke, 1996.

——, Law, V., Wilson, A., *et al.*, *Nation-building and Political Discourses of Identity Politics in the Baltic States*, Cambridge, Cambridge University Press, 1998.

Smith, J., Teague, E., (eds.), *Democracy in the New Europe. The Politics of Post-Communism*, London, Greycoat Press, 1999.

Sneidere, I., (ed.), *Occupation Regimes in Latvia in 1940–1956*, Riga, Research Commission of the History of Latvia, 2002.

Szczerbiak, A., Taggart, P., (eds.), *EU Enlargement and Referendums*, London, Routledge, 2005.

Thaden, E., (ed.), *Russification in the Baltic provinces and Finland 1955–1914*, Princeton, Princeton University Press, 1981.

Vardys, V.S., (ed.), *Lithuania under the Soviets: Portrait of a Nation 1940–1965*, New York, Praeger, 1965, pp. 141–169.

Von Hirschhausen, C., (ed.), *New Neighbours in Eastern Europe: Economic and Industrial Reform in Lithuania, Latvia and Estonia*, Paris, Presses de l'Ecole des Mines, 1998.

Walker, N., (ed.), *Sovereignty in Transition*, Oxford, Hart, 2003.

Westphal, K., (ed.), *A Focus on EU-Russia Relations*, Frankfurt am Main, Lang, 2005.

Zettermark, H., Hägg, M., Von Euler, C., (eds.), *The Baltic Room: Extending the Northern Wing of the European House*, Stockholm, Swedish National Defence College, 2000.

Zielonka, J., (ed.), *Democratic Consolidation in Eastern Europe*, Oxford, Oxford University Press, 2001.

——, (ed.), *Europe Unbound. Enlarging and Reshaping the Boundaries of the European Union*, London, Routledge, 2002.

Monographs

Aalto, P., *European Union and the Making of a Wider Northern Europe*, London—New York, Routledge, 2006.

Albi, A., *EU Enlargement and the Constitutions of Central and Eastern Europe*, Cambridge, Cambridge University Press, 2005.

Arnswald, S., *EU Enlargement and the Baltic States. The Incremental Making of New Members*, Helsinki, The Finnish Institute of International Affairs, 2000.

Avery, G., Cameron, F., *The Enlargement of the European Union*, Sheffield, Sheffield Academic Press, 1998.

Baldwin, R., *Towards an integrated Europe*, London, CEPR, 1994.

Barysch, K., *The EU and Russia. Strategic Partners or Squabbling Neighbours?*, London, Centre for European Reform, 2004.

Baun, M., *A Wider Europe. The Process and Politics of European Union Enlargement*, Lanham, Rowan & Littlefield, 2000.

Berglund, S., Aarebrot, F., *The Political History of Eastern Europe in the 20th Century: the Struggle between Democracy and Dictatorship*, Aldershot, Elgar, 1997.

Beurdeley, L., *L'élargissement de l'Union européenne aux pays d'Europe centrale et orientale et aux îles du bassin Méditerranéen*, Paris, L'Harmattan, 2003.

Bideleux, R., Jeffries, I., *A History of Eastern Europe: Crisis and Change*, London, Routledge, 1998.

Böcker, A., Guild, E., *Implementation of the Europe Agreements in France, Germany, the Netherlands and the UK: Movement of Persons*, London, Platinium, 2002.

Brownlie, I., *Principles of Public International Law*, Oxford, Clarendon Press, 2003.

Buhler, K.G., *State Succession and Membership in International Organisations. Legal Theories versus Political Pragmatism*, The Hague, Kluwer, 2001.

Bungs, D., *The Baltic States: Problems and Prospects of Membership in the European Union*, Baden-Baden, Nomos, 1998.

Clemens, W.C., *Baltic Independence and Russian Empire*, New York, St. Martin's Press, 1991.

——, *The Baltic Transformed. Complexity Theory and European Security*, Lanham, Rowan & Littlefield, 2001.

Crawford, J., *The Creation of States in International Law*, Oxford, Clarendon Press, 1979.

Creech, R., *Law and Language in the European Union. The Paradox of a Babel 'United in Diversity'*, Groningen, Europa Law Publishing, 2005.

Danjoux, O., *L'Etat C'est Pas Moi. Reframing Citizenship(s) in the Baltic Republics*, Lund, Lund University Press, 2002.

Dangerfield, M., *Subregional Economic Cooperation in Central and Eastern Europe. The Political Economy of CEFTA*, Cheltenham, Elgar, 2001.

Davies, N., *Europe, A History*, London, Pilmico, 1997.

De Chambon, H., *La Tragédie des Nations Baltiques*, Paris, Editions de la Revue Parlementaire, 1946.

Desai, P., *Perestroika in Perspective. The Design and Dilemmas of Soviet Reform*, London, Tauris, 1989.

De Vareness, F., *Language, Minorities and Human Rights*, The Hague, Kluwer, 1996.

Dreifelds, J., *Latvia in Transition*, Cambridge, Cambridge University Press, 1997.

Dunsdorfs, E., *The Baltic Dilemma. The Case of the de jure recognition by Australia of the incorporation of the Baltic States into the Soviet Union*, New York, Speller, 1975.

Elletson, H., *Baltic Independence and Russian Foreign Energy Policy*, London, GMB, 2006.

Fierro, E., *The EU's Approach to Human Rights Conditionality in Practice*, The Hague, Martinus Nijhoff, 2003.

Friis, L., Friis, A., *Countdown to Copenhagen: Big Bang or Fizzle in the EU's Enlargement Process*, Copenhagen, Danish Institute of International Affairs, 2002.

Galbreath, D., *Nation-Building and Minority Politics in Post-Socialist States. Interests, Influences and Identities in Estonia and Latvia*, Stuttgart, Ibidem Verlag, 2005.

Grabbe, H., Hughes, K., *Enlarging the EU Eastwards*, London, Royal Institute of International Affairs, 1998.

Henrard, K., *Devising an Adequate System of Minority Protection. Individual Human Rights, Minority Rights and the Right to Self-Determination*, The Hague, Martinus Nijhoff, 2000.

Hiden, J., *The Baltic States and Weimar Ostpolitik*, Cambridge, Cambridge University Press, 1987.

——, Salmon, P., *The Baltic Nations and Europe. Estonia, Latvia and Lithuania in the Twentieth Century*. London-New York, Longman, 1991.

Hughes, J., Sasse, G., Gordon, C., *Europeanization and Regionalization in the EU's Enlargement to Central and Eastern Europe. The Myth of Conditionality*, Houndmills, Palgrave, 2004.

Kasekamp, A., *The Radical Right in Interwar Estonia*, Houndmills, Macmillan, 2000.

Kelley, J., *Ethnic Politics in Europe. The Power of Norms and Incentives*, Princeton, Princeton University Press, 2004.

Kemp, W., *Quiet Diplomacy in Action: The OSCE High Commissioner on National Minorities*, The Hague, Kluwer Law International, 2001.

Kirby, D., *Northern Europe in the Early Modern Period. The Baltic World 1492–1772*, London—New York, Longman, 1990.

——, *The Baltic World 1772–1993. Europe's Northern Periphery in an Age of Change*, London—New York, Longman, 1995.

Klinge, M., *The Baltic World*, Helsinki, Otava, 1997.

Küng, A., *A Dream of Freedom: Four Decades of National Survival versus Russian Imperialism in Estonia, Latvia and Lithuania 1940–1980*, Cardiff, Boreas, 1981.

Laitin, D., *Identity in Formation. The Russian-speaking Population in the Near Abroad*, Ithaca, Cornell University Press, 1998.

Landsbergis, V., *Lithuania Independent Again*. Seattle, University of Washington Press, 2000.

Lane, T., *Lithuania Stepping Westward*, London, Routledge, 2001.

Lehti, M., *A Baltic League as a Construct of the New Europe. Envisioning a Baltic Region and Small State Sovereignty in the Aftermath of the First World War*, Frankfurt am Main, Lang, 1999.

Lenaerts, K., Van Nuffel, P., *Constitutional Law of the European Union*, London, Sweet & Maxwell, 2005.

Lieven, A., *The Baltic Revolution. Estonia, Latvia, Lithuania and the Path to Independence*, New Haven, Yale University Press, 1994.

Lippert, B. Umbach, G., *The Pressure of Europeanisation. From Post-Communist State Administrations to Normal Players in the EU System*, Baden-Baden, Nomos, 2005.

Löwenhardt, R., *The reincarnation of Russia. Struggling with the legacy of communism 1990–1994*, London, Longman, 1995.

Ludlow, P., *The Making of the New Europe. The European Councils in Brussels and Copenhagen 2002*, Brussels, EuroComment, 2004.

Lukowski, J., *The Partitions of Poland 1772, 1793, 1795*, Longman—New York, 1999.

Mälksoo, L., *Illegal Annexation and State Continuity: The Case of the Incorporation of the Baltic States by the USSR*, Leiden-Boston, Martinus Nijhoff, 2003.

Marek, K., *Identity and Continuity of States in Public International Law*, Geneva, Librairie Droz, 1968.

Mayhew, A., *Recreating Europe. The European Union's Policy Towards Central and Eastern Europe*, Cambridge, Cambridge University Press, 1998.

McHugh, J.T., Pacy, J.S., *Diplomats Without a Country. Baltic Diplomacy, International Law, and the Cold War*, Westport, Greenwood Press, 2001.

Meissner, B., *Die Sowjetunion, die baltischen Staaten und das Völkerrecht*, Köln, 1956.

Misiunas, R., Taagepera, R., *The Baltic States. Years of Dependence 1940–1990*, London, Hurst & Co, 1993, 400 p.

Moshes, A., *Overcoming Unfriendly Stability. Russian-Latvian Relations at the end of the 1990s*, Helsinki, The Finnish Institute of International Affairs, 1999.

Müllerson, R., *International law, rights and politics: developments in Eastern Europe and the CIS*. London, Routledge, 1994.

Nello, S., *The New Europe. Changing Economic Relations between East and West*, New York, Harvester Wheatsheaf, 1991.

Nies, S., *Les Etats baltes. Une longue dissidence*, Paris, Armand Collin, 2004.

Nissinen, M., *Latvia's Transition to a Market Economy. Political Determinants of Economic Reform Policy*, Houndmills, Macmillan, 1999.

O'Connor, K., *The History of the Baltic States*, Westport, Greenwood Press, 2003.

Open Society Institute, *Monitoring the EU Accession Process: Minority Protection (Vol. I). An Assessment of Selected Policies in the Candidate State*, Budapest, OSI, 2002.

Pabriks, A., Purs, A., *Latvia: The Challenges of Change*, London, Routledge, 2001.

Pentassuglia, G., *Minorities in International Law*. Strasbourg, Council of Europe Publishing, 2002.

Poleshchuk, V., *Advice Not Welcomed. Recommendations of the OSCE High Commissioner to Estonia and Latvia and the response*, Münster, Lit-Verlag, 2001.

Poole, P., *Europe Unites: The EU's Eastern Enlargement*, Westport, Praeger, 2003.

Puheloinen, A., *Russia's Geopolitical Interest in the Baltic Area*, Helsinki, National Defence College, 1999.

Puissochet, J.P., *L'élargissement des Communautés européennes*, Paris, Editions techniques et économiques, 1974.

Pullerits, A., *The Estonian Yearbook 1929*, Tallinn, 1929.

Raun, T.U., *Estonia and the Estonians*, Stanford, Hoover Institution Press, 2001.

Rodgers, H.J., *Search for Security. A Study in Baltic Diplomacy, 1920–1934*, Hamden, 1975.

Santamaria, Y., *1939, Le Pacte Germano-Soviétique*, Bruxelles, Editions Complexe, 1998.

Senn, A.E., *The Great Powers, Lithuania and the Vilna Question*, Leiden, Brill, 1966.

Sharlet, R., *The New Soviet Constitution of 1977. Analysis and Text*, Brunswick, King's Court Communications, 1985.

Shuibhne, N., *EC Law and Minority Language Policy. Language, Citizenship and Fundamental Rights*, The Hague, Kluwer Law International, 2002.

Smith, D., *Estonia. Independence and European Integration*, London, Routledge, 2002.

Smith, K., *The Making of EU Foreign Policy. The Case of Eastern Europe*, Houndmills, MacMillan, 1999.

——, *Russian Energy Politics in the Baltics, Poland and Ukraine: A New Stealth Imperialism*, Washington, Center for Strategic and International Studies, 2005.

Spohr Readman, K., *Germany and the Baltic Problem after the Cold War. The Development of a New Ostpolitik 1989–2000*, London—New York, Routledge, 2004.

Svensson, T., *The New Baltic Tigers*, Stockholm, Olaf Palme International Centre, 1995.

Swettenham, J.A., *The Tragedy of the Baltic States*, London, Hollis and Carter, 1952.

Szalay, K., *Scrutiny of EU Affairs in the National Parliaments of the New Member States. Comparative Analysis*, Budapest, Hungarian National Assembly, 2005.

Talmon, S., *Recognition of Governments in International Law*, Oxford, Clarendon Press, 1998.

Taube, C., *Constitutionalism in Estonia, Latvia and Lithuania. A Study in Comparative Constitutional Law*, Uppsala, Iustus Förlag, 2001.

Trenin, D., *Baltic Chance. The Baltic States, Russia and the West in the Emerging Greater Europe*, Washington, Carnegie Endowment for International Peace, 1997.

——, *The End of Eurasia. Russia on the Border Between Geopolitics and Globalisation*, Washington, Carnegie Endowment for International Peace, 2002.

Truscott, P., *Russia First. Breaking with the West*, London, Tauris Publishers, 1997.

Tucny, E., *L'Elargissement de l'Union Européenne aux pays d'Europe centrale et orientale. La conditionalité politique*, L'Harmattan, Paris, 2000.

Vardys, V.S., Sedaitis, J.B., *Lithuania: the Rebel Nation*, Boulder, Westview Press, 1997.
Von Rauch, G., *The Baltic States. The Years of Independence 1917–1940*, London, Hurst & Co, 1974.
Viscont, A., *La Lithuanie et la guerre*, Genève, Attar, 1917.
Vitas, R.A., *The United States and Lithuania: the Stimson Doctrine of non-recognition*, New York, Praeger, 1990.
Walker, E., *Dissolution. Sovereignty and the Breakup of the Soviet Union*, Lanham, Lowan and Littlefield, 2003.
X, *Question de Vilna. Consultations de MM. A. De Lapradelle, Louis Le Fur et André N. Mandelstam concernant la force obligatoire de la décision de la Conférence des Ambassadeurs du 15 mars 1923*, Paris, Jouve & Co, 1928.
Zaagman, R., *Conflict Prevention in the Baltic States: The OSCE High Commissioner on National Minorities in Estonia, Latvia and Lithuania*, Flensburg, ECMI, 1999.
Ziegler, C.E., *The History of Russia*, Westport, Greenwood Press, 1999.
Ziemele, I., *State Continuity and Nationality: The Baltic States and Russia. Past, Present and Future as Defined by International Law*, Leiden, Martinus Nijhoff, 2005.
Zukova, G., *Legal Aspects of Trade in Goods between the EU and its Candidate States: The Case of Latvia*, Riga, Latvijas Vestnesis, 2004.

Articles

Adinolfi, A., "Free Movement and Access to Work of Citizens of the New Member States: The Transitional Measures", 42 *Common Market Law Review* (2005), pp. 485–496.
Albi, A., "Estonia's Constitution and the EU: How and to What Extend to Amend It"?, *Juridica International* 7 (2002), pp. 39–48.
——, "EU Accession Referendums in the Baltic States", 11 *Tilburg Foreign Law Review* (2003) 3, pp. 653–670.
——, "Europe Articles in the Constitutions of Central and Eastern European Countries", 42 *Common Market Law Review* 2 (2005), pp. 399–423.
——, "Supremacy of EC Law in the New Member States: Bringing Parliaments into the Equation of Co-operative Constitutionalism", 2 *European Constitutional Law Review* 3 (2006), pp. 25–67.
——, Van Elsuwege, P., "The EU Constitution, National Constitutions and Sovereignty: An Assessment of a European Constitutional Order", 29 *European Law Review* 6 (2004), pp. 741–765.
Albi, K., "The Right to Use Minority Languages in the Public Sphere. Evaluation of Estonian Legislation in Light of the International Standards", 8 *Juridica International* (2003), pp. 151–161.
Anciuviene, M., "The Harmonisation of the Lithuanian Legal System with that of the European Union: Gains and Challenges", *Lithuanian Human Development Report* (1999), pp. 129–137.
Asmus, R., Nurick, R., "NATO Enlargement and the Baltic States", 38 *Survival* 2 (1996), pp. 121–142.
Avdeev, A., "Russian-Lithuanian Relations: An Overview", 3 *Lithuanian Foreign Policy Review* 2 (2000), http://www.lfpr.lt/uploads/File/2000–6/Avdeev.pdf.
Barrington, L.W., "Nations, States and Citizens: An Explanation of the Citizenship Policies in Estonia and Lithuania", 21 *Review of Central and East European Law* 2 (1995), pp. 103–148.
Bayou, C., "Les Etats baltes et l'Union européenne: un nouveau départ", *Le Courrier des Pays de l'Est* 1001 (2000), pp. 64–71.
Bildt, C., "The Baltic Litmus Test" 73 *Foreign Affairs* 5 (1994), pp. 72–85.

Birkavs, V., "Latvia between Madrid and Luxembourg and Beyond", 50 *Studia Diplomatica* 3 (1997), pp. 43–50.

Blackman, J.L., "State Successions and Statelessness: The Emerging Right to an Effective Nationality under International Law", 19 *Michigan Journal of International Law*, (1998), pp. 1141–1194.

Boelaert-Suominen, S., "Non-EU Nationals and Council Directive 2003/109/EC on the Status of Third-Country Nationals who are long-term residents: five paces forward and possibly three paces back", 42 *Common Market Law Review* 4 (2005), pp. 1011–1052.

Booss, D., Forman, J., "Enlargement: Legal and Procedural Aspects", 32 *Common Market Law Review* 1 (1995), pp. 95–130.

Brockelbank, W.J., "The Vilna Dispute", 20 *The American Journal of International Law* 3 (1926), pp. 483–501.

Bruggemann, K., "Leaving the 'Baltic' States and 'Welcome to Estonia': Re-regionalising Estonian identity", 10 *European Review of History* 2 (2003), pp. 343–360.

Burg, S.L., "The European Republics of the Soviet Union", *Current History* (1990), pp. 321–324.

Chan, J.M.M., "The Right to a Nationality as a Human Right. The Current Trend Towards Recognition", 12 *Human Rights Law Journal* 1 (1991), pp. 1–14.

Cremona, M., "EU Enlargement: Solidarity and Conditionality", 30 *European Law Review* 1 (2005), pp. 3–22.

Delcourt, C., "The *Acquis Communautaire*: Has the Concept Had Its Day?", 38 *Common Market Law Review* 4 (2001), pp. 829–870.

Ehin, P. "Determinants of public support for EU membership: Data from the Baltic countries", 40 *European Journal of Political Research* 5 (2001), pp. 31–56.

——, Willerton, J., "Baltic Diversity and Russian Power Interests: Policy Differentiation in an era of Change", 25 *The Soviet and Post-Soviet Review* (1998) 3, pp. 245–264.

Endzins, A., "The Position of the Constitutional Court of the Republic of Latvia following integration into the European Union", 60 *Zeitschrift für Öffentliches Recht* 3 (2005), pp. 507–516.

Evans, C., "Voluntary Harmonisation in Integration between the European Community and Eastern Europe", 22 *European Law Review* (1997), pp. 201–220.

Evtimov, E., "The Freedom of Movement for Workers under the Europe Agreements of the EC with the Central and Eastern European Countries", *The European Legal Forum* 4 (2002), pp. 235–239.

Fehervary, A., "Citizenship, Statelessness and Human Rights: Recent Developments in the Baltic States", 5 *International Journal on Refugee Law*, (1993), pp. 392–423.

Feldmann, M., "The Fast Track from the Soviet Union to the World Economy: External Liberalization in Estonia and Latvia", 36 *Government and Opposition* 4 (2001), pp. 544–545.

Feldmann, M., Sally, R., "From the Soviet Union to the European Union: Estonian Trade Policy, 1991–2000", 25 *The World Economy* 1 (2002), pp. 79–106.

Franckx, E., "The 1998 Estonia-Sweden Maritime Boundary Agreement: Lessons to be Learned in the Area of Continuity and/or Succession of States", 31 *Ocean Development and International Law* 3 (2000), pp. 269–284.

Garcia, P., "Le traité d'Athènes, un traité d'adhésion comme les autres?", *Revue du Marché commun et de l'Union européenne* 478 (2004), pp. 290–292.

Gautron, J.C., "Le Traité de Nice satisfait-il aux exigences de l'élargissement", 10 *Revue des Affaires Européenes* 4 (2000), pp. 353–363.

Ginter, C., "Constitutional review and EC law in Estonia", 31 *European Law Review* (2006), pp. 912–923.

Gomart, T., "Le Partenariat entre l'Union européenne et la Russie à l'épreuve de l'elargissement", *Revue du Marché commun et de l'Union européenne* (2004) 479, pp. 349–354.

Hanneman, A., "Independence and Group Rights in the Baltics: a Double Minority Problem", 35 *Virginia Journal of International Law* 2 (1995), pp. 485–528.

Henrard, K., "The impact of the enlargement process on the development of a minority protection policy within the EU: another aspect of responsibility/burden sharing?", 9 *Maastricht Journal of European and Comparative Law* (2002), pp. 357–391.

——, "Charting the Gradual Emergence of a More Robust Level of Minority Protection: Minority Specific Instruments and the European Union", 22 *Netherlands Quarterly of Human Rights* 4 (2004), pp. 559–584.

Hillion, C., "Enlargement of the European Union: The Discrepancy between Membership Obligations and Accession Conditions as regards the Protection of Minorities", 27 *Fordham International Law Journal* 2 (2003), pp. 715–740.

——, "The European Union in dead. Long live the European Union... A commentary on the Treaty of Accession 2003", 29 *European Law Review* (2004), pp. 583–612.

Himmer, S.E., "The Achievement of Independence in the Baltic States and its Justifications", 6 *Emory International Law Journal* (1992), pp. 253–291.

Holzapfel, M., "The Implications of Human Rights Abuses Currently Occurring in the Baltic States against the Ethnic Russian National Minority", *Buffalo Journal of International Law*, (1995–96), pp. 329–373.

Horng, D.C., "The Human Rights Clause in the European Union's External Trade and Development Agreements", 9 *European Law Journal* 5 (2003), pp. 677–701.

Hough, W.J.H., "The Annexation of the Baltic States and its effect on the Development of Law Prohibiting Forcible Seizure of Territory", 6 *New York Law School Journal of International and Comparative Law* 2 (1985), pp. 301–533.

Hughes, J., Sasse, G., "Monitoring the Monitors: EU Enlargement Conditionality and Minority Protection in the CEECs", *JEMIE* (2003), at http://www.ecmi.de/jemie/download/Focus1-2003_Hughes_Sasse.pdf.

Ilmjärv, M., "The Soviet Union, Lithuania and the Establishment of the Baltic Entente", *Lithuanian Foreign Policy Review* 2 (1998), pp. 87–109.

Ilves, T.H., "The Pleiades Join the Stars: Transatlanticism and Eastern Enlargement", 18 *Cambridge Review of International Affairs* 2 (2005), pp. 191–202.

Inglis, K., "The Europe Agreements compared in the light of their pre-accession reorientation", 37 *Common Market Law Review* 5 (2000), pp. 1189–1208.

——, "The Union's fifth Accession Treaty: New Means to Make Enlargement Possible", 41 *Common Market Law Review* (2004), pp. 937–971.

Järvelaid, P., "Estonian Legal Culture on the Threshold of the 21st Century", 29 *International Journal of Legal Information* 1 (2001), pp. 75–83.

Jubulis, M., "The External Dimension of Democratization in Latvia: the Impact of European Institutions", 13 *International Relations* (1996), pp. 59–73.

Kaleda, S.L., "The interim obligations of a state acceding to the European Union in the light of the inter-temporal jurisprudence of the Court of Justice", 26 *European Law Review* 7 (2001), pp. 599–604.

Kalvaitis, R., "Citizenship And Regional Identity in the Baltic States", 16 *Boston University International Law Journal* (1998), pp. 231–271.

Kerikmae, T., Vallikivi, H., "State Continuity in the Light of Estonian Treaties Concluded before World War II", *Juridica International* 5 (2000), pp. 30–39.

Kergandberg, E., "Role of the Constitutional Review Chamber of the Supreme Court of Estonia in the European Union", 60 *Zeitschrift für Öffentliches Recht* 3 (2005), pp. 469–476.

Kherad, R. "La Reconnaissance Internationale des Etats Baltes", 96 *Revue Générale de Droit International Public* 4 (1992), pp. 843–872.

Kimpe, I., Van Meurs, W., "A la frontière russo-estonienne", *Le Courrier des Pays de l'Est* (1999) 438, pp. 54–67.

Kionka, R., "La politique étrangère des états baltes", 59 *Politique Etrangère* 1 (1994), pp. 87–98.

Koskenniemi, M., Lehto, M., "La succession d'états dans l'ex-URSS en ce qui concerne particulièrement les relations avec la Finlande", 38 *Annuaire Français de.Droit International*, (1992), pp. 179–219.

Küris, E., "Role of the Constitutional Court of Lithuania in the European Union", 60 *Zeitschrift für Öffentliches Recht* 3 (2005), pp. 477–506.

Laffranque, J., "Influence of European Community Law on Estonian Law and, in Particular, Law-making", 4 *Juridica International* 1 (1999), pp. 86–92.

———, "Estonia's Association Agreement with the European Union: Legal and Constitutional Aspects", 8 *Juridica* 4 (2000), pp. 224–237.

———, "Constitution of the Republic of Estonia in the Light of Accession to the European Union", 6 *Juridica International* 1 (2001), pp. 207–221.

———, "Co-Existence of the Estonian Constitution and European Law", 7 *Juridica International* (2002), pp. 17–27.

———, "A Glance at the Estonian Legal Landscape in View of the Constitution Amendment Act", *Juridica International* (2007), pp. 55–66.

———, D'sa, M., "Domestic Implementation of EU Regulations in Estonia: A Flawed Methodology or Necessary Transposition?", 27 *European Law Review* (2002), pp. 91–99.

Laffranque, R., "Le contrôle parlementaire de la politique européenne du Gouvernement en République d'Estonie au regard des nouvelles dispositions du règlement intérieur du *Riigikogu*" *Juridica International* (2004), pp. 69–77.

Lagerspetz, M., "The Cross of the Virgin Mary's Land: A Study in the Construction of Estonia's Return to Europe", 6 *Finnish Review of Eastern European Studies* 3–4 (1999), pp. 17–28.

Lannon, E., "Le traité d'adhésion d'Athènes. Les négociations, les conditions de l'admission et les principales adaptations des traités résultant de l'élargissement de l'UE à vingt-cinq Etats membres", 40 *Cahiers de droit européen* 1–2 (2004), pp. 15–94.

Laserson, M., "The Recognition of Latvia", 37 *The American Journal of International Law*, 2 (1943), pp. 233–247.

Letki, N., "Lustration and Democratisation in East-Central Europe", 54 *East-Asia Studies* 4 (2002), pp. 529–552.

Levinsson, C., "The Long Shadow of History: Post-Soviet Border Disputes—The Case of Estonia, Latvia and Russia", 5 *Connections The Quarterly Journal* 2 (2006), pp. 98–109.

Lippert, B., Becker, P., "Structured Dialogue Revisited: the EU's Politics of Inclusion and Exclusion" 3 *European Foreign Affairs Review* (1998), pp. 341–365.

Loeber, D.A., "Regaining Independence—Constitutional Aspects: Estonia, Latvia, Lithuania", 24 *Review of Central and East European Law* 1 (1998), pp. 1–7.

———, "Consequences of the Molotov-Ribbentrop Pact for Lithuania of Today. International Law Aspects", *Lithuanian Foreign Policy Review* 4 (1999), pp. 95–105.

Mälksoo, L., "Professor Uluots, the Estonian Government in Exile and the Continuity of the Republic of Estonia in International Law", 69 *Nordic Journal of International Law* 3 (2000), pp. 289–316.

———, "Soviet genocide? Communist mass deportations in the Baltic States and international law", 14 *Leiden Journal of International Law* 4 (2001) pp. 757–787.

———, "Which Continuity: The Tartu Peace Treaty of 2 February 1920, the Estonian-Russian Border Treaties of 18 May 2005, and the Legal Debate about Estonia's Status in International Law", 10 *Juridica International* 1 (2005), pp. 144–149.

Mälksoo, M., "From Existential Politics Towards Normal Politics? The Baltic States in the Enlarged Europe", 37 *Security Dialogue* 3 (2006), pp. 275–297.

Maresceau, M., "EU-Central and Eastern Europe Relations at a Turning Point", 7 *Revue Des Affaires Européennes* 3 (1997), pp. 263–267.

———, Montaguti, E., "The relations between the European Union and Central and Eastern Europe: a legal appraisal", 32 *Common Market Law Review* (1995), pp. 1327–1367.

Maruste, R., "Democracy and the Rule of Law in Estonia: Progress Achieved and the Problems Remaining", 26 *Review of Central and East European Law* 3 (2000), pp. 311–327.

Mauring, L., Schaer, D., "The Effects of the Russian Energy Sector on the Security of the Baltic States", 8 *Baltic Security and Defence Review* (2006), pp. 66–80.

Mereckis, D., Morkvenas, R., "The 1991 Treaty as a Basis for Lithuanian-Russian Relations", 1 *Lithuanian Foreign Policy Review* 1 (1998), pp. 7–17.

Muiznieks, N., "The Influence of the Baltic Popular Movements on the Process of Soviet Disintegration", 47 *Europe-Asia Studies* 1 (1995), pp. 3–25.

Myrjord, A., "Governance Beyond the Union: EU Boundaries in the Barents Euro-Arctic Region", 8 *European Foreign Affairs Review* 2 (2003), pp. 239–257.

Nicolaides, P., "Negotiating Effectively for Accession to the European Union: Realistic Expectations, Feasible Targets, Credible Arguments", *Eipascope* 1 (1998), pp. 8–13.

Obradovic, D., "Community Law and the Doctrine of Divisible Sovereignty", 20 *Legal Issues of Economic Integration* (1993), pp. 1–20.

Ojanen, H., "The EU and its Northern Dimension: An Actor in Search of a Policy or a Policy in Search of an Actor?", 5 *European Foreign Affairs Review* 3 (2000), pp. 359–376.

Ott, A., "The Rights of Self-employed CEEC Citizens in the Member States under the Europe Agreements", *The European Legal Forum* (2001) pp. 497–501.

Ozolins, U., "The Impact of European Accession Upon Language Policy in the Baltic States", 2 *Language Policy* 3 (2003), pp. 217–238.

Park, A., "Ethnicity and Independence: The Case of Estonia in Comparative Perspective", 46 *Europe-Asia Studies* 1 (1994), pp. 69–87.

Peers, S., "The Queue for Accession Lengthens", 20 *European Law Review* 3 (1995), pp. 323–329.

——, "An ever closer waiting room?: The case for Eastern European accession to the European Economic Area", 32 (1995) 3 *CMLRev.*, pp. 187–213.

——, "Implementing Equality? The Directive on long-term resident third-country nationals", 29 *European Law Review* 4 (2004), pp. 437–460.

Pelkmans, J., Murphy, A., "Catapulted into Leadership: The Community's Trade and Aid Policies *vis à vis* Eastern Europe", 14 *Journal of European Integration* 2–3 (1990–1991), pp. 125–151.

Pentassuglia, G., "The EU and the Protection of Minorities: The Case of Eastern Europe", 12 *European Journal of International Law* 1 (2001), pp. 3–38.

Pettai, V., "Political Data in 2001: Estonia", 41 *European Journal of Political Research* 7–8 (2002), pp. 947–951.

Pisuke, H., "Estonia and the European Union: European Integration in Estonia", 1 *Juridica International* 1 (1996), pp. 2–4.

Plakans, A., "Peasants, Intellectuals and Nationalism in the Russian Baltic Provinces 1820–1890", 46 *Journal of Modern History* 3 (1974), pp. 445–475.

Pollet, K., "Human Rights Clauses in Agreements between the European Union and Central and Eastern European Countries", 7 *Revue des affaires européennes* 3 (1997), pp. 290–301.

Putins Peters, R., "Problems of Baltic Diplomacy in the League of Nations", 14 *Journal of Baltic Studies* 2 (1983), pp. 128–149.

Raun, T.U., "The Revolution of 1905 in the Baltic Provinces and Finland", 43 *Slavic Review* 3 (1984), pp. 453–467.

Reich, N., "The Constitutional Relevance of Citizenship and Free Movement in an Enlarged Union", 11 *European Law Journal* 6 (2005), pp. 675–698.

Rich, R., "Recognition of States: The Collapse of Yugoslavia and the Soviet Union", 4 *European Journal of International Law* (1993), pp. 36–65.

Rutenberg, G., "The Baltic States and the Soviet Union", 29 *The American Journal of International Law* 4 (1935), pp. 598–615.

Schinkel, M.P., Thielert, J., "Estonia's Competition Policy: A Critical Evaluation towards EU Accession", 24 *European Competition Law Review* 4 (2003), pp. 165–175.

Soldatos, P., Vandersanden, G., "L'admission dans la Communauté économique européenne. Essai d'interprétation juridique", 4 *Cahiers deDroit Européen* 6 (1968), pp. 674–707.

Sasse, G., "Securitization or Securing Rights? Exploring the Conceptual Foundations of Policies Towards Minorities and Migrants in Europe", 43 *Journal of Common Market Studies* 4 (2005), pp. 673–693.

Schlager, E., "The Right to have Rights: Citizenship in the Newly Independent OSCE Countries", 8 *Helsinki Monitor* 1 (1997), pp. 19–37.

Shemiatenkov, V., "The Relations between Russia and the EU", 7 *Revue des Affaires Européennes* 3 (1997), pp. 277–289.

Skolnick, J., "Grappling with the Legacy of Soviet Rule: Citizenship and Human Rights in the Baltic States", 54 *Toronto Faculty of Law Review* 2 (1996), pp. 387–417.

Smith, D.J., "Russia, Estonia and the Search for a Stable Ethno-Politics", 29 *Journal of Baltic Studies* 1 (1998) pp. 3–18.

Taagepera, R., "Baltic Population Changes 1950–1980", 12 *Journal of Baltic Studies* 1 (1981), pp. 35–57.

Taagepera, R., "Estonia in September 1988: Stalinists, Centrists and Restorationists", 20 *Journal of Baltic Studies* 2 (1989), pp. 175–186.

——, "The Baltic States", 9 *Electoral Studies* 4 (1990), pp. 303–311.

Taylor, T., "The International Legal Status of Gdansk, Klaipeda and the Former East Prussia", 41 *International and Comparative Law Quarterly* (1993), pp. 919–928.

Timmermans, W.A., "The Baltic States, the Soviet Union and the Netherlands: A Historical Note", 32 *Netherlands International Law Review* (1985), pp. 288–294.

Trapans, J.A., "The West and the Recognition of the Baltic States: 1919 and 1991. A Study of the Politics of the Major Powers", 25 *Journal of Baltic Studies* 2 (1994), pp. 153–173.

Tsilevich, B., "Development of the Language Legislation in the Baltic States", *Journal on Multicultural Societies*, 3, 2001, 2, http://www.unesco.org/most/vl3n2edi.htm.

Vadapalas, V., "Opinion of the Constitutional Court of the Republic of Lithuania in the Case Concerning the Conformity of the European Convention on Human Rights with the Constitution of Lithuania", *Zeitschrift für ausländisches öffentliches Recht und Völkerrecht* 4 (1995), pp. 1077–1094.

Vallens, D., "The Law on Aliens Controversy in the Baltic States", *The International Commission of Jurists Review* (1995) 54, pp. 12–21.

Van Den Vyver, J.D., "Statehood in International Law", 5 *Emory International Law Review* 9 (1991), pp. 28–31.

Van Elsuwege, P., "The Baltic States on the road to EU Accession. Opportunities and Challenges", 7 *European Foreign Affairs Review* 2 (2002), pp. 171–192.

——, "The Process of Constitutional Revision in the light of Lithuania's accession to the European Union", 44 *Jurisprudencija* 36 (2003), pp. 59–69.

——, "State Continuity and its Consequences: The Case of the Baltic States", 16 *Leiden Journal of International Law* (2003), pp. 377–388.

Van Ham, P., "The Baltic States and *Zwischeneuropa*: Geography is Destiny?" 14 *International Relations* 2 (1998), pp. 47–59.

Van Ooik, R., "Freedom of Self-Employed Persons and the Europe Agreements", 4 *European Journal of Migration and Law* 3 (2002), pp. 377–393.

Vilpisauskas, R., "The Impact of the European Union on Intra-Baltic Economic Co-operation", *Lithuanian Foreign Policy Review* 3 (1999), pp. 97–124.

Visek, R., "Creating the Ethnic Electorate Through Legal Restorationism: Citizenship Rights in Estonia", 38 *Harvard International Law Journal* 2 (1997), pp. 315–373.

Vitkus, G., "National Parliamentary Control of EU Policy in Lithuania", 1 *Lithuanian Foreign Policy Review* 2 (1999), pp. 65–76.

Von Staden, B., "Die Baltischen Staaten und Europa", 46 *Europa-Archiv* 9 (1991), pp. 275–281.

Williams, A., "Enlargement of the Union and Human Rights Conditionality: A Policy of Distinction?", 25 *European Law Review* (2000), pp. 601–617.

X, "Estonian SSR Legislation on Sovereignty", 5 *Baltic Forum* 2 (1988), pp. 74–79.

Yakemtchouk, R., "Les Républiques baltes et la crise du fédéralisme Soviétique", *Studia Diplomatica*, 43, 1990, 4–5–6, pp. 1–408.

Zalimas, D. "Legal and Political Issues on the Continuity of the Republic of Lithuania", *Lithuanian Foreign Policy Review* 4 (1999), pp. 107–118.

Yearbooks and Collected Courses

Fitzmaurice, G., "The General Principles of International Law Considered from the Standpoint of the Rule of Law", 92 *Academie de Droit International The Hague, Recueil des Cours* (1957) II, pp. 1–227.

Handoll, J., "The Long-Term Residents Directive", 4 *European Yearbook of Minority Issues* (2004/5), pp. 389–410.

Jakstonyte, S., Cvelich, M., "Constitutional and International Documents Concerning the International Legal Status of Lithuania", 1 *Baltic Yearbook of International Law*, (2001), pp. 301–312.

Kononenko, V., "Normal neighbours or trouble-makers? The Baltic States in the Context of Russia-EU Relations", *Estonian Foreign Policy Yearbook 2006*, Tallinn, Estonian Foreign Policy Institute, 2006, pp. 69–84.

Laffranque, J., "The Constitution of Estonia and Estonia's Accession to the European Union", 4 *Baltic Yearbook of International Law* (2004), pp. 1–20.

Lobjakas, A., "Estonia Adrift: Caught in the Crosswinds of the EU's Constitutional Debate", *Estonian Foreign Policy Yearbook* (2004), pp. 85–98.

Loeber, D.A., "Legal Consequences of the Molotov-Ribbentrop Pact for the Baltic States on the Obligation to Overcome the Problems Inherited from the Past", 1 *Baltic Yearbook of International Law* (2001), pp. 85–98.

Maresceau, M., "Bilateral Agreements Concluded by the European Community", *Academie de Droit International The Hague, Recueil des Cours* (2004), pp. 129–451.

Salulaid, J., "Restoration of the Effect of Estonian International Treaties", 1 *Baltic Yearbook of International Law* (2001), pp. 225–232.

Satkauskas, R., "Subrogation of State Responsibility? The Baltic Legations in Paris", 5 *Baltic Yearbook of International Law* (2005), pp. 133–145.

Stern, B., "La Succession d'Etats", *Recueil des Cours. Academie de Droit International The Hague* (1996), pp. 9–438.

Vilpisauskas, R., "Baltic States Negotiating The EU Entry: Process, Patterns and Results", *Lithuanian Political Science Yearbook* (2002), pp. 119–141.

Yakemtchouk, R., "Les républiques baltes en droit international. Echec d'une annexion opérée en violation du droit des gens", 37 *Annuaire Français du Droit International*, (1991), pp. 259–287.

Zalimas, D. "Legal Issues on the Continuity of the Republic of Lithuania", 1 *Baltic Yearbook of International Law* (2001), pp. 1–21.

——, "Commentary to the Law of the Republic of Lithuania on Compensation of Damage Resulting from the Occupation of the USSR", 3 *Baltic Yearbook of International Law* (2003), pp. 97–163.

——, "The Soviet Aggression against Lithuania in January 1991: International Legal Aspects", *Baltic Yearbook of International Law* (2006), pp. 293–343.

Ziemele, I., "State Continuity, Succession and Responsibility: Reparations to the Baltic States and their Peoples?", 3 *Baltic Yearbook of International Law* (2003), pp. 165–189.

——, "The Application of International Law in the Baltic States", 40 *German Yearbook of International Law* (1997), pp. 243–279.

Working Papers and Special Reports

De Schutter, O., *European Union Legislation and the Norms of the Framework Convention for the Protection of National Minorities*, Report of the Committee of Experts on Issues Relating to the Protection of National Minorities, DH-MIN (2006) 019, Strasbourg, 23 October 2006.

De Witte, B., *Politics Versus Law in the EU's Approach to Ethnic Minorities*, EUI Working Papers (2000) 4.

Dorodnova, J., *EU Concerns in Estonia and Latvia: Implications of Enlargement for Russia's Behaviour Towards the Russian-speaking Minorities*, EUI Working Papers (2000) 40.

——, *Challenging Democracy: Implementation of the Recommendations of the OSCE High Commissioner on National Minorities to Latvia, 1993–2001*, CORE Working Paper (2003) 10.

Feldmann, M., *Understanding the Baltic and Estonian Puzzles: The Political Economy of Rapid External Liberalization in Estonia and Latvia*, BOFIT Papers (2000) 11.

Heineman-Grüder, A., *Small States—Big Worries. Choice and Purpose in the Security Policies of the Baltic States*, Bonn, Bonn International Center For Conversion, 2002.

Kaitila, V., Widgren, M., *Revealed Comparative Advantage in Trade between the European Union and the Baltic Countries*, EUI Working Papers (2001) 2.

Löfgren, J., Herd, G., *Estonia and the EU. Integration and Societal Security in the Baltic Context*, Tampere Peace Research Institute Research Report (2000).

Moshes, A., *The Double Enlargement, Russia and the Baltic States*, DUPI Working Paper (2002) 4.

Ozolina, Z., *The Impact of the European Union on Baltic Co-operation*, COPRI Working Papers (1999) 3.

Paulauskas, K., *The Baltics: From Nation States to Member States*, Institute For Security Studies, Occasional Paper (2006) 62.

Sasse, G., *EU Conditionality and Minority Rights: Translating the Copenhagen Criterion into Policy*, EUI Working Papers (2005) 16.

Smith, K., *The Use of Political Conditionality in the EU's Relations with Third Countries*, EUI Working Papers (1997) 7.

Spokeveciute, R., *The impact of EU Membership on the Lithuanian budget*, SEI Working Paper (2003) 63.

Thiele, C., *The Criterion of Citizenship for Minorities: The Example of Estonia*, ECMI Working Papers (1999) 5.

Van Elsuwege, P., *EU Enlargement and its Consequences for EU-Russia Relations: The Limits of a Fair Weather Strategy*, Chair Interbrew-Baillet Latour Working Papers (2002) 14.

——, *Russian-speaking minorities in Estonia and Latvia: Challenges at the threshold of the European Union*, ECMI Working Papers (2004) 20.

Vinokurov, E., *Kaliningrad in the Framework of EU-Russia Relations: Moving Toward Common Spaces*, Chair Interbrew—Baillet Latour Working Papers (2004) 20.

Newspapers and Press Releases

Alas, J., "Russia bans EU fish imports", *The Baltic Times*, 29 November 2006.

Celms, E., "Roma woman breaks legal barrier for minorities", *The Baltic Times*, 31 May 2006.

Cronin, D. "Ethnic Russian status must improve", *European Voice*, 27 February 2003.

Johansson, J., "Vike-Feiberga initiates further language changes", *The Baltic Times*, 13 Dec. 2001.

Kolb, M., "Looking for the truth behind Lihula", *The Baltic Times*, 27 April 2005.

Kovalick, M., "High Costs of Closing Down Ignalina Plant", *The Baltic Times*, 25 April 2002.

Mann, M., "Lithuania warns EU on nuclear plant closure", *Financial Times*, 1 April 2002.

Parker, G., "Russia says new Member States damaging EU relationship", *Financial Times*, 21 May 2006.

Racas, A., "Conservatives ask Russia to compensate for Jan. 13 victims", *The Baltic Times*, 10 January 2007.

Raubisko, I., "NATO: Robertson urges Latvia to amend election laws", *RFE/RL*, 22 Feb. 2002.

Repson, K., "Border Treaty requires new negotiations", *The Baltic Times*, 29 June 2005.

Toth, S., "Russia condemns partisan trial underway in Valga court", *The Baltic Times*, 22–28 August 2002.

X, "Kallas Talk of 'Russian Card' Triggers Debate", *The Baltic Times*, 21 August 2003;
——, "Gas Pipeline Triggers New Backlash", *The Baltic Times*, 3 May 2006.

Internet

European Court of Justice, http://www.curia.europa.eu.
European Court of Human Rights, http://www.coe.int.
European Union, http://europa.eu.
EUObserver, http://www.euobserver.com.
Estonian Ministry of Foreign Affairs, http://www.vm.ee.
Latvian Ministry of Foreign Affairs, http://www.am.gov.lv.
Lithuanian Ministry of Foreign Affairs, http://www.urm.lt.
Russian Ministry of Foreign Affairs, http://www.ln.mid.ru.
Citizenship and Migration Board of the Republic of Estonia, http://www.mig.ee.
Naturalization Board of the Republic of Latvia, http://www.ng.gov.lv.
Latvian Office of Citizenship and Migration Affairs, http://www.ocma.gov.lv.
Estonian EU Information Agency, http://www.eib.ee.
Latvian EU Information Agency, http://www.eib.gov.lv.
Lithuanian EU Information Agency, http://www.euro.lt.
Parliament of the Republic of Estonia, http://www.riigikogu.ee.
Parliament of the Republic of Latvia, http://www.saeima.lv.
Parliament of the Republic of Lithuania, http://www.lrs.lt.
The Council of the Baltic Sea States (CBSS), http://www.cbss.st.
Statistical Office of Estonia, http://www.stat.ee.
Statistical Office of Latvia, http://old.csb.gov.lv/Satr/aorg.htm.
Statistical Office of Lithuania, http://www.stat.gov.lt.
Statistical Office of the European Union, http://epp.eurostat.ec.europa.eu.
Estonian National Electoral Committee, http://www.vvk.ee.
Latvian National Electoral Committee, http://web.cvk.lv.
Lithuanian National Electoral Committee, http://www.lrs.lt.
Estonian Legal Language Centre, http://www.legaltext.ee.
Latvian Translation and Terminology Centre, http://www.ttc.lv.

Case Law

European Court of Justice

Case 26/62, *Van Gent en Loos v. Nederlandse Administratie der Belastingen* [1963] ECR 1.
Case 6/64, *Flaminio Costa v. Enel* [1964] ECR 585.
Case 11/70, *Internationale Handelsgesellschaft GmbH v. Einfuhr- und Vorratstelle für Getreide und Futtermittel* [1970] ECR 1125.

Case 181/73, *Haegeman v. Belgian State* [1974] ECR 447.
Case 185/73, *Hauptzollamt Bielefeld* v. *OHG Koenig* [1974] ECR 607.
Case 8/74 *Dassonville* [1974] ECR 837.
Opinion 1/75 *OECD Local Costs Standard* [1975] ECR 1355.
Case 94/77 *Zerbone* [1978] ECR 99.
Case 106/77, *Simmenthal SpA v. Adminstrazione delle Finanze dello Stato* [1978] ECR 629.
Case 87/75, *Bresciani* v *Amministrazione delle Finanze* [1976] ECR 129.
Opinion 1/78, *International Agreement on Natural Rubber* [1979] ECR 2871.
Case 93/78, *Mattheus v. Doego* [1978] ECR 2203.
Case 120/78 *Rewe* v. *Bundesmonopolverwaltung für Branntwein* [1979] ECR 649.
Case 149/79 *Commission* v. *Belgium* [1980] ECR 3881.
Case 270/80 *Polydor* [1982] ECR 329.
Case 17/81, *Pabst & Richarz* [1982] ECR 1331.
Case 104/81, *Kupferberg* [1982] ECR 3641.
Joint cases 115 and 116/81, *Adoui and Cornuaille* [1982] ECR I-1665.
Case 258/81 *Metallurgiki Halyps A.E.* v. *Commission* [1982] ECR 4261.
Case 11/82, *SA Piraiki-Patraiki* [1985] ECR 207.
Case 238/83, *Meade* [1984] ECR 2631.
Case 44/84, *Hurd* v. *Jones* [1986] ECR 29.
Joint Cases 194/85 and 241/85, *Commission v. Greece* [1988] ECR 1037.
Case 12/86 *Meryem Demirel* v. *Stadt Schwäbisch Gmünd* ECR [1987] 3719.
Joint Cases 31/86 and 35/86, *LAISA* v. *Council* [1988] ECR 2285.
Case 45/86 *Commission* v. *Council* [1987] ECR 1493.
Joint Cases 46/87 and 227/88 *Hoechst* v. *Commission* [1989] ECR 2859.
Case C-305/87, *Commission v. Greece* [1989] ECR 1461.
Case 374/87 *Orkem* v. *Commission* [1989] ECR 3283.
Case C-379/87, *Groener* v. *Minister for Education* [1989] ECR 3987.
Joined Cases C-297/88 and C-197/89 *Dzodzi* [1990] ECR I-3763.
Case C-113/89, *Rush Portuguesa* [1990] ECR I-1417.
Case C-192/89, *Sevince* v. *Staatssecretaris van Justitie* [1990] ECR I-3461.
Case C-18/90, *Kziber* [1991] ECR 199.
Case C-62/90, *Germany* v. *Commission* ECR [1992] I-2575.
Case C-369/90, *Mario Vicente Micheletti and Others* v. *Delegation del Gobierno and Cantabria* [1992] ECR I-4239.
Opinion 1/91 *on the creation of the European Economic Area* [1991] ECR 6079.
Case C-106/91 *Ramrath* [1992] ECR I-3351.
Case C-312/91 *Metalsa* [1993] ECR I-3751.
Case 327/91 *France vs. Commission* [1994] ECR I-3641.
Case C-316/91, *Parliament v. Council* [1994] ECR I-659.
Case C-43/93, *Vander Elst* [1994] ECR I-3803.
Case C-58/93, *Yousfi* v. *Belgium* [1994] ECR I-1353.
Case C-434/93 *Bozkurt* v. *Staatssecretaris van Justitie* [1995] ECR I-1475.
Case C-469/93 *Amministrazione delle Finanze dello Stato* v *Chiquita Italia* [1995] ECR I-4533.
Opinion 1/94 *on the competence of the Community to conclude international agreements concerning services and the protection of intellectual property* [1994] ECR I-5267.
Opinion 2/94 *on Accession by the Community to the ECHR* [1996] ECR I-1759.
Case C-70/94, *Werner* [1995] ECR 3189.
Case C-83/94 *Leifer* [1995] ECR I-3231.
Case C-103/94 *Krid* v. *CNAVTS* [1995] ECR I-719.
Case C-107/94 *Asscher* [1996] ECR I-3089.
Case C-268/94 *Portugal* v. *Council* [1996] ECR I-6177.
Case C-259/95, *European Parliament* v. *Council* [1997] ECR I-5303.
Case C-265/95, *Commission* v. *France* [1997] ECR I-6959.
Case C-368/95 *Familiapress* [1997] ECR I-3689.

Case C-27/96, *Danisco Sugar* [1997] ECR I-6653.
Case C-129/96, *Inter-Environnement Wallonie* [1997], ECR I-7411.
Case C-170/96, *Commission v. Council* [1998], ECR I-2763.
Case C-262/96, *Sürul* [1999] ECR I-2685.
Case C-249/96 *Grant* [1998] ECR I-621.
Case C-233/97 *KappAhl Oy* [1998] ECR I-8069.
Case C-302/97, *Klaus Konle v. Republik Österreich* [1999] ECR I-3099.
Case C-424/97, *Haim v. Kassenzahnärztliche Vereinigung Nordrhein* [2000] ECR I-5123.
Case C-224/98, *D'Hoop*, [2002] ECR I-6191.
Case C-233/98, *Hauptzollambt Neubrandburg v. Lensing & Brockhausen GmbH* [1999] ECR
    I-7365.
Case C-29/99, *Commission v. Council* [2002] ECR I-11221.
Case C-63/99, *Gloszczcuk* [2001] ECR I-6369.
Case C-66/99, *D. Wandel GmbH v. Hauptzollambt Bremen* [2001] ECR I-873.
Joint cases C-95/99 to C98/99 and C-180/99, *Khalil and others*[2001] ECR I-7413.
Case C-184/99, *Grzelczyk* [2001] ECR I-6193.
Case C-235/99 *Kondova* [2001] ECR I-6427.
Case C-257/99, *Barkoci and Malik* [2001] ECR I-6567.
Case C-268/99 *Jany and others* [2001] ECR I-8615.
Case C-274/99 P *Connolly v Commission* [2001] ECR I-1611.
Case C-294/99 *Athinaiki Zihopiaa* [2001] ECR I-6797.
Case C-481/99 *Heininger* [2001] ECR I-9945.
Case, C-60/00, *Carpente*, [2002] ECR I-6279.
Case C-94/00 *Roquette Frères* [2002] ECR I-9011.
Case C-112/00, *Schmidberger* [2003] ECR I-5659.
Case C-162/00 *Pokrzeptowitcz-Meyer* [2002] ECR I-1071.
Case C-179/00, *Weidacher* [2002] ECR I-501.
Case C-438/00 *Deutscher Handballbund* [2003] ECR I-4135.
Case C-444/00 *Mayer Parry Recycling* [2003] ECR I-6163.
Case C-445/00, *Austria v. Council* [2003] ECR 8549.
Case C-58/01 *Océ Van Der Grinten* [2003] ECR I-9809.
Case 109/01, *Akrich* [2003] ECR I-9607.
Case C-148/02, *Garcia Avello* [2003] ECR I-1161.
Case 233/02, *France vs. Commission* [2004] ECR I-2759.
Case C-327/02 *Panayotova and others* [2004] ECR I-11055.
Case C-105/03 *Pupino* [2005] ECR I-5285.
Case C-209/03, *Bidar* [2005] ECR I-2119.
Case C-265/03 *Simutenkov* [2005] ECR 2579.
Case C-320/03, *Commission v. Austria* [2005] ECR I-9871.
Case C-540/03 *Parliament v. Council* [2006] ECR I-5769.
Case C-145/04, *Spain v. United Kingdom* [2006] ECR I-7917.
Case C-300/04, *Eman and Sevinger* [2006] ECR I-8055.
Case C-413/04, *European Parliament v. Council* [2006] ECR I-11221.
Case C-303/05, *Advocaten van de Wereld VZW v. Leden van de Ministerraad* [2007] ECR
    I-3633.
Case C-341/05, *Laval un Parteneri Ltd v. Svenska Byggnadsarbetareförbundet*, judgment of
    18 December 2007, nyr.
Case C-438/05, *The International Transport Workers' Federation and The Finnish Seamen's
    Union v. Viking Line*, judgment of 11 December 2007, nyr.

Court of First Instance

Case T-115/94, *Opel Austria v. Council* ECR [1997] II-39.
Case T-66/99 *ESF Elbe-Stahlwerke Feralpi v. Commission* [2001] ECR II-1523.
Case T-256/01, *Pyres v. Commission* [2005] ECR II-99.

Joint Cases T-219/02 and T-337/02, *Lutz Herrera v. Commission* [2004] ECR II-1407.
Case T-257/04, *Poland v. Commission*, OJ (2004) C 251/20, pending.
Case T-258/04, *Poland v. Commission*, OJ (2004) C 251/21, pending.
Case T-324/05, *Estonia v. Commission*, OJ (2005) C 271/24, pending.

European Court of Human Rights

Belgian Linguistics v. Belgium, 23 July 1968, Series A, No. 6.
App. 24833/94, *Matthews v. The United Kingdom*, 18 February 1999, CEDH, 1999-I.
App. 25781/94, *Cyprus v. Turkey*, 10 May 2001, CEDH 2001-IV.
App. 31414/96, *Karassev and Family v. Finland*, 14 April 1998, CEDH 1999-II.
App. 44158/98, *Gorzelik and Others v. Poland*, 17 February 2004, CEDH, 2004-I.
App. 46726/99, *Podkolzina v. Latvia*, 9 April 2002, CEDH 2002-II.
App. 48321/99, *Slivenko v. Latvia*, 9 October 2003, CEDH 2003-X.
App. 50183/99, *Kolosovskiy v. Latvia*, 29 January 2004.
App. 55480/00 and 59330/00, *Sidabras and Dziautas v. Lithuania*, 27 July 2004, CEDG 2004-VIII.
App. 58278/00, *Zdanoka v. Latvia*, 17 June 2004 (First Section).
App. 58278/00, *Zdanoka v. Latvia*, 16 March 2006 (Grand Chamber).
App. 59643/00, *Kaftailova v. Latvia*, 22 June 2006.
App. 60654/00, *Sisojeva v. Latvia*, 15 January 2007.
App. 69405/01, *Fedorova and Others v. Latvia*, 9 October 2003.
App. 70665/01 and 74345/01, *Rainys and Gasparavicius v. Lithuania*, 7 April 2005.
App. 36117/02, *Grisankova and Grisankovs v. Latvia*, 13 February 2003, ECHR, 2003-II.

INDEX

Studies in EU External Relations

Editor
Marc Maresceau

ISSN: 1875-0451

1. Rasch, M.B. *The European Union at the United Nations.* The Functioning and Coherence of EU External Representation in a State-centric environment. 2008. ISBN 978 90 04 16714 8
2. Van Elsuwege, P. *From Soviet Republics to EU Member States.* A Legal and Political Assessment of the Baltic States' Accession to the EU. 2008. ISBN 978 90 04 16845 6